Introducing
Roseville Pottery

Mark Bassett

4880 Lower Valley Rd. Atglen, PA 19310

Panel. 10" vase, floral, brown; 12" vase, floral, green. *Shannon collection.* **$275–325, $375–450**

Library of Congress Cataloging-in-Publication Data

Bassett, Mark T.
 Introducing Roseville Pottery/Mark Bassett.
  p. cm.
 Includes bibliographical references and index.
 ISBN 0-7643-0921-8
 1. Roseville Pottery Company. 2. Pottery, American--Collectors
and collecting Handbooks, manuals, etc. I. Title.
 NK4510.R58B37
  738.3'09771'91--dc21   99-15193
                               CIP

Designed by "Sue"
Type set in University Roman Bd Bt/Humanst 521 BT

ISBN: 0-7643-0921-8
Printed in China
1 2 3 4

Title page photo
Creamware (Decorated). 545-8" jardiniere, green bands and hand-painted decorations, large die-impressed shape number 545, hand-lettered marks (black ink) reading "The Roseville Pottery Co., – MERCIAN–, 545-8." *Hoppe collection.* **$400–500**

Published by Schiffer Publishing Ltd.
4880 Lower Valley Road
Atglen, PA 19310
Phone: (610) 593-1777; Fax: (610) 593-2002
E-mail: Schifferbk@aol.com
Please visit our web site catalog at **www.schifferbooks.com**
or write for a free catalog.
This book may be purchased from the publisher.
Please include $3.95 for shipping.

In Europe, Schiffer books are distributed by
Bushwood Books
6 Marksbury Rd.
Kew Gardens
Surrey TW9 4JF England
Phone: 44 (0)181 392-8585; Fax: 44 (0)181 392-9876
E-mail: Bushwd@aol.com

Please try your bookstore first.

We are interested in hearing from authors
with book ideas on related subjects.

Acknowledgments

This book is dedicated to my mother Donna Ruth Lima Bassett and to her mother Margaret-Kathryn Read Lima, both of whom are now deceased. Through the nurturing of these two artistically inclined women, I developed an early love for the decorative and the fine arts. Without them, I would not have written about American art pottery.

M.K.'s house in Oklahoma City was chock full of knick-knacks. An old black-and-white Kodak print captured me, at the age of five or six, giving a recitation on Granny's carved alabaster bookends, shaped like stylized Mexicans on siesta. On summer vacations, our family sometimes stopped at a working pottery for a tour and a souvenir. When I was a child, we visited Van Briggle and Frankoma. An earlier generation made pilgrimages to U.N.D., Rosemeade, Camark, and Niloak. When Granny died, I inherited my first examples of American art pottery—including a 12" Weller vase in the 1930s Ardsley pattern (cattails!). In the mid 1980s I began to collect Roseville and other Art Deco period ceramics.

My mother's influence is harder to define, partly because she died of breast cancer when I was only 10. She played the piano, sang in the church choir, and pursued her avocation as an artist, usually working in charcoal or pastel (colored chalk). Like me, she had a divided mind, also harboring more "masculine" interests in the sciences.

Research for Introducing Roseville Pottery was conducted at the Corning Museum of Glass (Corning, NY); the Library of Congress (Washington, DC); the Ohio Historical Society (Columbus, OH); and the Zanesville (OH) Public Library. The staffs of these invaluable institutions made my work easy and my stay pleasant. A special thanks also goes to Moses Mesre and to Ed and June Wagner, who allowed me to study rare factory publications from their personal collections.

Photographs are essential to documenting the history of the Roseville Pottery. Unless otherwise noted, all photographs in Introducing Roseville Pottery are the work of the author. Some of the credit for their quality must go to Victoria Naumann Peltz, from whom I learned much while we worked together on Cowan Pottery and the Cleveland School (Schiffer, 1997). I also thank Peter Schiffer, Douglas Congdon-Martin, and Jeffrey B. Snyder for advice and instruction in the purchase and use of professional photographic equipment. Once again I am grateful for the fine photo finishing and related services of Dodd Camera and Video (Fairview Park, OH).

Two museums in Zanesville, Ohio, allowed me to photograph pottery in their collections (or provided other assistance). For their friendly interest and their hospitality, I would like to acknowledge Philip Alan LaDouceur (director) and the rest of the staff at the Zanesville Art Center. At the National Road and Zane Grey Museum, museum manager Alan D. King assisted me in photographing pieces on loan from private collectors.

The collectors, dealers, antiques shops, and auction houses who generously allowed pottery to be photographed for this book include the following: Anonymous; Dave Auclair (Madison, WI); Mark Bassett (Lakewood, OH); Joyce and Rich Bennett; Robert Bettinger; William M. Bilsland III (Cedar Rapids, IA); Len Boucher; Jack Brooks; Joanne H. Calkins; Cedar Hill Collection (St. Charles, IA); Cincinnati Art Galleries; Clarabelle Antiques (Zanesville, OH); C. George Cooper; Cowan Pottery Museum at Rocky River (OH) Public Library; Joseph Davis, Joseph Davis Antiques (Lakewood, OH); John Ross Dougar; Dick Downey; James and Jennifer Fairfield; Jim Grandin (Hamilton, IN); Norm Haas; Eric and Shelly Hansen; Mark and Barb Harris; Berek and Emma Haus; Heart of Ohio Antique Center (Springfield, OH); Gordon and Sue Hoppe; Hardy Hudson (Winter Park, FL); Paul Jacklitch; Bobby and Joan Joray; Vera Kaufman, Buried Treasures/Vintage Vera (Manchester, NH); Greg Koster; the George Krause family; Jane Langol Antiques (Medina, OH); Mark and Marie Latta; Mike McAllister, McAllister Auctions (Grand Ledge, MI); Tony McCormack; Elaine Mastromatteo; Medina Antique Mall (Medina, OH); Robert T. Merritt, Memories Galore (Bay City, MI); Moses Mesre; Mike Nickel and Cindy Horvath (Portland, MI); David Rago Auctions (Lambertville, NJ); Jack and Karen Ready; Mrs. Robert Ross; Phil and Nanci Ruhoff, P & N's Potts, Etc. (Minneapolis, MN); Jerry and Marsha Scheytt; Mike and Leita Schultz; Len Senior; Frank Shannon; Jeanette (Mrs. Marvin) Stofft; John and Brenda Stofft; Robert Swartz; Treadway Gallery, Inc. (Cincinnati, OH); Mark Valloric; Ed and June Wagner; Betty Ward, White Pillars Antique Mall (Zanesville, OH); and Webb's Antique Mall (Centerville, IN).

Several people allowed me to reprint their photographs in this book, and are acknowledged in the captions too: William Acevedo (Olmsted Township, OH); Bernard Banet (Ann Arbor, MI); Jeremy J. Caddigan, Caddigan Auctioneers, Inc. (Hanover, MA); Gordon Hoppe; and Mike McAllister, McAllister Auctions (Grand Ledge, MI). Photographs bearing the legend "Hoppe photograph" depict items in the Gordon and Sue Hoppe collection that were photographed by Gordon Hoppe.

For their willingness to comment on early drafts, I thank Dave Auclair; my partner C. George Cooper; James Fairfield; Gordon and Sue Hoppe; Mark and Marie Latta; Mike Nickel; Jerry Scheytt; Frank Shannon; and Jeanette Stofft. Both my publisher Peter Schiffer and my editor Jeffrey B. Snyder showed admirable patience, offering valuable suggestions and constructive criticism. The designers at Schiffer Publishing are also due my thanks for once again putting together a beautiful book.

Last, I wish to express my appreciation to the dealers and collectors who patiently answered many questions when I began attending the pottery shows. You were enthusiastic and knowledgeable when my curiosity was overshadowed only by my naïveté. Perhaps you will find, in some small way, that this book helps to repay the debt I owe to you.

Contents

Introduction

If you are new to Roseville, this book is for you! If you have been buying and selling Roseville for decades, this book is for you too. *Introducing Roseville Pottery* was written for beginners—those who have not yet begun to collect or deal in American art pottery. But as the title implies, in some sense "we are all beginners."

We've certainly come a long way since 1968, when Richard A. Clifford published the first book on *Roseville Art Pottery*. Like many authors who followed him, Clifford confused two Roseville lines made during two different decades. He claimed that Pine Cone was "sold from 1913 to 1952 in various forms; the glossy pine cone being later. It was again revived in 1952 but did not sell well in the cheap form" (4). My research clarifies the history of the two Pine Cone lines and distinguishes between them. (For the details, see Chapter 5.)

Pine Cone was not Roseville's only success story. Other lines are equally plausible candidates for the title "big seller." Judging only by factory records (in the collection of the Ohio Historical Society, Columbus), we can nominate nine more product lines, each offering over 100 different shapes: Matt Green (302 shapes), Rozane Royal (246 shapes), Majolica (232 shapes), Creamware (203 or shapes, or more), Ivory (179 shapes), Romafin (a Utility Ware line, in 150 shapes), Donatello (109 shapes), Carnelian (103 shapes), and Rosecraft (102 shapes). Interestingly, there were 104 different Della Robbia designs, even though this hand-carved line is rare today.

Between 1890 and 1954, the Roseville Pottery Company designed and manufactured 132 different product lines, an average of two lines a year for 65 years. Not counting variations in color and shape, *Introducing Roseville Pottery* illustrates and values examples of each product, arranged from A to Z, along with at least 50 variations on the basic lines.

In the collection of the Ohio Historical Society are a large sample of "factory stock pages." The archival fuel behind *all* the Roseville books, these "pages" are actually oversized black and white photographs that have been mounted on cloth backings and hand-painted in watercolors. These factory photographs apparently functioned as a record-keeping tool for Roseville executives, not as a tool for marketing current lines. They were probably used primarily "in house," although they may have been seen by a few V.I.P. visitors to the factory. To market new products, Roseville participated in major trade shows and placed advertisements in trade journals and interior decorating magazines. Between 1927 and 1941, a small factory pamphlet titled *Pottery* illustrated representative examples of current lines. From time to time, another factory booklet could serve as a marketing aid.

After about 1947, no oversized hand-colored photographs were produced at the factory. Under Robert Windisch's presidency, the new Roseville lines were typically photographed for illustration in a "factory brochure" that served *both* a record-keeping and a marketing function. Designed so that (when folded properly) they would fit into a regular business envelope, these brochures were printed with a limited amount of color. They appear to have been distributed free upon request, even to those casually responding to a Roseville advertisement.

In *Introducing Roseville Pottery*, distinctions are always carefully made between the factory stock pages and the factory brochures. Because of new research, the Roseville line dates indicated—and sometimes the names—do not always agree with earlier books on the Pottery. When a "collector nickname" is known to refer to a given line, this name is also cited, along with its first known printed reference. The index will help Roseville lovers locate the line in question.

How did I arrive at conclusions so different from those of earlier writers? Graduate training at the University of Missouri taught me to read the cataloging notes at the Ohio Historical Society, where I studied the original Roseville factory stock pages. In 1980 the librarians in charge of cataloging the Robert Windisch collection penned this warning: "The dates supplied in the collection inventory appear in pencil on the side of the corresponding page (supplied by a person or persons unknown) and should be used with caution."

I began by assuming that *all* pencil notations on the factory stock pages—including line names—might be erroneous. Then I set out to answer two questions about each line: WHAT was it called? WHEN was it made? To me, answering these two questions is as essential to art history as learning to count is to calculus. How could a plausible history of the Roseville factory be written without the answers to those two questions? For that reason, when I spoke at the Zanesville Art Center in July 1998, I compared my task to the child's counting game "One Potato, Two Potato." In real life, the job was somewhat more difficult.

Through research at the Corning Museum of Glass and the Library of Congress, I verified some details and corrected others. Sometimes all I can offer is an educated guess. Whenever possible, published references are provided as documentation. This book is not meant to be "the final word" on Roseville Pottery. Despite the best intentions, any researcher can make errors or misinterpret evidence.

In Chapter 6 are shape lists for many of the Roseville lines. These shape lists were drawn *exclusively* from factory documents, even in cases when I have been able to photograph Roseville pieces that do not appear in any factory listing. If you know of additional Roseville shapes—other than those listed or illustrated here—please let me know. I plan to update the shape lists in future publications from Schiffer.

The values shown in *Introducing Roseville Pottery* are intended to be average retail figures for items in mint condition. Actual prices a seller might obtain can vary from region to region, from year to year, and from collector to collector. Neither the author nor the publisher can assume responsibility for losses (or gains) made by the use of the values offered.

Like the figures shown in any price guide, these estimates represent the educated opinion of the author at the time the book was compiled for publication. I supplemented my own 15 years' experience in valuing Roseville pottery by consulting with several long-time Roseville lovers (both dealers and collectors). Despite this preparation, certain rare Roseville examples come up for sale so infrequently that an accurate market price can be difficult (or impossible) to predict. For these rare pieces, I have used the abbreviation **NPD** to mean "no price determined." In mint condition, these items are likely to sell for at least $1000. Out of professional courtesy, examples from the Zanesville Art Center collection were also marked **NPD** (regardless of rarity).

Please let me know if you conduct additional research on Roseville, or if you find mistakes in this text. **Write me at this address**: Mark Bassett, P.O. Box 771233, Lakewood, OH 44107, or care of the publisher. My website at <www.angelfire.com/oh/markbassett> illustrates some of the American art pottery that I buy, which includes Roseville, Weller, Rookwood, Cowan, Muncie Ruba Rombic, AMACO, "Federal Art Project" figurines from Cleveland, WPA ceramics, art deco Lenox figures, and many others. Photographs and descriptions are helpful, as are reports of condition.

Because of my busy schedule, I cannot always fulfill complicated personal requests. **Sorry, but no free appraisals can be made.** Enclosing SASE's is a courtesy, when asking for another person's time. I look forward to hearing from you.

Chapter 1
COLLECTING ROSEVILLE POTTERY

So Many Pots ... So Little Time!

Buying and selling Roseville Pottery is big business. It is no longer surprising to see examples of Roseville on the cover of *American Bungalow* or to hear of prices well over $1000 for a single piece. At the Internet auction site <www.ebay.com>, over 1200 Roseville items are usually being offered at all times.

Roseville pottery lovers begin collecting for various reasons. While writing this book, I spoke with a retired shoe salesman who began with the purchase of a Freesia basket. Until he bought that first piece, he thought of Roseville as something "fussy," appealing mainly to "the ladies." Now he takes great pleasure in the soft matte colors and sculptural details that characterize the typical Roseville pot.

Most Roseville collectors begin collecting without any particular goal or ambition. They may have inherited a piece or two, and now wish to add new pieces to the grouping. Others wish to purchase a few useful and decorative examples with which to adorn their home. In time, most collectors decide upon an individual goal. Many dream of owning one example from every Roseville line.

A fairly common goal is to collect "an entire line." The collector picks a specific Roseville pattern and sets out to purchase an example of every known shape in, say, Mostique or Fuchsia. Over time, the hunt can offer as much pleasure and fascination as the collection itself. But watch out: those collections have a way of "growing on you!" Before you know it, your basement is full of Roseville.

One collector has fully shelved the crawl space underneath his house, allowing enough storage for rows and rows of Roseville, all arranged by pattern. To retrieve a group of pots for display in the living room, he still uses his beloved red wagon of childhood, now refurbished with a lining made from carpet remnants. Other collectors house their pieces in an assortment of china cabinets, shelving units, and bookcases. Roseville executives hardly had such arrangements in mind when they wrote, in 1947, "Keep flower bowls not in use carefully stored in your flower cupboard!" (quotation from *How to Decorate with Art Pottery*).

The Basement. Roseville collections can outgrow your china cabinet!

A Few of My Favorite Shapes

Some Roseville collectors prefer to collect a particular shape. They might decide to collect baskets, in various patterns and colors. Book lovers may prefer Roseville bookends. Flower frogs are an interesting and affordable choice for those with limited display space. Almost everyone loves a good "jard and ped." (Imagine the impression you could make with four or five!)

The larger the piece, the more spectacular the decorations. At least, that's what floor vase collectors believe. Apartment dwellers, on the other hand, can be perfectly satisfied with a collection of 6" and 7" bud vases. Wall pockets and window boxes can make an appealing display on an otherwise empty wall space or window sill.

The photographs illustrate some of the shapes Roseville collectors associate with the company, and a variety of Roseville patterns and colors.

Decorating with Roseville

Most Roseville lovers are also flower lovers. As Barbara A. Perry writes, "The name Roseville is most appropriate for this pottery, established by George F. Young, because its wares were decorated to a great extent with floral motifs of some kind. The manufactory originated in Roseville, Ohio (hence its name), but moved to Zanesville six years later in 1898" [see *American Art Pottery: From the Collection of Everson Museum of Art* (New York: Abrams, 1997), page 56].

Few collectors are content to leave their pots stored away in boxes. In addition to displaying them as part of a room's decoration, from time to time it is appropriate to use your pots as they were intended. Those who wish to avoid the potential for water stains and hard-water deposits might try silk or dried flowers. If groupings of pottery can be arranged to harmonize with your other decor, a charming corner can be presented—say, on the subject of "chicks."

Ephemera from the Pottery are also valued by collectors. A collector who contributed photographs to this book sometimes decorates with original Roseville advertising. The advertisement is first matted in the color of a favorite glaze, and the framed piece can then be displayed alongside the actual pottery pieces that are pictured in black and white.

Because paper can fade or be damaged by accidental spills, others prefer to keep Roseville "paper" in a drawer or small box. Original booklets, catalogs, calling cards, stationery, postcards, and other paper items can enhance one's understanding of the factory's relationship with its buyers. Generous collectors have aided many a researcher (including this one!) by sharing these paper collectibles.

One example of Roseville correspondence turned up at a country auction in Ellsworth, Kansas, held on June 24, 1989. The Roseville collector who bought the dealer sign that day became its second owner in over fifty years. Soon afterward, at a Kansas City antiques mall, the same collector purchased a Roseville Pottery business letter dated May 18, 1940, addressed to the owner of the country store and signed by F.S. Clement. It had gone to a dealer attending the 1989 Ellsworth auction. The letter reads, "In reply to your postal of the 15th instant, we are pleased to advise that your order was shipped May 16th." The lucky collector argues convincingly that this letter dates his dealer sign to 1940.

Roseville collectors can treasure even the most insignificant reminders of the factory's history. A number of years ago, one couple visited the original factory dump site in Zanesville, Ohio, and—with permission—collected a basket full of pottery shards. The trek was made strictly for sentimental reasons. No unusual colors or designs were turned up that day, and none were expected. The dump site was used by the factory for disposing of "seconds." **Caution:** In the interest of both privacy and safety, the current property owner hereby requests that *no one* trespass on the old Roseville Pottery site without prior written permission!

The Many Roseville Books!

If you are looking for an accurate survey of Roseville products and advice about buying and selling American art pottery, *Introducing Roseville Pottery* will ground you on these subjects. I hope you will recommend its purchase to your friends. However, one book cannot answer every question you may have about a company that operated for almost 65 years! Soon you will want to expand your library—if you have not already done so.

Since 1968, over a dozen books on Roseville have been published. Because the progress of scholarship is sometimes slow, many simply duplicate the ideas of earlier authors. Most offer

Baskets. Morning Glory 340-10" basket, green; Blackberry 334-6.5" basket; Cosmos 357-10" basket, blue. *Hoppe collection.* **$950–1200, $800–900, $375–425**

photographs of items not readily available in other books. Virginia Hillway Buxton, author of *Roseville Pottery ... for Love or Money*, has an engaging writing style and an intriguing method of rating desirability. *The Collectors Encyclopedia of Roseville Pottery, Second Series*, by Sharon and Bob Huxford, illustrates a good variety of wall pockets, Experimental pieces, Della Robbia, and Creamware. Futura collectors will value the detailed discussions and full-page photographs in Randy Monsen's *Collectors' Compendium of Roseville Pottery, Volume I*.

Two books are strongly recommended as supplements to *Introducing Roseville Pottery*. First, when it becomes available (expected during the year 2000), please read my forthcoming *Understanding Roseville Pottery*. That volume will discuss the factory's products in more depth, focusing on the early art products—like Modern Art, Decorated Artware, Rozane Royal, Azurean, Della Robbia, Mara, Mongol, Egypto, Chloron, Crystalis, Olympic, Aztec, Crocus, Cremo, Cameo, etc.—plus Pauleo, Matt Green, Carnelian (Glazes), unusual Creamware, Experimentals and Trial Glaze pieces. The illustrations will include a number of outstanding museum-

quality items and the collection of the George Krause family. You will also want to own a copy of Jack and Nancy Bomm's *Roseville Pottery in All Its Splendor*, an important reference work that reprints hundreds of original factory records.

Every Roseville lover must also develop some method of gauging current values. Several annual price guides are available to aid in this process, notably Gloria and James Mollring's *Roseville Pottery: Collector's Price Guide* and John W. Humphries' *A Price Guide to Roseville Pottery by the Numbers*. These will soon be joined by *Bassett's Guide to Roseville Pottery Prices*, the first edition of which is expected during the year 2000.

Buyers who participate in the nationally advertised auctions can measure changing values by studying the hammer prices, reported in a computer printout after each auction. Just one of the professional auction catalogs, unfortunately, can cost more than a comprehensive Roseville price guide. A **free** and up-to-the-minute price guide is constantly available on the Internet: just register at <www.ebay.com> and then conduct a SEARCH for "Roseville" among "Completed Auctions."

Bookends. Pair, Snowberry IBE bookends, green; pair, Foxglove 10 bookends, blue. *Hoppe collection.* **$200–250, $275–325**

Cider Set. Magnolia 1327 cider pitcher, brown, and six 3-3" cider mugs, brown. *Shannon collection.* **$350–400 (pitcher), $75–100 (mugs, each).** Roseville's cider sets and stein sets (including Creamware) were originally sold with six mugs (or steins).

Cookie Jars. *Top*: Freesia 4-8" cookie jar, green; Water Lily 1-8" cookie jar, brown. **$450–500, $450–500.** *Bottom*: Clematis 3-8" cookie jar, brown; Magnolia 2-8" cookie jar, blue; Zephyr Lily 5-8" cookie jar, brown. *Shannon collection.* **$500–550, $500–550, $450–500.** Produced during the 1940s, these cookie jar designs are numbered 1 through 5, allowing the company to market them as a line of cookie jars. Each shape was available in each of the three standard colorings for that floral pattern.

Floor Vases. Freesia 129-18" vase, brown; Cosmos 958-18" vase, blue. *Hoppe collection.* **$800–900, $950–1200**

Flower Frogs. Cosmos 39 flower frog, blue; Ixia 34 flower frog, yellow; Rozane Pattern 44 flower frog, blue; Iris 38 flower frog, blue; Poppy 35 flower frog, green. *Hoppe collection.* **$150–175, $100–125, $100–125, $150–175, $125–150.** Like the Roseville cookie jars, these flower frogs were numbered in a sequence that allowed them to be marketed as a line of decorative accessories for flower arranging.

Flower Pots. Ixia 641-5" flower pot (separate saucer), yellow; Ferella 620-5" flower pot (attached saucer), brown. *Hoppe collection.* **$150–200, $750–950**

Performing a Marriage. In November 1989, Frank Shannon (left) and Gordon Hoppe (right) were able to "marry" a stray jardiniere with an appropriate pedestal. A good marriage is considered to involve a proper fit and well-matched color and mold.

"The Happy Couple." Mostique 10" jardiniere and 18" pedestal, in Majolica (Blended) colors. *Hoppe photograph.* **$800–900**

Left:
Jardinieres and Pedestals. Bleeding Heart 651-8" jardiniere and pedestal, blue. *Stofft collection.* **$1500–1800**

Wall Pockets. Matt Green 1206-5" wall pocket, die-impressed 1206; 7.25" wall pocket, attributed to Roseville, unmarked. *Hoppe collection.* **$150–175, $175–225**

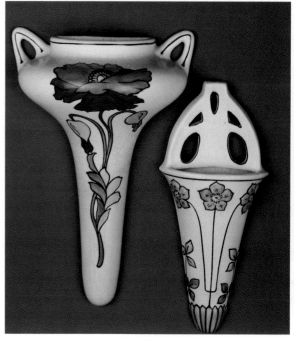

Wall Pockets. Creamware (Persian) 11.5" wall pocket, hand-painted decoration of red poppy and two closed buds; Creamware (Traced and Decorated) 328-10.75" wall pocket, molded phlox design. *Hoppe collection.* **$450–550 (each)**

Below:
Window Boxes. Vista 368-10" window box, with original liner. *Courtesy of Treadway Gallery.* **$950–1200.** This example is marked with a blue inkstamp shape number. (Nearly illegible; the shape number shown may be in error.) The window box interior measures 10" x 3.75"; overall it is 11.75" x 4.5" x 6.25" tall.

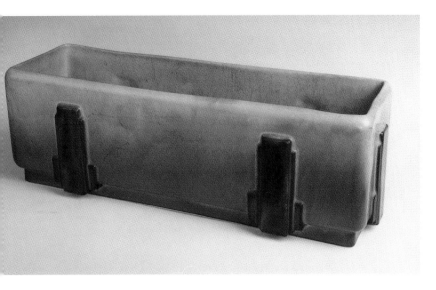

Window Boxes. Futura 376-15" x 4" x 6" window box, unmarked. *Courtesy of Cincinnati Art Galleries.* **$1200–1500**

Cut Flowers in a Vase with Complementary Colors. Early Carnelian 8" vase, attributed to Roseville. *Hoppe collection.* **$100–125 (vase only)**

Decorating with a Jardiniere and Pedestal. Creamware (Persian) 462-12" x 33" jardiniere and pedestal, stylized lotus motifs within unusually ornate pattern, multicolor. *Hoppe collection.* **$2000–2500.** Nothing makes a more impressive visual statement to friends and family than a Roseville "J and P" in use.

A Cactus Garden. Mostique 7" comport. *Shannon collection.* **$200–250 (comport only)**

Decorating with Silk Flowers. Pair, Freesia 1160-2" candlesticks, blue; 7-10" bowl, blue. *Shannon collection.* **$100–125 (pair), $200–250 (bowl only)**

Using Dried Flowers with Roseville. Teasel 885-8" fan vase, peach, with dried teasel pods. *Shannon collection.* **$175–225 (vase only)**

A Covey of Chicks. An assortment of Creamware (Juvenile chick) pieces, displayed with a yard-long print of chicks, a Bon Ami tin with chicks on the lid, and a period Easter postcard of chicks. *Private collection.*

Original Roseville Advertising. An original 1945 Roseville advertisement, matted in rust-colored paper; Freesia 464-6" bowl, brown; Freesia 198-8" cornucopia, brown. *Hoppe photograph.* **$30–40 (framed and matted advertisement), $100–125, $100–125**

Collectible Roseville Paper Items. A reprint of the 1905 catalog; a 1970 reprint of the 1906 catalog; an original 1931 booklet; and (foreground) an original salesman's calling card, ca. 1940. *Shannon collection.* **$25–30 (reprint of 1905 catalog), $30–40 (reprint of 1906 catalog), $50–60 (factory booklet), $15–20 (calling card)**

Roseville Dealer Sign. *Hoppe photograph.* **$2500–3000.**

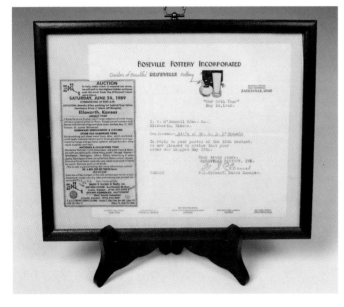

Factory Letter, Signed by F.S. Clement. An original letter (on factory stationery) from Roseville Pottery Incorporated, to the T.G. O'Donnell Hardware Company, Ellsworth, Kansas (site of a June 24, 1989 auction). *Shannon collection.* **$50–60 (factory letter only)**

Basket of Roseville Pottery Shards. *Shannon collection.* **No market value.**

Group of Roseville Dealer Signs. Moderne 9.5" x 3.5" sign, aqua; Ivory 5.5" x 1.5" sign; 5.5" x 1.5" sign, green and orange; 6.25" x 2" sign, pink. *Hoppe collection.* **$2500–3000, $2000–2500, $2200–2700, $1800–2200**

13

Chapter 2
POTTERY COLLECTOR'S ETIQUETTE

This chapter deals with etiquette, ethics, common practices, and expectations. It will prepare you to study actual examples of Roseville and other pottery. There is no substitute for "seeing the real thing." When you have questions, just ask. That's how we learn.

Most pottery dealers are eager to teach others about their favorite subject. If you politely ask to see an example with minor damage or restoration, most would be happy to oblige. If you are concerned about the difference between legitimate Roseville marks and the "forged" marks on recent fake and fantasy pieces, perhaps you can find an example of both at the next show.

As you begin to study Roseville pottery in person, remember to use "pottery collector's etiquette." *A beginner should not handle pottery without the owner's permission* (and possibly assistance). When the seller is not busy with another customer, identify yourself as a beginner. It is customary (and polite) to converse a bit before asking to handle anything. Even with permission, do *not* pick up a piece of pottery by the handle—especially not baskets or teapots. If other pieces of pottery are close by, you may need to move something first—or ask the seller to do so.

Remove the lid carefully (if there is one), and use both hands to grasp the body of the pot. When setting a pot down again, carefully lower it so that one end of the piece touches the surface first (and gently). Then you can use the weight of the piece to your advantage, enabling you to center the pot and stand it upright again. Do not let go until you are sure the piece is stable. Moving your hand away slowly, you can avoid a collision with the next pot over—and the collector behind you.

Delicate figurines may require even more caution. Your motto must be: *Handle with care!* If you damage anything, expect to pay compensation. (*You break, you buy!*)

Bottoms Up!

At antiques shows everywhere, you can see pottery lovers turning pots over and studying their bottoms. Why?

First, most potteries marked their wares on the bottom. Turning a pot over allows a potential buyer to study the marks, as an indicator of maker, age, shape number, or pattern. With practice, you will soon learn to recognize a "typical" Roseville bottom—including a piece that has no factory mark. (For Roseville marks, see Chapter 7. For fake and fantasy pieces, including marks, see Appendix 2.)

Even an unmarked bottom reveals much to the trained eye. Study the photograph captioned "The Bottom of an Unmarked Earlam Piece." Can you see the faint crayon shape number 519? This number was hand-written onto the base after the vase was bisque-fired.

Note the unglazed "ring" of buff-colored clay around the bottom. This is the "foot," the surface upon which the pot rests. The buff color is significant because the clay that can be found in the Zanesville area "fires to buff." Pottery lovers interpret the buff

clay on an unmarked pot as a clue that the piece may have been made at Roseville, Weller, Owens, McCoy, or another Zanesville-area pottery. (One exception is Peters and Reed, whose clay typically fired to a brick red.)

On this pot, you can find several different glazes—a translucent ivory underglaze on the bottom, a matte brown glaze near the foot, and a mottled blue-green matte glaze over that. The foot was intentionally left unglazed, through a process called "dry-footing." When applying glaze a factory worker, using a damp sponge or cloth, carefully removed all glaze from the pot's foot before it had time to dry. Eventually, a group of pots was arranged inside a round clay box (or "sagger") and loaded into the kiln. Dry-footing prevented the glazed pottery from sticking to the sagger. (Saggers were used to increase kiln capacity and to control both the heat and the firing atmosphere.)

Another pot can offer evidence of another method of manufacture. Study the photograph captioned "The Bottom of an Unmarked Matt Green Piece." Do you see that the L-shaped feet of this pot are covered in a thick green glaze? This pot was *not* dry-footed.

As the small white spots indicate, this piece was first covered with an opaque white glaze to neutralize the buff color of the clay. This "underglaze" enabled the primary glazes to fire at their "true" colors. In contrast to the Earlam example, this Matt Green piece has primary glaze on the bottom too—which would obscure any crayon shape number that might have been written there after the bisque firing.

The buff Zanesville clay is visible in only one small spot, which again is the key to understanding how this piece was loaded into the sagger. Before firing, because this piece was *not* dry-footed, it had to be placed atop a small bisque support. This pot was supported by a widely used type of "kiln furniture," a small Y-shaped piece called a "stilt."

The diamond-shaped ends of a stilt enable it to support a pot on three tiny points. Because of its Y-shaped design, a stilt is strong and stable enough to hold a vessel aloft during firing. When the kiln has cooled, and the saggers are opened, grasping the pot and giving it a slight twist will break the stilt, freeing the pot from the sagger. Any bits that still cling to the pot or sagger can easily be broken off with a small hammer. On the bottom of a pot, the broken stilts leave behind three small unglazed "chips" in the shape of an equilateral triangle. (Only one of these "stilt marks," or "stilt pulls," is visible in the photograph under discussion.)

Sometimes glaze runs down from the pot to the stilt or sagger before solidifying. When this occurs, a worker must grind the bottom of the pot enough to allow it to stand level. Tiny "grinding chips" can occur during this process, on the bottom or around the outer edge of the foot. Important: *the "stilt marks" and "grinding chips" associated with using stilts are a normal part of the manufacturing process—not damage.*

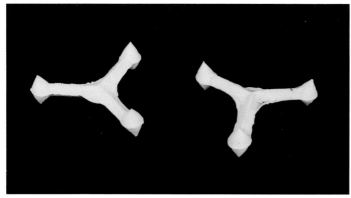

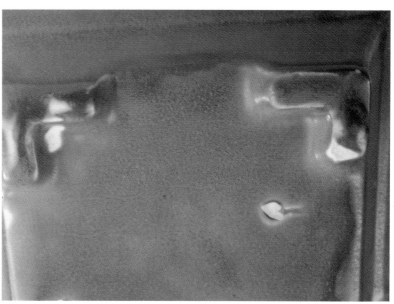

Stilts. These two stilts are small enough to hold a pot whose base is only 3" across. *Courtesy of the Cowan Pottery Museum at Rocky River (OH) Public Library.*

The Bottom of an Unmarked Earlam Piece.

The Bottom of an Unmarked Matt Green Piece.

Damage, Restoration, Preservation

Only a few years ago, many Roseville collectors shunned pieces with even the most minor damage—and sometimes pieces with inconsequential factory flaws. Today most collectors recognize that ceramics have an inherent potential for damage. The typical collector *does* expect every seller to make a "full disclosure" of condition. In other words, he or she requires a complete description of any distracting factory flaws and of *all* damage (or restoration) that occurred after a piece left the factory. With an adjustment in price, collectors are often willing to add defective pieces to a collection. Many hope to upgrade the collection later, when a better example is acquired and the earlier example can be resold.

Over time, a vocabulary has emerged with which to discuss these matters. A "glaze chip" is usually so small that it is *not noticeable* from a distance of about two to three feet away. As the term implies, a glaze chip should not involve any damage to the clay body of the piece—only to the glaze itself.

When describing small nicks and chips, it is sometimes useful to "measure" by making comparisons to some readily available object—the head of a straight pin, a mustard seed, a grain of rice, a small English pea, a person's smallest fingernail, a dime, and so on. Look at the photograph of a brown Orian vase. The glaze chip on this pot's left handle is a bit narrower and longer than the head of a straight pin. (Incidentally, did you notice the smaller glaze chip on the other handle?)

An Orian Vase with Minor Damage.

The Matt Green fern dish with cherub heads has two small "nicks" on the rim, each about the size of a mustard seed. The term "nick" implies that some clay may have been damaged along with the glaze, but that the damage is self-contained and less than 0.25" across. (The grayish buff spots inside and along the outer shoulder are hard-water deposits, which can probably be removed with a little effort and the proper cleaning solution.)

More serious to collectors than either glaze chips or nicks are "chips" and "hairlines" (or "cracks"), both of which are illustrated in the photograph captioned "Detail from a Futura Vase." To the best of your ability, describe what you see. This time the chip is roughly 0.125" tall by 0.25" wide and located horizontally along the outer rim, about halfway between the handles. You could say that the chip is about the size of two grains of rice laid side by side. Running down through the chip is a hairline crack, starting at the "mouth" of the piece (the inside rim, or "lip") and extending about 1.25".

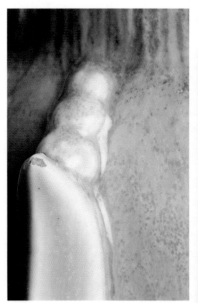

A Glaze Chip (detail).

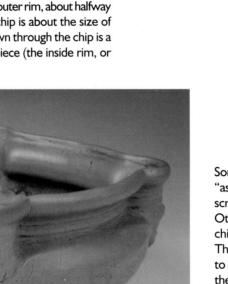

A Matt Green Fern Dish with Minor Nicks. Matt Green 319-7" fern dish, winged and crowned cherub heads at each corner, die-impressed 319. *Courtesy of Mark Bassett Antiques.* **$200–250 "as is"** (or $300–400 in mint condition)

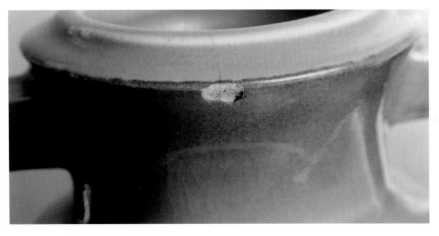

Detail from a Futura Vase.

Collectors differ over the need for restoration. Some purists believe every piece should be left in its "as found" condition, revealing all the dents and scratches, bumps and bruises that come with age. Others choose to have professional restorers fill in chips and hairlines with two-part epoxy cement. Then the epoxy repair is painted (typically in acrylics) to blend with the glazes or decorations surrounding the damage. An application of acetone can remove both the acrylic paint and the epoxy without harm to either clay or glaze. Most restorers expect their work to last for about five years.

Restoration is motivated primarily for cosmetic reasons. If a properly restored pot looks substantially like it was originally intended to look, and the restoration is "reversible," there are fewer objections. Dealers may even find it easier to sell a properly restored example than to sell a piece with minor (but unrestored) damage. When restoration has occurred, full disclosure is particularly important.

If you believe a piece to be restored, and suspect that the seller is not being honest, **do not** disturb the surface in any manner without prior permission. If you scratch off a bit of paint with your nail, or apply acetone to the surface (for example, in the form of nail polish remover on a facial tissue), be prepared to have the piece restored again—at your own expense!

Instead, there are various non-obtrusive methods of determining whether a pot has been restored. Look at the photograph captioned "A Rozane Royal (Dark) Miniature." From a normal distance of several feet, this piece looks fine. "It displays well." Yet a chip about half the size of a dime was restored on the rim. Close up, one can see where the dark brown paint has been applied. In one spot, the restorer accidentally left a drippy section of paint. The top view also is not perfectly round, an indication that the epoxy repair was hand-shaped by the restorer. Daylight (or a table

Restoration (detail). Note the drip of paint just beneath the lip. Another sign of restoration is the transition in color from an opaque chocolate brown (airbrushed paint) to a translucent golden brown (fired glaze).

Restoration (detail). Roughly the top 1/4 of the lip of this Rozane Royal (Dark) bud vase was missing, due to a chip about half the size of a dime. The restorer has hand-modeled the missing section and painted it dark brown. Note the slightly out-of-round edge and the brush strokes.

A Miniature Roseville Vase. Rozane Royal (Dark) 925A-3.5" vase, pansies, die-impressed ROZANE marks, including shape number 925. *Cooper collection.* **$40–50 "as is" (or $75–100 in mint condition).** Note that this restored vase makes a perfectly attractive "shelf piece." The restorer charged a reasonable $15, and the unrestored vase cost $10 in 1998—bringing the total investment to $25. Because most professional restorers charge a minimum fee of $50 or more, some damaged Roseville is still impractical to restore.

lamp with a 75-watt bulb or stronger) is an effective aid to inspection. (Fluorescent lights can distort colors and textures, even in close-up.) Some buyers rely on more specialized methods, such as black lights or dental X-rays.

Respect is paramount in these matters. Museum curators remind us that the decorative objects we collect may very well survive our own death, making us simply their caretakers, not their "owners." With that possibility in mind, it is advisable to consider the proper conservation of your beloved pottery too—in addition to more selfish concerns.

The proper care of a collection requires some thought. Dust, smoke, extreme temperature changes, abrasive cleaning solutions—all these can damage pottery too, or prevent its full enjoyment. To safeguard your investment, keep your collection in a temperature- and humidity-controlled environment. Regular cleaning should be done, at least once a year, even if no more than rinsing with lukewarm water and drying with a clean, soft cloth. Some glazes are sturdy; others are delicate. Until you know the difference, use extreme caution! Specialized pottery dealers have usually cleaned their pots properly before presenting them for sale. If you have questions about cleaning a piece, they are usually pleased to help.

Grade versus Condition

During the firing process, glazes become liquid, change color, and gradually cool to form a decorative and protective coating for the piece. When things went wrong, the potteries might label a particular pot a "factory second," instead of "first quality" production. Each pottery defined its own goals and standards. Today, practically everyone agrees that manufacturing flaws are to be left alone. They are not to be altered by a restorer.

At most American art potteries, including Roseville, we do not know precisely what "defects" necessitated a pot's being labeled a factory second. Unlike Rookwood (who marked factory seconds with a hand-incised "X" on the base), Roseville did *not* use any special mark to indicate their factory seconds. If a factory second was particularly objectionable, it was probably destroyed in the pottery's dump site. Otherwise, as was the common practice among the potteries, a factory second with a minor flaw might be sold at half the usual price. Sometimes an employee may have retrieved an unbroken example from the dump site.

Today both factory seconds and first-quality pieces sit side by side in the antiques shows. Like the original factory workers, we can only inspect them one by one, and judge for ourselves whether a piece "passes our inspection." Only you can set the standards for your personal collection.

Even among the factory's first-quality products, some examples of Roseville have crisper details or brighter colors than others of the same design. What happened? There might have been a fortunate coincidence of humidity and air pressure that morning, along with well-rested staff and a newly mixed vat of glaze. Maybe the caster had just poured the first series of pieces made in a brand-new mold. Perhaps the man firing the kiln turned down the oxygen at just the right time, or cooling proceeded in a "textbook" fashion, producing the most desirable gradations of hue or texture. These are matters of *grade,* not condition.

The making of pottery was always partly an art, even though improved by a working knowledge of glaze chemistry. It is unreasonable to apply an impossibly obsessive standard of "perfection" to one's purchases. Consider the following list of "oddities" one might encounter on a particular pot (a few of which are illustrated in the photographs):

—glaze "crawling" (the glaze curls back a bit, exposing the clay body);

—unexpected color variations;

—seam lines showing through a thinly applied glaze (some factories deemed this problem grounds for the label "factory second"; others did not worry much about seam lines; Roseville's view of the subject is unclear);

—"crazing" (a finely crackled surface, produced during firing if the glaze and clay body cool at different rates);

—uneven bases, so that a piece does not stand perfectly level;

—"slumping" (the piece does not stand perfectly straight because some part of it warped during firing);

—handles of slightly different dimensions, or applied at slightly different heights;

—lids that don't fit properly;

—burst air bubbles in the glaze;

—"kiln kisses" (small dents or losses on glazed and fired ware, caused while the saggers were being loaded into the kiln and a pot touched the sagger wall or another piece of ware);

—"glazed-over chips" (small chips on the greenware or bisque ware that have been glazed over and fired);

—"firing lines" (cracks that occurred during firing, usually along a stress line in the piece—not damage caused after leaving the factory);

—"peppering" (small black specks of mica or iron in a glaze intended to be white or light in color); or

—bits of clay fired onto an otherwise smooth surface (these were to be smoothed away before the bisque firing).

Such vagaries of the manufacturing process are useful in determining the "grade" of a particular pot. In general, the more "oddities" on a given piece, the lower the grade.

Glaze Spot (detail). The tan spot on the shoulder of this Della Robbia teapot appears to have spattered onto a previously colored green section.

Glaze Pooling (detail). During firing, the green glaze on this Primrose leaf flowed into the pink background.

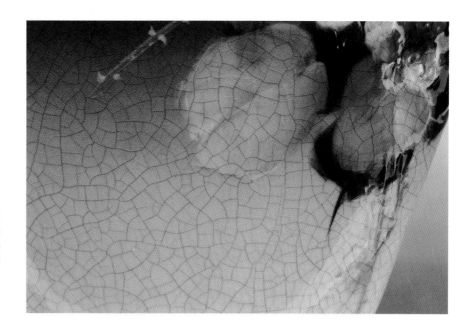

Crazing (detail). Rozane Royal, Azurean, and Decorated Artware pieces often have some amount of crazing. If the crazing can easily be seen from a distance of about two feet, many collectors view it as an unpleasant distraction.

Firing Crack (detail). During firing, weaknesses in the wall of a pot can cause it to separate, leaving a firing crack. Look for such fissures near the holes introduced into wall pockets or hanging baskets (like the Vista example shown). They are also common at the joints of pieces which were assembled, before firing, from separately molded parts.

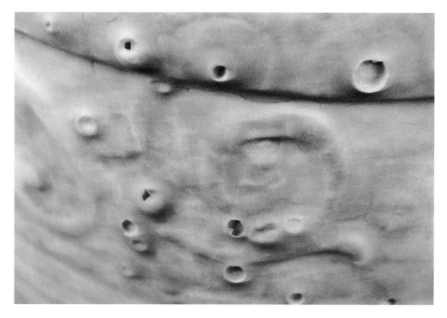

Burst Air Bubbles (detail). During firing, air bubbles can drift to the surface and burst, releasing oxygen into the kiln atmosphere. In this instance, the glaze began to cool before these air bubbles had all been released.

Collectors like pieces with "good color." But what they mean by that phrase varies from one person to the next. The photographs show several examples of color variation. Another important consideration is the relative sharpness of molded details. "How is the mold?" one often hears collectors ask. Again, this kind of judgment is completely subjective. Even more than condition, answering questions about color and mold is better accomplished through personal inspection.

Photographs can be a useful aid, but they can also be deceiving. With professional lighting and other equipment, a crisp photograph can make a pot seem better than it really looks under typical indoor lighting. On the other hand, improper lighting or focus can change colors and surface details—a problem one encounters fairly often when buying Roseville on-line. Digital cameras are fun and quick, but they too can produce inferior results.

Variations in Color (Iris). Iris 131-6" cornucopia, blue; Iris 918-7" bud vase, blue. *Shannon collection.* **$125–150, $150–175.** Such dramatic color variations are known in many Roseville lines. Only personal taste can determine which coloring is preferable.

Variations in Color (Futura). Three Futura 393-12" vases, with minor differences in color. *Courtesy of Greg Koster; Bassett collection; courtesy of Bob Swartz.* **$950–1200 (each).** The amount of translucent white overglaze varies in these three examples. Only the individual collector can determine which piece is "the most attractive" (or "most successful").

Variations in Color (Vista). Two Vista 589-10" jardinieres. *Hoppe photograph.* **$750–950, $650–750.** One example has lavender details in the foliage, as do most examples of Vista. The light-colored example (without any lavender) would be less desirable.

Variations in Color (Montacello). Montacello 557-5" vase, turquoise; Montacello 563-8" vase, turquoise. *Hoppe photograph.* **$375–425, $575–650.** Glaze flow during firing can cause dramatically different "looks" in certain lines. Montacello collectors enjoy the resulting variety in the appearance of various examples.

Variations in "Mold" (Pine Cone and Pine Cone Modern). Pine Cone 112-7" bud vase, brown, *courtesy of Tony McCormack;* Pine Cone Modern 479-7" bud vase, blue, *courtesy of Bobby and Joan Joray.* **$125–150, $150–175.** Note the unusually sharp definition on the pine cone, branch, and needles of the blue vase.

Variations in "Mold" (Clemana). Clemana 750-6" vase, green; Clemana 123-7" pillow vase, green; Clemana 752-7" vase, green. *Hoppe photograph.* **$275–325, $275–325, $300–350.** The center example is less detailed than the other two pieces, and would therefore be slower to sell.

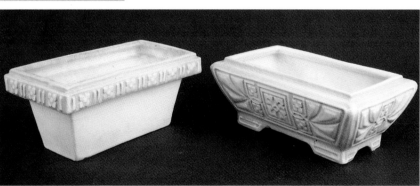

A Pot with Multiple Parts. Old Ivory (Tinted) 210-4" x 8" combination planter, pale green, liner die-impressed 210. *Scheytt collection.* **$175–225 (complete, or $95–125 without liner).** Beginners sometimes overlook the possibility that a Roseville piece may have been intended to have another part—whether a liner, a lid, or an underplate.

An Old Ivory (Tinted) Combination Planter. Here is the two-part planter, correctly assembled.

21

Worn Hand-Painted Trim. Two Creamware 8" rolled-edge plates, with Nursery Rhyme decals of "Hickory, Dickory Dock," both unmarked. *Scheytt collection.* **$125–175, $95–125.** One example is colorful; most of its narrow green banding is intact. In the other case, the Baby's Plate legend is almost entirely worn away (through repeated use and cleaning).

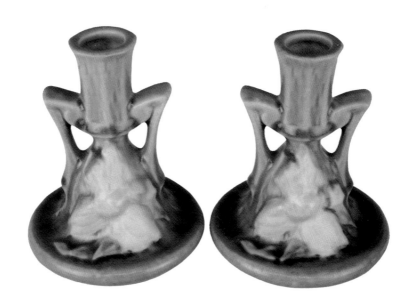

Factory Seconds? Pair, Clematis 1159-4.5" candlesticks, blue. *Courtesy of Treadway Gallery.* **$75–95 (pair).** The glassy dark blue glaze on the surface of these candlesticks is an indication of overfiring. The pieces may have been considered factory seconds.

What is "Mint Condition"?

In its most widely accepted meaning, the term "mint condition" (when used by pottery dealers and collectors) means "factory new." In other words, the term *mint* refers *only* to condition; it should *not* be used to describe the *grade* of a piece.

If an item is in mint condition, it is presumed to have all of its original parts. An item in mint condition does not have glaze nicks, chips, hairlines, or repairs of any kind. If a hole was drilled through the bottom or side of a vase (after leaving the factory) to allow use as a lamp base, it is *not* in mint condition! (For more information about Roseville lamps, see "Lamps," in Chapter 6.) Mint-condition examples do *not* have worn decals or scratched lustre glazes.

On the other hand, factory seconds and inferior pots can also be found in mint condition. As long as no damage occurred after the piece was sold by the factory, the term "mint" still applies. For this reason, most collectors buying by mail will ask questions about *both* condition and grade.

The Pottery Shows

If you love Roseville, then reserve the third week of July to attend the annual Pottery Lovers Reunion (Zanesville/Cambridge, Ohio). This major event is a must for pottery lovers—held in the town where Roseville was made! Activities generally begin the first full weekend after July 4th, with buying and selling of American art pottery (of all kinds) in the east-end Zanesville hotels (chiefly the Holiday Inn, Days Inn, and Red Roof Inn). The easiest way to learn about next year's reunion is to subscribe to the informal "Pottery Lovers" newsletter. Send $5 (check payable to "Pottery Lovers") to Mrs. Pat Sallaz, 4969 Hudson Drive, Stow, OH 44224.

Pottery lovers should also know about the American Art Pottery Association (abbreviated AAPA). Every year this non-profit organization publishes an educational *Journal of the American Art Pottery Association* and an annual "Directory of Membership" (useful for contacting both dealers and collectors). In the spring, the AAPA hosts a national convention that combines slide presentations with a show and sale of American art pottery. For AAPA membership information, write to the AAPA Secretary, Patti Bourgeois, P.O. Box 834, Westport, MA 02790–0697. On the Internet, visit the AAPA website at <www.AmArtPot.org>.

Another major annual show is APEC, an abbreviation for American Pottery, Earthenware, and China. This one-day show is held in Springfield, Illinois, at the Illinois State Fairgrounds on one Saturday every fall (usually the last Saturday in September). The show features American art pottery, collectible American dinnerware, Russel Wright accessories, Hall teapots, and American studio pottery and tiles. To contact the show promoter, write Norm Haas, 264 Clizbe Road, Quincy, MI 49082; or call (517) 639-8537.

Regional shows and conventions are popping up all over. In Florida, the collector club Rosevilles of the Past sponsors a show during a January or February weekend. In 1998 club founders and show promoters Jack and Nancy Bomm published their useful reference volume *Roseville in All Its Splendor*. For information about the club and show, write Nancy Bomm, P.O. Box 656, Clarcona, FL 32710; or call (407) 294-3980.

Two major pottery shows take place in California. The longest running is called simply "The Pottery Show," held in Glendale in mid-October. The San Jose Pottery Show is a February event (like the Arts and Crafts Conference, in Asheville, North Carolina). The Madison-based Wisconsin Pottery Association now has a pottery show in late August every year. In Cleveland, the Cowan Pottery Museum Associates are currently planning an annual fall show of American pottery and china.

The AAPA Code of Ethics

Whether you buy or sell Roseville Pottery as a hobby or as a livelihood, you need to know about the "Code of Ethics" of the American Art Pottery Association, reprinted below. Good "business" practices are good for all of us!

1. Contracts for pottery sales or trades are binding, whether written or verbal. A seller* shall not agree to a transaction and later make a more favorable contract on the same piece of pottery. A buyer** shall not renege on an agreement except as provided herein.

2. Sellers must truthfully and accurately represent pieces for sales as to authenticity and condition, point out all damage, alterations, repairs and missing parts.

3. Sellers must clearly price all pottery for sale.

4. Sellers must provide buyers with their names or business names, addresses and telephone numbers if requested. This information must be provided on all sales receipts and business documents.

5. Sellers must give any buyer who purchases pottery in person the privilege of return of any piece if invisible repairs or alterations are discovered. When a piece is bought sight unseen, the buyer must be allowed to return the piece for any reason. The amount of

time allowed to the buyer to return pieces must be clearly stated by the seller at the time of the transaction, preferably in writing. Unless actually agreed to otherwise, buyers must return piece in substantially the same condition as when purchased.

6. Sellers and buyer must conduct their business dealings with honesty, integrity and in accordance with the law among themselves and with the public.

*A "seller" is defined as any person offering any item of pottery for sale or trade, regardless of whether that person is a full-time or part-time dealer by profession or a collector.

**A "buyer" is defined as any person interested in acquiring an item of pottery by purchase or trade, regardless of whether that person is a collector, or a full-time or part-time dealer by profession.

These basic tenets can be consulted for guidance when a transaction goes awry, as occasionally happens to the best of us. If a buyer cannot see a piece personally before a purchase is made, disagreements over authenticity and condition sometimes occur. Upon receipt (and certainly within the next day or two), every mail-order package should be carefully unpacked and inspected.

If the buyer is satisfied, it is polite to send a thank-you. If the seller does *not* receive a telephone call, telegram, or e-mail message *immediately* after receipt, he or she can assume that the buyer is satisfied. Beyond a reasonable period (often defined as "within three business days of receipt"), the seller no longer has an obligation to allow returns.

Despite the current fascination with computers, disputes about authenticity or condition are better handled on the telephone. Bite the bullet, and give your transaction a personal flavor while working out these sensitive issues. (Some pottery lovers are not on-line, even if they buy and sell on the Internet. While writing this book, for example, your author has had on-line connections only at a friend's house or at the local public library, which has excellent facilities. Just after Christmas of 1998, I ran almost 80 auctions on <www.ebay.com> during a single week!)

Buyer and seller now compare their impressions and opinions. Both parties already know that—according to AAPA rule 5—the buyer can return the piece for a refund if not satisfied. When a return is made for personal reasons, the buyer cannot expect to be refunded the costs of selling, shipping, or insurance. An example: a buyer decides that a Russco vase does not have "large" crystals in the glaze, after all.

When the seller can be shown to have made an error (in authenticity or condition), then the buyer must be refunded the shipping and insurance costs (for shipping both ways). One example: a piece turns out to have been restored, although it was advertised as being in "mint" condition. Another example: the buyer can document with a die-impressed example that a matte green pottery jardiniere was made by Weller, not Roseville.

Buyers, keep this in mind: If the dispute is not settled amicably, you may have to pay for the return shipping and insurance charges. (You may also lose the original shipping and insurance charges.) It's a hard lesson to learn. We are sometimes better off to buy from knowledgeable sellers, and from those willing to admit mistakes. (We all make them!)

Dealing with Dealers

If you plan to buy or sell Roseville on the Internet, you'll be glad to know that sales tax is not usually due on mail-order transactions that cross state lines. Some Pottery Lovers and AAPA members who sell pottery as hobbyists are essentially upgrading their personal collections. In such a case, you may not always be required to pay sales tax.

However, within their home state, many Roseville dealers are *required* to collect and pay the state sales tax (even on transactions made by mail or Internet). Those who cannot prove that a transaction was made properly must be willing to pay the sales tax (plus interest and penalties). Few sellers are willing to risk such financial losses in order to make one sale.

Everyone enjoys finding a bargain. The good news is that pottery sellers often collect pottery themselves. So most sellers at the major pottery shows are happy to negotiate their asking prices a bit. Flourishing a copy of your favorite price guide is not likely to improve your chances. Instead, try a smile and an honest expression of interest in purchasing the piece.

Don't be afraid to ask questions, but use a little common sense. It can be tiresome to spend hours with someone who never actually makes a purchase, hires an appraisal, or offers something for sale to the generous "pottery expert." An important part of your education will come when you begin to invest your own money into your collection (or inventory). Building a library of reference books is also important.

Upgrading Your Collection

In time, many collectors find the need to sell an occasional piece from their collection. Some choose to purchase duplicates whenever a rare or desirable item is encountered in a price range that seems appropriate (or reasonable). Back at home, a collector can make comparisons thoughtfully, keeping the "better" example and using the duplicate for trading or investment purposes.

Since the early 1980s, American art pottery has been a growing market, and prices have steadily risen. Perhaps the urge to sell will come only when you feel a need to raise funds for another purchase. In Zanesville, at the Pottery Lovers Reunion—or at the other specialized American ceramic shows—you may soon find lots of tempting reasons to "upgrade"!

Fantasy Piece. 9" vase, partly glazed in semigloss black, unmarked. *Courtesy of McAllister Auctions.* **$25–30.** This piece appears to be loosely based on the Roseville Sunflower 487-7" vase. No known example of Sunflower has a smooth background; none are known to have been partly glazed in such a manner.

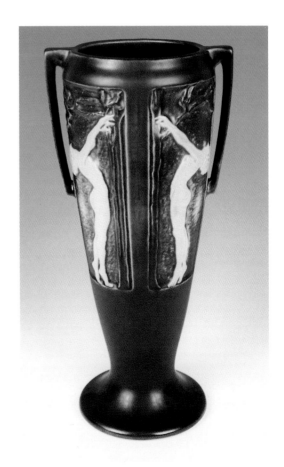

Panel. 298-11" vase, green, blue Rv inkstamp. *Schultz collection.* **$1200–1500**

Chapter 3
EXPERIMENTAL AND TRIAL GLAZE PIECES

Experimental and Trial Glaze pieces were used to assist Roseville executives in developing new product lines. The decision-making process involved two stages, described below. Today, collectors avidly seek these unusual shapes and colors. The pieces are rare enough to rate values significantly higher than those of regular production items.

Experimentals

Experimental pieces often began with a slip-cast molded vase. Classical shapes were used (and perhaps designed) for this purpose. Because of this standardization, many Experimentals share the same underlying vase shape. Look beyond the applied and carved details to see the basic shape with which an Experimental piece began. (There are also Experimentals that were wheel-thrown, slab-built, and/or hand-modeled.)

After the greenware had dried to the "leather hard" stage, the vase was ready for further design work. Frank Barks, chief modeler for many years, would apply sculpted blossoms and leaves to the vase, using slip as adhesive. ("Slip" is a slurry made by mixing additional water into a sample of the clay body.) Fine tooling was carried out on the petals and stems when these had dried enough to allow handling again. Additional low-relief details were often carved into the background surface.

Most collectors believe that Roseville Experimentals approach being one of a kind. For this reason, they are inevitably in demand, and usually make good investments—despite their initially high cost. In today's market, it is typical for an Experimental piece to sell for several thousand dollars—despite the minor damage that seems typical of these items.

Some Experimental pieces showcase ideas that were never developed further. Occasionally, an Experimental seems to be the prototype for a standard production line, although in non-standard colors on a non-standard shape. Such pieces are naturally somewhat less interesting (and therefore less expensive) than those with subjects that were never put into production. Many Experimentals have hand-incised legends on one side, naming the flower depicted and recommending particular colors. Other examples are completely unmarked.

Experimental (Amaryllis). 8" vase, pink and green. *Hoppe photograph.* Obverse is hand-incised "Amaryllis, Scarlet, white or pink striped flowers."
$3000–3500

Obverse of Experimental (Amaryllis). *Hoppe photograph.*

Experimental (Dahlia and Silhouette). 10" vase, pink and green; 10" vase, rust, black crayon glaze notations. *Hoppe photograph.* **$2500–3000, $2000–2500.** The obverse of the first piece is hand-incised "Dahlia, most any color, yellow centre."

Experimental (Freesia). 9" vase, green and tan, black crayon notations "58 / 84 / 14" and 923. *Courtesy of Mike Nickel and Cindy Horvath.* Obverse is hand-incised "Freesia, White or Pink or Yellow Flowers." **$2500–3000**

Crayon Glaze Notations from Experimental "Silhouette" Vase. *Hoppe photograph.*

Experimentals. 8" vase, blue Rv inkstamp, die-impressed M; 8" vase, blue Rv inkstamp, die-impressed II. *Hoppe collection.* **$2000–2500, $2500–3000.** The first piece is ribbed in the manner of Lombardy, but glazed in Carnelian (Drip) colors. The second piece has incised designs reminiscent of Savona.

Experimental. 12.25" vase, carved with floral tree, unmarked. *Nickel and Horvath collection.* **$3000–3500.** This shape is reminiscent of Victorian Art Pottery, and the colors of Panel.

Trial Glazes

When a motif was approved for production, the general style was also decided upon—whether classical or Modernistic, and whether backgrounds would be smooth or textured. Perhaps the line's signature handles and rims were chosen at this time. Designer Frank Ferrell (or another artist) then began to prepare detailed drawings of the shapes to be produced for the line.

Parallel to these activities, in another department, the factory was constantly experimenting with new glazes and underglaze colors for use in hand decoration. Some of these glaze trials were conducted on miniature bud vases (designed during the Rozane Royal period), plates, or small tiles. But when a new line was to be introduced, Trial Glaze pieces were also executed—for consideration by Roseville's board of directors, stylists, and important buyers. For this purpose, the 8" vase shape was often selected from the line's repertoire.

Trial Glaze pieces are examples of standard production shapes, but glazed with non-standard colors. They usually have indelible blue or black crayon markings on the base to indicate the glazes used, although these abbreviations have little or no meaning to the average person. Such glaze notations are usually covered with a

Trial Glazes (Primrose and Corinthian). Primrose 767-8" vase, glossy blue; Primrose 767-8" vase, pink (a standard coloring); Corinthian 217-8" vase (standard coloring); Corinthian 217-8" vase, rust and brown. *Shannon collection.* **$250–300, $200–250, $150–200, $500–600.** The blue Primrose vase has no crayon glaze notations. Instead of a Trial Glaze, it may represent an overfired factory second. In any case, because the glaze is unusual, most collectors consider it slightly more valuable than the standard production piece.

Trial Glazes [Water Lily and Dogwood (Smooth)]. Water Lily 77-8" vase, pink and brown; Water Lily 77-8" vase, brown (a standard coloring); Dogwood (Smooth) 135-8" vase (standard coloring); Dogwood (Smooth) 135-8" vase, dark and light brown. *Shannon collection.* **$350–400, $150–200, $175–225, $375–450**

Trial Glazes (Silhouette and Mock Orange). Silhouette 785-9" vase, rust (a standard coloring); Silhouette 785-9" vase, peach and green (obverse has brown in recessed design); Mock Orange 982-7" vase, pink (a standard coloring); Mock Orange 982-8" vase, mustard yellow and green, high gloss. *Shannon collection.* **$150–175, $350–400, $150–175, $400–500**

transparent or translucent glaze. Similar glaze notations can appear on Experimentals. (**Caution:** Roseville lamps were often marked with orange or red crayon shape numbers. Although the factory lamps can have interesting and innovative glazes, they should not be considered Trial Glaze pieces.)

Less valuable than Experimentals, Trial Glaze pieces are more readily available in the market. Like Experimentals, Trial Glazes are essentially one of a kind. Occasionally, one encounters several examples with striking similarities. Close inspection often reveals a flower painted differently, or some other minor variation in decoration.

Trial Glazes in colors very similar to the regular production line have less value to collectors than those in bright, unexpected hues. The most spectacular examples—a subjective judgment—can bring 3-4 times the price of the same piece in standard production colors. Because Trial Glazes sometimes go unnoticed in the booths of general-line antiques dealers, many Roseville collectors place this category on their "wish list."

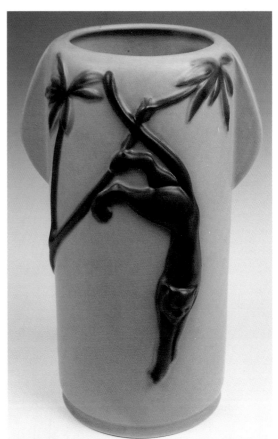

Trial Glaze (Wincraft). 290-11" vase, matte colors, background blends from pale orange to rose, artist monogram GK (George Krause), dated 1947, both hand-incised and crayon trial glaze notations. *Ross collection.* **NPD**

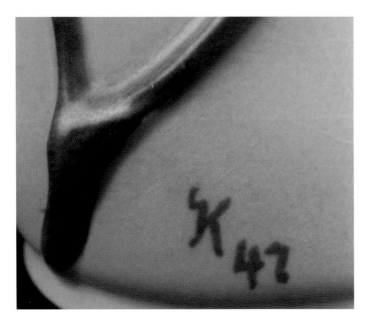

Detail of Trial Glaze (Wincraft).

Marks on Trial Glaze (Wincraft). Note that a Roseville employee has called this cat a "tiger" instead of a panther.

Chapter 4
GLAZE AND SHAPE: TIPS FOR IDENTIFYING ROSEVILLE LINES

Until they get the hang of it, beginners sometimes need a little help distinguishing similar Roseville pieces from each other. This chapter demonstrates the point and will help you avoid some potential confusion. When in doubt, consult the shape lists in Chapter 6.

Glaze Before Shape

Some Roseville pieces are difficult for beginners to identify correctly because their shape appears in more than one line. The general rule is this: Glaze before shape. In other words, if you find a Futura shape that is white all over and has die-impressed marks, then your piece is from the Ivory line—even if the shape number is not listed under Ivory in the Roseville books.

Caution: Not all legitimate Roseville shapes are shown or listed in factory documents. The photographs in this book document most of the Roseville products, some of which may have had a "short shelf life." Others were probably made after the factory stock pages were already completed.

The "glaze before shape" rule applies even if a different line name was die-impressed onto the bottom of a piece, as shown in the case of the Rozane Royal (Dark) ewer incorrectly marked "Azurean." Collectors sometimes find a piece whose Rozane wafer (shown in Chapter 7) does not accurately describe the glaze—for example, a Mongol wafer on a vase with Hand Decorated artwork. (Thankfully, Roseville collectors do not often encounter this type of marking error. Weller collectors often find Eocean marked Etna, Louwelsa marked Floretta, and so on.)

Trial Glaze pieces reverse this rule—making *shape* (not glaze) the key to identifying a line. (For details, see Chapter 3.)

As this chapter's photographs of pitchers indicate, Roseville sometimes reused an earlier shape. Such decisions were made after studying recent buying trends and professional market forecasts—not out of whim or caprice. It is not quite accurate to make the statement, as we sometimes do, "Oh yeah, they were *always* doing that!"

Before 1910, classically inspired Roseville shapes appealed to the decorators or designers of more than one line. Most collectors know that Rozane Royal (Dark) and Rozane Royal (Light) share many shapes. When glancing through a Roseville book, it may be less obvious that Woodland, for example, can share shapes with Rozane Royal, Matt Green, and Fudji.

Many Matt Green shapes were available as Old Ivory (Tinted), and vice versa. Some 1950s Pine Cone Modern shapes are either reissues or adaptations of 1930s Pine Cone designs. (This accounts for the different shape numbers one can find on those shapes.) Carnelian (Drip) pieces are sometimes confused with Carnelian (Glazes).

Made in the 1930s, the Tourmaline line introduced new shapes and revived others from earlier lines. Because of their different values, pieces glazed in one of Tourmaline's four standard colorings should be distinguished from Futura, Earlam, and Imperial (Glazes).

Related Shapes and Glazes

Sometimes, two shapes are not identical, but so similar that one gives every sign of having been derived from the other. Study the photographs that compare a Rozane Royal (Dark) vase with an example of Chloron/Egypto, and an Early Carnelian jardiniere with a related Vista piece. Fortunately, these lines are distinct enough to cause little confusion. (If you're wondering how to tell Chloron from Egypto, welcome to the club!)

Many beginners confuse the Ivory reissues of Volpato with the earlier line. Note that Volpato has a transparent glossy glaze. The buff-colored clay easily shows through the Volpato finish. In contrast, Ivory is an opaque semimatte white. Ivory's buff-colored clay can only peek through the glaze on the high points of a molded design (if at all).

Three of Roseville's semigloss or semimatte rosy red shades are easily confused with one another. Two of these glazes are from the lines Rosecraft and Solid Colors. The third was used on a group of fluted "ivy pots"—not a full-fledged line, but simply another money-making idea during the Great Depression. Similarly, a drippy green glaze occurs in both Pasadena Planters and Keynote.

By incorporating more than one floral motif into a single line, Artwood, Futura, and Wincraft are not typical Roseville products. Do not confuse these lines! Because of Futura's great variety and high value in the marketplace, recognizing unmarked examples of Futura can only be beneficial. The photographs illustrate a few of the similarities between these and other floral lines.

Inaccurate Markings. Rozane Royal (Dark) 858-15" ewer, leaves and berries, artist initialed J.I. (by Josephine Imlay), incorrectly die-impressed AZUREAN, also die-impressed 858/R P Co and 5. *Fairfield collection.* **$950–1200**

•**Group of 550-4" Jardinieres.** At least three Roseville "lines" are represented in this assortment: Ivory (center), Antique Matt Green (left center, and right center), and Solid Colors. The rose-colored example may be Rosecraft, although that shape does not appear in the Rosecraft factory stock pages. *Fairfield collection.* **$75–95 (Ivory), $95–125 (Antique Matt Green), $65–85 (other lines, each).** These pieces are unmarked. Some have foil labels.

Utility Ware (Landscape Pitchers). Majolica (Hand Decorated) 7.5" pitcher; Majolica (Blended Colors) 7.5" pitcher. *Hoppe photograph.* **$175–225, $150–200.** These decorative pitchers are located under Utility Ware in Chapter 5, but the examples shown are typical in having Majolica glazes. These pieces are unmarked.

Utility Ware ("Ideal" Pitcher) and Pauleo. Utility Ware ("Ideal") 3-5.5" pitcher, opaque pink and white enamels, gilt trim; Pauleo 6-7.25" pitcher, mottled matte brown. *Hoppe photograph.* **$150–200, $550–650.** These pieces are unmarked.

Utility Ware (Pitchers). Cornelian 5" pitcher, blue; Majolica (Solid Colors) 6.5" pitcher, brown; Cornelian 8" pitcher, pink. *Shannon collection.* **$75–95, $75–95, $95–125.** All three examples have a translucent ivory underglaze. The Majolica example was next dipped partly into a brown glaze. The Cornelian pitchers were mottled in gray, blue, and pink, applied with a sponge or cloth. These pieces are unmarked.

Della Robbia and Rozane Royal (Light). Della Robbia 34-6.75" pitcher, stylized florals, artist initials G.B., no factory mark; Rozane Royal (Light) 7.25" pitcher, nasturtiums, ornate stippled decorations on rim and handle, artist initials M.E., Rozane Ware wafer, die-impressed 7. *Stofft collection.* **$4000–5000, $2500–3000**

Left:
Rozane Royal (Dark) and Rozane Royal (Light). Rozane Royal (Dark) 815-20" vase, roses, attributed to Walter Myers, die-impressed ROZANE marks; Rozane Royal (Light) 815-20" vase, roses, hand-painted artist signature "W. Myers," die-impressed 7. *Stofft collection.* **$1500–1800, $3000–3500**

Right:
Rozane Royal (Dark) and Woodland. Rozane Royal (Dark) 822-15.75" vase, lilies of the valley, hand-painted artist signature "W. Myers," die-impressed marks; Woodland 822-15.75" vase, hollyhocks, hand-incised artist initials ET, Woodland wafer. *Stofft collection.* **$1500–1800, $2000–2500**

Matt Green and Woodland. Matt Green 10.5"
vase; Woodland 10.5" vase. *Hoppe photograph.*
$175–225, $750–950

Fudji and Woodland. Fudji 970-10" vase,
squeezebag artist monogram GF (Gazo Foudji),
Rozane Ware wafer, die-impressed 5; Woodland
970-10" vase, Woodland wafer. *Stofft collection.*
$2500–3000, $950–1200

**Old Ivory (Tinted) and
Matt Green.** Old Ivory
(Tinted) 1205-7" wall
pocket, die-impressed
1205; Matt Green 1205-7"
wall pocket, die-impressed
1205. *Hoppe collection.*
$150–200, $225–275

Pine Cone and Pine Cone Modern. Pine Cone 632-6" jardiniere, brown; Pine Cone Modern 401-6" jardiniere, brown. *Schultz collection.* **$275–325 (each).** The examples shown have slightly different handles. In the 1930s, brown Pine Cone had a dark green lining; the 1950s line gave brown Pine Cone Modern a brown lining too.

Right:
Carnelian (Drip) and Carnelian (Glazes). Carnelian (Drip) 312-8" vase, mustard drip on tan; Carnelian (Glazes) 312-8" vase, mottled green and lavender. *Shannon collection.* **$200–250, $275–325.** In a Carnelian (Drip) piece, the drip glaze contrasts with the solid color underneath. Carnelian (Glazes) examples are usually mottled from mouth to foot. These pieces are unmarked.

Below:
Tourmaline and Futura. Tourmaline A435-10" vase, Futura shape, mottled blue and white; Futura 435-10" vase. *Hoppe collection.* **$275–325, $1500–1800.** Don't forget that each Tourmaline shape can be found in all four standard Tourmaline glazes. These pieces are unmarked.

Earlam and Tourmaline. Earlam 517-5.5" vase, mottled blend of tan and blue, crayon 517; Earlam 517-5.5" vase, mottled blend of green and blue, tan lining, unmarked; Tourmaline A517-6" vase, glossy mottled blend of two-tone blue, white, and gold, crayon A517; Tourmaline A517-6" vase, mottled rust and gold, crayon A517. *Fairfield collection.* **$225–275, $200–250, $100–125, $125–150.** Earlam glazes can run to tan or to blue-green, although most are a blend of these colors. Note the different measurements used by the factory for this shape. Many Roseville shape numbers include rounded-off measurements.

Imperial (Glazes) and Carnelian (Glazes). Imperial (Glazes) 200-4.5" vase, standard coloring; Carnelian (Glazes) 1064-3" candlestick, mottled lavender and turquoise (one of many possible Carnelian glazes). *Courtesy of Cincinnati Art Galleries.* **$250–300, $95–125.** As shape A200, this Imperial (Glazes) shape was also made in the four standard Tourmaline glazes.

Rozane Royal (Dark) and Chloron/Egypto. Rozane Royal (Dark) 5.5" vase, roses, hand-painted artist signature "W. Myers," Rozane Royal wafer; Chloron (or Egypto?) 5.5" vase, pears (obverse shows cherries), no mark. *Private collection.* **$300–350, $400–500**

Volpato and Ivory. Volpato 3-8" covered vase (missing its cover); Ivory 12-8 x 4.5" bowl. *Shannon collection.* **$175–225 (or $300–350 with the cover), $125–150.** These pieces are unmarked.

Early Carnelian and Vista. Early Carnelian 581-10" jardiniere; Vista 589-10" jardiniere, blue inkstamp shape number. *Hoppe collection.* **$400–500, $750–950.** In a late 1998 Internet auction at <www.ebay.com>, an example of this Early Carnelian jardiniere was sold. Its black crayon number 581 matches a shape number in the July 1916 price list.

A Fluted Ivy Pot. 630-4" ivy pot, semigloss red, foil label. *Auclair collection.* **$50–60.** According to a trade notice in the March 29, 1934, issue of *Pottery, Glass and Brass Salesman,* "These pots are fluted and come in a matt glaze, in ivory, red, green, and yellow. They are very popular in price, the 4-inch to retail for 50 cents and the 5-inch for 75 cents" (page 8). The shape appears only in one of the factory stock pages for Ivory.

Rosecraft and Solid Colors. Rosecraft 180-10" vase, glossy old rose; Solid Colors 625-5" vase, semigloss raspberry. *Fairfield collection.* **$250–300, $95–125.** These pieces are unmarked.

Pasadena Planters and Keynote. 3.75" Pasadena -31 planter, green, *courtesy of Mark Bassett Antiques;* Keynote 306-12" bowl, green, *courtesy of McAllister Auctions.* **$30–35, $40–50**

Teasel and Futura. Teasel 884-8" vase, rust; Futura 427-8" vase, teasel motif. *Shannon collection.* **$175–225, $750–950.** The Futura 438-15" vase (not shown) also has a teasel design.

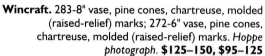

Wincraft. 283-8" vase, pine cones, chartreuse, molded (raised-relief) marks; 272-6" vase, pine cones, chartreuse, molded (raised-relief) marks. *Hoppe photograph.* **$125–150, $95–125**

Pine Cone. 711-10" vase, green, die-impressed marks, foil label. *Hoppe photograph.* **$600–700**

Futura Shapes with Floral Motifs. Futura 437-12" vase, Weeping Tulip; Futura 433-10" vase, Pine Cone. *Courtesy of McAllister Auctions.* **$1500–1800, $950–1200.** The Futura vase with a pine cone motif has Carnelian-style handles and a speckled green glaze overall. Note: there are also another Futura and an Artwood shape that have tulip motifs.

Chapter 5
A TIMELINE
OF ROSEVILLE PRODUCTS

The following chronology reflects the current state of research. Many Roseville lines were introduced to United States pottery buyers through trade notices in a professional journal. This kind of document is typically the report of a journalist after having attended a major trade show, such as the annual Pittsburgh glass and china shows, held in January. Other products were announced to the trade in a factory advertisement shortly before being advertised in the interior decorating (or "women's") magazines.

In some cases, no published reference to a given line has been located. Using all available research material, in combination with typical marks, glazes, and overall style, I have estimated the year of introduction for these "undocumented" lines.

Any such report is subject to further research and correction. Please let me know if you locate published references predating those listed below.

Year Introduced	Line (or Glaze)	Earliest Known Published Reference

EARLY LINES (Presidency of George Young, and earlier)

Year Introduced	Line (or Glaze)	Earliest Known Published Reference
by 1898	Utility Ware (Venitian)	Shards of Venitian have been located at the original plant site in Roseville, Ohio
by 1901	Majolica	Trade notice, *China, Glass and Lamps*, November 9, 1901: 9
by 1901	Rozane Royal	Frank S. Parmelee advertisement, *Crockery and Glass Journal*, December 12, 1901: 58
by 1902	Decorated Artware	Advertisement, *Crockery and Glass Journal*, August 21, 1902: 40
by 1902	Cornelian	Trade notice, *China, Glass and Lamps*, October 18, 1902: 7
1903	Azurean	Trade notice, *China, Glass and Lamps*, January 17, 1903: 12
ca. 1903	Vase Assortment	*No published reference has been located
1904	Modern Art	Trade notice, *China, Glass and Lamps*, January 9, 1904: 34
1905	Chloron	Trade notice, *China, Glass and Lamps*, January 14, 1905: 25
1905	Old Ivory	Trade notice, *China, Glass and Lamps*, January 14, 1905: 25
1905	Fujiyama	Trade notice, *China, Glass and Lamps*, March 18, 1905: 4
1905	Egypto	1905 "Rozane" catalog (see trade notice, *China, Glass and Lamps*, May 20, 1905: 4)
1905	Mara	"Rozane" catalog (see trade notice, *China, Glass and Lamps*, May 20, 1905" 4)
1905	Mongol	1905 "Rozane" catalog; see trade notice, *China, Glass and Lamps*, May 20, 1905: 4)
1905	Woodland	1905 "Rozane" catalog; see trade notice, *China, Glass and Lamps*, May 20, 1905: 4)

Year Introduced	Line (or Glaze)	Earliest Known Published Reference
ca. 1905	Aztec	*No published reference has been located, but examples are known with a Rozane Ware wafer
ca. 1905	Crocus	*No published reference has been located, but examples are known with a Rozane Ware wafer
ca. 1905	Cremo	*No published reference has been located
1906	Crystalis	1906 "Rozane" catalog; see trade notice, *China, Glass and Lamps*, August 4, 1906: 17)
1906	Della Robbia	1906 "Rozane" catalog; see trade notice, *China, Glass and Lamps*, August 4, 1906: 17)
by 1906	Fudji	1906 "Rozane" catalog; see trade notice, *China, Glass and Lamps*, August 4, 1906: 17)
ca. 1906	Olympic	*No contemporary published reference has been located
1907	Decorated Landscape	Trade notice, *China, Glass and Lamps*, January 12, 1907: 8
1907	Decorated Matt	Trade notice, *China, Glass and Lamps*, January 12, 1907: 8
by 1907	Matt Green	Trade notice, *China, Glass and Lamps*, January 12, 1907: 8
1908	Blue Porcelain	Trade notice, *China, Glass and Lamps*, January 11, 1908: 11
1908	Cameo	Trade notice, *China, Glass and Lamps*, January 11, 1908: 11
by 1910	Creamware	Factory stock page (Moses Mesre collection)
ca. 1910	Autumn	*No published reference has been located
by 1914	Romafin	Illustrated in *Theobald's Premium Catalogue*, September 1914 (Wagner collection)
ca. 1914	Pauleo	Trade notice, *Pottery, Glass and Brass Salesman*, December 17, 1914: 109; see also the "Pauleo" booklet, dated April 1916
by 1916	Early Carnelian	Advertisement, *Pottery, Glass and Brass Salesman*, December 14, 1916: 80
by 1916	Donatello	Advertisement, *Pottery, Glass and Brass Salesman*, December 14, 1916: 80; listed in a typewritten Roseville price list, dated July 1916 (at Ohio Historical Society)
by 1916	Solid Colors	Advertisement, *Pottery, Glass and Brass Salesman*, December 14, 1916: 80
by 1916	Antique Matt Green	Advertisement, *Pottery, Glass and Brass Salesman*, December 14, 1916: 80; listed in a typewritten Roseville price list, dated July 1916 (at Ohio Historical Society)
by 1916	Early Velmoss	Photograph, *Pottery, Glass and Brass Salesman*, August 15, 1918: 20; listed in a typewritten Roseville price list, dated July 1916 (at Ohio Historical Society)
by 1917	Mostique	Advertisement, *Pottery, Glass and Brass Salesman*, December 13, 1917: 27
by 1917	Early Rosecraft	Advertisement, *Pottery, Glass and Brass Salesman*, December 13, 1917: 27

Year Introduced	Line (or Glaze)	Earliest Known Published Reference
MIDDLE PERIOD LINES (Presidencies of Russell T. Young and Anna M. Young)		
by 1920	Dogwood (Smooth)	Advertisement, *Pottery, Glass and Brass Salesman*, December 11, 1919: 65
by 1920	Rozane Line	Advertisement, *Pottery, Glass and Brass Salesman*, December 11, 1919: 65
by 1920	Sylvan	Advertisement, *Pottery, Glass and Brass Salesman*, December 11, 1919: 65
ca. 1920	Vista	*No published reference has been located
by 1921	Rosecraft	Trade notice, *Pottery, Glass and Brass Salesman*, July 13, 1922: 15
ca. 1921	Black Tea Pots	Advertisement, *Pottery, Glass and Brass Salesman*, December 16, 1920: 130
1921	Imperial (Textured)	Advertisement, *Pottery, Glass and Brass Salesman*, December 16, 1920: 130
by 1922	Lustre	Directory listing, *Crockery and Glass Journal*, December 14, 1922
1922	Volpato	Trade notice, *Pottery, Glass and Brass Salesman*, July 13, 1922: 15
1923	Corinthian	Trade notice, *Pottery, Glass and Brass Salesman*, July 12, 1923: 53
1924	Florentine	Trade notice, *Pottery, Glass and Brass Salesman*, May 8, 1924: 17
1924	Juvenile (Glossy)	Trade notice, *Pottery, Glass and Brass Salesman*, July 3, 1924: 15
1924	La Rose	Trade notice, *Pottery, Glass and Brass Salesman*, July 3, 1924: 15
1925	Hexagon	Trade notice, *Pottery, Glass and Brass Salesman*, August 20, 1925: 17
1925	Vintage	Trade notice, *Pottery, Glass and Brass Salesman*, August 20, 1925: 17
ca. 1925	Victorian Art Pottery	*No published reference has been located
1926	Dogwood (Textured)	Trade notice, *Pottery, Glass and Brass Salesman*, March 25, 1926: 30
1926	Carnelian (Drip)	Trade notice, *Pottery, Glass and Brass Salesman*, July 8, 1926: 15
by 1926	Panel	M.E. Moortgat Co. advertisement, *Gift and Art Shop*, November 1926: 194
ca. 1926	Lombardy	*No published reference has been located
1927	Tuscany	Advertisement, *House Beautiful*, September 1927: LOOK UP
1927	Garden Pottery	Directory listing, *Crockery and Glass Journal*, December 15, 1927: 205
ca. 1928	Normandy	*No published reference has been located
by 1928	Cremona	Advertisement, *House Beautiful*, March 1928: 340
by 1928	Dahlrose	California Artificial Flower Co. advertisement, *Gift and Art Shop*, May 1928: 194
1928	Futura	Advertisement, *House and Garden*, October 1928: 140
by 1928	Carnelian (Glazes)	California Artificial Flower Co. advertisement, *Gift and Art Shop*, November 1928: 174
1929	Savona	Advertisement, *House and Garden*, April 1929: 152
1930	Imperial (Glazes)	Advertisement, *House and Garden*, March 1930: 124
1930	Earlam	Trade notice, *Crockery and Glass Journal*, August 1930: 71
1930	Ferella	Trade notice, *Crockery and Glass Journal*, August 1930: 71
ca. 1930	Sunflower	*No published reference has been located
1931	Montacello	Trade notice, *Pottery, Glass and Brass Salesman*, August 13, 1931: 13
1931	Windsor	Trade notice, *Pottery, Glass and Brass Salesman*, August 13, 1931: 13
ca. 1931	Jonquil	*No published reference has been located
1932	Ivory	Trade notice, *Crockery and Glass Journal*, April 1932: 20
1932	Baneda	Advertisement, *Crockery and Glass Journal*, July 1932: 24
ca. 1932	Blackberry	*No published reference has been located
1933	Cherry Blossom	Trade notice, *Crockery and Glass Journal*, March 1933: 25–26
1933	Tourmaline	Trade notice, *Crockery and Glass Journal*, March 1933: 25–26
1933	Artcraft	Trade notice, *Pottery, Glass and Brass Salesman*, August 17, 1933: 9
1933	Falline	Trade notice, *Pottery, Glass and Brass Salesman*, August 17, 1933: 9
1933	Wisteria	Trade notice, *Pottery, Glass and Brass Salesman*, August 17, 1933: 9
1934	Laurel	Trade notice, *Crockery and Glass Journal*, February 1934: 29
1934	Topeo	Advertisement, *Pottery, Glass and Brass Salesman*, February 15, 1934: 14
1934	Luffa	Trade notice, *Crockery and Glass Journal*, September 1934: 23
1934	Russco	Trade notice, *Crockery and Glass Journal*, September 1934: 23
1935	Pine Cone	Trade notice, *Pottery, Glass and Brass Salesman*, January 10, 1935: 8
1935	Velmoss	Trade notice, *Pottery, Glass and Brass Salesman*, January 10, 1935: 8
1935	Morning Glory	Trade notice, *Pottery, Glass and Brass Salesman*, August 15, 1935: 7
1935	Orian	Trade notice, *Pottery, Glass and Brass Salesman*, August 15, 1935: 7
1936	Clemana	Trade notice, *Crockery and Glass Journal*, January 1936: 65
1936	Primrose	Trade notice, *Crockery and Glass Journal*, January 1936: 65
1936	Moderne	Trade notice, *Pottery, Glass and Brass Salesman*, September 1936: 20
1936	Moss	Trade notice, *Pottery, Glass and Brass Salesman*, September 1936: 20
1937	Thorn Apple	Trade notice, *Gift and Art Buyer*, January 1937: 21
1937	Dawn	Advertisement, *Gift and Art Buyer*, April 1937: 10
1937	Ixia	Advertisement, *Gift and Art Buyer*, October 1937: 2
1938	Poppy	Advertisement, *Gift and Art Buyer*, January 1938: 2
1938	Teasel	Advertisement, *Gift and Art Buyer*, April 1938: 2
1938	Fuchsia	Advertisement, *Gift and Art Buyer*, June 1938: 2
LATE LINES (Presidencies of F.S. Clement and Robert Windisch)		
1939	Iris	Advertisement, *Gift and Art Buyer*, December 1938: 2
1939	Cosmos	Advertisement, *Gift and Art Buyer*, June 1939: 2
ca. 1939	Crystal Green	See Ivory advertisement, *Gift and Art Buyer*, August 1939: 2
1940	Bleeding Heart	Advertisement, *Gift and Art Buyer*, December 1939: 2
1940	White Rose	Advertisement, *Gift and Art Buyer*, June 1940: 2
1941	Columbine	Advertisement, *Gift and Art Buyer*, December 1940: 2
1941	Rozane Pattern	Advertisement, *Gift and Art Buyer*, December 1940: 2
1941	Bushberry	Advertisement, *Gift and Art Buyer*, May 1941: 2
1942	Foxglove	Advertisement, *Gift and Art Buyer*, December 1941: 2
1942	Peony	Advertisement, *Gift and Art Buyer*, May 1942: 2
1943	Water Lily	Advertisement, *Gift and Art Buyer*, January 1943: 2

Year Introduced	Line (or Glaze)	Earliest Known Published Reference
1943	Magnolia	Advertisement, *Gift and Art Buyer*, June 1943: 2
1944	Clematis	Advertisement, *Gift and Art Buyer*, June 1944: 2
1945	Freesia	Advertisement, *Gift and Art Buyer*, January 1945: 2
1946	Zephyr Lily	Advertisement, *Gift and Art Buyer*, January 1946: 2
1947	Snowberry	Advertisement, *Gift and Art Buyer*, December 1946: 2
1948	Wincraft	Advertisement, *Gift and Art Buyer*, December 1947: 2
1949	Apple Blossom	Advertisement, *Gift and Art Buyer*, December 1948: 2
1949	Ming Tree	Advertisement, *Gift and Art Buyer*, June 1949: 2
ca. 1949	Florane	*No published reference has been located
1950	Gardenia	Advertisement, *Gift and Art Buyer*, December 1949: 2
1950	Silhouette	Advertisement, *Gift and Art Buyer*, June 1950: 2
1950	Burmese	Advertisement, *Gift and Art Buyer*, September 1950: 2
ca. 1950	Mock Orange	*No published reference has been located
1951	Bittersweet	Advertisement, *Gift and Art Buyer*, December 1950: 2
1951	Artwood	Advertisement, *Gift and Art Buyer*, December 1950: 2
1952	Mayfair	Advertisement, *Gift and Art Buyer*, December 1951: 2
1952	Lotus	Advertisement, *Gift and Art Buyer*, January 1952: 2
1952	Raymor Modern Stoneware	Richards Morgenthau & Co. advertisement, *Gift and Art Buyer*, June 1952: 157
1953	Raymor Modern Artware	Mentioned in board of directors minutes, July 20, 1953
1953	Raymor Two-Tone Casual	Mentioned in board of directors minutes, July 20, 1953
ca. 1953	Capri	*No published reference has been located
ca. 1953	Commercial work	*No published reference has been located
1953	Pine Cone Modern	Advertisement, *Gift and Art Buyer*, August 1953: 27
ca. 1954	Pasadena Planters	*No published reference has been located
ca. 1954	Late Capri	*No published reference has been located
ca. 1954	Royal Capri	*No published reference has been located
ca. 1954	Keynote	Undated brochure (Banet collection)

*Except for Roseville factory records

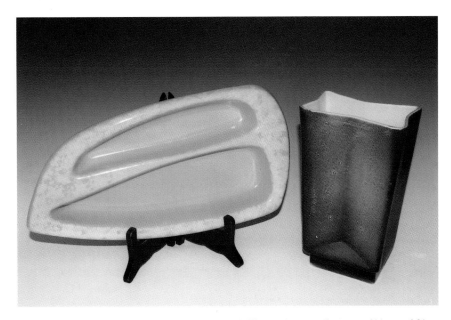

Keynote. 204-13" compartment tray, aqua; 602-8" vase, brown. *Courtesy of Heart of Ohio Antique Center.* **$40–50, $95–125**

Chapter 6
ROSEVILLE POTTERY LINES, A TO Z

This chapter discusses each Roseville product line, with photographs showing the standard glazes and/or decorations. For some lines, the pieces available for photography were mainly blue, or mainly pink. Readers should not interpret this to mean that a particular color is more popular or more available today. The photographs in any book about pottery reflect the personalities of the collectors who participated in the project.

Many Roseville lines have come to be known by various names and nicknames. If you have trouble locating a particular product, don't forget to use the index too! For important information about values and references, see the Introduction.

Because this book is intended primarily for beginners, I opted for breadth over depth of coverage. For unusual pieces and more new shapes, watch for my next book, *Understanding Roseville Pottery*.

ANTIQUE MATT GREEN
An Early Glaze, introduced by 1916

Factory Name(s): Antique; Antique Green Matt (which can be read as "Antique Green, Matt")
Collector Nickname(s): Antique Matt Green (see Huxford, 1976)
Style: Arts and Crafts
Standard Color(s): Matte blend of yellowish green and dark green, sometimes with a "rusty" cast
Typical Marks: Unmarked. Some pieces may have a die-impressed shape number.

Antique Matt Green was often used on symmetrical shapes of a vaguely Roman inspiration. Some pieces may predate 1916. The glaze was offered as late as 1921, indicating that the Arts and Crafts style was still popular among homeowners then (see advertisement, *Crockery and Glass Journal* December 16, 1920: 164). Today, it is difficult to locate large examples of this glaze.

Caution: Other companies may have produced a similar glaze. If you cannot locate a shape in a Roseville stock page or other factory publication, use the term "attribution" when you believe Roseville to be the maker.

In the factory stock pages, 13 examples of Antique Matt Green are shown. An additional 29 shapes are mentioned in the July 1916 price list as being available in Antique Matt Green.

ANTIQUE MATT GREEN

Shape No.	Description	Reference/Notes
220	-9" window box, diamond shape	See July 1916 price list
220	-6.5" window box, diamond shape	See July 1916 price list
226	-4" fern dish	See July 1916 price list
226	-5" fern dish	See July 1916 price list
226	-6" fern dish	See July 1916 price list
363	-11" x 6.5" window box	See July 1916 price list
363	-12" x 8" window box	See July 1916 price list
363	-16" x 8.5" window box	See July 1916 price list
550	-4" jardiniere	Also in July 1916 price list
550	-5" jardiniere	
550	-6" jardiniere	Also in July 1916 price list
550	-7" jardiniere	Also in July 1916 price list
550	-8" jardiniere	Also in July 1916 price list
550	-9" jardiniere	Also in July 1916 price list
550	-10" jardiniere	Also in July 1916 price list
550	-10" jardiniere & pedestal	
550	-12" jardiniere	Also in July 1916 price list
550	-12" jardiniere & pedestal	
550	-14" jardiniere	See July 1916 price list
558	-6" jardiniere	See July 1916 price list
558	-8" jardiniere	See July 1916 price list
558	-10" jardiniere	See July 1916 price list
558	-12" jardiniere	See July 1916 price list
558	-10" x 28" jardiniere and pedestal	Bomm 389; also in July 1916 price list
558	-12" x 33" jardiniere & pedestal	See July 1916 price list
560	-6" jardiniere	See July 1916 price list
560	-8" jardiniere	See July 1916 price list
560	-9" jardiniere	See July 1916 price list
560	-10" jardiniere	See July 1916 price list
565	-8" jardiniere	See July 1916 price list
565	-9" jardiniere	See July 1916 price list
565	-10" jardiniere	See July 1916 price list
565	-12" jardiniere	See July 1916 price list
741	-21" umbrella stand	Bomm 173, lower left; also in July 1916 price list
742	-21" umbrella stand	Bomm 173, lower right; also in July 1916 price list
1208	-12" x 6.5" wall pocket	See July 1916 price list
1209	-10" x 5" wall pocket	See July 1916 price list
1210	-10" wall pocket	See July 1916 price list
1210	-12" wall pocket	See July 1916 price list
1211	-10" wall pocket	See July 1916 price list
1211	-12" wall pocket	See July 1916 price list
1213	wall pocket	See July 1916 price list

Antique Matt Green. 550-4"
jardiniere; 909-9.75" cuspidor. *Hoppe
photograph.* **$100–125,
$350–450**

Antique Matt Green. 12.75" x 6.25" wall pocket,
attributed to Roseville, unmarked; 1211-12.5" x 6"
wall pocket, square paper label. *Hoppe collection.*
$300–400 (each)

Antique Matt Green. 550-12"
jardiniere. *Hoppe collection.*
$650–750

APPLE BLOSSOM
A Late Line, introduced in 1949

Factory Name(s): Apple Blossom
Alternate Spelling(s): Appleblossom (see Clifford, 1968)
Style: Realistic; some examples in the Mid-Century Modern style
Standard Color(s): Apple Green ("green"), Aqua Blue ("blue"), or Coral ("pink")
Typical Marks: Molded (raised-relief) marks, including "Roseville" (script), shape number, and size

Apple Blossom depicts a flowering branch from an apple tree, complete with "dainty pink-and-white blooms and rustic twig handles" (advertisement, *Gift and Art Buyer* March 1949: 2). A perennial favorite with buyers, the semigloss line stayed in production at least through 1952, with new shapes added from year to year. Many Apple Blossom shapes are symmetrical, although the handles can be set "akimbo." Contours tend to be curvilinear.

Today, this lovely pattern is still plentiful. Most collectors prefer the blue or pink pieces to the green. Early advertisements claimed that the line began with 45 shapes, but only 41 appear in the factory brochure. (There are no known factory stock pages.) The original wall pocket—which is now rare—has a blossom on the handle, but none on the body of the piece.

APPLE BLOSSOM

Shape No.	Description	Shape No.	Description
300	-4" planter	359	bookends
301	-6" vase	361	-5" hanging basket
302	-8" jardiniere	366	-8" wall pocket
305	-8" jardiniere & pedestal	368	-8" planter
309	-8" basket	369	-12" window box
310	-10" basket	371	-C cream
311	-12" basket	371	-P teapot
316	-8" ewer	371	-S sugar
318	-15" ewer	373	-7" vase
321	-6" cornucopia	379	-7" vase
323	-8" cornucopia	381	-6" vase
326	-6" bowl	382	-7" vase
328	-8" bowl	385	-8" vase
329	-10" bowl	387	-9" vase
330	-10" bowl	388	-10" vase
331	-12" bowl	389	-10" vase
333	-14" bowl	390	-12" vase
342	-6" rose bowl	391	-12" vase
351	-2" candlestick	392	-15" vase
352	-4.5" candlestick	393	-18" vase
356	-5" flower pot and saucer		

Apple Blossom. 331-12" bowl, blue; pair, 351 candlesticks, blue; 329-10" bowl, blue. *Courtesy of McAllister Auctions.* **$225–275, $125–150 (pair), $175–225**

Apple Blossom. 323-8" cornucopia, pink; 382-7" vase, blue; 389-10" vase, pink; pair, 352-4.5" candlesticks, green. *Shannon collection.* **$125–150, $150–175, $275–325, $150–175 (pair)**

Apple Blossom. 342-6" rose bowl, green; 318-15" ewer, green; 310-10" basket, green. *Courtesy of McAllister Auctions.* **$125–150, $750–850, $250–300**

Apple Blossom. 385-8" vase, pink; 393-18" floor vase, pink; 368-8" window box, pink. *Hoppe photograph.* **$150–175, $950–1250, $150–175**

Artcraft. 18" vase, glossy mottled aqua. *Courtesy of Len Boucher.*
$2500–3000. This glaze was used on several Imperial (Glazes) vases.

ARTCRAFT
A Middle Period Line, introduced in 1933

Factory Name(s): Artcraft
Style: Art Deco shapes, often having Arts and Crafts glazes
Standard Color(s): Matte mottled green or tan; or glossy solid colors
Typical Marks: Foil labels. (These could be lost, leaving the piece unmarked.) Some may have hand-written (crayon) shape numbers.

Earlier researchers have viewed Artcraft as a single jardiniere (and pedestal) shape, a rounded form with a stepped-down rim and attached handles. In August 1933, these "semi-modernistic" Artcraft jardinieres were offered to the trade in two semi-matt colorings: "the green is brown lined and the brown is green lined." The jardinieres were accompanied by "a new line of vases in 'Artcraft' ware," to "come in 12, 16 and 18 inch types and in a choice of six colors, there being two greens, two blues and two browns, together with black and ivory" (trade notice, *Pottery, Glass and Brass Salesman*, August 17, 1933: 9). Another trade journal described the colors as "ivory, black, turquoise, tan, green and a windsor blue in a glossy glaze—seemingly a porcelain finish" (*Crockery and Glass Journal*, September 1933).

Clearly, the Artcraft line has not yet been fully identified. The line seems to include a group of modernistic vase shapes that were also decorated as Carnelian (Glazes). No one yet knows which glaze treatment was first used on these rare designs. No Artcraft shape numbers are listed in known factory documents or advertising.

The jardinieres are also known in glazes more typical of other Roseville lines—including the glossy red glaze of Topeo and a glossy mottled aqua sometimes used for Imperial (Glazes). Without knowledge of the 1933 notices, Monsen (1995) classified them as being either Earlam or Futura (page 100). Most books on Roseville do not illustrate or mention them at all.

If you feel confused, you're in good company! Regardless, Artcraft is extremely popular among collectors.

Caution: Do not confuse Artcraft with the 1950s floral Artwood line!

Artcraft. 629-4" jardiniere, tan; 629-6" jardiniere, green; 629-4" jardiniere, blue-green. *Hoppe photograph.* **$250–300, $300–400, $250–300**

Artcraft. 16.25" vase, matte mottled
tan, green lining. *Koster collection.*
$1500–2000

ARTWOOD

A Late Line, introduced in 1951

Factory Name(s): Artwood
Style: Mid-Century Modern
Standard Color(s): Emerald Green ("green"), Poppy Yellow ("yellow"), or Stone Grey ("gray")
Typical Marks: Molded (raised-relief) marks, including "Roseville" (script), shape number, and size

Roseville described Artwood as "smart, ultramodern art pottery shapes in newest fashionable colors! And accented by a rich, lustrous glaze finish" (advertisement, *Gift and Art Buyer,* April 1951: 2). Each of Artwood's geometrical and biomorphic shapes features a "picture window" cutout section. Motifs range from the buckeye (the Ohio state flower) to the ubiquitous palm (a totem of 1950s kitsch). Even Frank Ferrell's beloved pine cone gets a chance to be recast as an Artwood vase.

Perhaps because this "short" line includes only 13 shapes, Artwood has relatively few devotees. Asking prices often tend toward the affordable, although a renewed interest in Mid-Century Modern design indicates that values will rise. The pattern makes a splendid complement to Heywood Wakefield furniture.

Caution: Do not confuse Artwood (which has cutouts) and Wincraft (which does not)! (This mistaken identity problem occurred in Huxford, 1976.)

There are no known factory stock pages, but all 13 Artwood shapes appear in factory advertising:

ARTWOOD

Shape No.	Description	Shape No.	Description
1050	-3" planter	1057	-8" double vase
1051	-6" vase	1058	-9" planter
1052	-8" vase	1059	-10" vase
1053	-8" vase	1060	-12" double vase
1054	-8.5" vase	1061	-10" bowl
1055	-9" planter	1062	-12" bowl
1056	-10" vase		

Artwood. 3-pc. set, 1051-6" vase (center) and two 1050-4" planters, all gray; 1052-8" vase, yellow. *Shannon collection.* **$150–200 (3-pc. set), $125–150**

Artwood. 1053-8" circle vase, green; 1062-12" planter, green. *Hoppe photograph.* **$125–150, $175–225**

Artwood. 1061-10" planter, green. *Hoppe photograph.* **$150–200**

AUTUMN
An Early Decorative Motif, introduced ca. 1910

Factory Name(s): Autumn
Style: Simplified utilitarian shapes, with "Arts and Crafts" colors
Standard Color(s): Black decals on an airbrushed red and yellow-orange background
Typical Marks: Most pieces are unmarked. Some have a die-impressed shape number.

Autumn's air-brushed backgrounds are always dramatic. As if to represent a fall sunset, the colors shade from a rich reddish orange to a buttercup yellow. Each example is decorated with black decals of trees beside a river. Scenes can vary according to the size of a piece. Because of its early date and method of manufacture, Autumn can be viewed as a variety of Decorated Artware.

Most collectors of early Roseville like to boast of having at least one example. Surfaces are easily scratched or worn. If this kind of damage is clearly noticeable, buyers expect some adjustment in the asking price.

The factory stock pages show only 15 shapes (either jardinieres or toilet articles) decorated with Autumn motifs:

AUTUMN

Shape No.	Description	Reference/Notes
480	-7" jardiniere	
480	-8" jardiniere	
480	-9" jardiniere	
480	-10" jardiniere	
498	-7" jardiniere	
498	-8" jardiniere	
498	-9" jardiniere	
498	-10" jardiniere	
	brush holder	
	chamber (covered)	
	combinette (covered)	
	ewer and basin	
	mouth ewer	
	shaving mug	
	soap dish (covered)	
	10-pc. toilet set	See July 1916 price list
	12-pc. toilet set	See July 1916 price list

Autumn. 480-8.25" jardiniere, die-impressed 480. *Wagner collection.* **$750–850**

Autumn. 12" ewer. *Fairfield collection.* **$850–950**

Autumn. 14.5" basin. *Ready collection.* **$500–600**

AZTEC
An Early Line, introduced ca. 1905

Factory Name(s): Aztec
Collector Nickname(s): Aztec (see Alexander, 1970); Aztec Art, or
    Egyptian (see Buxton, 1977)
Style: Arts and Crafts, or Art Nouveau
Standard Color(s): Backgrounds in a solid semigloss color, such as
    coral, blue, or gray
Typical Marks: Usually unmarked (or marked only with a die-
    impressed numeral, meaning unknown). A few bear the Rozane
    Ware wafer. Some have a single artist initial.

Aztec pieces were individually decorated in Art Nouveau or
geometrical squeezebag (that is, tube-line) motifs. Stylistic influences
are difficult to define, although the term "Aztec" often seems
inappropriate. The decorations were applied in complementary or
contrasting matte colors, such as white, blue, gray, or dark red.
Because of the hand decoration, variations in color and motif can
be found on the same shape.

Today, Aztec is scarce and in high demand among collectors. At
auction, the highest prices go to ornately decorated examples with
strong color contrasts. Most buyers will overlook minor nicks on
the decoration, although a higher price can be demanded for mint-
condition examples.

Some Aztec examples—perhaps the earliest—use a shape
borrowed from the Rozane Royal line. Other shapes are shared
with Della Robbia or Cremo. (Everyone wonders which of these
lines preceded the others.) In the factory stock pages, the following
27 shapes are illustrated with Aztec decorations:

AZTEC

Shape No.	Description	Shape No.	Description
1	-5" pitcher	11	-12" vase
1	-11" vase	12	-10.5" vase
2	-6" pitcher	13	-8.5" vase
2	-11" vase	14	-8" vase
3	-5" pitcher	15	-6" vase
3	-11" vase	16	-10" vase
4	-10" vase	17	-9" vase
5	-11" vase, kerosene	18	-9" vase
	lamp shape	19	-9" vase
6	-11" vase	20	-9" vase
7	-10" vase	21	-8.5" vase
8	-11" vase	22	-8" vase
9	-10.5" vase	23	-8" vase
10	-10" vase	24	-8" vase

Aztec. 3-11" vase, gray; 20-9" vase, tan. *Scheytt collection.*
$650–750, $550–650

Aztec. 6-11" vase, dark blue, die-impressed 5; 2-11" vase,
light blue, artist initial "R." *Courtesy of McAllister Auctions.*
$450–500, $400–450

Aztec. 15-6" vase, gray; 23-8" vase, gray; 1-11" vase, light blue; 2-6" pitcher, dark blue. *Shannon collection.* **$400–450, $450–500, $500–600, $450–500**

Aztec. 3-5" pitcher, gray; 17-9" vase, dark blue, artist initial "C," die-impressed 8; 4-10" vase, gray; 1-5" pitcher, dark blue, artist initial "L." *Courtesy of Clarabelle Antiques.* **$300–350, $450–500, $400–450, $400–450**

AZUREAN

An Early Line, introduced in 1903

Factory Name(s): Azurean; Rozane Art Blue

Collector Nickname(s): Blue Ware (see Huxford, 1976)

Style: Late Victorian

Standard Color(s): Backgrounds airbrushed in a blend of blue, gray, and white, with underglaze slip decoration in shades of blue and gray

Typical Marks: Most examples have a die-impressed line name "AZUREAN" (although the line name can be omitted), "R.P. Co.," the shape number, and often other numerals (whose meaning is unknown). Some pieces are unmarked. Examples can have hand-painted artist initials or an artist's signature.

Roseville introduced "Rozane art blue" at the 1903 Pittsburgh glass and china show. One reviewer reported the new ware "is attracting much attention with many expressions of pleasant surprise" (*China, Glass and Lamps,* January 17, 1903: 12). Inspired by Rookwood's 1895 Aerial Blue and Weller's Blue Louwelsa, Azurean featured floral sprays and landscapes—especially sea and lake scenes. Rare examples featuring a portrait are also known.

Azurean. 818-11.75" vase, landscape, artist initials "AD," *Downey collection;* 835-10.75" vase, landscape, *Zanesville Art Center Permanent Collection, Gift of Mr. & Mrs. Stephen E. Prout, 1984.* **$3000-4000, NPD**

Azurean. 865-18" floor vase, nasturtiums, artist initials "V.A." *Hoppe collection.* **$2000–2500**

Marks parallel those found on Rozane Royal. An example with a Rozane Ware wafer would not be surprising. Azurean is often artist-signed or initialed, and portraits can be titled too.

Today, Azurean is extremely difficult to locate. Judging from its scarcity, collectors assume that this line was made for a briefer period than either the Dark or Light varieties of Rozane Royal. In the factory stock pages, 27 shapes are shown decorated as Azurean.

Caution: Do not confuse Azurean (the blue equivalent of Rozane Royal) with Azurine (a Rosecraft color). (This mistaken identity problem occurred in Purviance and Schneider, 1970.)

AZUREAN

Shape No.	Description	Shape No.	Description
812	-12" vase	893	-13" vase
813	-7.75" vase	900	-6" tyge (three-handled drinking cup)
814	-9.25" vase	921	-11" tankard
821	-8.5" vase	931	-14.75" vase
832	-15.5" vase	933	-15.25" vase
835	-10.75" bud vase	935	-5.75" teapot
845	-11.5" vase	936	-8" chocolate pot
855	-14" tankard	937	-8" pitcher
856	-4" stein	955	-17" vase
865	-17.75" vase	956	-8.5" vase
882	-9" pillow vase	957	-16.5" vase
888	-4" pitcher	958	-11" vase
891	-14" vase	959	-7" vase
892	-8.5" vase		

Azurean. 936-8" chocolate pot, die-impressed marks. *Latta collection.* **$1500–1800.** Including the lid (and measuring to the top of its handle), this piece stands 9.75" tall. Perhaps Roseville measured such pieces without their lids.

Azurean. 834-6.5" vase, pansies; 8.5" vase, floral motif; 851-6" vase, clover, die-impressed marks. *Hoppe collection.* **$750–950, $950–1200, $600–750.** The handled vase is similar to Vase Assortment 105, which has molded floral decorations.

Azurean. 956-8" vase, grapes, no mark. *Downey collection.* **$1200–1500**

BANEDA

A Middle Period Line, introduced in 1932

Factory Name(s): Baneda
Style: Arts and Crafts (green) or Art Deco (pink)
Standard Color(s): Green, or pink
Typical Marks: Paper or foil labels. (These could be lost, leaving the piece unmarked.) Some examples have a hand-written (crayon) shape number.

In 1932, buyers demanded a good value for their Depression-era dollars. For that reason, Roseville marketed Baneda as offering "practical shapes that are not only delightfully artistic, but also thoroughly useful … in keeping with the times!" The new line made a sensation with buyers, and was expanded in the spring of 1933: "it is doubtful if Roseville ever before put out such a rich and pleasing line at such a popular price" (trade notice, *The Pottery, Glass and Brass Salesman*, August 11, 1932: 11).

Each example features a low-relief band of pumpkins (both fruit and flowers), still on the vine. These motifs are hand-decorated in orange and yellow on a blue background. The smooth surfaces outside this decorated band were colored—in either green or pink—with glazes having a distinct texture and appeal.

Green Baneda looks back to the Arts and Crafts period, with a matte mottled glaze of the sort used on Earlam. Its appearance varies according to the sharpness of the molded design, and the patterns created by the flowing glazes. Most collectors prefer pieces with a lot of blue "drip" into the green areas.

In contrast, Art Deco lovers prefer Pink Baneda because of its bright semigloss strawberry pink color, which is lightly stippled in white. Seldom do the colors in Pink Baneda run into one another, allowing for stronger color contrasts and a more "modern" feel. Both varieties are in great demand today, although the green pieces may be slightly more expensive in the current marketplace.

In the factory stock pages, 36 Baneda shapes are shown:

BANEDA

Shape No.	Description	Shape No.	Description
232	-6" bowl	600	-15" vase
233	-8" bowl	601	-5" vase
234	-10" bowl	602	-6" vase
235	-5" rose bowl	603	-4" vase
237	-12" bowl	604	-7" vase
587	-4" vase	605	-6" vase
588	-6" vase	606	-7" vase
589	-6" vase	610	-7" vase
590	-7" vase	626	-4" jardiniere
591	-6" vase	626	-5" jardiniere
592	-7" vase	626	-6" jardiniere
593	-8" vase	626	-7" jardiniere
594	-9" vase	626	-8" jardiniere & pedestal
595	-8" vase	626	-9" jardiniere
596	-9" vase	626	-10" jardiniere & pedestal
597	-10" vase	1087	-5" candlestick
598	-12" vase	1088	-4" candlestick
599	-12" vase	1269	-8" wall pocket

Baneda. 601-5" vase, green; 235-5" rose bowl, pink. *Shannon collection.* **$400–450, $400–450**

Baneda. 592-7" vase, pink; 605-6" vase, pink. *Bassett collection.* **$450–500, $600–700**

Baneda. 594-9" vase, green; 598-12" vase, green. *Hoppe photograph.* **$800–900, $1500–2000**

Baneda. 596-9" vase, green. *Courtesy of McAllister Auctions.* **$950–1200**

Baneda. 600-15" floor vase, pink. *Courtesy of Treadway Gallery.* **$2500–3000**

BITTERSWEET

A Late Line, introduced in 1951

Factory Name(s): Bittersweet
Style: Realistic
Standard Color(s): Dawn Grey ("gray"), Marsh Green ("green"), or Saffron Yellow ("yellow")
Typical Marks: Molded (raised-relief) marks, including "Roseville" (script), shape number, and size

Bittersweet depicts the berry-laden branch of the bittersweet, or woody nightshade (*Solanum dulcamara*), a shrub native to Great Britain. Although the line hints at the Mid-Century Modern style, its shapes are usually symmetrical, and the matte-glazed colors are subdued. Perhaps the conservative Bittersweet line was marketed as an alternative to the more radical Artwood, also offered in yellow, gray, or green. The two lines were announced in the same advertisement (*Gift and Art Buyer*, December 1950: 2).

There are no known factory stock pages for Bittersweet. However, a Bittersweet factory brochure shows the 42 shapes that inaugurated the line:

BITTERSWEET

Shape No.	Description	Shape No.	Description
800	-4" vase	859	bookends
801	-6" vase	861	-5" vase
802	-8" jardiniere	863	-4" vase
805	-8" jardiniere & pedestal	866	-7" wall pocket
808	-6" basket	868	-8" planter
809	-8" basket	869	-12" window box
810	-10" basket	871	-C cream
811	-10" basket	871	-P teapot
816	-8" ewer	871	-S sugar
822	-8" cornucopia	872	-5" vase
826	-6" bowl	873	-6" double vase
827	-8" bowl	874	-7" pillow vase
828	-10" planter	879	-7" vase
829	-12" bowl	881	-6" vase
830	-14" bowl	882	-6" vase
841	-5" vase	883	-8" vase
842	-7" vase	884	-8" vase
851	-3" candlestick	885	-10" vase
856	-7" flower pot and saucer	886	-12" vase
857	4" cornucopia	887	-14" vase
858	double planter	888	-16" vase

Bittersweet. 884-8" vase, gray; 811-10" basket, green. *Shannon collection.* **$175–225, $275–325**

Bittersweet. 886-12" vase, gray; 887-14" vase, green; 883-8" vase, yellow. *Fairfield collection.* **$200–250, $350–400, $150–175**

Bittersweet. 863-4" comport, yellow; 830-14" planter, yellow; 879-7" bud vase, yellow. *Hoppe collection.* **$100–125, $150–175, $125–150**

BLACKBERRY
A Middle Period Line, introduced ca. 1932

Factory Name(s): Blackberry; Blackberry Ware
Style: Realistic
Standard Color(s): One standard coloring, as described below
Typical Marks: Paper or foil labels. (These could be lost, leaving the piece unmarked.) Some examples have a hand-written (crayon) shape number.

A perennial favorite among collectors, Blackberry depicts blackberries on the vine, decorated in semigloss colors. The berries are a natural bluish black, and the vine green. Leaves are in fall colors of yellow, orange, and green. The irregularly modeled background—which may represent bark—is glazed in shades of green and brown.

Blackberry shapes are usually somewhat bulbous. The baskets and wall pocket have the most stylized handles. Blackberry lovers know each piece by heart—each minor variation in the placement of leaves, vine, and berry clusters. Differences in size are clearly easier to notice. Market forecasters think Blackberry may be headed up in value again soon.

The factory stock pages show 29 Blackberry shapes:

BLACKBERRY

Shape No.	Description	Shape No.	Description
226	-6" bowl	575	-8" vase
227	-8" bowl	576	-8" vase
228	-10" bowl	577	-10" vase
334	-6.5" basket	578	-12" vase
335	-7" basket	623	-4" jardiniere
336	-8" basket	623	-5" jardiniere
348	-5" hanging basket	623	-6" jardiniere
567	-4" vase	623	-7" jardiniere
568	-4" vase	623	-8" jardiniere
569	-5" vase	623	-9" jardiniere
570	-5" vase	623	-10" jardiniere & pedestal
571	-6" vase	623	-12" jardiniere
572	-6" vase	1086	-4.5" candlestick
573	-6" vase	1267	-8" wall pocket
574	-6" vase		

Blackberry. 573-6" vase, flower pot shape; 578-12.5" vase. *Hoppe photograph.* **$650–750, $1500–1750**

Blackberry. 568-4" vase; 576-8" vase; 570-5" vase. *Hoppe photograph.* **$400–500, $800–900, $500–600**

Blackberry. 348-5" hanging basket; 577-10" vase; 569-5" vase, volcano shape; 571-6" vase. *Courtesy of McAllister Auctions.* **$950–1200, $1200–1400, $500–600, $600–700**

BLEEDING HEART
A Late Line, introduced in 1940

Factory Name(s): Bleeding Heart
Style: Realistic, with Art Deco features in many shapes
Standard Color(s): Garden Red ("pink"), Leaf Green ("green"), or Sea Blue ("blue")
Typical Marks: Molded (raised-relief) marks, including "Roseville" (script), shape number, and size

Bleeding Heart was said to have "the beauty of fine sculpture": "Six points—so outstanding in the architectural design of 'Bleeding Heart'—are subtly molded to form the lips of the vases, border of the plate and mouth of the bowls" (advertisement, *The Gift and Art Buyer,* January 1940: 2). According to factory advertisements, the new line's

subtle color shades intimating the ever changing hues of the garden … will blend superbly with all interiors. GARDEN RED skillfully combines those favored warm shades of delicate coral and shell pink which gradually turn to a deep burgundy. LEAF GREEN is pleasingly neutral with a light bud green gently shading

into a fully developed deep green. The leaves have a tint of sun yellow and petals of the Bleeding Heart suggest a pale rose. SEA BLUE is a soft grey which matures in depth to a deep rich blue. Highlighted with beige, Sea Blue provides a smart contrast for the coral pink flowers of the motif (February 1940: 2).

Today, collectors show some preference for the pink and blue colors, over the green. Yet green Bleeding Heart also allows a pleasing contrast between flowers and background.

The factory stock pages show 48 Bleeding Heart shapes:

BLEEDING HEART

Shape No.	Description	Shape No.	Description
6	bookends	651	-10" jardiniere & pedestal
40	flower frog	652	-5" flower pot and saucer
138	-4" vase	961	-4" vase
139	-8" vase	962	-5" vase
140	-4.5" gate	963	-6" ewer
141	-6" cornucopia	964	-6" vase
142	-8" cornucopia	965	-7" vase
359	-8" basket	966	-7" vase
360	-10" basket	967	-7" vase
361	-12" basket	968	-8" vase
362	-5" hanging basket	969	-8" vase
377	-4" vase	970	-9" vase
378	-6" vase	971	-9" vase
379	-6" bowl	972	-10" ewer
380	-8" bowl	973	-10" vase
381	-10" plate	974	-12" vase
382	-10" bowl	975	-15" ewer
383	-12" bowl	976	-15" vase
384	-14" bowl	977	-18" vase
651	-3" jardiniere	1139	-4.5" candlestick
651	-4" jardiniere	1140	candlestick
651	-5" jardiniere	1287	-8" wall pocket
651	-6" jardiniere	1323	pitcher
651	-7" jardiniere		
651	-8" jardiniere & pedestal		

Bleeding Heart. 977-18" floor vase, blue. *Stofft collection.* **$1500–1800**

Bleeding Heart. 651-8"
jardiniere and pedestal, green.
Courtesy of McAllister Auctions.
$1200–1400

Bleeding Heart. 141-6" cornucopia, pink; 965-7"
vase, pink; 967-7" bud vase, pink. *Shannon collection.*
$125–150, $200–250, $150–200

Bleeding Heart. 968-8" fan vase, green; 359-8"
basket, pink; 962-5" vase, blue. *Shannon collection.*
$225–275, $325–375, $150–200

BURMESE

A Late Line, introduced in 1950

Factory Name(s): Burmese
Collector Nickname(s): Burmese Green (see Purviance and Schneider, 1970)
Style: Chinese Modern
Standard Color(s): Antique Copper Green ("green"), Gun Metal Black ("black"), or Ivory ("white")
Typical Marks: Molded (raised-relief) marks, including "Roseville" (script), shape number, and size

Burmese was a short-lived Roseville line, although factory advertising expressed optimism: "Kwan Singh and Mayatreya are adolescent Buddhist disciples now immortalized in lifelike masks in which youthful charm combines hauntingly with the calm stoicism of the Orient. A Roseville exclusive for collectors of the truly dramatic in ceramic originals" (advertisement, *The Gift and Art Buyer*, September 1950: 2). Even today, Burmese has relatively few devoted collectors. The wall pockets (or masks) are the preferred shape.

Black examples are usually semigloss, although firing variations can cause pieces to tend toward the matte or the high gloss. The green matte glaze is similar (or identical) to Moderne's "Patina," having tan highlights along the rim. White Burmese pieces are glossy, a glaze that was also used on late Rozane Pattern.

No factory stock pages are known for Burmese. Only 5 shapes appear in factory advertising:

BURMESE

Shape No.	Description
70B	candlestick (female)
72B	wall pocket (female)
81B	bookend (male)
82B	wall pocket (male)
90B	-10" window box

Burmese. 70B candleholder (female), white; 80B candleholder (male), white. *Fairfield collection.* **$250–300 (pair).** Both are 7.5" tall.

Burmese. 81B bookend (female), black; 71B bookend (male), black. *Hoppe photograph.* **$300–350 (pair)**

Burmese. Pair, 76B candlesticks, matt light green; 90B-10" window box, black. *Fairfield collection.* **$75–100 (pair), $100–125**

Burmese. 92B-14.75" window box, black. *Scheytt collection.* **$125–150**

BUSHBERRY
A Late Line, introduced in 1941

Factory Name(s): Bushberry; Bushberry Pattern
Style: Life-like berry designs, often on Mid-Century Modern shapes
Standard Color(s): Blue, Green, or Woodland Orange (or "Orange")
Typical Marks: Molded (raised-relief) marks, including "Roseville" (script), shape number, and size

Bushberry appeals to lovers of the Mid-Century Modern style. In 1941, a factory advertisement remarked that Bushberry "blends naturally with reed or metal furniture" (*Gift and Art Buyer*, June 1941: 2). The line depicts "large spreading leaves carefully detailed and berries that are delightfully realistic." These are set across "a background of wood textured finish"—all in all, a line that Roseville thought "exceptionally smart" (advertisement, *Gift and Art Buyer*, May 1941: 2).

The berries of Bushberry do not seem to have any real-life reference. The term "bushberry" does not appear in the *Oxford English Dictionary*. It was probably coined from the words "bush" and "berry." Not that collectors seem to care! All three colors have followers in today's market.

Early advertising mentions 64 shapes, but only 61 are shown in the factory stock pages:

BUSHBERRY

Shape No.	Description	Shape No.	Description
1	-3.5" mug	157	-8" vase
1	-6" ewer	158	-4.5" gate
1	-10" comport	369	-6.5" basket
2	-C cream	370	-8" basket
2	-S sugar	371	-10" basket
2	-T teapot	372	-12" basket
2	-10" ewer	383	-6" planter
3	cornucopia	384	-8" window box
3	-15" ewer	385	-10" bowl
9	bookend	411	-4" rose bowl
26	ashtray	411	-6" rose bowl
28	-4" vase	411	-8" rose bowl
29	-6" vase	412	-6" comport
30	-6" vase	414	-10" bowl
31	-7" vase	415	-10" bowl
32	-7" vase	416	-12" bowl
33	-8" vase	417	-14" bowl
34	-8" vase	465	-5" hanging basket
35	-9" vase	657	-3" jardiniere
36	-9" vase	657	-4" jardiniere
37	-10" vase	657	-5" jardiniere
38	-12" vase	657	-6" jardiniere
39	-14" vase	657	-8" jardiniere & pedestal
40	-15" vase	657	-10" jardiniere & pedestal
45	flower frog	658	-5" flower pot and saucer
152	-7" bud vase	778	-14" sand jar
153	-6" cornucopia	779	-20" umbrella stand
154	-8" cornucopia	1147	candlestick
155	-8" double cornucopia	1148	-4.5" candlestick
156	-6" vase	1291	-8" wall pocket
		1325	ball pitcher

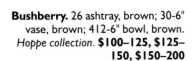

Bushberry. 35-9" vase, blue; 37-10" vase, brown; 34-8" vase, green. *Shannon collection.* **$225–275, $250–300, $200–250**

Bushberry. 26 ashtray, brown; 30-6" vase, brown; 412-6" bowl, brown. *Hoppe collection.* **$100–125, $125–150, $150–200**

Bushberry. 1-6" ewer, green; 411-8" rose bowl, green; 370-8" basket, green. *Auclair collection.* **$150–200, $200–250, $225–275**

Bushberry. 156-6" vase, blue; pair, 9 bookends, blue; 39-14" vase, blue; 371-10" basket, blue. *Auclair collection.* **$150–200, $325–375 (pair), $400–500, $275–325**

CAMEO

An Early Line, introduced in 1908

Factory Name(s): Cameo
Collector Nickname(s): Chloron (see Purviance and Schneider, 1970); Matt Green (see Huxford, 1980)
Style: Arts and Crafts, or Art Nouveau
Standard Color(s): One standard coloring, as described below
Typical Marks: Unmarked. Some examples have a die-impressed shape number.

Cameo pieces borrow two glazes from earlier Roseville lines. Their "cameo" sections are modeled in low relief and glazed in Old Ivory (Tinted). The rest of these pieces usually have a mottled matte green glaze, in the manner of Chloron or Egypto. Introduced at the 1908 Pittsburgh glass and china show, the Cameo line drew a notice from the press, who thought its "mission effects" so novel that the line could "only be appreciated by a person seeing the real goods" (trade notice, *China, Glass and Lamps,* January 11, 1908: 11).

Caution: Do not confuse hand-decorated Old Ivory (Decorated) with Cameo, as many Roseville researchers have done!

This line is quite rare today, and may have had a brief marketing. Collectors can be passionate about the line's wall pockets. Factory stock pages show only 4 items glazed as Cameo:

CAMEO

Shape No.	Description	Reference/Notes
337	-15.75" wall pocket	Bomm 93
339	-12.5" wall pocket	Bomm 93
488	-13" x 42" jardiniere and pedestal	Bomm 79 lower left, item 2
489	-12" x 41.5" jardiniere and pedestal	Bomm 79 lower left, item 1

Cameo. 416-6" planter, die-impressed 416. *Courtesy of Joyce and Rich Bennett.* **$350–450.** The motif of geese in flight echoes a Frederick H. Rhead tubeline design for Roseville—Decorated Landscape.

Cameo. 10" x 30" jardiniere and pedestal, profile of young woman on jardiniere, poppies and pods on pedestal, unmarked. *Courtesy of Treadway Gallery.* **$2000–2500**

Cameo. 489-7" jardiniere, Bacchantes in the forest. *Hoppe photograph.* **$750–950**

Cameo. 339-12" wall sconce, owl with spread wings, *Hoppe photograph.* **$2500–3000.** The legend in molded letters reads "Licht Mehr Licht" (a well-known exclamation of the German poet Goethe as he began to lose his eyesight: "Light! More light!").

A Late Line, introduced ca. 1953

Factory Name(s): Capri
Collector Nickname(s): Late unnamed line (see Purviance and Schneider, 1970); Unnamed line, or Crystal Green (see Huxford, 1976); Capri (see Huxford, 1980); Mayfair/Capri (see Monsen, 1995), Capri/Mayfair (see Monsen, 1997)
Style: Mid-Century Modern
Standard Color(s): Cactus Green ("green"), Metallic Red ("red"), or Sandalwood Yellow ("yellow")
Typical Marks: Molded (raised-relief) marks, including "Roseville" (script), shape number, and size

Like Ben Seibel's two Raymor lines, most Capri pieces evoke the Mid-Century Modern style. The name "Capri" is derived from "caprice," which implies "a freak," "a whim," or "a work of irregular and sportive fancy" (according to the *Oxford English Dictionary*). The Roseville factory brochure describes many of Capri's bowl and planter shapes as "odd" (instead of round or oblong).

Such fantastic biomorphic designs seem atypical of art director Frank Ferrell, then in his mid-seventies. Capri (and the more restrained Mayfair) may be the work of Smith and Scheer, designers of the 1952 Roseville line Lotus. Minutes of the April 4, 1952, Board of Directors meeting indeed record that "Smith & Scherr [*sic*] were being considered for the designers of the new 1953 line." On the other hand, one can also notice a movement toward embracing the Mid-Century style in several known Ferrell designs—from Lozane Pattern to Mock Orange to Wincraft.

When Capri borrows a shape from the somewhat earlier line Mayfair, the Capri shape number begins with a "C." The mottled yellow glaze may be a revival of (or based on) one of the Tourmaline glazes.

Probably because Roseville made so few Mid-Century Modern lines, Capri is still one of the most affordable of Roseville products today.

No factory stock pages are known. An undated factory brochure for Capri shows 31 shapes:

Capri. C1004-9" vase, yellow. *Shannon collection.* **$100–125**

CAPRI

Shape No.	Description		Shape No.	Description
508	-7" basket		586	-12" vase
509	-8" basket		597	-7" ashtray
510	-10" basket		598	-9" ashtray
526	-7" bowl		599	-13" ashtray
527	-7" bowl		C1003	-8" vase (Mayfair shape)
529	-9" bowl		C1004	-9" vase (Mayfair shape)
531	-14" bowl		C1009	-8" bowl (Mayfair shape)
532	-15" bowl		C1010	-10" bowl (Mayfair shape)
555	-7" planter		C1012	-10" basket (Mayfair shape)
556	-6" cornucopia		C1016	-10" vase (Mayfair shape)
557	-7" vase		C1017	-12" vase (Mayfair shape)
558	planter		C1118	shell (Mayfair shape)
569	-10" window box		C1119	shell (Mayfair shape)
572	-8" planter vase		C1120	shell (Mayfair shape)
580	-6" vase		C1151	shell candlestick (Mayfair shape)
582	-9" vase			

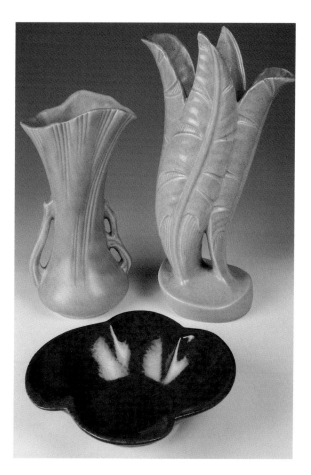

Capri. 582-9" vase, green; 527-7" bowl, red; 586-12" vase, yellow. *Fairfield collection.* **$100–125, $50–60, $150–175**

Capri. 580-6" vase, red; 509-8" basket, green. *Shannon collection.* **$100–125, $125–150**

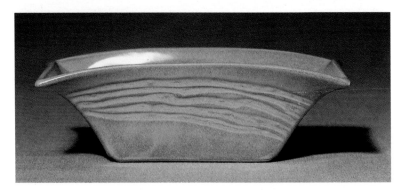

Capri. 569-10 window box, yellow. *Hoppe photograph.* **$75–100**

CARNELIAN
A Middle Period Line, introduced in 1926

Factory Name(s): Carnelian

Collector Nickname(s): Carnelian (First) and Carnelian (Second) [see Alexander, 1970]; Carnelian I and Carnelian II (see Huxford, 1976); Futura Carnelian (see Monsen, 1997)

Style: Arts and Crafts; or Modernistic

Standard Color(s): Various matte or semigloss glazes, as described below

Typical Marks: Carnelian (Drip) examples can be unmarked, but usually have a blue inkstamp Rv logo. If such pieces were reglazed as Carnelian (Glazes), the old inkstamp mark would still be present. (In some cases, a thick glaze may obscure the inkstamp mark.) Examples of Carnelian (Glazes) were usually marked with paper labels. (These could be lost, leaving the piece unmarked—or marked only with the earlier inkstamp.) Some examples have hand-written (usually crayon) shape numbers.

Carnelian (Drip). 309-6" vase, dark on medium green; 62-3.5" combination candlestick and flower frog, dark on light blue; 167-12" x 9" bowl, dark on light blue. *Fairfield collection.* **$150–175, $125–150, $200–250**

The first Carnelian (Drip) pieces were matte glazed, with either dark bluish green dripping over medium turquoise, or yellowish tan dripping over light tan ("on the taupe order"). A 1926 observer admired "the artistic fashion in which two shades of the same color are made to blend into each other in an irregular line, the darker tone invariably occupying the upper portion" (trade notice, *Pottery, Glass and Brass Salesman,* July 8, 1926: 15). Other colorings—such as dark blue over pink, and dark blue over light blue—came later.

The line had some sales, but did not fare as well as expected. By 1928, Roseville began to reglaze their unsold Carnelian (Drip) inventory. Thick matte and semigloss glazes of rose, purple, lavender, tan, peach, green, or blue were applied and pieces refired until deemed "finished." In the manner of Early Carnelian or Egypto, the new Carnelian (Glazes) allowed one layer of color to show through another, creating irregular and pleasing textures. Gradually, a new inventory of Carnelian (Glazes) accumulated, and the glazes sold themselves.

Caution: It is easy for a beginner to confuse Carnelian (Glazes) with Imperial (Glazes). Both Alexander (1970) and Huxford (1976) include a mistake of this sort. When in doubt, refer to the shape lists.

The factory stock pages show 103 Carnelian shapes. Sometimes a shape number was corrected in the stock pages, making it hard to read. Only shapes 439 through 461 appear in the factory records as Carnelian (Glazes); the others are glazed in Carnelian (Drip).

CARNELIAN

Shape No.	Description	Reference/Notes
15	-2.5" flower block	
15	-3.5" flower block	
17	-2" x 3.5" flower block	
17	-3" x 4.5" flower block	
50	-4" flower holder	
51	-5" fan vase	Bomm 84 (top, row 5, item 1)
52	-6" fan vase	Bomm 84 (top, row 4, item 1)
53	-5" pillow vase	Bomm 84 (top, row 4, item 5)
54	-8" fan vase	Bomm 84 (top, row 6, item 4)
55	-6" pillow vase	Bomm 84 (top, row 6, item 5)
56	-5" double bud vase, gate shape	Bomm 84 (top, row 1, item 6)
57	-3" candlestick/flower frog	
58	-3.5" flower frog	
59	-3.5" flower holder	
60	-6" rock flower frog	
61	-6" x 2.5" planter	
62	-3.5" candlestick/flower holder	
63	-5.5" flower holder	
64	-5" vase	
65	-6" vase	
152	-4" bowl	
152	-5" bowl	
152	-6" bowl	
152	-7" bowl	
153	-5" comport	
154	-6" bowl	
155	-8" bowl	
156	-12" bowl	Bomm 84 (top, row 6, item 3)
157	-14" bowl	Bomm 84 (top, row 5, item 2)
158	-5" vase	Bomm 84 (top, row 6, item 1)
159	-6" bowl	
160	-7" bowl	
161	-7" bowl	
162	-8" bowl	
163	-8" bowl	
164	-9" bowl	
165	-9" bowl	
166	-10" bowl	
167	-12" bowl	
168	-10" bowl	
169	-12" bowl	
170	-14" bowl	
306	-6" bud vase	Bomm 84 (bottom, row 2, item 3)
307	-6" vase	Bomm 84 (bottom, row 1, item 3)
308	-7" vase	Bomm 84 (bottom, row 1, item 4)
309	-8" vase	Bomm 84 (bottom, row 2, item 5)
310	-7" vase	Bomm 84 (bottom, row 1, item 5)
311	-7" vase	Bomm 84 (bottom, row 1, item 2)
312	-8" vase	Bomm 84 (bottom, row 2, item 4)
313	-9" vase	Bomm 84 (bottom, row 2, item 2)
314	-9" vase	Bomm 84 (bottom, row 2, item 1)
315	-10" vase	Bomm 84 (bottom, row 3, item 3)

Shape No.	Description	Reference/Notes
316	-10" vase	Bomm 84 (bottom, row 3, item 4)
317	-10" vase	Bomm 84 (bottom, row 3, item 2)
318	-8" vase	
319	-9" vase	Bomm 84 (bottom, row 1, item 1)
320	-12" vase	Bomm 84 (bottom, row 3, item 5)
321	-15" vase	Bomm 84 (bottom, row 3, item 1)
322	-18" floor vase	Bomm 84 (bottom, row 3, item 6)
331	-7" vase	
332	-8" vase	
333	-6" vase	
334	-8" vase	
335	-8" vase	
336	-9" vase	
337	-10" vase	
338	-12" vase	
339	-15" vase	
340	-18" vase	
439	-9" vase	
440	-8" vase	
441	-8" vase	
442	-12" vase	
443	-12" vase	
444	-12" vase	
445	-12" vase	
446	-12" vase	
450	-14" vase	
456	-20" vase	
457	-24" vase	
458	-24" vase	
459	-28" vase	
460	-28" vase	
461	-28" vase	
1058	-2" candlestick	
1059	-2.5" candlestick	
1060	-3" candlestick	
1063	-3" candlestick	
1064	-3" candlestick	
1065	-4" candlestick	
1246	-7" wall pocket	
1247	-8" wall pocket	Bomm 84 (top, row 4, item 2)
1248	-8" wall pocket	Bomm 84 (top, row 4, item 4)
1249	-9" wall pocket	
1251	-8" wall pocket	
1252	-8" wall pocket	
1253	-8" wall pocket	
1311	-10" ewer	
1312	-10" ewer	
1313	-12" ewer	
1314	-8" ewer	
1315	-15" ewer	
1316	-18" ewer	

Left:
Carnelian (Drip). *Top Row:* Pair, 1064-3" candlesticks, dark on light blue; 333-6" urn, dark on light blue. **$175–225 (pair), $250–300.** *Bottom Row:* 335-8" vase, dark on light blue; 336-9" vase, dark on light blue. *Shannon collection.* **$300–350, $300–350**

Carnelian (Drip). 1315-15" ewer, blue on pink; 1311-10" ewer, blue on pink. *Senior collection; courtesy of Jeanette Stofft.* **$700–800, $400–450**

Carnelian (Drip). 54-8" fan vase, tan on mustard yellow; 58-3.5" vase with holes for flower arranging, blue on pink; 319-10" vase, tan on light green; 153-5" comport, blue on blue green. *Shannon collection.* **$150–175, $100–125, $250–300, $125–150**

Carnelian (Glazes). 450-14" vase, originally fired as Carnelian (Drip). *Hoppe collection.* **$2500–3000**

Carnelian (Glazes). 310-7" vase, originally fired as Carnelian (Drip); 334-8" vase; 310-7" vase, originally fired as Carnelian (Drip). *Shannon collection.* **$300–350, $375–450, $300–350**

Carnelian (Glazes). 158-5" urn; 314-9" vase, originally fired as Carnelian (Drip); 441-8" vase, originally fired as Carnelian (Drip). *Fairfield collection.* **$250–300, $275–350, $700–800**

Carnelian (Glazes). 446-12" vase, originally fired as Carnelian (Drip), crayon shape number 446. *Courtesy of Mike Nickel and Cindy Horvath.* **$3000–4000**

Carnelian (Glazes). 337-10" vase, originally fired as Carnelian (Drip); 339-15" vase, originally fired as Carnelian (Drip); 152-7" bowl. *Courtesy of Cincinnati Art Galleries.* **$600–700, $1200–1500, $175–225**

Carnelian (Glazes). 452-16" vase; 443-12" vase. *Shannon collection.* **$2000–2500, $1500–2000**

CHERRY BLOSSOM
A Middle Period Line, introduced in 1933

Factory Name(s): Cherry Blossom
Style: Art Deco
Standard Color(s): Brown ("tan with white") or pink ("green with pink")
Typical Marks: Foil labels. (These could be lost, leaving the piece unmarked.) Some have hand-written (crayon) shape numbers.

A splendid Middle Period line, Cherry Blossom has long had admirers. A 1933 trade notice says it all:

This excellent bit of potting is very gay and spring-like with graceful floral sprays trailing over a trellis-like effect. The body is worked out in sort of a moire feeling that affords an excellent background for the dainty sprays and the crisp trellis.... The colors soft and subtle with rather a mother-of-pearl feeling. There are vases, flower bowls and wall pockets to retail from $1.00 to $3.50, console sets of flat bowl and candlesticks to retail at $5.00, and a special huge 15-inch vase to retail at $7.50, and a range of jardinieres and pedestals in which the design has been worked out with specially good decorative results (trade notice, *Crockery and Glass Journal*, March 1933: 25–26).

Most collectors prefer the pink variety, although both have devoted followers. The factory stock pages show 25 Cherry Blossom shapes:

CHERRY BLOSSOM

Shape No.	Description	Shape No.	Description
239	-5" vase	627	-4" jardiniere
240	-8" bowl	627	-5" jardiniere
350	-5" hanging basket	627	-6" jardiniere
617	-3.5" vase	627	-7" jardiniere
618	-5" vase	627	-8" jardiniere & pedestal
619	-5" vase	627	-9" jardiniere
620	-7" vase	627	-10" jardiniere
621	-6" vase	627	-10" jardiniere & pedestal
622	-7" vase	627	-12" vase
623	-7" vase	628	-15" vase
624	-8" vase	1090	-4" candlestick
625	-8" vase	1270	-8" wall pocket
626	-10" vase		

Cherry Blossom. 621-6" vase, brown; pair, 1090-4" candlesticks, pink; 617-3.5" vase, brown. *Fairfield collection.* **$450–500, $600–700 (pair), $300–350**

Cherry Blossom. 620-7" vase, pink. *Courtesy of McAllister Auctions.* **$600–700**

Cherry Blossom. 627-7" jardiniere, brown; 627-5" jardiniere, brown; 627-6" jardiniere, brown. *Hoppe collection.* **$500–600, $400–450, $450–500.** Reminder: Always measure the inside diameter (across the opening) of a Roseville jardiniere (not its height).

Cherry Blossom. 628-15" floor vase, brown. *Hoppe photograph.* **$1500–1800**

CHLORON

An Early Line, introduced in 1905

Factory Name(s): Chloron
Style: Art Nouveau
Standard Color(s): Matte green
Typical Marks: This line can be definitively identified only by the presence of a distinctive inkstamp reading "Chloron" (in artistic script-like lettering). This mark is also known in a die-impressed version.

A 1905 reviewer admired Roseville's "exceedingly artistic new line of Chloron pottery." Showing Roseville's wares at the Pittsburgh glass and china show, factory sales representative Frank Pletcher called Chloron "a line of vases in antique styles, of a soft, rich green color." According to the reporter, "The decorations, floral, mostly, and most artistically done, are raised slightly, and are more or less indistinct. They are most attractive" (trade notice, *China, Glass and Lamps,* January 14, 1905: 25).

The name Chloron echoes the Greek word for "green." It is therefore more accurate than the name Egypto, which was applied to a similar line at Roseville later that year. Because many shapes appear in both lines, unmarked examples can only be "attributed" to one or the other Roseville line. Some may instead belong properly to the early Matt Green line.

Mistakenly thinking Chloron to be a later production than Egypto, many collectors currently value Egypto more highly. In any case, marked examples are slightly better at auction. Savvy collectors weigh more substantial characteristics, including design and glaze quality. The matte green glaze varies in coloring, texture, and degree of variation.

The only known Chloron factory stock page shows 19 shapes, many of which were quickly revived in the Egypto and Mara lines:

Chloron. C15-8.25" vase, foliage, "Chloron" inkstamp, TRPCo inkstamp. *Courtesy of White Pillars Antique Mall.* **$750–850**

Shape No.	Description	Shape No.	Description
C10	-8.5" vase	C20	-4.5" ewer
C11	-9" vase	C21	-6.5" vase
C12	-10.5" vase	C22	-8.5" vase
C13	-3.5" bowl	C23	-8" vase
C14	-8.5" ewer	C24	-4.5" vase
C15	-8.5" vase	C25	-5.5" vase
C16	-6.5" vase	C26	-2.5" bowl
C17	-5.5" vase	C27	-2.5" bowl
C18	-3.5" bowl	C28	-2" candlestick
C19	-5.5" vase		

Chloron. C19-5.5" vase, flowers in arch-like arrangement, unmarked. *Courtesy of Treadway Gallery.* **$450–550**

Chloron. C21-6.5" vase, floral vine, "Chloron" inkstamp; C16-6.5" vase, berries and foliage, die-impressed "Chloron." *Hoppe photograph.* **$400–500, $500–600**

CLEMANA
A Middle Period Line, introduced in 1936

Factory Name(s): Clemana
Alternate Spelling(s): Clemena (see Buxton, 1977)
Style: Art Deco
Standard Color(s): Blue, green, or tan
Typical Marks: Early pieces have a foil label. (These can be lost, leaving the piece unmarked). Pieces made in 1937 or later have die-impressed marks, including "Roseville" (script), shape number, and size.

Oral history does not recount the origin of the name Clemana. Like Pauleo and Wincraft, this line may be named for a member of the George F. Young family—namely, Fenwick S. Clement, husband to Young's daughter Leota. The line name is spelled "Clemena" in a January 1936 notice in *Crockery and Glass Journal.* With the other 1936 line, Primrose, Clemana was said to "offer quite a variety and with the colorful florals as the decor, the pieces make excellent decorative accents for any type of home, whether it be modern or classic."

Clemana. 749-6" vase, blue; 756-9" vase, green; 23-4" flower frog, brown. *Shannon collection.* **$250–300, $350–400, $125–150**

The stylized geometrical motifs appeal to Art Deco lovers. Each flower has a tiny pink center, and the petals are heart-shaped. Although factory records show Clemana pieces with white linings, most examples are lined in the same glaze used on the background.

Clemana is fairly scarce today. Many surviving examples have minor damage. The only known factory stock page shows the following 18 Clemana shapes:

CLEMANA

Shape No.	Description	Shape No.	Description
122	-7" vase	752	-7" vase
123	-7" vase	753	-8" vase
280	-6" vase	754	-8" vase
281	-5" bowl	755	-9" vase
282	-8" bowl	756	-9" vase
283	-12" bowl	757	-10" vase
749	-6" vase	758	-12" vase
750	-6" vase	759	-14" vase
751	-7" vase	1104	-4.5" candlestick

Clemana. 752-7" vase, green; 754-8" vase, brown; 122-7" vase, blue. *Auclair collection.* **$275–325, $400–450, $350–400.** Note the differences in grade: the middle piece has the sharpest background details; using the colloquial expression, a collector might say, "it has the best mold."

Below:
Clemana. 751-7" vase, green. *Courtesy of Mark Bassett Antiques.* **$325–375.** Most Clemana pieces have an interior in the same color as the background. This example is lined in matte white instead. (See also the hand-colored factory stock page in Bomm, where the linings are shown in white.)

Clemana. 759-14" vase, blue; 281-5" bowl, brown; 753-8" vase, green. *Auclair collection.* **$600–700, $175–225, $350–400**

CLEMATIS

A Late Line, introduced in 1944

Factory Name(s): Clematis
Style: Realistic
Standard Color(s): Autumn Brown ("brown"), Ciel Blue ("blue"), or Forest Green ("green")
Typical Marks: Molded (raised-relief) marks, including "Roseville" (script), shape number, and size

Named for a climbing vine popular in the 1940s, Clematis today has more appeal to gardeners than to the typical Roseville collector. In 1944, Roseville advertisements boasted that "in this lovely new creation, the inviting beauty of Clematis is faithfully translated to variegated art forms of charming design" (*Gift and Art Buyer,* June 1944: 2). In the best examples, Clematis has a highly detailed textural background, which offers contrast to the large, fairly smooth petals of the flower.

Unfortunately, the wartime economy forced Roseville to use Clematis molds longer than would normally be advisable. As a result, the Clematis pieces in today's market often have poorly defined details—in both flower and background. Collectors seem to have a slight preference for green and brown over blue.

The factory stock pages show 47 shapes in the Clematis line:

CLEMATIS

Shape No.	Description	Shape No.	Description
3	-8" cookie jar	191	-8" cornucopia
5	-C cream	192	-5" vase
5	-S sugar	193	-6" vase
5	teapot	194	-5" gate
6	-10" bowl	387	-7" basket
14	bookend	388	-8" basket
16	-6" ewer	389	-10" basket
17	-10" ewer	391	-8" window box
18	-15" ewer	455	-4" bowl
50	flower holder	456	-6" bowl
102	-6" vase	457	-8" bowl
103	-6" vase	458	-10" bowl
105	-7" vase	459	-10" bowl
106	-7" vase	460	-12" bowl
107	-8" vase	461	-14" bowl
108	-8" vase	470	-5" hanging basket
109	-9" vase	667	-4" jardiniere
110	-9" vase	667	-5" jardiniere
111	-10" vase	667	-8" jardiniere & pedestal
112	-12" vase	668	-5" flower pot and saucer
114	-15" vase	1158	-2" candlestick
187	-7" bud vase	1159	-4.5" candlestick
188	-6" vase	1290	-8" wall pocket
190	-6" cornucopia		

Clematis. 17-10" ewer, brown; 112-12" vase, blue; 387-7" basket, green. *Shannon collection.* **$200–250, $275–325, $175–200**

Clematis. 109-9" vase, green; 50 flower arranger, green; 110-9" vase, green; 103-6" vase, green. *Courtesy of McAllister Auctions.* **$150–175, $75–100, $175–200, $100–125**

Left:
Clematis. 457-8" bowl, brown; 388-8" basket, brown; 460-12" bowl, brown. *Courtesy of McAllister Auctions.* **$150–175, $200–250, $175–200**

Clematis. 108-8" vase, blue; 111-10" vase, blue; 391-8" window box, blue. *Hoppe photograph.* **$125–150, $225–275, $100–125**

COLUMBINE

A Late Line, introduced in 1941

Factory Name(s): Columbine
Style: Realistic
Standard Color(s): Frost Blue ("blue"), Red ("pink"), or Sand Brown ("brown")
Typical Marks: Molded (raised-relief) marks, including "Roseville" (script), shape number, and size

In factory advertising, Roseville claimed "tremendous success" for Columbine: "It is the fine detail of this pattern skillfully molded to the contour of each vase which makes Roseville's latest creation so greatly in demand" (advertisement, *Gift and Art Buyer,* February 1941: 2).

The most conservative of Roseville's three 1941 patterns (the others being Bushberry and Rozane Pattern), Columbine pieces are typically symmetrical. Smooth, classical shapes provide the background for the floral motifs, modeled with considerable restraint. Mildly angular handles appear on many items, but only the three baskets and the flower frog are clearly Mid-Century Modern shapes.

The traditionalist bent of Columbine may have served to keep prices fairly moderate for today's collector. All three colors are successful, although blue may cost slightly more.

Roseville advertising mentions 46 shapes, but only 44 appear in the factory stock pages:

COLUMBINE

Shape No.	Description	Shape No.	Description
8	planter bookend	366	-8" basket
12	-4" vase	367	-10" basket
13	-6" vase	368	-12" basket
14	-6" vase	399	-4" vase
15	-7" bud vase	400	-6" rose bowl
16	-7" vase	401	-6" bowl
17	-7" vase	402	-8" bowl
18	-7" ewer	403	-10" bowl
19	-8" vase	404	-10" bowl
20	-8" vase	405	-12" bowl
21	-9" vase	406	-14" bowl
22	-9" vase	464	-5" hanging basket
23	-10" vase	655	-3" jardiniere
24	-10" vase	655	-4" jardiniere
25	-12" vase	655	-5" jardiniere
26	-14" vase	655	-6" jardiniere
27	-16" vase	655	-8" jardiniere & pedestal
42	flower frog	655	-10" jardiniere & pedestal
149	-6" cornucopia	656	-5" flower pot and saucer
150	-6" vase	1145	-2.5" candlestick
151	-8" vase	1146	-4.5" candlestick
365	-7" basket	1291	-8" wall pocket

Columbine. 656-5" flower pot (and separate saucer), blue; 21-9" vase, blue; 16-7" vase, blue. *Hoppe photograph.* **$175–225, $175–225, $150–175**

Columbine. 367-10" basket, blue; 13-6" vase, blue. *Hoppe photograph.* **$325–375, $125–150**

Columbine. 150-6" vase, brown; pair, 8 bookends, brown; 23-10" vase, brown; 18-7" ewer, brown. *Auclair collection.* **$125–150, $275–325 (pair), $275–325, $200–250**

Columbine. Pair, 1145-2.5" candlesticks, pink; 406-14" bowl, pink; 42 flower frog, pink. *Stofft collection.* **$125–150 (pair), $200–250, $125–150**

Columbine. 365-7" basket, pink; 19-8" pillow vase, brown; 15-7" bud vase, pink. *Shannon collection.* **$225–275, $150–175, $125–150**

COMMERCIAL
A Generic Term useful for referring to Several Late Corporate Jobs

Factory Name(s): Various, including Hyde Park
Style: Mid-Century Modern
Standard Color(s): Various glossy colors
Typical Marks: Molded (raised relief) marks, usually including the "brand name" and shape number. On Hyde Park pieces, the marks are "Hyde Park" and shape number.

Little is known about the commercial jobs Roseville appears to have undertaken in 1953 and 1954. Huxford (1980) shows several examples of this kind of work. If Hyde Park is the best-known such commission, Borden's Elsie sets are certainly the most desirable to collectors. (The Borden's sets are mentioned in the Board of Directors minutes dated September 8, 1954). Additional commissions are said to have been executed for "Vernco" and "Cal Art," although such products have not been located for study.

Caution: The Haeger Potteries also conducted work for Hyde Park. Roseville examples can be identified by their white-speckled glazes and buff clay body. They also weigh relatively more than the more brittle Haeger product.

No factory stock pages for these Commercial wares have been located.

Commercial (Borden's Set). B3 cereal bowl. *Hoppe photograph.* **$150–200**

Commercial (Borden's Set). B2-7.5" plate; B1 cup. *Hoppe photograph.* **$300–350, $125–150**

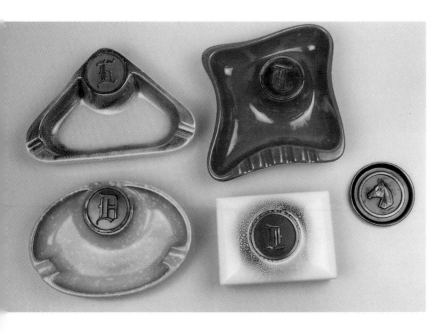

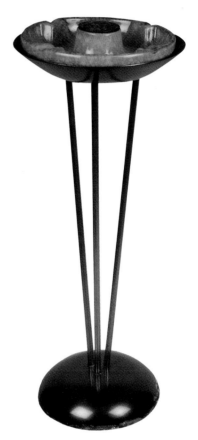

Commercial (Hyde Park). 1900 ashtray, green, typical molded marks, on 22.25" metal stand, unmarked. *Fairfield collection.* **$125–150**

Commercial (Hyde Park). (Clockwise from lower left) 1950 ashtray, yellow; 1940 ashtray, lime; 1930 ashtray, rust; horse ashtray (metal, not a Roseville product), marked Hyde Park; 1510 cigarette box, white pottery lid, metal box. *Fairfield collection.* **$20–25, $20–25, $25–30, $5–10, $30–35**

CORINTHIAN

A Middle Period Line, introduced in 1923

Factory Name(s): Corinthian

Style: Greek Revival, or Italianate

Standard Color(s): One standard coloring, as described below

Typical Marks: Some examples are unmarked. Others have a blue inkstamp Rv logo.

Roseville's Corinthian line has a fluted body, the grooves being tinted green in the manner of the earlier Donatello. At the mouth, "each piece is finished with a real Italian Renaissance border," observed one contemporary reviewer (trade notice, *Pottery, Glass and Brass Salesman*, July 12, 1923: 53). Just beneath the rim, a well-modeled band of grapevines is decorated in natural colors of brown, green, and purple.

Most shapes were fairly traditional, although the 24-inch jardiniere & pedestal was considered "particularly suitable for use in restaurants, and in large and imposing showrooms, such as for automobiles."

Caution: Do not confuse Corinthian and Normandy, another fluted 1920s line.

CORINTHIAN

Shape No.	Description	Reference/Notes
14	-2.5" flower block	(Donatello shape; see also La Rose)
14	-3.5" flower block	(Donatello shape; see also La Rose)
15	-8" comport	
37	gate	
42	gate	
121	-5" bowl	
121	-6" bowl	
121	-7" bowl	
212	-6" vase	
213	-6" vase	
214	-6" vase	

Shape No.	Description
336	-6" hanging basket
336	-8" hanging basket
601	-5" jardiniere
601	-6" jardiniere
601	-7" jardiniere
601	-8" jardiniere
601	-9" jardiniere
601	-10" jardiniere & pedestal
601	-12" jardiniere & pedestal
603	-5" flower pot and saucer
603	-6" flower pot and saucer
1048	-8" candlestick
1228	-10" wall pocket
1229	-12" wall pocket
1232	-8" wall pocket

Shape No.	Description
215	-7" vase
216	-7" vase
217	-8" vase
218	-8" vase
219	-10" vase
220	-12" vase
235	-6" vase
235	-8" vase
235	-10" vase
235	-12" vase
235	-15" vase
255	-5" planter
255	-6" planter
256	-5" planter
256	-6" planter

Corinthian. 212-6" vase; 219-10" vase; 235-6" vase. *Hoppe photograph.* **$150–175, $225–275, $150–175**

Corinthian. 121-5" bowl; 121-8" bowl. *Hoppe photograph.* **$100–125, $125–150**

Corinthian. 603-5" flower pot (and separate saucer); 215-7" vase. *Hoppe photograph.* **$200–250, $175–200**

Corinthian. 601-5" jardiniere; 213-6" vase. *Hoppe photograph.* **$150–175, $175–200**

CORNELIAN

An Early Glaze, introduced by 1902

Factory Name(s): Cornelian; Cornelian Twist; Our Leader; Colonial
Collector Nickname(s): Cornelian Ware (see Buxton, 1977)
Style: Early American
Standard Color(s): Glossy spongeware glazes in blue, brown, pink, or yellow on ivory, with gilt rim and other details
Typical Marks: Unmarked

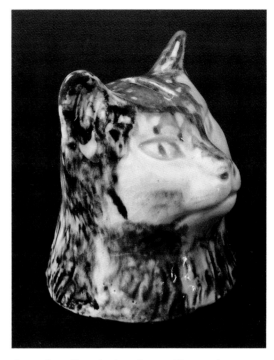

Cornelian. 4" cat bank, yellow and brown. *Latta collection.* **$250–300.** This bank has a handwritten date on the bottom (January 23, 1909), presumably added by the first owner when the piece was purchased or received as a gift.

One early reviewer commented of Cornelian, "as the name implies, the decoration given the ware has all the appearance of marble of that name. It is canary yellow, the marble effect being produced in rich brown and green, finished off in gold" (*China, Glass and Lamps* October 18, 1902: 7). Other mottled spongeware colors were soon added to the line, notably blue and pink.

In about 1903, Roseville published a small catalog titled "Cornelian Ware." This booklet illustrates a number of items available in the Cornelian glazes, including utility ware, cuspidors, fern dishes, 12 figural banks, jardinieres, and two toilet sets ("Our Leader"—which in 1904 or later was renamed "Colonial"—and simply "Cornelian").

In one factory stock page, three jardinieres (shapes 1419, 1421, and 1427) are touted as "Our Leaders for 1903." These and other shapes available in Cornelian glazes were probably also produced in Majolica—either in Blended, Hand Decorated, or Solid Colors. It is unclear how long Cornelian was produced, but toilet sets of some kind were being sold in 1911 and perhaps later (Boston showroom listing, *Crockery and Glass Journal,* December 22, 1910: 213).

Cornelian often goes unidentified into the collections of those who decorate in an American "country" or folk style. Prices are generally reasonable. (For more examples, see "Utility Ware.") In the factory stock pages, 94 shapes are shown decorated in Cornelian glazes:

Cornelian. 11.75" Colonial combinette, blue. *Fairfield collection.* **$300–400.** A combinette (also called a "waste jar") was used to store waste water overnight, after washing, brushing one's teeth, etc.

CORNELIAN

Banks, Cuspidors, Fern Dishes, Jardinieres

Shape No.	Description	Reference/Notes
313	-7" fern dish	Bomm 138 (row 3, item 1)
318	-8" fern dish	Bomm 138 (row 4, item 2)
318	-9" fern dish	Huxford (1977), page 33
607	cuspidor	Bomm 111 (row 5)
609	cuspidor	Bomm 111 (row 6)
610	cuspidor	Bomm 111 (row 4)
1419	-6" jardiniere	Bomm 376
1419	-7" jardiniere	Bomm 376
1419	-8" jardiniere	Bomm 376
1419	-9" jardiniere	Bomm 376
1421	-6" jardiniere	Bomm 376
1421	-7" jardiniere	Bomm 376
1421	-8" jardiniere	Bomm 376
1421	-9" jardiniere	Bomm 376
1427	-6" jardiniere	Bomm 376
1427	-7" jardiniere	Bomm 376
1427	-8" jardiniere	Bomm 376
1427	-9" jardiniere	Bomm 376
	beehive bank, large	
	beehive bank, small	
	buffalo bank	
	cat bank	
	dog bank	
	eagle bank	
	hawk bank	
	lion bank	
	pig bank, large	
	pig bank, small	
	pig bank, standing	
	Uncle Sam bank	

Colonial (or "Our Leader") Toilet Set

Shape No.	Description	Reference/Notes
	brush holder	
	chamber pot (covered)	
	combinette (covered)	
	ewer and basin	
	mouth ewer	
	shaving mug	
	soap dish (covered)	

Cornelian Toilet Set

Shape No.	Description	Reference/Notes
	brush holder	
	chamber pot (covered)	
	combinette (covered)	
	ewer and basin	
	mouth ewer	
	shaving mug	
	soap dish (covered)	

Utility Ware

Shape No.	Description	Reference/Notes
3	1-pt. pitcher ("Cornelian Twist")	Huxford (1977), page 43
3	2-pt. pitcher ("Cornelian Twist")	Huxford (1977), page 43
3	5-pt. pitcher ("Cornelian Twist")	Huxford (1977), page 43
10	-7" mixing bowl	
10	-8" mixing bowl	
10	-9" mixing bowl	
10	-10" mixing bowl	
10	-12" mixing bowl	
10	-14" mixing bowl	
11	-4" pudding dish	
11	-5" pudding dish	
11	-6" pudding dish	
11	-7" pudding dish	
11	-8" pudding dish	
11	-9" pudding dish	
11	-10" pudding dish	
11	-12" pudding dish	
12	cracker jar	
B3	pitcher	Huxford (1977), page 33
C1	pitcher ("The Wild Rose")	Bomm 132
C2	pitcher ("The Golden Rod")	Bomm 132
C5	pitcher ("The Wild Rose")	Bomm 132
C6	pitcher ("The Golden Rod")	Bomm 132
D2	pitcher ("Poppy")	Buxton 43
D3	pitcher ("Poppy")	Buxton 43
E1	pitcher	Bomm 104
E2	pitcher	Bomm 104
E3	pitcher	Bomm 104
E4	pitcher	Bomm 104
E5	pitcher	Bomm 104
	berry set (serving bowl, six bowls, and six underplates)	Buxton 43
	bread and milk set (milk pitcher, bowl, and underplate)	Buxton 43
	butter dish (covered)	
	fruit bowl	
	oatmeal set (milk pitcher and bowl)	
	1-pt. pitcher	
	2-pt. pitcher	
	3-pt. pitcher	
	6-pt. pitcher	
	punch bowl	
	4" shirred eggs bowl	
	5" shirred eggs bowl	
	tobacco jar (covered)	Buxton 43

Cornelian. I-pt. milk pitcher, 4" tall; 10" x 4" fruit bowl; 7.25" x 2" bowl, attributed to Roseville; 8" mouth ewer, from toilet set. *Shannon collection.* **$75–95, $95–125, $75–95, $150–200**

Cornelian. 15" pedestal for #421 jardiniere. *Mastromatteo collection.* **$200–250**

Cornelian. 8" Colonial mouth ewer, blue; 8" Colonial mouth ewer, cream. *Shannon collection.* **$175-200, $150-175.** A mouth ewer was used to store clean (perhaps "purified") drinking water.

Cornelian. 5" milk pitcher from bread and milk set, embossed wheat design, ivory; 6" pitcher, embossed corn design, tan; 5" pitcher, embossed corn design, blue. *Shannon collection.* **$95-125, $125-150, $125-150.** Five corn-decorated pitchers appear in the factory stock pages (shapes E1 through E5), but no dimensions are given, making it difficult to assign shape numbers accurately.

COSMOS

A Late Line, introduced in 1939

Factory Name(s): Cosmos
Style: Realistic, with Art Deco features in many shapes
Standard Color(s): Ice Blue ("blue"), Sepia Brown ("brown"), or
Sunlight Green ("green")
Typical Marks: Die-impressed marks, including "Roseville" (script),
shape number, and size

Roseville advertising boasted of the Cosmos line, "the fragile detail of each petal has been carried out in minute reproduction of the real Cosmos" (*Gift and Art Buyer*, June 1939: 2). In Cosmos, several blossoms are modeled against a textured band. The background is usually partly smooth and partly "pebbled" in look and feel. Colors are pastel, and easily run down into the neighboring areas of a design—in the manner of green Baneda.

In spirit, Cosmos has much in common with Roseville's next line, Bleeding Heart. The 10" Cosmos vase even has a six-pointed lip of the kind that characterizes the Bleeding Heart style. But most Cosmos shapes have sculptural pleated mouths that are divided into multiples of four.

The blue color tends to be the most popular today. Although advertisements mention 48 items, only 45 Cosmos shapes appear in the factory stock pages:

COSMOS

Shape No.	Description	Shape No.	Description
39	flower frog	649	-10" jardiniere & pedestal
133	gate	650	-5" flower pot and saucer
134	-4" vase	944	-4" vase
135	-8" vase	945	-5" vase
136	-6" cornucopia	946	-6" vase
137	-8" cornucopia	947	-6" vase
357	-10" basket	948	-7" vase
358	-12" basket	949	-7" vase
361	-5" hanging basket	950	-8" vase
369	-6" bowl	951	-8" vase
370	-8" bowl	952	-9" vase
371	-10" bowl	953	-9" vase
372	-10" bowl	954	-10" vase
373	-12" bowl	955	-10" ewer
374	-14" bowl	956	-12" vase
375	-4" bowl	957	-15" ewer
376	-6" vase	958	-18" floor vase
381	-9" window box	959	-7" bud vase
649	-3" jardiniere	1136	candlestick
649	-4" jardiniere	1137	-4.5" candlestick
649	-5" jardiniere	1285	-6" wall pocket
649	-6" jardiniere	1286	-8" wall pocket
649	-8" jardiniere & pedestal		

Cosmos. 953-9" vase, blue. *Shannon collection.* **$275–325**

Cosmos. 133-4" double bud vase, gate shape, green, die-impressed marks, gold foil label. *Courtesy of McAllister Auctions.* **$175–225**

Cosmos. 373-12" bowl, green. *Shannon collection.* **$250–300.** Note the unusually large tan section on this example of green Cosmos.

Cosmos. 947-6" vase, tan; 948-7" vase, green; 952-9" vase, tan. *Shannon collection.* **$125–150, $225–275, $250–300**

Cosmos. 381-9" window box, blue; pair, 1136 candlesticks, blue; 946-6" vase, blue. *Hoppe collection.* **$250–300, $175–225 (pair), $150–175**

CREAMWARE
An Early Product Category, introduced by 1910

Factory Name(s): Various, including Coat of Arms, Conventional, Decorated and Gold Traced, Decorated Persian, Dutch, Eagle, Elk, Forget Me Not, Gibson Girls, Gold Traced, Green and Gold, Holly, Indian, Jeanette, Juvenile, K of P (Knights of Pythias), Medallion and Gold, Moose, Novelties, Nursery Line, Orange or Blue Bands, Rozane, Tourist, and perhaps others

Collector Nickname(s): Various, including Persian (see Purviance and Schneider, 1970); Bordeaux Gardens, Cherry Jubilee, Cupidon, Quaker, and Tally Ho (see Buxton, 1977); Stylized Crocus (see Huxford, 1980); and Rosalie (see Bomm, 1998).

Style: Utilitarian (often with an Edwardian-era decal)

Standard Color(s): Old Ivory (that is, cream), usually matte glazed, with decorations in various hand-painted colors or applied by decal

Typical Marks: Unmarked. Early Creamware advertising novelties often have a red three-line inkstamp reading "ROSEVILLE POTTERY" or "ROSEVILLE POTTERY CO." and "ZANESVILLE, O." One particular motif bears the hand-written name "MERCIAN," whose meaning is unknown. Starting in about 1923, examples of banded Utility Ware were marked with a black inkstamp Rv logo. In 1924 and later, this mark was used on the new glossy Juvenile wares. Three late 1930s Juvenile pieces (sold as a set) have molded (raised-relief) marks, consisting of an "R" and the shape number.

Roseville's Creamware lines are a fascinating field of collecting. Experiments in Creamware seem to have begun about 1906, as indicated by a dated stein with a Rozane Ware wafer. Although the stein may represent a private commission, Roseville soon began offering Creamware-style vases with artwork by Charles Dana Gibson, dubbed the Gibson Girls line.

The year 1910 saw Roseville's introduction of Creamware wall pockets. One reviewer recommended "a wall pocket of decorated pottery which is proving highly popular as a flower holder for cut flowers in automobiles. It can be hung in a corner of the auto. The decorative treatment is a point which tends to popularize this pocket. Combination flower pots and jardinieres are shown at this [New York] display room in a variety of designs and decorations" (trade notice, *Pottery, Glass and Brass Salesman*, April 7, 1910: 27).

Other Creamware products were soon introduced, such as coordinated dresser sets, smoker's sets, tea sets, and toilet sets. Methods of decoration included hand-painted banding, hand-colored details, gilt tracing, stippling, applied decals, and pouncing (a technique for transferring a simple design by sifting black pigment through a perforated sheet of onionskin paper).

Creamware advertising novelties were also a popular offering of the factory. A little-known Creamware factory stock page (*courtesy of the Moses Mesre collection*) shows a hanging match holder with lettering that reads "KNOXVILLE, 1910." In 1913, this line garnered a notice from one reviewer, who noticed a variety of "trays (in a number of shapes and sizes), mugs, steins, match holders,

etc., all of which the concern stand ready to furnish with the addition of names or monograms. The samples displayed of items that have been turned out with special names show some very attractive embossed lettering. Articles of the character of those mentioned above are also suitable for restaurants, clubs, etc., as well as for advertising purposes" (*PGBS*, June 19, 1913: 17).

As early as 1905, Roseville sometimes used the term "Rozane" to indicate their entire assortment of art goods, including Creamware. Of some Creamware items introduced by 1911, one reviewer commented: "The coral decorations on the cream colored ware form a very pronounced contrast that is at once pleasing and striking" (*PGBS*, March 23, 1911: 31). The same reviewer also admired a group of Creamware items with stippled decoration, applied by squeezebag. Again, the factory had revived an earlier term to describe this technique—namely, "Aztec." The reviewer remarked: "The 'Aztec' design is of a festoon order with turquoise and brown dots; this is a very good pattern.... The shapes are round and octagonal, and all are fitted with finished liners." In the July 1916 price list, both products were still being offered. For some shapes, buyers could choose: "Aztec–Coral" (that is, either "Aztec" or "Coral" hand decoration on Creamware).

Faced with this enormous body of product (and occasionally inconsistent terminology), Roseville researchers have understandably differed in their treatment of Creamware. Unfortunately, many of the terms suggested in earlier Roseville books now seem more confusing than helpful. It is probably simpler and more accurate to view Creamware as an innovative category of wares, instead of attempting to subdivide and assign nicknames to every conceivable variant in decoration.

By 1916, a line of Creamware products for the nursery was being manufactured (advertisement, *PGBS*, December 14, 1916: 80). Sometimes the factory used the terms Juvenile and Nursery interchangeably. These lines were extremely long-lived, and children's Creamware items were offered for more than twenty years.

In 1924 Roseville began using the Volpato clay body and glossy cream-colored glaze on its Juvenile ware. One reviewer noted "The line is naturally short, with baby plate, cup and saucer, etc., as leading items. The nursery ware carried four decorations—a duck, a dog, a little girl [Sunbonnet Baby] and Santa Claus. These are all fantastic and well calculated to appeal to the juvenile imagination and sense of color" (trade notice, *PGBS*, July 3, 1924: 15).

Caution: Creamware shapes and decorations can be confused with one another. Witness the decades-long confusion about Creamware decorations Jeanette and Gibson Girls. The numbering system for Creamware (Juvenile) is particularly illogical. When in doubt, take a photograph (or try—carefully—making a "quick copy" with a photocopy machine).

In the following shape list, Juvenile-decorated shapes have been listed separately from other Creamware. The factory stock pages (including those from the Moses Mesre collection) show 203 items as Creamware (in decorations other than Juvenile), and 52 items decorated as Juvenile:

CREAMWARE

Various Decorations (not Juvenile)

Shape No.	Description	Reference/Notes
1	-3" bouquet holder (covered)	See July 1916 price list (mentioned as "Decorated")
1	-4" bouquet holder (covered)	See July 1916 price list (mentioned as "Decorated")
1	-6" bouquet holder (covered)	See July 1916 price list (mentioned as "Decorated")
1	-10" cemetery vase	Bomm 88
1	cigarette holder	Not reprinted
1	dresser set (hair receiver, covered powder dish, ring holder, and tray)	Bomm 127; also in July 1916 price list (as "Forget Me Not," "Holly," and "Medallion")
1	lemonade set (pitcher, six mugs)	Bomm 207; also in July 1916 price list (mentioned as "Conventional," "Dutch," "Holly," and "Landscape")
1	teapot	Bomm 129
1	smoker's set (straight-sided tobacco jar, match holder, ashtray, and tray)	See Bomm 332 for shapes; also in July 1916 price list (as "Holly")
1	tobacco jar, no lid	See July 1916 price list (mentioned as "Dutch"); perhaps for cigars
1	tobacco jar, with lid	See July 1916 price list (mentioned as "Dutch")
1B	smoker's set (straight-sided tobacco jar, match holder, ashtray, and tray)	Bomm 332; also in July 1916 price list (as "Coat of Arms")
2	-3" bouquet holder (covered)	See July 1916 price list (mentioned as "Decorated")
2	-4" bouquet holder (covered)	See July 1916 price list (mentioned as "Decorated")
2	-12" cemetery vase	Bomm 88
2	combination ashtray	Bomm 332; also in July 1916 price list (as "Green and Gold")
2	lemonade set (pitcher, four mugs)	Bomm 207
2	teapot	Bomm 129
2	tobacco jar	See July 1916 price list (mentioned as "Dutch")
2B	tobacco jar	Bomm 332; also in July 1916 price list (as "Coat of Arms"); same shape as the Rozane Royal 897-5.5" tobacco jar
3	lemonade set (pitcher, six 1 soda glasses)	Not reprinted
3	tea set (creamer, sugar, teapot)	Bomm 343, 344; also in July 1916 price list (as "Ceramic," "Conventional C," "Conventional D," "Conventional E," "Decorated," "Dutch," "Landscape, Blue," and "Landscape, Brown")
3	teapot	Bomm 129
3	ashtray	See Bomm 332 for shape; also in July 1916 price list (as "Holly")
3A	ashtray	Bomm 332; also in July 1916 price list (as "A, B, or C Decoration")
3C	ashtray	Bomm 332; also in July 1916 price list (as "A, B, or C Decoration")
4	-3" bouquet holder (covered)	See July 1916 price list (mentioned as "Decorated")
4	-2" match holder	See July 1916 price list (mentioned as "Dutch")
4	combination ashtray	Bomm 332; also in July 1916 price list (as "Green and Gold")
4	tea set (creamer, sugar, teapot)	See July 1916 price list (mentioned as "Ceramic")
4	teapot	Bomm 129
4B	smoker's combination	Bomm 332; also in July 1916 price list (as "Coat of Arms")
5	-6" bouquet holder (covered)	See July 1916 price list (mentioned as "Decorated")
5	teapot	Bomm 129
5	ashtray	See Bomm 332 for shape; also in July 1916 price list (as "Holly")
5B	ashtray	Bomm 332; also in July 1916 price list (as "A, B, or C Decoration")
5C	ashtray	Bomm 332; also in July 1916 price list (as "A, B, or C Decoration")
6	-4" bouquet holder (covered)	See July 1916 price list (mentioned as "Decorated")
6	-7.5" "florist" vase, underglaze striped	See July 1916 price list
6	-9" "florist" vase, underglaze striped	See July 1916 price list
6	-11" "florist" vase, underglaze striped	See July 1916 price list
6	-14" "florist" vase, underglaze striped	See July 1916 price list
6	stein	Bomm 174
6	teapot	Bomm 129
6A	combination ashtray	Bomm 332; also in July 1916 price list (as "A Decoration")
6B	combination ashtray	Bomm 332; also in July 1916 price list (as "B Green and Gold")
7	combination ashtray	Not reprinted
7A	smoker's combination	Bomm 332; also in July 1916 price list (as "Indian")
7B	smoker's combination	Bomm 332; also in July 1916 price list (as "Green and Gold")
8	combination ashtray	Not reprinted
8	stein	Bomm 174
8	tea set (creamer, sugar, teapot)	See July 1916 price list (mentioned as "Holly," "Landscape, Blue," and "Landscape, Brown")
8A	smoker's combination	Bomm 332; also in July 1916 price list (as "Indian")
8B	smoker's combination	Bomm 332; also in July 1916 price list (as "Green and Gold")
9	hanging match holder	Not reprinted
9	stein	Bomm 174
9A	smoker's combination	Bomm 332; also in July 1916 price list (as "Indian")
10	-0.5 pt. milk pitcher	Not reprinted
10	-1 pt. milk pitcher	Not reprinted
10	-2 pt. pitcher	Not reprinted
10	hanging match holder	Not reprinted
10A	smoker's combination	Bomm 332; also in July 1916 price list (as "Indian")
10B	smoker's combination	Bomm 332; also in July 1916 price list (as "Green and Gold")
11	-1 pt. pitcher	Not reprinted
11	combination ashtray	See July 1916 price list (mentioned as "Black with Gold Lines" and "Matt White and Decorated")
12	-1 pt. milk pitcher	Not reprinted
13	-1 pt. milk pitcher	Not reprinted
13	teapot	Bomm 129; also in July 1916 price list (as "Conventional Decoration")
14	-1 pt. milk pitcher	Not reprinted
14	teapot	Bomm 129
15	stein	Bomm 174
15	teapot	Bomm 129
16	stein	Bomm 174

Shape No.	Description	Reference/Notes
17	teapot	Bomm 129
203	-4" fern dish	Bomm 90; also in July 1916 price list (as "Landscape")
203	-5" fern dish	Bomm 90; also in July 1916 price list (as "Landscape")
203	-6" fern dish	Bomm 90; also in July 1916 price list (as "Landscape")
203	-7" fern dish	See July 1916 price list (mentioned as "Landscape")
204	-3" fern dish	Bomm 90; also in July 1916 price list (as "Medallion & Gold")
204	-4" fern dish	Bomm 90; also in July 1916 price list (as "Medallion & Gold")
204	-5" fern dish	Bomm 90; also in July 1916 price list (as "Medallion & Gold")
205	-3" fern dish	See July 1916 price list (mentioned as "Holly")
206	-4" fern dish	Bomm 90; also in July 1916 price list (as "Medallion & Gold" and "Conv'l. Decoration")
206	-5" fern dish	Bomm 90; also in July 1916 price list (as "Medallion & Gold" and "Conv'l. Decoration")
206	-6" fern dish	Bomm 90; also in July 1916 price list (as "Medallion & Gold" and "Conv'l. Decoration")
206	-7" fern dish	Bomm 90; also in July 1916 price list (as "Conv'l. Decoration")
213	-3.5" combination planter	Bomm 90; also in July 1916 price list (as "Aztec" or "Coral")
213	-4.25" combination planter	Bomm 90; also in July 1916 price list (as "Aztec" or "Coral")
213	-5.25" combination planter	Bomm 90; also in July 1916 price list (as "Aztec" or "Coral")
214	-4" combination planter	Bomm 90; also in July 1916 price list (as "Ceramic")
214	-5" combination planter	Bomm 90; also in July 1916 price list (as "Ceramic")
215	-4" combination planter	Bomm 90; also in July 1916 price list (as "Coral")
215	-5" combination planter	Bomm 90; also in July 1916 price list (as "Coral")
216	-4" fern dish	See July 1916 price list (mentioned as "Decorated")
217	-5" fern dish	See July 1916 price list (mentioned as "Decorated")
218	-3" or -3.25" combination planter	Bomm 90; also in July 1916 price list (as "Coral")
218	-4" combination planter	Bomm 90; also in July 1916 price list (as "Coral")
218	-5" combination planter	Bomm 90; also in July 1916 price list (as "Coral")
226	-4" fern dish	See July 1916 price list (mentioned as "Tourist")
226	-5" fern dish	See July 1916 price list (mentioned as "Tourist")
226	-6" fern dish	See July 1916 price list (mentioned as "Tourist")
226	pitcher	See July 1916 price list (mentioned as "Decorated")
315	-4" hanging basket	Bomm 253; also in July 1916 price list (as "Decorated")
315	-5" hanging basket	Bomm 253; also in July 1916 price list (as "Decorated")
315	-6" hanging basket	Bomm 253; also in July 1916 price list (as "Decorated")
315	-7" hanging basket	Bomm 253; also in July 1916 price list (as "Decorated")
315	-8" hanging basket	See July 1916 price list (mentioned as "Decorated")
316	-6" fern dish	See July 1916 price list (mentioned as "Holly")
316	-7" fern dish	See July 1916 price list (mentioned as "Holly")
316	-8" fern dish	See July 1916 price list (mentioned as "Holly")
326	-5" hanging basket	See July 1916 price list (mentioned as "Tourist")
326	-6.5" hanging basket	See July 1916 price list (mentioned as "Tourist")
326	-8.5" hanging basket	See July 1916 price list (mentioned as "Tourist")
326	-10" wall pocket	Bomm 88; also in July 1916 price list (as "Decorated")
328	-10.5" or -11" wall pocket	Bomm 88; also in July 1916 price list (as "Decorated")
330	-11" wall pocket	Bomm 88
331	-10.5" wall pocket	Bomm 88
334	-14" wall pocket	Bomm 88
335	-13" wall pocket	Bomm 88
336	-18" corner wall pocket	Bomm 88
338	-17" wall pocket	Bomm 88
343	-5.75" wall sconce	Bomm 169
344	-12" corner wall sconce	Bomm 169
347	-15.25" quadruple candelabra	Bomm 169
351	-13.5" x 5.75" x 6.5" window box	Bomm 169
353	-9" candlestick	Bomm 168; also in July 1916 price list (as "Gold Traced" and "Decorated & Gold Traced")
354	-9" candlestick	Bomm 168
355	-9" candlestick	Bomm 168; also in July 1916 price list (as "Gold Traced," "Decorated & Gold Traced," and "Holly")
356	-9" candlestick	Bomm 168
357	-9" candlestick	Bomm 168; also in July 1916 price list (as "Gold Traced" and "Decorated & Gold Traced")
360	stacking tea set (including teapot, creamer, cup)	See July 1916 price list
361	-9" candlestick	Bomm 168
362	-11" x 6.5" window box	See July 1916 price list (mentioned as "Tourist")
362	-12" candlestick	Bomm 169; also in July 1916 price list (as "Decorated")
362	-14" x 8" window box	See July 1916 price list (mentioned as "Tourist")
362	-16" x 8.5" window box	See July 1916 price list (mentioned as "Tourist")
462	-3" jardiniere	See July 1916 price list (mentioned as "Dec–Jeanette")
462	-5" jardiniere	Bomm 89, 252; also in July 1916 price list (as "Dec–Jeanette")
462	-6" jardiniere	Bomm 89, 252; also in July 1916 price list (as "Dec–Jeanette")
462	-7" jardiniere;	Bomm 89, 252; also in July 1916 price list (as "Dec–Jeanette")
462	-8" jardiniere	Bomm 89, 252; also in July 1916 price list (as "Dec–Jeanette")
462	-9" jardiniere	Bomm 89, 252; also in July 1916 price list (as "Dec–Jeanette")
462	-10" jardiniere	Bomm 89; also in July 1916 price list (as "Dec–Jeanette")
462	-10" x 27" jardiniere & pedestal	Bomm 252; also in July 1916 price list (as "Decorated")
462	-12" jardiniere	Bomm 89; also in July 1916 price list (as "Dec–Jeanette")
462	-12" x 33" jardiniere & pedestal	Bomm 252; also in July 1916 price list (as "Decorated")
511	-10" jardiniere	See July 1916 price list (mentioned as "Decorated"—perhaps an abbreviation for "Decorated Persian")

Shape No.	Description	Reference/Notes
523	-4" combination jardiniere	Bomm 89
523	-5" combination jardiniere	Bomm 89
523	-6" combination jardiniere	Bomm 89
523	-7" combination jardiniere	Bomm 89
523	-8" combination jardiniere	Bomm 89
523	-9" combination jardiniere	Bomm 89
523	-10" combination jardiniere	Bomm 89
526	-6" combination jardiniere	See July 1916 price list (mentioned as "Decorated"—perhaps an abbreviation for "Decorated Persian")
526	-8.5" combination jardiniere	See July 1916 price list (mentioned as "Decorated"—perhaps an abbreviation for "Decorated Persian")
527	-4" combination jardiniere	See July 1916 price list (mentioned as "Decorated"—perhaps an abbreviation for "Decorated Persian")
527	-6" combination jardiniere	See July 1916 price list (mentioned as "Decorated"—perhaps an abbreviation for "Decorated Persian")
527	-8" combination jardiniere	See July 1916 price list (mentioned as "Decorated"—perhaps an abbreviation for "Decorated Persian")
545	-10" x 30" jardiniere & pedestal	See July 1916 price list (mentioned as "Jeanette")
557	-6" jardiniere	See July 1916 price list (mentioned as "Decorated Persian")
557	-8" jardiniere	See July 1916 price list (mentioned as "Decorated Persian")
557	-10" jardiniere	See July 1916 price list (mentioned as "Decorated Persian")
569	-7" jardiniere	See July 1916 price list (mentioned as "Tourist")
569	-8" jardiniere	See July 1916 price list (mentioned as "Tourist")
569	-9" jardiniere	See July 1916 price list (mentioned as "Tourist")
569	-10" jardiniere	See July 1916 price list (mentioned as "Tourist")
569	-12" jardiniere	See July 1916 price list (mentioned as "Tourist")
569	-12" x 33" jardiniere & pedestal	See July 1916 price list (mentioned as "Tourist")
626	cuspidor	See July 1916 price list (mentioned as "Decorated" and "Jeanette")
723	-21" x 9" umbrella stand	Bomm 382 (for "Jeanette" example); also in July 1916 price list (as "Jeanette")
725	-23" x 10" umbrella stand	See July 1916 price list (mentioned as "Tourist")
856	stein	Bomm 174
909	-9.75" cuspidor	Bomm 111; also in July 1916 price list (mentioned as "Decorated," "Jeanette," and "Tourist")
921	-11" tankard	Bomm 183; also in July 1916 price list (as "Dutch," "Eagle," "Elk," "Indian," "K of P," "Monk," and "Moose")
1004	bedside candlestick	See July 1916 price list (mentioned as "Decorated" and "Holly")
1007	candlestick	See July 1916 price list (mentioned as "Decorated")
1209	-10" x 5" wall pocket	See July 1916 price list (mentioned as "Tourist")
1303	pitcher	See July 1916 price list (mentioned as "Decorated")
1304	pitcher	See July 1916 price list (mentioned as "Decorated")
1305	pitcher	See July 1916 price list (mentioned as "Decorated")
1306	pitcher	See July 1916 price list (mentioned as "Decorated")

Shape No.	Description	Reference/Notes
E60	-3.75" candlestick (Egypto shape)	Bomm 169
	bedroom set (candlestick, match receiver, pitcher, tray)	See July 1916 price list (mentioned as "Orange or Blue Bands")
	brush holder	Bomm 128
	chamber pot (covered)	Bomm 128
	child's mug	See July 1916 price list (mentioned as "Holly")
	combinette (covered)	Bomm 128
	creamer	See July 1916 price list (mentioned as "Holly")
	ewer and basin	Bomm 128
	individual teapot	Bomm 129; also in July 1916 price list (as "Dutch Decoration" and "Holly")
	mouth ewer	Bomm 128
	novelty steins	Bomm 243; also in July 1916 price list
	pitcher no. 1	Bomm 174
	pitcher no. 2	Bomm 174
	shaving mug	Bomm 128
	soap dish (covered)	Bomm 128
	8-oz. stein, "flagon shape"	See July 1916 price list (mentioned as "Hoster Flagon Steins–White Lined")
	10-oz. stein, "flagon shape"	See July 1916 price list (mentioned as "Hoster Flagon Steins–White Lined")
	12-oz. stein, "flagon shape"	See July 1916 price list (mentioned as "Hoster Flagon Steins–White Lined")
	steins	See July 1916 price list (mentioned as "Dutch," "Eagle," "Elk," "Indian," "K of P," "Monk," and "Moose")
	tankard set (tankard, six steins)	See July 1916 price list (mentioned as "Dutch," "Eagle," "Elk," "Indian," "K of P," "Monk," and "Moose")
	12-pc. toilet set	See July 1916 price list (mentioned as "Dutch," "Lily of the Valley," and "Osiris")

Decorated as Juvenile

Shape No.	Description	Reference/Notes
1	-3" mug	For shape, see Bomm 200 (ca. late 1930s)
1	-7.5" rolled edge plate	Bomm 199
1	bread and milk set	Bomm 199; also in July 1916 price list
1	chamber pot	Bomm 199
1	creamer	See July 1916 price list
1	egg cup	Bomm 199
1	ewer and basin	Bomm 199
1	flat plate	See July 1916 price list
1	mug	See July 1916 price list
1	soda glass	Bomm 199 (previously termed #2 mug); also in July 1916 price list
1	soap dish	Bomm 199
2	-6" bowl	For shape, see Bomm 200 (ca. late 1930s)
2	-6.75" flat plate	Bomm 199; also in July 1916 price list
2	bread and milk set	Bomm 199; also in July 1916 price list
2	chamber pot	Bomm 199
2	egg cup	Bomm 199
2	mug	Bomm 199; also in July 1916 price list
2	tea set (cream, sugar, teapot)	Bomm 344; also in July 1916 price list
3	-7" rolled edge plate	For shape, see Bomm 200 (ca. late 1930s)
3	-8.25" flat plate	Bomm 199; also in July 1916 price list
3	bread and milk set	Bomm 199; also in July 1916 price list
3	mug	Bomm 199 (later termed #6 mug)
4	-5.75" flat plate	Bomm 199
4	bread and milk set	Bomm 199; also in July 1916 price list
5	-6.5" rolled edge plate	Bomm 199
5	bread and milk set	Bomm 199; also in July 1916 price list

Shape No.	Description	Reference/Notes
5	mug	Bomm 200
6	-6" rolled edge plate	Bomm 200
6	bread and milk set	Bomm 200
6	cup and saucer	Bomm 199; also in July 1916 price list
7	-7.875" flat plate	Bomm 200
7	bread and milk set	Bomm 199
7	cup and saucer	Bomm 199
7	mug	Bomm 198
8	-6.25" straight edge plate	Bomm 198
8	bread and milk set	Bomm 199
8	cup and saucer	Bomm 200
8	tea set (teapot, cream, sugar)	See July 1916 price list
9	-9" compartment plate	Bomm 198
9	bread and milk set	Bomm 199
10	.25-pt. creamer	See July 1916 price list
10	.5-pt. creamer	See July 1916 price list
13	bread and milk set	Bomm 200
13	creamer	See July 1916 price list
14	bowl	Bomm 198
14	creamer	See July 1916 price list
42	ramekin	See July 1916 price list
50 or 51	custard	Bomm 199; also in July 1916 price list
181	casserole	See July 1916 price list
1004	bedside candlestick	For shape, see Bomm 172; also in July 1916 price list (as "Good Night Candlestick")
	child's set (no. 1 baby plate, no. 1 bread and milk)	See July 1916 price list
	individual tea pot	See July 1916 price list

**Vase with "Gibson Girl,"
ca. 1906.** 810-8.75" vase,
Rozane Royal shape, black
drawing transferred by
pouncing (?), hand-filled in
yellow, lavender, pink, and
beige, gilt stenciling around lip,
white crackle glaze overall,
molded (raised-relief) 10.
Scheytt collection. **NPD**

1906 Shriner Stein, Early Creamware. 965-6.5"
stein, white crackle glaze, overglaze hand-decoration
of Shriners fez and "Aladdin Patrol," gilt trim, fancy
gilt lettering "Al. G. Field" and dated "Aug. 6 - 06,"
Rozane Ware wafer, die-impressed 21. *Scheytt
collection.* **$550–650**

Creamware (various decorations). 3.5" shaving mug, scroll decal, thin black line painted
on rim; 4" sugar bowl, narrow green bands, outlined in black, and rose decals; pair, 2"
chambersticks, one with narrow orange band, outlined in black, thin black lines,
geometrical black and blue decal, and the other with narrow orange and green bands,
outlined in black, thin black lines; E60-3.75" candlestick, Egypto shape, gilt tracing over
molded designs and quotation "More Light – Goethe"; 3.5" covered oval pin box, narrow
blue band, outlined in black, rose decals, geometrical black and blue decal; 4" pitcher,
"ideal" shape; 3.5" side-pour pitcher, thin blue lines, black Greek key design applied over
narrow gilt band. *Scheytt collection.* **$125–175, $75–95, $125–175 (each), $200–250,
$200–250, $60–75, $95–125**

Creamware (Advertising). 2" ashtray, Glacier National Park; 2" ashtray, Billie O'Hern, Minneapolis; 2" ashtray, Cincinnati General Hospital. *Hoppe photograph.* **$75–125 (each)**

Creamware (Baby Bunting). 8" rolled-edge plate, Baby's Plate lettering, decal reads "Baby Bunting runs away And joins the little pigs at play"; 8" rolled-edge plate, Baby's Plate lettering, decal reads "Baby Bunting takes his hoe And tries to help the flowers grow." *Courtesy of Mike Nickel and Cindy Horvath.* **$250–300 (each)**

Right:

Creamware (Coat of Arms). 6" tobacco humidor; 10" tray. *Scheytt collection.* **$300–400, $200–250.** Both shapes have pounced lettering and design for "The Bachelors Coat of Arms." The motto around the tray's border reads, "It is better to smoke in this world than in the next." The other two items in a complete 1B smoker's set are a match holder and an ashtray.

Creamware (decorating techniques). 9" candlestick, hand-painted gilt "tracing"; 3.25" planter and liner, red and blue squeezebag (or "stippled") trim, liner hand-incised 213. *Fairfield collection.* **$125–150, $95–125.** Note: both "tracing" and "stippling" accentuate the details of a molded design.

Creamware (Conventional Floral Motifs). 4" tumbler; 60-8.5" teapot; 4" soda glass; 6.5" pitcher. *Private collection.* **$95–125, $300–400, $95–125, $200–250.** This is one of several different "conventional" designs in Roseville creamware. During the Arts and Crafts period, some designers preferred to use idealized (or "conventionalized")— instead of naturalistic—portrayals of flowers, animals, ships, and other motifs.

Creamware (Dutch). 5" toothbrush holder, boy smoking; 1-7.5" pitcher, girl with doll bed; 5.5" powder box, various decals, boy skating, girl standing, girl waving; 13-8" teapot, various decals, boy skating, girl with hoop, girl waving; 2.75" side-spout milk pitcher, baby kneeling (may properly be part of the Baby Bunting group, instead of Dutch). *Scheytt collection.* **$125–150, $275–325, $175–225, $300–400, $95–125.** These smaller Dutch decals are believed to be earlier than the more detailed Dutch scenes.

Creamware (Dutch). 10.25" tray; 15-5" stein; 856-4.5" stein; 7.5" pitcher, flared rim; 3.5" shaving mug; 7" bedside candlestick. *Shannon collection.* **$175–225, $95–125, $95–125, $200–300, $125–175, $275–325.** Dutch uses a wide variety of colorful decals showing children at play, families working together, and similar scenes.

Creamware (Forget Me Not). 3" d. powder dish; 3" d. hair receiver (lid missing); 10" tray. *Hoppe photograph.* **$125–150, $75–95 (or $125–150 with lid), $125–175.** Oddly, this decal was often applied upside down, with the ribbons hanging "upward," as shown here.

Creamware (Fraternal Societies). 15-5" stein, Knights of Pythias; 856-4.5" stein, Knights Templar. *Hoppe collection.* **$125–150, $150–175.** The "K of P" stein has a legend reading "Merry Xmas 1915, Anthony Wayne, No. 141, K of P, Toledo, Ohio." The "K.T." stein has several legends: "Souvenir, 1000 Members, Englewood Commandery No. 59, K.T., J.A. Lozier, Commander, Sept. 11th, 1913." Such legends date these wares and offer intriguing hints about their provenance.

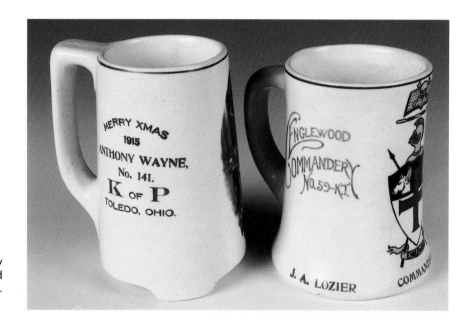

Creamware (Fraternal Societies). Another view of the Knights of Pythias and Englewood Commandery steins.

Creamware (Fraternal Societies). Complete 7-pc. stein set, Loyal Order of Moose, also bearing slogan "Howdy Pap." Set includes an 821-11" tankard and six 856-4.5" steins. *Courtesy of Medina Antique Mall.* **$95–125 (stein, each), $150–200 (tankard)**

Creamware (Fraternal Societies). Four Shriner (Masonic) items, each with a black and yellow Shriner emblem, and a red fez bearing yellow lettering that denotes the particular temple: 856-4.5" stein, Osman Temple; 206-4" planter and liner, Syrian Temple, Cincinnati, O., souvenir of "Imperial Council Meeting, Rochester [NY], July 1911"; 821-11" tankard, Alhambra Temple; 856-4.5" stein, K.E.M. Temple. *Scheytt collection.* **$150–175, $175–225, $325–375, $150–175**

Creamware (Holly). 3.5" side-pour pitcher; 205-4" planter. *Merritt collection.* **$225–275, $175–225.** In the factory stock pages, the pitcher shape appears (in the Juvenile line) as part of the No. 1 bread and milk set.

Creamware (Jeanette). 545-6" jardiniere. *Shannon collection.* **$175–225**

Creamware (Juvenile). 8" rolled-edge plate, Sunbonnet Babies; 7" rolled-edge plate, Sitting Rabbit, Baby's Plate lettering; 8" rolled-edge plate, Dog. *Hoppe photograph.* **$125–150, $125–150, $150–200**

Left:
Creamware (Juvenile). Two items from a boxed 3-piece "No. 1" Juvenile set, ca. early 1940s—the 3-7" plate, Jack Rabbit, molded (raised-relief) R, shape 3, and U.S.A.; the 1-3" mug, Puddle Duck, molded (raised-relief) R, shape 1, and U.S.A. *Harris collection.* **$175–200, $125–150.** The third item (not shown) is the 2-6" bowl, usually decorated with the Happy Puppy. No other Creamware shapes are known to have molded (raised-relief) marks.

Creamware (Juvenile). Assortment of rabbit designs, most with narrow green bands, and decorated with three different motifs: standing rabbit, rabbit head, and jack rabbit in red waistcoat. Clockwise from Baby's Plate (upper right): 8" rolled-edge plate, orange and green bands, legend "Baby's Plate," unmarked; 3.75" sugar bowl, molded (raised-relief) 8; 5.5" bowl, red inkstamp "No. 2"; 2" creamer, red inkstamp 10; 6" bowl, black inkstamp 11; 3" side-pour creamer, unmarked; 2.25" cup, unmarked, with 5.25" saucer, red inkstamp 6; 4.5" bowl, unmarked; 6.75" plate, black inkstamp 2; 3.5" milk pitcher, black inkstamp 6; 3" mug, jack rabbit in red waistcoat, black Rv inkstamp. *Scheytt collection.* **$150–175, $150–175, $95–125, $125–150, $75–95, $95–125, $150–175 (set), $75–95, $95–125, $125–150, $150–175**

Creamware (Juvenile). 7.75" rolled-edge plate, Puppies, Baby's Plate lettering in orange band; 3.75" de-pour pitcher, Bear. *Courtesy of Mike Nickel and Cindy Horvath.* **$250–300, $225–275.** This plate shape is more typically found with Baby Bunting decals.

Creamware (Landscape). 2.75" cream, hand-incised 8; 4.5" teapot. *Scheytt collection.* **$125–150, $200–250.** These two items are from the 8 tea set. The ca. 1910 decals might be dubbed "Early Landscape" to distinguish them from the later "Landscape" decals.

Creamware (Landscape). 9.5" coffeepot, blue; 3.5" ramekin, blue; 8" chocolate pot, brown. *Scheytt collection.* **$325–375, $95–125, $250–300.** These three scenes appear in various combinations on Creamware (Landscape) pieces. Factory records term the sailboat decals "Landscape A," and the windmill and trees decals (collectively) "Landscape B." Some examples have both.

Creamware (Medallion). 3" creamer; 6.5" chocolate pot; 3.5" sugar bowl. *Scheytt collection.* **$95–125, $200–250, $95–125.** This motif depicts several Greek (or Roman) soldiers in an oval cameo, consisting of a dark green decal. Other elements of the design are gilt; some were applied by decal, and others by tracing handles, spout, and feet. Factory records term this design "Decoration D."

Creamware (Monk). 15-4.5" stein, monk holding tankard and stein, legend reading "Should Auld Acquaintance Be Forgot." *Scheytt collection.* **$350–400**

Creamware (Novelty Steins). 856-4.5" stein, "Try It on the Dog" (Novelty decal 5); 8-4.5" stein, "Do It Now" (Novelty decal 3). *Harris collection.* **$175–225 (each).** Photographic records at the Ohio Historical Society show that twelve different scenes were available on any of six standard stein shapes (6, 8, 9, 15, 16, and 856).

Creamware (Nursery Rhyme). 8" rolled-edge plate, green band, "Old Woman, Old Woman" decal, black Rv inkstamp; 8" rolled-edge plate, green band, "Little Jack Horner" decal, unmarked. *Scheytt collection.* **$125–175, $125–175**

Creamware (Nursery Rhyme). 8" rolled-edge plate, Baby's Plate legend, "Higgledy Piggledy" decal, unmarked; 6.5" rolled-edge plate, Baby's Plate legend, "Little Bopeep" decal, unmarked. *Scheytt collection.* **$125–175, $125–150**

Creamware (Persian). 462-5" jardiniere, leaf and berry design; 462-8" jardiniere, poppies. *Hoppe photograph.* **$275–325, $475–550**

Creamware (Persian). 315-5" hanging basket. *Courtesy of Robert Bettinger.* **$400–450**

Creamware (Persian). 523-10" combination jardiniere, unmarked. *Calkins collection.* **$600–700.** The interior of the liner measures 10"; the jardiniere is 9.5". The shape also came in sizes of 4", 5", 6", 7", 8" and 9". The "523" refers to the shape, not the decoration.

Creamware (Quaker). 897-5.5" humidor (4.5" without its lid); 12" tankard; 4.75" teapot. *Shannon collection.* **$150–175 (or $275–350 with lid), $350–400, $225–275.** Quaker men usually appear on smoking articles, and women on tea sets. Watch for the powdered wigs.

Creamware (Persian). 3" creamer; 3.5" sugar, both decorated in a conventional design through pouncing. *Fairfield collection.* **$125–150 (each)**

Creamware (Tourist). 9.5" jardiniere, horse pulling touring car, sign reads "Garage 10 Miles," *Calkins collection;* 8.5" jardiniere, touring car stalled because of bucking horse ahead, *Wagner collection.* **$2500–2800, $2200–2500**

Creamware (Tourist). 13" window box; 7" jardiniere. *Hoppe collection.* **$2800–3200, 2000–2200.** Both examples use the same illustration, featuring a cow blocking the roadway. The jardiniere is turned to show the rest of the landscape, a scene typical of the back of other Tourist pieces.

Creamware (Tourist). 9" vase, touring car scaring two geese off the road. *Wagner collection.* **$1500–2000**

Creamware (Tourist). 226-5" fern dish. *Ross collection.* **$950–1200**

CREMO
An Early Line, introduced ca. 1905

Factory Name(s): Cremo Vases
Style: Art Nouveau
Standard Color(s): One standard coloring, as described below
Typical Marks: Unmarked

Cremo's squeezebag (tube-line) decoration is attributed to Frederick Hurten Rhead (or to his brother Harry). This rare line is probably contemporary with Aztec, also decorated in squeezebag. The whiplash curves on each Cremo piece are in the archetypal Art Nouveau style. The green lines represent stems, and stylized blue and yellow flowers are also applied to complete the raised designs. Backgrounds are opaque enamels (which Roseville spelled "opac enamels"), blending from pink to yellow to green.

The name "Cremo" seems to call for an association with cream. Its origin and meaning are otherwise unknown. Even without much pedigree, collectors avidly seek an example of Cremo for their collections—and damage (if present) has to be overlooked.

Many a Cremo design began life as a Rozane Royal shape. Only one known factory stock page shows Cremo, a total of 12 shapes:

CREMO

Shape No.	Description	Shape No.	Description
1	-9" vase	7	-6.5" vase
2	-9.25" vase	8	-6" vase
3	-9.5" vase	9	-5" vase
4	-6.5" vase	10	-8.25" vase
5	-4" jardiniere	11	-7.5" vase
6	-9" vase	12	-8" vase

Cremo. 4-7" vase. *Shannon collection.* **$1200–1500**

Cremo. 9-5" vase. *Hoppe photograph.*
$950–1200

CREMONA
A Middle Period Line, introduced in 1928

Factory Name(s): Cremona, Cremona Ware
Style: Art Deco
Standard Color(s): Green, or pink
Typical Marks: Paper labels. (These could be lost, leaving the piece unmarked.)

According to the *Oxford English Dictionary,* Cremona is a town in Lombardy, Italy, "where the art of violin-making reached its highest perfection in the 17th and early 18th century." The Cremona line thus appears to have an Italianate name, like several other 1920s lines—notably Florentine and Volpato.

Advertised as having "embossed modernistic floral designs" (*House Beautiful,* May 1928), Cremona is Art Deco in the most French sense—feminine, even dainty, and seldom geometrical. The low-relief decorations are conventionalized. Glazes are matte mottled pastel shades of green or pink. A few examples have handles; most shapes are symmetrical. Values tend to be moderate.

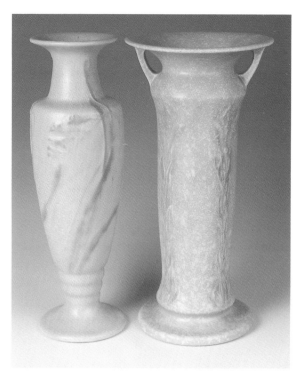

Cremona. 361-12" vase, green; 362-12" vase, pink. *Shannon collection.* **$350–400 (each)**

Cremona. 359-10" vase, green; 355-8" vase, pink. *Courtesy of McAllister Auctions.* **$325–375, $250–300**

Cremona. 351-4" vase, green; 360-10" vase, pink; 73-5" fan vase, green. *Fairfield collection.* **$175–225, $275–325, $150–200**

The only known factory stock page shows 20 shapes in Cremona:

CREMONA

Shape No.	Description	Shape No.	Description
2	-4" vase	354	-7" vase
3	-5" vase	355	-8" vase
4	-6" vase	356	-8" vase
5	flower frog	357	-8" vase
76	-6" comport	358	-10" vase
77	-8" bowl	359	-10" vase
78	-8" bowl	360	-10" vase
51	-4" vase	361	-12" vase
52	-5" vase	362	-12" vase
53	-5" planter	1068	-4" candlestick

CROCUS

An Early Line, introduced ca. 1905

Factory Name(s): Unknown (perhaps Egyptian)

Collector Nickname(s): Conventional Landscape, or Shiny Aztec (see Buxton, 1977); Crocus (see Huxford, 1980)

Style: Arts and Crafts

Standard Color(s): Unknown; typical colors are described below

Typical Marks: Usually unmarked (or marked only with a die-impressed numeral, meaning unknown). A few bear the Rozane Ware wafer. Some examples have slip-painted artist initials.

Like Aztec and Cremo, this slip-decorated line is attributed to Frederick Hurten Rhead (or his brother Harry). Before coming to the U.S., F.H. Rhead is known to have produced similar work, ca. 1899, at the Wardle Pottery, England (see Dale 21). Shapes tend to be shared with Aztec.

Each example alternates between stylized flowers and their buds, all with conventionalized stems and leaves. Background colors can be dark or light,

with the floral motifs in either a different shade or a contrasting color. Collectors tend to refer to pieces by their background—often brown, dark blue, or dark green.

The so-called "Crocus" motifs seem an odd subject matter to have maintained such a hold on Rhead's (and the various potteries') imagination. Instead of a "crocus," perhaps these pieces depict the Egyptian lotus, which symbolizes the soul. An unsigned and undated typewritten list of Roseville line names at the Ohio Historical Society does include the name "Egyptian."

No factory stock pages are known for Crocus.

Crocus. 6" vase, dark green, die-impressed 4. *Merritt collection.* **$500–600**

Below:
Crocus. 9" vase, olive green, die-impressed 6 (or 9), artist initials "F.M."; 9.5" vase, brown, die-impressed 6 (or 9). *Fairfield collection.* **$650–750 (each)**

Crocus. 9" vase, gray, artist initials "F.H." *Scheytt collection.* **$600–700**

Crocus. 456-6" jardiniere, sienna brown, unmarked. *Shannon collection.* **$350–400**

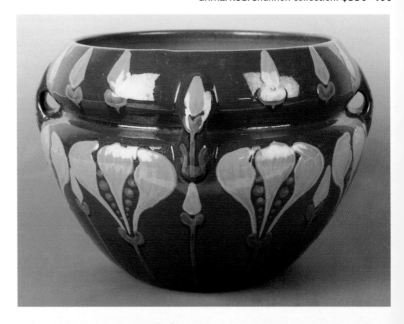

CRYSTAL GREEN
A Late Line, introduced ca. 1939

Factory Name(s): Unknown (perhaps Crystal Green)
Collector Nickname(s): Crystal Green (see Purviance and Schneider, 1970)
Style: Arts and Crafts glaze; Art Deco shapes
Standard Color(s): Semimatte mottled light green
Typical Marks: Die-impressed marks, including "Roseville" (script), shape number, and size

This little-known line has a Laurel- or Velmoss-style leaf and berry decoration. Shapes often have pleated rims similar to those in Cosmos, also a 1939 line. The shapes seem to have been introduced initially as an addition to Ivory. In the factory stock pages, they appear only there. But pieces have also been located in a mottled crystalline light green glaze that many collectors call Crystal Green. (One light blue variation has also been located.)

The name "Crystal Green" appears in an unsigned and undated typewritten list of Roseville line names (Norris Schneider collection, Ohio Historical Society). However, this document is known to be incomplete, and includes a few puzzling misspellings and references to additional otherwise unknown lines. The listing's value is therefore questionable.

Crystal Green prices tend to parallel those for green Velmoss, which this line closely resembles.

For a list of Crystal Green shapes appearing in the factory stock pages, see Ivory.

Crystal Green. 3-4.5" x 5.5" wall shelf; 356-8" basket. *Private collection.* **$250–350, $325–375**

Crystal Green. 941-10" ewer; 357-6" bowl. *Hoppe photograph.* **$175–225, $95–125**

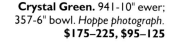

Crystal Green. 936-8" vase. *Hoppe collection.* **$125–175**

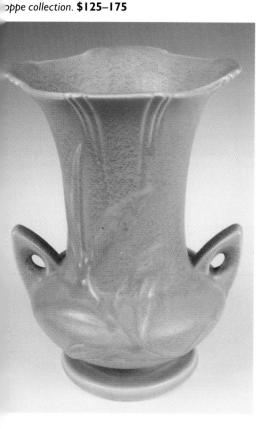

Crystal Green. 942-8" pillow vase; 368-10" bowl; 934-8" fan vase; 932-7" vase. *Hoppe collection.* **$150–200, $150–200, $175–225, $150–200**

CRYSTALIS
An Early Line, introduced in 1906

Factory Name(s): Rozane Crystalis
Collector Nickname(s): Crystalis (see Huxford, 1976)
Alternate Spelling(s): Crystallis (see Alexander, 1970)
Style: Arts and Crafts
Standard Color(s): Blue, green, orange, and red examples are known
Typical Marks: Unmarked. Some have a Rozane Ware logo paper label. (These could be lost, leaving the piece unmarked.) Others have a Rozane Ware wafer, or a Mongol wafer.

Crystalline glazes are one of the fascinations that working potters have with their art. Careful study of this early Roseville line shows why. Place a strong light above you, when you are able to examine a piece closely. Most (or all) of the surface will be scattered with snowlike crystals of various sizes and hues.

Roseville does not seem to have manufactured Crystalis for many years, although some examples are known on shapes typically associated with Pauleo. Collector demand for the line has always been high, so expect to pay a premium when you encounter a piece—once in a blue moon.

The Crystalis pages of the 1906 Rozane Ware catalog show 14 examples. In Bomm, these pages can be found under "Rozane–Crystalis."

CRYSTALIS

Shape No.	Description	Shape No.	Description
C12	-13.25" vase	C20	-8.5" vase
C13	-11" vase	C22	-5" x 12" ferner
C14	-12" vase	C23	-14" vase
C15	-7.25" ewer	C24	-11.25" vase
C16	-11" vase	C25	-8" vase
C17	-8" vase	C26	-14" vase
C19	-12.5" vase	E64	-14.75" vase

Crystalis. 10.5" vase, green with gold highlights, Mongol wafer. *Hoppe collection.* **$1500–2000**

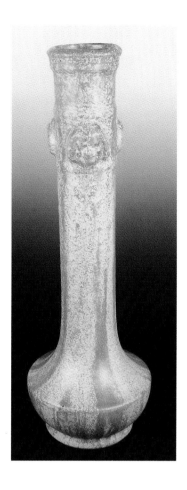

Crystalis. E64-14.75" vase, mottled brown and gold rutile glaze, unmarked. *Merritt collection.* **$2500–3000**

Crystalis. E58-14.5" basket, reddish orange, Egypto wafer. *Hoppe collection.* **$2800–3500**

Crystalis. C12-13.25" vase, dark and light blue with gold highlights, unmarked. *Nickel and Horvath collection.* **NPD**

Crystalis. 6.75" ewer, blue with pale gray and gold highlights, oval red and white paper price tag, otherwise unmarked. *Wagner collection.* **$950–1200**

DAHLROSE
A Middle Period Line, introduced by 1928

Factory Name(s): Dahlrose
Style: Arts and Crafts
Standard Color(s): One standard coloring, described below
Typical Marks: Paper labels. (These could be lost, leaving the piece unmarked.)

The origin of the name "Dahlrose" is unclear. The flower depicted in this line resembles a daisy, with wide yellow petals and serrated green leaves. The motifs are conventionalized to form a repeating border design, modeled in low relief. Backgrounds are textured, with a greenish brown wash.

Despite its similarity to Sunflower, Dahlrose has remained a relatively inexpensive Middle-Period line. Shapes tend to be round and symmetrical, but some are square or rectangular, and others surprisingly modernistic.

The factory stock pages show 26 shapes for Dahlrose:

DAHLROSE

Shape No.	Description	Shape No.	Description
76	-6" triple vase	369	-10" vase
77	-7" vase	370	-12" vase
78	-8" vase	375	-10" window box
79	-6" gate	375	-14" window box
179	-8" bowl	614	-6" jardiniere
180	-8" bowl	614	-7" jardiniere
343	-6" hanging basket	614	-8" jardiniere & pedestal
363	-6" vase	614	-9" jardiniere
364	-6" vase	614	-10" jardiniere & pedestal
365	-8" vase	614	-12" jardiniere
366	-8" vase	1069	-3" candlestick
367	-8" vase	1258	-8" wall pocket
368	-10" vase	1259	-10" wall pocket

Dahlrose. 76-6" triple bud vase; 6" vase, square; 77-7" bud vase. *Stofft collection.* **$125–150, $250–300, $125–175**

Dahlrose. 10" vase; 464-9" vase, orange crayon shape number, black paper label. *Hoppe collection.* **$450–500, $350–450**

Dahlrose. 5" hanging basket; 6" hanging basket. *Hoppe collection.* **$350–450, $300–350.** The smaller piece is incorrectly termed a 7.5" hanging basket in Huxford (1980), because the outermost diameter was measured instead of the inside opening.

Dahlrose. 8" vase; 7" bowl; 370-12" vase; 4" flower pot (saucer missing); 6" x 8.25" pillow vase. *Hoppe collection.* **$300–350, $175–225, $650–750, $125–150 (or $200–250 with saucer), $200–250**

Dahlrose. 8" bowl, oval; 7" jardiniere; 4" vase, urn shape; 8.25" vase. *Hoppe collection.* **$125–175, $200–250, $150–175, $200–250**

DAWN

A Middle Period Line, introduced in 1937

Factory Name(s): Dawn
Style: Art Deco
Standard Color(s): Yellow, green, or pink
Typical Marks: Die-impressed marks, including "Roseville" (script), shape number, and size

With Dawn, Roseville offered buyers "a touch of spring" (advertisement, *Gift and Art Buyer,* April 1937: 10). The three matte "pastel shades" enliven the Art Deco shapes, which tend to be round bodies with angular handles. Each piece has a sgrafitto-style leaf design, hand-tinted in either green or white.

Except for the spectacular modernistic bookends, Dawn tends to be a more reasonably priced Art Deco line than either Futura or Moderne.

The only known factory stock page shows 18 Dawn shapes:

DAWN

Shape No.	Description	Shape No.	Description
4	-5" bookend	827	-6" vase
31	-4" flower frog	828	-8" bud vase
315	-4" rose bowl	829	-8" vase
316	-6" rose bowl	830	-8" vase
317	-10" bowl	831	-9" vase
318	-14" bowl	832	-10" vase
319	-6" centerpiece	833	-12" vase
345	-8" basket	834	-15" ewer
826	-6" vase	1121	-2" candlestick

Dawn. 829-8" vase, green; 828-8" bud vase, green. *Hoppe photograph.* **$200–250, $175–225**

Dawn. 826-6" vase, pink; 827-6" vase, yellow. *Shannon collection.* **$150–200 (each)**

Dawn. 31 flower frog, green; 317-10" console bowl, green; 1121-2" candlestick, green. *Hoppe photograph.* **$125–150, $150–200, $65–75**

Dawn. 319 centerpiece (measures 6.25" x 10.25" x 5.25"), pink. *Courtesy of McAllister Auctions.* **$300–350**

DECORATED ARTWARE
A Generic Term for an Early Product Category, introduced by 1902

Factory Name(s): Various, including Ceramic Art Ware, Decorated, Special, Unique, and perhaps others

Collector Nickname(s): Blue Tea Pots (see Huxford, 1976); Special, Decorated Art, or Decorated (see Buxton, 1977). Unique (see Huxford, 1977). Gold and Silver Decorated (see Huxford, 1980). Conventional Landscape, or Decorated Mongol (see Buxton, rev. ed., ca. 1996). Rozane–Decorated Art (see Bomm, 1998)

Style: Late Victorian

Standard Color(s): Various, as described below

Typical Marks: Most pieces are unmarked. Some have a die-impressed shape number.

"Decorated Artware" is a group of varied wares offering decorative alternatives to Majolica and Rozane Royal. Many examples have an ivory- or cream-colored interior. Decorations are hand-painted or applied by decal (or both), and backgrounds often have a blend of air-brushed pastel colors.

This definition can be seen to fit Autumn, which most authors (including this one) treat as a distinct line. Likewise, the seldom-recognized Art Nouveau line Modern Art could be viewed as a sub-category of Decorated Artware. Some writers have used the term "Special" to indicate those wares which have an air-brushed background and decal decorations.

The earliest documented Decorated Artware line was dubbed "Ceramic Art Ware" (advertisement, *Crockery and Glass Journal*, August 21, 1902: 40). Decorated Artware was also a major part of the Roseville Pottery display at the 1904 Pittsburgh glass and china show, where undecorated Rozane Royal (Dark) was also shown, perhaps for the first time.

A 1906 trade notice helps us date another species of Decorated Artware—called Imperial at the pottery. A reviewer for *China, Glass and Lamps* studied the Roseville display at the Pittsburgh glass and china show, noting, "There was one jardiniere & pedestal that struck me as particularly handsome, and that was the one finished in matte green with a gold dragon" (January 13, 1906: 17). For the factory stock page that illustrates this item, see Bomm (page 179).

In 1907 a large group of similar items with stenciled gold decorations was shown in Pittsburgh. One reviewer noted, "A new line with a lustre effect is also a leader; in fact, in my estimation *the* leader. The finish is smooth and perfect and the decoration is neither gold nor gilt" (trade notice, *China, Glass and Lamps*, January 12, 1907: 8).

At the 1908 Pittsburgh show, one reviewer noticed "a new line of teapots in very original and antique shapes, as well as a full line of rare and matchless steins, quite as odd, finished in a very dark blue, with gold and white effects" (trade notice, *China, Glass and Lamps*, January 11, 1908: 11).

Like Imperial, these decorative serving pieces were first glazed in an opaque enamel (or "opac enamel," to use the factory term). Dark cobalt blue is the usual color (thus the nickname "Blue Porcelain"), but an example in old rose has also been located. The wares were then decorated with either gilt hand-painted florals or decal-transferred gilt trim (or both). Most also have stippling or hand-painted white decoration, and a few use small amounts of squeezebag decoration in other colors.

According to factory advertisements, Decorated Artware was manufactured as late as 1920 (*Crockery and Glass Journal*, December 18, 1919: 86). The factory stock pages show 44 shapes finished in a style that could be so classified. Another 5 shapes are mentioned in the July 1916 price list.

DECORATED ARTWARE

Shape No.	Description	Reference/Notes
403	jardiniere	Bomm 376
405	-10" jardiniere	Bomm 384
405	-34" jardiniere & pedestal	Not reprinted
409	jardiniere	Bomm 375
410	jardiniere	Bomm 374
410	-22" jardiniere & pedestal	Bomm 230
410	-38" jardiniere & pedestal	Bomm 230
411	-8" jardiniere	Bomm 384
411	-22" jardiniere & pedestal	Bomm 230
411	-38" jardiniere & pedestal	Bomm 230
414	-14" x 23" jardiniere & pedestal	Bomm 116

Shape No.	Description	Reference/Notes
414	-33" jardiniere & pedestal	Not reprinted (for shape, see Bomm 386)
416	-28" jardiniere & pedestal	Bomm 394
419	-7" jardiniere	Bomm 384
421	jardiniere	Bomm 114
422	-9" jardiniere	Bomm 384
422	-29" jardiniere & pedestal	Bomm 394
423	jardiniere	Bomm 114
424	12" x 32" jardiniere & pedestal (Rozane Royal shape)	Bomm 179
429	-10.5" x 26" jardiniere & pedestal	Bomm 229
438	-7" jardiniere (Rozane Royal shape)	Bomm 302; also in July 1916 price list (as "Art")
438	-8" jardiniere (Rozane Royal shape)	Bomm 302; also in July 1916 price list (as "Art")
438	-9" jardiniere (Rozane Royal shape)	Bomm 302; also in July 1916 price list (as "Art")
438	-9" x 22" jardiniere & pedestal	See July 1916 price list (as "Art")
438	-10" jardiniere (Rozane Royal shape)	Bomm 302; also in July 1916 price list (as "Art")
438	-10" x 24" jardiniere & pedestal	See July 1916 price list (as "Art")
438	-12" jardiniere (Rozane Royal shape)	Bomm 302; also in July 1916 price list (as "Art")
438	-12" x 28" jardiniere & pedestal	See July 1916 price list (as "Art")
438	-14" jardiniere (Rozane Royal shape)	See July 1916 price list (as "Art")
438	-14" x 32" jardiniere & pedestal	See July 1916 price list (as "Art")
439	-13" x 34" jardiniere & pedestal	Bomm 116
440	-15" x 12" x 45" jardiniere and pedestal	Bomm 116
441	-9" x 12" x 37" jardiniere & pedestal	Bomm 115
444	-8" jardiniere	Bomm 179
444	-9" jardiniere	Bomm 179
444	-10" jardiniere	Bomm 179
444	-12" jardiniere	Bomm 179
523	-4" combination jardiniere, squeezebag water lilies	Bomm 89; also in July 1916 price list (as "Ceramic")
523	-5" combination jardiniere, squeezebag water lilies	Bomm 89; also in July 1916 price list (as "Ceramic")
523	-6" combination jardiniere, squeezebag water lilies	Bomm 89; also in July 1916 price list (as "Ceramic")
523	-7" combination jardiniere, squeezebag water lilies	Bomm 89; also in July 1916 price list (as "Ceramic")
523	-8" combination jardiniere, squeezebag water lilies	Bomm 89; also in July 1916 price list (as "Ceramic")
523	-9" combination jardiniere, squeezebag water lilies	Bomm 89; also in July 1916 price list (as "Ceramic")
523	-10" combination jardiniere, squeezebag water lilies	Bomm 89; also in July 1916 price list (as "Ceramic")
743	-20" x 10" umbrella stand	See 1916 price list (mentioned as "Bl. Porcelain")

Shape No.	Description	Reference/Notes
744	-21" x 10" umbrella stand	See 1916 price list (mentioned as "Bl. Porcelain")
745	-19" x 10" umbrella stand	See 1916 price list (mentioned as "Bl. Porcelain")
746	-20" x 9" umbrella stand	See 1916 price list (mentioned as "Bl. Porcelain")
747	-19" x 10" umbrella stand	See 1916 price list (mentioned as "Bl. Porcelain")
748	-20" x 10" umbrella stand	See 1916 price list (mentioned as "Bl. Porcelain")
749	-21" x 10" umbrella stand	See 1916 price list (mentioned as "Bl. Porcelain")
807	-12.75" vase (Rozane Royal shape)	Bomm 302
822	-16" vase (Rozane Royal shape)	Bomm 302
884	-15" or -16" tankard (Rozane Royal shape)	Bomm 337
886	-5" stein (Rozane Royal shape)	Bomm 337
893	-12.75" vase (Rozane Royal shape)	Bomm 302
900	-6" tyge (Rozane Royal shape)	Bomm 302
910	-22" umbrella stand	Bomm 142
956	-8.5" vase (Rozane Royal shape)	Bomm 302
961	-10.5" vase (Rozane Royal shape)	Bomm 302
964	-16.5" tankard (Rozane Royal shape)	Bomm 337
965	-6.5" stein (Rozane Royal shape)	Bomm 337
966	-14.5" tankard (Rozane Royal shape)	Bomm 337

Decorated Artware. 15" vase, attributed to Roseville, hand-painted grape clusters, unmarked. *Latta collection.* **$300–400.** An almost identical design (vase shape 987) is shown as Rozane Royal in the 1906 catalog.

Decorated Artware. 10.5" vase, hand-painted pink roses, Mongol wafer. *Fairfield collection.* **NPD**

Decorated Artware. 409-8" jardiniere, pink roses. *Hoppe collection.* **$250–300**

Decorated Artware. 422-8" jardiniere, azalea. *Hoppe photograph.* **$250–300**

Decorated Artware (Blue Porcelain). 4" teapot; 6" mug, both with sprigged-on white decoration and gilt decals. *Hoppe photograph.* **$175–225, $125–150.** The teapot shape was also decorated as Creamware (see Huxford, Series 2, pages 53, 65).

Decorated Artware. 429-8" jardiniere, wild roses. *Hoppe photograph.* **$200–250**

Decorated Artware (Special). 414-14" jardiniere, lion head handles, paw feet, unmarked. *Courtesy of Riverfront Antique Mall.* **$500–600.** To prepare a "Special" variation of jardiniere 414, a worker first removed some of the embossed scrollwork and foliage from the original design. (For an example of the original design, see Majolica.) A new set of molds was made, so that multiples of the simplified jardiniere could be cast. The new version of the jardiniere featured a large, unadorned central section that was decorated with airbrushed colors and decals. The 414 pedestal was also reworked into a "Special" variation.

Decorated Artware (Blue Porcelain). 6.75" teapot. *Scheytt collection.* **$225–275**

Decorated Artware (Special). 886-5" stein, decal of grapes, unmarked. *Scheytt collection.* **$125–175.** Magenta colored decal over an air-brushed brown to ivory background.

Detail of Stein. To distinguish decal-applied from hand-painted decorations, examine a small section with a magnifying glass. If closely spaced horizontal lines or dots are used anywhere to create gradations of color, the decoration was applied by decal transfer (as shown here).

DECORATED LANDSCAPE
An Early Motif, introduced in 1907

Factory Name(s): Unknown
Style: Arts and Crafts
Standard Color(s): One standard coloring, as described below
Typical Marks: Unmarked. Some examples have a die-impressed shape number.

In 1907, the Roseville display at the annual Pittsburgh glass and china show included a striking design that collectors call Decorated Landscape. An enthusiastic reviewer predicted success for this "new effect in Art Nouveau. One particularly strong feature is that the finish is smooth and hard and there is no crazing about it.... This line is in jardinieres and pedestals and has a very Jappy [Japanese] appearance and is beautiful withal. It is made with a light background and the decorations stand out with a telling appearance" (trade notice, *China, Glass and Lamps,* January 12, 1907: 8).

Frederick Hurten Rhead is certain to be the artistic genius behind Decorated Landscape, which features a combination of squeezebag, sgrafitto, and hand-painted details. The conventional landscape has elements reminiscent of several Vance/Avon designs, where F.H. Rhead worked as a designer during 1902 and 1903, before going to Weller (and then Roseville). The background is a glossy brown, and other details are colored in shades of burnt orange, green, ivory, and yellow.

It is not known whether these pieces were part of a larger line, or simply an attractive jardiniere design. A comparably decorated umbrella stand has been attributed to Roseville (see Huxford, 1980, page 178), but its shape does not appear in factory stock pages.

The only known factory stock page to show the Decorated Landscape motif illustrates 8 related items:

DECORATED LANDSCAPE

Shape No.	Description	Shape No.	Description
456	-5" jardiniere	456	-9" jardiniere
456	-6" jardiniere	456	-10" jardiniere
456	-7" jardiniere	456	-10" jardiniere & pedestal
456	-8" jardiniere	456	-12" jardiniere & pedestal

Decorated Landscape. 456-12" x 42" jardiniere and pedestal. *Nickel and Horvath collection.* **$5000–6000.** Most Roseville collectors love green plants and flowers. Somehow they always seem able to make room for another "J and P."

Decorated Landscape. 456-7" jardiniere. *Hoppe collection.* **$700–800**

DECORATED MATT
An Early Line, introduced in 1907

Factory Name(s): Unknown (perhaps Aztec)
Collector Nickname(s): Peacock (see Purviance and Schneider, 1970); Decor Matt (see Buxton, 1977)
Style: Arts and Crafts (or Art Nouveau)
Standard Color(s): Unknown; backgrounds seem to be brown, gray, or light blue
Typical Marks: Unmarked. Some examples have a die-impressed shape number.

Besides Decorated Landscape, also introduced at the 1907 Pittsburgh glass and china show was the ware known as Decorated Matt. A 1907 reviewer remarked, "In Pompeiian and old Grecian designs there are eight or ten new effects. This is a new and original line produced in gray and brown, the jardinieres running in size from 5 to 12 inches. The pedestals are probably the unique feature of this line, being in odd shapes and designed after the order of mission furniture" (trade notice, *China, Glass and Lamps,* January 12, 1907: 8).

Like Decorated Landscape, this little-known line is also believed to be the work of Frederick Hurten Rhead. At the factory, these Decorated Matt items may have been viewed as extensions of the Aztec line. Both feature squeezebag decorations on matte-glazed (or semigloss) backgrounds in a solid color.

Decorated Matt is characterized by conventionalized landscapes or geometrical motifs, in a variety of colors. The extent of the line is not known. Only 2 umbrella stands appear in the factory stock pages with Decorated Matt decoration:

DECORATED MATT

Shape No.	Description
723	-21.5" umbrella stand
724	-20.25" umbrella stand

Decorated Matt. 468-6" jardiniere, geometrical band. *Hoppe photograph.* **$500–600**

Decorated Matt. 12" x 42" jardiniere and pedestal, attributed to Roseville, decorated with lotus and other floral motifs, artist initials "HR" (Harry Rhead). *Photograph by Mike McAllister, McAllister Auctions.* **$5000–6000.**

Detail of Decorated Matt umbrella stand.

Decorated Matt. 724-20.25" umbrella stand, peacock in tree, berry and vine borders, unmarked. *Nickel and Horvath collection.* **$3500–4500**

DELLA ROBBIA

An Early Line, introduced in 1906

Factory Name(s): Della Robbia; Rozane Della Robbia

Style: Arts and Crafts (often with echoes of an older culture, such as Pre-Raphaelite, Celtic, and the like)

Standard Color(s): Various; can be as simple as two shades of a single color, or hand decorated in as many as twelve colors

Typical Marks: Unmarked. Some examples have a Rozane Ware wafer. Artist signatures or initials can be found on many pieces.

Many Della Robbia designs began life as a Rozane Royal or Cremo shape, to which Frederick Hurten Rhead added carefully worked-out decorations. More than any other Roseville line, Della Robbia is considered a virtuoso Arts and Crafts achievement—both for Rhead personally and for the factory. Few (if any) other Roseville products are more expensive in today's market.

Because the 1906 Rozane Ware catalog was not reprinted until recently (see Bomm), many collectors did not realize that Della Robbia motifs were once offered as factory-standard decorations. The catalog shows that Della Robbia shape numbers apply to both a shape and a particular decoration. Yet because each example was carved, excised, detailed, and colored by hand, Della Robbia pieces also have individual personalities.

Values are hard to estimate, although demand is highest for pieces requiring a variety of colors. Decorations involving people (or animals) are preferred over floral motifs, and size matters. Yet almost every Roseville collector yearns for the day when he or she can brag about even a two-color Della Robbia teapot, the least expensive possibility.

The factory stock pages show 3 teapot and 18 vase shapes in the Della Robbia line, and an additional 83 designs appear in the 1906 Rozane Ware catalog. In Bomm, Della Robbia is located under "Rozane–Della Robbia."

DELLA ROBBIA

Shape No.	Description	Shape No.	Description	Shape No.	Description
1	-18" vase	23	-8" ferner	55	-13.25" vase
1	teapot	24	-11.25" vase	56	-4" ferner
2	-16.25" vase	25	-8" vase	57	-5.5" ewer
2	teapot	26	-6.5" stein	58	-10.5" vase
3	-6.5" vase	27	-9.75" vase	59	-7" vase
3	teapot	28	-19" vase	60	-4.5" vase
4	-15" vase	29	-9.25" vase	61	-20" vase
4	teapot	30	-19" vase	62	-10" vase
5	-7" pillow vase	31	-9" vase	63	-13.25" vase
5	teapot	32	-10" tankard	64	-3" vase
6	-11.5" vase	33	-17.75" vase	65	-11.75" vase
6	teapot	34	-6.75" pitcher	66	-11.25" vase
7	-8.5" vase	35	-7.5" humidor	67	-17.5" vase
7	teapot	36	-11" vase	68	-11.5" vase
8	-10" vase	37	-14.75" vase	69	-13.5" vase
8	teapot	38	-6.25" ewer	70	-7.5" vase
9	-10.25" vase	39	-7.25" vase	D1	vase
9	teapot	40	-7.5" pitcher	D2	vase
10	-9" vase	41	-9" covered vase	D3	vase
10	teapot			D4	vase
11	-10.5" vase	42	-6.25" tyge	D5	vase
11	teapot	43	-11.5" vase	D6	vase
12	-10.25" vase	44	-5" toby jug	D7	vase
12	teapot	45	-9.25" vase	D8	vase
13	-18" vase	46	-9.5" vase	D9	vase
14	-15" vase	47	-16" vase	D10	vase
15	-14" vase	48	-11.25" vase	D11	vase
16	-12.75" vase	49	-14" vase	D12	vase
17	-12" vase	50	-3.5" pillow vase	D13	vase
18	-12" vase			D14	vase
19	-9" vase	51	-6" ferner	D15	vase
20	-16.5" vase	51	-7" ferner	D16	vase
21	-13.25" vase	51	-8" ferner	D17	vase
22	-6" vase	52	-16" vase	D18	vase
23	-6" ferner	53	-14" vase		
23	-7" ferner	54	-7" vase		

Della Robbia. 43-11.5" vase, Japanese-influenced floral, five colors, hand-incised artist signature "E. Caton," no factory mark. *Courtesy of Treadway Gallery.* **$7500–8500**

Della Robbia. 16-12.25" vase, reticulated rim, cherries on branch, hand-incised artist signature "H Smith," Rozane Ware wafer, *courtesy of Steve Schoneck;* 51-7" planter (or hanging basket), Egyptian-style lotuses and scallops, artist initials "H L" (Harry Larzalere), die-impressed 316 (a number assigned earlier to this shape, when executed in Matt Green or Creamware), *courtesy of David Rago.* **$4000–5000, $2500–3000**

Detail of Della Robbia. The motifs that decorate Della Robbia are always carved by hand. To identify this line, watch for minor slips of the knife, slightly uneven lines, improvised elements in a design, and similar traces of hand craftsmanship.

Della Robbia. 9-10.25" vase, conventional floral, two colors. *Hoppe collection.* **$1500–2000.** To decorate this vase, the outlines of three long rectangular panels were first incised. The flower shapes were then created by excising away the background. Carefully incised lines were added to give each petal definition.

Della Robbia. 8-5.75" teapot, stylized roses, Rozane Ware wafer. *Cannon collection.* **$1800–2200**

Della Robbia. D17-8" vase, penguins and evergreen trees, hand-incised artist initials GA, Rozane Ware wafer. *Courtesy of Mark Valloric.* **$2500–3000**

Della Robbia. 5-8" teapot, conventional floral, two colors. *Hoppe collection.* **$1800–2200**

Della Robbia. 61-20" vase, Art Nouveau figural, twelve colors, artist initials EC. *Nickel and Horvath collection.* **NPD**

Another view of Della Robbia figural vase.

DOGWOOD (Smooth)
A Middle Period Line, introduced by 1920

Factory Name(s): Dogwood
Collector Nickname(s): Dogwood (Second) [see Alexander, 1970]; Dogwood II (see Huxford 1976)
Style: Realistic
Standard Color(s): One standard coloring, as described below
Typical Marks: Unmarked. Some examples have a blue inkstamp mark giving the shape number and size (only).

Announcing Dogwood to the trade, Roseville proclaimed, "Everything points to the fact that this new line eclipses our previous efforts in art pottery. A distinctive design that offers great possibilities in the pottery world" (advertisement, *Pottery, Glass and Brass Salesman,* December 11, 1919: 65). The pattern features realistically modeled flowering Dogwood branches, hand decorated in black and ivory, against a smooth semigloss dark green background.

Many Dogwood (Smooth) shapes have reticulated openings at the rim, particularly where the woody stems are allowed to lift above the mouth of a vessel. Baskets typically have irregular branch-shaped handles. Roseville designer Frank Ferrell undoubtedly thought this product line to be quite

novel—even quaint (in the good sense, meaning "a conversation piece").

Today's collectors show a distinct preference for this version of the line, and the more unusual shapes demand the strongest prices.

In the factory stock pages, only 13 shapes in Dogwood (Smooth) are shown:

Dogwood (Smooth). 8" basket; 265-6" basket. *Hoppe photograph.* **$200–250, $175–225**

DOGWOOD (SMOOTH)

Shape No.	Description
135	-8" vase
136	-8" vase
137	-10" vase
138	-10" vase
139	-12" vase
140	-15" vase
590	-6" jardiniere
590	-7" jardiniere
590	-8" jardiniere
590	-9" jardiniere
590	-10" jardiniere & pedestal
590	-12" jardiniere & pedestal
758	-21" umbrella stand

Dogwood (Smooth). 269(?)-12" x 5.75" oval planter, blue inkstamp 269(?)-12. *Fairfield collection.* **$300–400.** The inkstamp on this planter resembles one more commonly found on Vista.

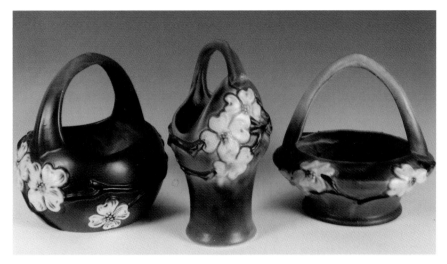

Dogwood (Smooth). 8" basket; 9" basket; 8" basket. *Shannon collection.* **$175–225, $200–250, $175–225**

Dogwood (Smooth). 9" basket; 7.75" basket; 9" basket. *Shannon collection.* **$275–350, 225–275, $275–350**

DOGWOOD (Textured)
A Middle Period Line, introduced in 1926

Factory Name(s): Dogwood

Collector Nickname(s): First Dogwood (see Purviance and Schneider, 1970); Dogwood (see Alexander, 1970); Dogwood I (see Huxford 1976)

Style: Realistic

Standard Color(s): One standard coloring, as described below

Typical Marks: Most examples have a blue inkstamp Rv logo, although some are unmarked. (In other cases, the inkstamp mark may be obscured by a thick glaze.)

In 1926, Roseville remodeled Dogwood (Smooth). According to one account, "The pattern has been a popular one for some time, but it appeared to the management that it could be improved by sharpening both the body color and the decoration. This has been done, with results that are highly satisfactory. The line is shown principally in jardinieres and other large pieces" (trade notice, *Pottery, Glass and Brass Salesman,* March 25, 1926: 30). Perhaps another 1921 line—Imperial (Textured)—had outsold its contemporary, Dogwood (Smooth).

Like many of the Frank Ferrell lines that would follow it, Dogwood (Textured) featured a sculptural floral design at a slightly higher relief than the overall textured background, which was given a contrasting color. The blossoms of Dogwood (Textured) are tooled more carefully, and the color of the branches is softer than that used in the earlier Dogwood line. It is uncertain whether these changes produced positive results for the factory. Most present-day collectors prefer the original Dogwood line!

Caution: Most earlier Roseville authors have confused the order of these two Dogwood lines, mistakenly thinking Dogwood (Smooth) came after Dogwood (Textured).

The factory stock pages show 22 Dogwood (Textured) shapes:

DOGWOOD (TEXTURED)

Shape No.	Description	Shape No.	Description
150	-4" bowl	340	-5" hanging basket
150	-5" bowl	340	-6" hanging basket
150	-6" bowl	374	-10" window box
150	-7" bowl	608	-5" jardiniere
151	-4" bowl	608	-6" jardiniere
300	-6" vase	608	-7" jardiniere
301	-7" vase	608	-8" jardiniere
302	-8" vase	608	-9" jardiniere
303	-9" vase	608	-10" jardiniere & pedestal
304	-10" vase	766	-20" umbrella stand
305	-12" vase	1245	-9" wall pocket

Dogwood (Textured). 301-7" vase. *Hoppe photograph.* **$225–275**

Dogwood (Textured). 150-4" bowl, blue Rv inkstamp; 340-5" hanging basket, blue Rv inkstamp. *Merritt collection.* **$125–150, $250–300**

Dogwood (Textured). 305-12" vase. *Fairfield collection.* **$400–500.** Few examples of Dogwood (Textured) have handles.

Dogwood (Textured). 300-6" vase; 151-4" bowl. *Courtesy of Treadway Gallery.* **$200–250, $150–175**

DONATELLO

An Early Line, introduced by 1916

Factory Name(s): Donatello

Style: Italianate

Standard Color(s): Green and white; or gray

Typical Marks: Early examples are unmarked. A few have a molded (raised-relief) mark that is specific to this line—the line name "DONATELLO" in a semi-circle. About 1920, some examples were marked with a blue inkstamp giving the shape number and size (only). Donatello pieces made in 1923 or later (if any) would be marked with the blue inkstamp Rv logo.

Like Volpato and Florentine, Donatello is an Italianate Roseville line. Each example has a fluted body. The principal decoration is a low-relief sculptural frieze of cupids or putti ("infants") at play. The double bud vase features a child satyr instead, and some of the putti have adult preoccupations with painting, sculpting, music, or other endeavors.

The standard coloring is matte green and white, with a brown wash on the frieze to color its background. Some shapes were available in a matte gray variation, which also has a (dark) brown frieze. Some shapes began life as Early Carnelian pieces.

Donatello was offered as late as 1921 (source: factory advertisement, *Crockery and Glass Journal,* December 16, 1920: 164). In 1975, collectors Josh and Anna Snook found the line intriguing enough to publish a small spiral-bound paperback on Donatello. This had the distinction of being the third book published strictly about Roseville products.

The factory stock pages show 91 Donatello shapes, and an additional 18 are mentioned in the July 1916 price list:

Donatello. 5.75" basket; 8.5" basket; 115-10" bud vase; 230-7" comport. *Shannon collection.* **$225–275, $325–375, $175–225, $175–225**

Donatello. 104-8" vase, gray; 111-12" vase. *Shannon collection.* **$250–300, $275–350**

DONATELLO

Shape No.	Description	Reference/Notes
1	jewel box (covered)	Also in July 1916 price list
2	jewel box (covered)	Also in July 1916 price list
8	double bud vase, gate shape	Also in July 1916 price list
9	double bud vase, gate shape	Also in July 1916 price list
9	-9" comport	
14	-2.5" flower block	Also in July 1916 price list
14	-3.5" flower block	Also in July 1916 price list
15	ashtray	Also in July 1916 price list
16	ashtray	Also in July 1916 price list
17	ashtray	Also in July 1916 price list
36	-10" bud vase	
53	-6" bowl	
53	-7" bowl	Also in July 1916 price list
54	-8" bowl	Also in July 1916 price list
55	-10" bowl	Also in July 1916 price list
60	-6" bowl	Also in July 1916 price list
60	-8" bowl	Also in July 1916 price list
60	-10" bowl	Also in July 1916 price list
60	-12" bowl	Also in July 1916 price list
61	-6" plate (or low bowl)	Also in July 1916 price list
61	-8" plate (or low bowl)	Also in July 1916 price list
61	-10" plate (or low bowl)	See July 1916 price list
88	vase	
89	bowl	
90	bowl	
91	bowl	
92	bowl	
101	-8" vase	Also in July 1916 price list
102	-8" vase	Also in July 1916 price list
103	-8" vase	Also in July 1916 price list
104	-8" vase	Also in July 1916 price list
105	-10" vase	Also in July 1916 price list
106	-10" vase	Also in July 1916 price list
107	-10" vase	Also in July 1916 price list
108	-10" vase	Also in July 1916 price list
109	-12" vase	Also in July 1916 price list
110	-12" vase	Also in July 1916 price list
111	-12" vase	Also in July 1916 price list
112	-12" vase	Also in July 1916 price list
113	-7" vase	Also in July 1916 price list
113	-8" vase	Also in July 1916 price list
113	-10" vase	Also in July 1916 price list
113	-12" vase	Also in July 1916 price list
113	-15" vase	Also in July 1916 price list
114	-7" vase	Also in July 1916 price list
115	-10" bud vase	Also in July 1916 price list
116	-6" bud vase	Also in July 1916 price list
118	-6" vase	
118	-8" vase	
184	-6" vase	
184	-8" vase	
184	-10" vase	
184	-12" vase	
227	-4" fern dish	Also in July 1916 price list
227	-5" fern dish	Also in July 1916 price list
227	-6" fern dish	Also in July 1916 price list
228	-6" x 6" footed fern dish	Also in July 1916 price list
229	-9" x 4" footed fern dish	Also in July 1916 price list
230	-7" x 3" footed fern dish	Also in July 1916 price list
231	-4" x 3" footed fern dish	Also in July 1916 price list
231	-5" footed fern dish	Also in July 1916 price list
231	-6" footed fern dish	Also in July 1916 price list
232	-8" footed fern dish	Also in July 1916 price list
233	-5" basket	See July 1916 price list
233	-6" basket	See July 1916 price list
233	-7" basket	See July 1916 price list
233	-8" basket	
238	-5" ferner	
238	-6" ferner	
238	-7" ferner	
301	-9" basket	
302	-10.5" basket	
303	-11" basket	
304	-12" basket	
305	-14" basket	
306	-14" basket	
327	-6" hanging basket	Also in July 1916 price list
327	-8" hanging basket	Also in July 1916 price list
364	-10.5" x 4.5" window box	See July 1916 price list
364	-14" x 5" window box	See July 1916 price list
575	-4" jardiniere	Also in July 1916 price list
575	-5" jardiniere	Also in July 1916 price list
575	-6" jardiniere	See July 1916 price list
575	-6" x 18" jardiniere & pedestal	See July 1916 price list
575	-7" jardiniere	See July 1916 price list
575	-8" jardiniere	See July 1916 price list
575	-8" x 24" jardiniere & pedestal	See July 1916 price list
575	-9" jardiniere	See July 1916 price list
575	-10" jardiniere	See July 1916 price list
575	-10" x 28" jardiniere & pedestal	See July 1916 price list
579	-6" jardiniere	Also in July 1916 price list
579	-8" jardiniere	Also in July 1916 price list
579	-10" jardiniere	Also in July 1916 price list
579	-10" x 28" jardiniere & pedestal	See July 1916 price list
579	-12" jardiniere	Also in July 1916 price list
579	-12" x 34" jardiniere & pedestal	See July 1916 price list
580	-4" flower pot and saucer	Also in July 1916 price list
580	-5" flower pot and saucer	Also in July 1916 price list
580	-6" flower pot and saucer	Also in July 1916 price list
628	cuspidor	See July 1916 price list
753	-21" x 10" umbrella stand	See July 1916 price list
1008	-7.5" candlestick	Also in July 1916 price list
1009	-6" bedside candlestick	Also in July 1916 price list
1011	bedside candlestick	Also in July 1916 price list
1022	-10" candlestick	
1212	-10" wall pocket	Also in July 1916 price list (misprinted as shape 1210 in stock page)
1212	-12" wall pocket	Also in July 1916 price list
1307	pitcher	Also in July 1916 price list

Donatello. 105-10" vase, gray, *Ross collection*; 12.5" vase, *courtesy of Mike Nickel and Cindy Horvath.* **$350–400, $700–800**

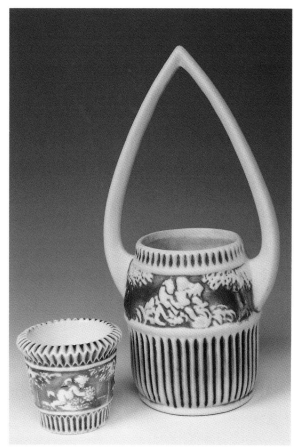

Donatello. 3" vase, flower pot shape; 303-11" basket. *Shannon collection.* **$65–75 (or $95–125 with flower frog), $500–600.** A circular ridge about halfway down the vase serves to hold a separate "T" shaped flower frog in place

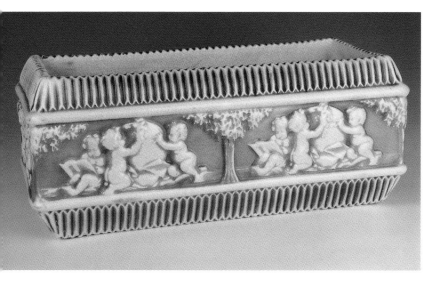

Left:
Donatello. 14" x 4.75" (opening) x 6.75" window box. *Calkins collection.* **$300–400**

ARLAM

A Middle Period Line, introduced in 1930

Factory Name(s): Earlam

Alternate Spelling(s): Earlham (see Purviance and Schneider, 1970)

Style: Early American, or Arts and Crafts

Standard Color(s): Matte mottled glaze, usually green and tan, or tan and purple

Typical Marks: Paper labels. (These could be lost, leaving the piece unmarked.) Some examples have a hand-written (crayon) shape number.

Roseville's 1930 line Earlam was praised from the start for its "soft colors with brown and green predominating" (trade notice, *Crockery and Glass Journal,* August 1930: 71). "Especially noteworthy in Earlam ware," remarked the commentator—as if speaking for present-day collectors—"are table strawberry jars in new and interesting shapes, as well as a hanging flower basket in strawberry jar effect."

The origin of the name Earlam is not known. In appearance, the rounded strap-like handles are reminiscent of Colonial wares. The pleasant matte glazes are also attractive in an Arts and Crafts interior, making this line doubly appealing to collectors.

The factory stock pages show 23 items in the Earlam line:

Shape No.	Description	Reference/Notes
15	-2.5" flower block	
15	-3.5" flower block	
88	-10" fan vase	
89	-8" planter	
90	-8" strawberry jar	
91	-8" strawberry jar	
92	-9" strawberry jar	
217	-4" bowl	
218	-9" ferner	
347	-6" hanging basket (strawberry jar)	
515	-4" rose bowl	
516	-4.5" vase	
517	-5.5" vase	
518	-6" vase	
519	-7" vase	
520	-8" vase	
521	-7" vase	
522	-9" vase	
769	-14" x 11.5" sand jar	Bomm 383
1059	-3" candlestick	
1080	-4" bedside candlestick	
1081	-4" candlestick	
1263	wall pocket (Imperial Glazes shape)	

Earlam. Pair, 1081-4" candlesticks. *Hoppe photograph.* **$275–325 (pair)**

Earlam. 521-7" urn; 517-5.5" vase. *Hoppe photograph.* **$400–500, $200–250**

Earlam. 516-4.5" vase. *Harris collection.* **$250–300**

Earlam. 517-5.5" vase; 519-7" vase. *Shannon collection.* **$200–250, $325–375**

EARLY CARNELIAN
An Early Line, introduced by 1916

Factory Name(s): Carnelian
Collector Nickname(s): Blended (see Buxton, 1977); Rosecraft Blended (see Huxford, 1980)
Style: Arts and Crafts
Standard Color(s): Mottled blue, green, pink or purple
Typical Marks: Unmarked. Some examples have a hand-incised shape number (only).

Today, the preferred Early Carnelian glaze is a matte mottled green and brown, which somewhat resembles Antique Matt Green. During 1916 the term "Carnelian" perhaps referred *only* to this particular glaze effect. In the typewritten July 1916 price list (at the Ohio Historical Society), shapes available in "Carnelian" were generally also available in Black, Blue, Red, and Yellow. (Some are instead available in three matte green colorings—Early Carnelian's green and brown glaze, Matt Green, or Antique Matt Green.)

The mottled green and brown of Early Carnelian was achieved by first dipping a bisque-fired example in a reddish brown glaze and allowing it to dry. Then a matte yellowish green glaze was applied thickly. The bottom was dried before firing, so the earlier brown glaze remained visible underneath. During firing, the green glaze separated in irregular patterns, allowing some of the underglaze to show through.

The other Early Carnelian glazes line were a mixture of semigloss white and either blue, pink, or purple. These pieces also have unpredictable mottled or veined patterns. Bottoms are not dry-footed, so the base is typically the same color as the surface elsewhere.

Early Carnelian was offered as late as 1921 (advertisement, *Crockery and Glass Journal,* December 16, 1920: 164). Occasionally, an Early Carnelian glaze is encountered on an unexpected shape and credited to another line. Bomm (1998) shows the mottled green and brown glaze on a Rozane Royal 893-12.5" vase shape (page 249, item 2). Huxford (1980) shows this glaze on a Carnelian (Glazes) 455-18" vase shape (page 72, row 3, item 1).

The only known factory stock page shows 28 Early Carnelian shapes. An additional 85 shapes are mentioned in the July 1916 price list. (Shapes 1 through 40 may be planters, jardinieres, or bowls instead of vases, as described below). In Bomm—as in most earlier Roseville books—this line is located under "Rosecraft Blended":

Early Carnelian. 45-8" vase, *courtesy of Mark Bassett Antiques;* 46-8" vase, *Fairfield collection;* 74-7" bowl and 15-3.5" flower block, *courtesy of Mark Bassett Antiques.* **$125–175, $150–200, $75–95 (bowl), $20–25 (flower block)**

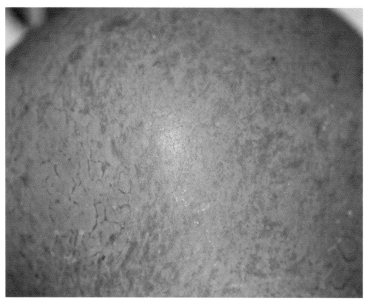

Detail of the Early Carnelian Green and Brown Glaze. Note that these pieces were first glazed a solid matte burnt orange (resembling the base color of Rosecraft's burnt orange). The thick green overglaze then flowed irregularly over the surface, allowing the reddish brown color to show through.

Early Carnelian. 36-5.75" bud vase, mottled wine and blue, hand-incised "36"; 234-7" basket, mottled blue and white. *Hoppe collection.* **$95–125, $175–225**

117

EARLY CARNELIAN

Shape No.	Description	Reference/Notes
1	-14" vase, 5.25" opening	See July 1916 price list
2	-11" vase, 5.25" opening	See July 1916 price list
3	-9" vase, 5" opening	See July 1916 price list
4	-7" vase, 5.75" opening	See July 1916 price list
5	-10" vase, 5.5" opening	See July 1916 price list
6	-9" vase, 4.5" opening	See July 1916 price list
7	-12" vase, 4.5" opening	See July 1916 price list
8	-8" vase, 4.25" opening	See July 1916 price list
9	-8.5" vase, 4" opening	See July 1916 price list
10	-5.5" vase, 4.5" opening	See July 1916 price list
11	-9" vase, 4.5" opening	See July 1916 price list
12	-9" vase, 4" opening	See July 1916 price list
12	frog-shaped flower holder	See July 1916 price list
13	-9.5" vase, 3.5" opening	See July 1916 price list
13	turtle-shaped flower holder	See July 1916 price list
14	-10" vase, 3.5" opening	See July 1916 price list
15	-8.5" vase, 4" opening	See July 1916 price list
16	-9.5" vase, 3.5" opening	See July 1916 price list
16	double bud vase, gate shape	Also in July 1916 price list
17	-8.5" vase, 3.25" opening	See July 1916 price list
17	fish-shaped flower holder	See July 1916 price list
18	-8" vase, 3.5" opening	See July 1916 price list
18	toad-shaped flower holder	See July 1916 price list
19	-7.25" vase, 3.5" opening	See July 1916 price list
20	-8.5" vase, 4.25" opening	See July 1916 price list
21	-9.25" vase, 3.25" opening	See July 1916 price list
22	-9.25" vase, 3.25" opening	See July 1916 price list
23	-6.5" vase, 3" opening	See July 1916 price list
24	-6" vase, 2.75" opening	See July 1916 price list
25	-5.5" vase, 3.25" opening	See July 1916 price list
26	-4" vase, 3.5" opening	See July 1916 price list
27	-5.75" vase, 3.25" opening	See July 1916 price list
28	-5.75" vase, 3" opening	See July 1916 price list
29	-5.75" vase, 2.75" opening	See July 1916 price list
30	-3.5" vase, 3" opening	See July 1916 price list
31	-4.75" vase, 3.5" opening	See July 1916 price list
32	-7.5" vase, 2.67" opening	See July 1916 price list
33	-6" vase	
33	-7" vase, 6" opening	See July 1916 price list
34	-5.75" vase, 5" opening	See July 1916 price list
34	-8" vase	
35	-4.5" vase, 4" opening	See July 1916 price list
35	-10" vase	
36	-2.25" vase, 5.5" opening	See July 1916 price list
36	-6" bud vase	
37	-1.75" vase, 4.25" opening	See July 1916 price list
37	-5" vase	
38	-2.75" vase, 2.5" x 8" opening	See July 1916 price list
38	-5" vase	
39	-5.25" vase, 2.5" x 7" opening	See July 1916 price list
39	-6" vase	
40	-6" bowl, oval	See July 1916 price list
40	-6" vase	
41	-6" vase	
41	-8" bowl, oval	See July 1916 price list
42	-6" bud vase	
42	-12" bowl, oval	See July 1916 price list
43	-4" x 2" bowl, round	See July 1916 price list
43	-8" vase	

Shape No.	Description	Reference/Notes
44	-5" x 2" bowl, round	See July 1916 price list
44	-8" vase	
45	-5" x 3" bowl, round	See July 1916 price list
45	-8" vase	
46	-6" x 2" bowl, round	See July 1916 price list
46	-8" vase	
47	-10" bowl, round, footed	See July 1916 price list
48	-12" bowl, round, footed	See July 1916 price list
49	-14" bowl, round, footed	See July 1916 price list
50	-10" bowl, round	See July 1916 price list
51	-12" bowl, round	See July 1916 price list
52	-14" bowl, round	See July 1916 price list
53	-10" vase	See July 1916 price list
54	-12" vase	See July 1916 price list
59	-6" bowl, round, flared	See July 1916 price list
59	-8" bowl, round, flared	See July 1916 price list
59	-10" bowl, round, flared	See July 1916 price list
59	-12" bowl, round, flared	See July 1916 price list
59	-14" bowl, round, flared	See July 1916 price list
62	-10" bowl, oval	See July 1916 price list
66	-4" bowl, round	See July 1916 price list
66	-5" bowl, round	See July 1916 price list
66	-6" bowl, round	See July 1916 price list
66	-7" bowl, round	See July 1916 price list
66	-8" bowl, round	See July 1916 price list
234	-5" basket	Also in July 1916 price list
234	-6" basket	Also in July 1916 price list
234	-7" basket	Also in July 1916 price list
236	-8" centerpiece	Also in July 1916 price list
550	-10" x 28" jardiniere & pedestal	See July 1916 price list
550	-12" x 33" jardiniere & pedestal	See July 1916 price list
574	-7" jardiniere	See July 1916 price list
574	-8" jardiniere	See July 1916 price list
574	-9" jardiniere	See July 1916 price list
574	-10" jardiniere	See July 1916 price list
574	-10" x 29" jardiniere & pedestal	See July 1916 price list
574	-12" x 33" jardiniere & pedestal	See July 1916 price list
581	-8" jardiniere	See July 1916 price list
581	-9" jardiniere	See July 1916 price list
581	-10" jardiniere	See July 1916 price list
581	-12" jardiniere	See July 1916 price list
581	-14" jardiniere	See July 1916 price list
582	-4" flower pot and separate saucer	Also in July 1916 price list
582	-5" flower pot and separate saucer	Also in July 1916 price list
582	-6" flower pot and separate saucer	Also in July 1916 price list
583	-3" jardiniere	Also in July 1916 price list
583	-4" jardiniere	Also in July 1916 price list
583	-5" jardiniere	Also in July 1916 price list
1012	-5" candlestick	Also in July 1916 price list
1013	-7" candlestick	Also in July 1916 price list
1014	-9" candlestick	Also in July 1916 price list

Opposite page, top left:
Early Carnelian. 440-8" vase. *Hansen collection.* **$600–700** As this example demonstrates, Early Carnelian's green and brown glaze was sometimes used on shapes thought to have been produced in the late 1920s.

Detail from Early Carnelian vase.

Early Carnelian. 41-6" vase, mottled brown; 35-10" trumpet vase, mottled pink; 7.5" bowl, mottled blue, *courtesy of Mark Bassett Antiques;* 44-8" vase, mottled green and blue; 234-8" basket, mottled pink, *courtesy of Mark Bassett Antiques.* All *Fairfield collection* (except as noted). **$95–125, $150–200, $60–70, $125–150, $200–250**

Early Carnelian. 742-27" umbrella stand. *Hoppe collection.* **$750–950**

Early Carnelian. 583-9" jardiniere, mottled wine and blue. *Courtesy of Cincinnati Art Galleries.* **$375–450**

EARLY ROSECRAFT
An Early Line, introduced by 1917

Factory Name(s): Unknown (believed to be Rosecraft)
Collector Nickname(s): Velmoss I (see Purviance and Schneider, 1970); Velmoss Scroll (see Buxton, 1977)
Alternate Spelling(s): Velmos (see Clifford, 1968); Velmoss Schroll (see Alexander, 1970)
Style: Arts and Crafts
Standard Color(s): One standard coloring, as described below
Typical Marks: Unmarked

This line depicts the Arts and Crafts "English rose" on a thorny vine. The conventionalized floral decoration is impressed into the creamware body, as if in sgrafitto. Natural coloring, in red and green, was applied quickly and then wiped off the background with a cloth.

Because the rose motif bears no resemblance to the leaves and berries of the Early Velmoss and Velmoss lines, it is surprising that researchers have persisted in nicknaming this line "Velmoss." A more plausible possibility is that it was given the name "Rosecraft," a variation on the nearly generic term "Rozane," then in use for Rozane Royal.

An early Rosecraft line is indeed mentioned (but not illustrated) in a 1917 factory advertisement (*Pottery, Glass and Brass Salesman,* December 13, 1917: 27). This timing significantly predates the 1922 trade notice describing another Rosecraft line, first offered in the colors Azurine, Orchid, and Turquoise (see Rosecraft).

The factory stock pages show 33 shapes in the Early Rosecraft line. In Bomm, Early Rosecraft shapes are located under "Velmoss 1."

EARLY ROSECRAFT

Shape No.	Description	Shape No.	Description
14	-8" comport	202	-10" vase
115	-5" bowl	203	-10" vase
115	-6" bowl	204	-10" vase
115	-7" bowl	205	-12" vase
116	-5" ferner	254	-6" fern dish
116	-6" ferner	335	-6" hanging basket
117	-6" bowl	600	-5" jardiniere
118	-6" bowl	600	-6" jardiniere
193	-5" vase	600	-7" jardiniere
194	-6" vase	600	-8" jardiniere
195	-6" vase	600	-9" jardiniere
196	-6" vase	600	-10" jardiniere & pedestal
197	-8" vase	1044	-8" candlestick
198	-8" vase	1045	-10" candlestick
199	-8" vase	1226	-11" wall pocket
200	-8" vase	1227	-12" wall pocket
201	-10" vase		

Early Rosecraft. 199-8" vase; 203-10" vase; 197-8" vase. *Hoppe photograph.* **$275–325, $325–375, $275–325**

Early Rosecraft. 193-5" vase; 14-8" comport; 195-6" vase. *Merritt collection.* **$175–225, $175–225, $225–250**

Early Rosecraft. 115-5" bowl; 204-10" vase; 194-6" vase. *Hoppe photograph.* **$125–150, $350–400, $225–250**

Left:
Early Rosecraft. Pair, 1044-8" candlesticks; 254-6" fern dish; 1045-10" candlestick. *Hoppe photograph.* **$350–400 (pair), $150–200, $175–225**. Few examples of Early Rosecraft have handles.

EARLY VELMOSS

An Early Line, introduced by 1916

Factory Name(s): Velmoss
Style: Arts and Crafts, or Art Nouveau
Standard Color(s): Matte mottled green—either alone, or with a matte mottled "tobacco" yellowish tan
Typical Marks: Unmarked. Some examples have a hand-written (crayon) shape number and size.

Early Velmoss uses a mottled green and brown glaze that first appeared in Roseville's Early Carnelian line. The shapes involve curvilinear leaf and bud motifs, or severely geometrical blade-like leaves. Some examples are hand decorated with a tobacco-colored matte blend of yellow and tan, in combination with the mottled green.

Long a mystery to pottery collectors, this Roseville line was finally identified by Bill Martin and Jim Blanchard, who located an example marked "Velmoss" in black crayon (under the glaze). Its shape numbers are listed in a 1916 Roseville price list at the Ohio Historical Society. Occasionally an example is marked (in crayon) with the shape number or the original retail price.

Even without authentication, the strong Arts and Crafts look of this line has generated considerable interest among collectors in recent years. Prices may soar again when the maker's name becomes more widely known.

There are no known factory stock pages for Early Velmoss, but 31 shape numbers are given in the typewritten July 1916 price list:

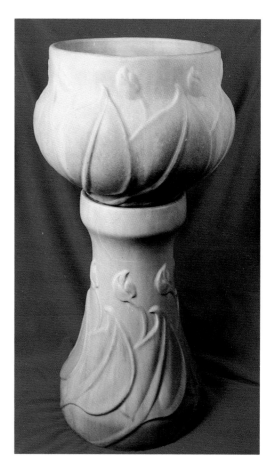

Early Velmoss. 577-10" x 27" jardiniere and pedestal, black paper label. *Hoppe collection.* **$2500–3000.** The Early Velmoss line is believed to have been made during a period when Roseville did not use paper labels. As pottery lovers know, paper labels are sometimes soaked off, allowed to dry, and then glued onto a different pot. (For an example of a piece of Monmouth Pottery bearing a Roseville paper label, see Appendix 2.)

Early Velmoss. 7.75" vase; 10" bowl; Early Carnelian 15-3.5" flower block; 5.75" vase. *Hoppe collection.* **$500–600, $200–250, $20–25, $400–500**

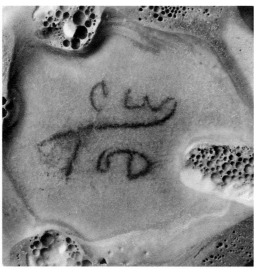

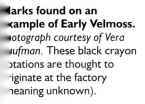

Marks found on an example of Early Velmoss. *Photograph courtesy of Vera Kaufman.* These black crayon notations are thought to originate at the factory (meaning unknown).

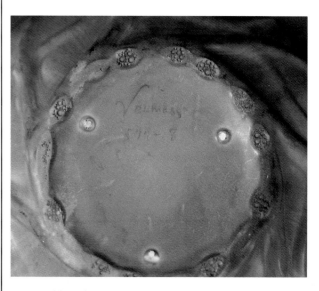

Mark found on an example of Early Velmoss. *Photograph by Jim Blanchard, Primarily Pottery, Jacksonville, FL.*

Shape No.	Description	Shape No.	Description
54	-8" bowl	138	-12" vase
55	-10" bowl	139	-12" vase
56	-6" bowl	140	-12" vase
125	-6" vase	577	-7" jardiniere
126	-6" vase	577	-8" jardiniere
127	-6" vase	577	-9" jardiniere
128	-6" vase	577	-10" jardiniere
129	-8" vase	577	-10" jardiniere & pedestal
130	-8" vase	577	-12" jardiniere
131	-8" vase	577	-12" jardiniere & pedestal
132	-8" vase	578	-7" jardiniere
133	-10" vase	578	-8" jardiniere
134	-10" vase	578	-9" jardiniere
135	-10" vase	578	-10" jardiniere
136	-10" vase	754	-21" x 10" umbrella stand
137	-12" vase		

Early Velmoss. 8" vase. *Hoppe collection.* **$600–700**

Early Velmoss. 10" vase; 10" vase. *Hoppe collection.* **$650–750 (each)**

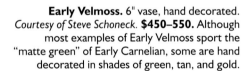

Early Velmoss. 6" vase, hand decorated.
Courtesy of Steve Schoneck. **$450–550**. Although
most examples of Early Velmoss sport the
"matte green" of Early Carnelian, some are hand
decorated in shades of green, tan, and gold.

EGYPTO

An Early Line, introduced in 1905

Factory Name(s): Rozane Egypto
Style: Arts and Crafts (often reminiscent of ancient cultures, such as Egyptian, Roman, Celtic, etc.)
Standard Color(s): Matte green
Typical Marks: This line can be definitively identified only by the presence of an Egypto wafer. Unmarked examples can be "attributed" to Egypto, but may instead be early Matt Green pieces (made by reusing an Egypto or Chloron mold).

Egypto is a more elaborate line than the slightly earlier Chloron, from which it borrows at least 7 shapes. Attributed to Christian Nielson (see Karin Coleman, "Egypto," *Antiques and Collecting*, June 1996: 16–19), Egypto is described in the 1905 Rozane Ware catalog as "one of the oddest styles of Rozane, although its soft finish and coloring, in varying shades of old greens, suggest … some of the rarest and most ancient potteries of old Egypt." Later commentators have remarked that the Egyptian influence on Egypto is tenuous at best.

Close examination reveals variations in the Egypto glaze(s), indicating that Roseville glaze chemists continued to experiment with matte green. At the 1906 Pittsburgh china and glass show—even before the 1906 Rozane Ware catalog was published!—the factory introduced a new, organic matte green glaze. One contemporary observer remarked that the most memorable Roseville product that year

was the new matte green with clouded effect. This is an improvement over the Egypto matte green and a gentleman who goes to Europe every six months in search of things, the most artistic, told me he did not know where he could find anything the equal of this. Great praise for American art, isn't it? (trade notice, *China, Glass and Lamps,* January 13, 1906: 17).

The term "Egypto" appears to have been used as a generic description of Roseville's matte green line as late as 1911 (Boston showroom listing, *Crockery and Glass Journal,* December 22, 1910: 13). Pieces made after 1906, however, are believed not to be marked with the Egypto wafer.

Today, Arts and Crafts lovers avidly seek Egypto shapes. These are not shown in any known factory stock page. But 38 Egypto items appear in the 1905 and/or 1906 Rozane Ware catalogs. One additional shape (the "Goethe" candlestick) appears on a piece of card-stock, formerly in the C.E. Offinger collection (*courtesy of Moses Mesre*) and illustrated with color photographs. This document was folded in thirds, evidently to fit Mr. Offinger's wallet. In Bomm, the line is located under "Rozane–Egypto."

EGYPTO

Shape No.	Description	Reference/Notes
E10	-8.5" vase (same as Chloron C10)	1905 and 1906 catalogs (Bomm 300, 297)
E11	-9.5" footed ferner	1906 catalog (Bomm 296)
E12	-10.5" vase (same as Chloron C12)	1905 and 1906 catalogs (Bomm 299, 296)
E15	-8.25" vase (same as Chloron C15)	1905 and 1906 catalogs (Bomm 300, 297)
E17	-6" vase (same as Chloron C17)	1905 and 1906 catalogs (Bomm 300, 296)
E19	-5.5" vase (same as Chloron C19)	1906 catalog (Bomm 296)
E20	-7.5" ewer (same as Chloron C20)	1905 and 1906 catalogs (Bomm 300, 297)
E21	-6.5" vase (same as Chloron C21)	1905 and 1906 catalogs (Bomm 299, 296)
E29	-5.25" ewer	1906 catalog (Bomm 297)
E30	-4.25" pitcher	1906 catalog (Bomm 296)
E31	-7" basket	1906 catalog (Bomm 296)
E32	-5.5" basket	1906 catalog (Bomm 297)
E33	-5.25" pitcher	1906 catalog (Bomm 297)
E34	-3.5" pitcher	1906 catalog (Bomm 297)
E35	-5.25" oil lamp	1906 catalog (Bomm 297)
E36	-10.5" ewer	1906 catalog (Bomm 296)
E37	-10" oil lamp	1906 catalog (Bomm 296)
E38	-7" vase	1906 catalog (Bomm 297)
E39	-6" vase	1906 catalog (Bomm 297)
E40	-9" vase	1906 catalog (Bomm 297)
E41	-12.25" vase	1906 catalog (Bomm 297)
E42	-5.5" bud vase	1906 catalog (Bomm 297)
E43	-7" vase	1906 catalog (Bomm 297)
E44	-6" vase	1906 catalog (Bomm 296)
E45	-12.75" ewer	1906 catalog (Bomm 297)
E46	-12.5" bud vase	1906 catalog (Bomm 296)
E47	-12.5" vase	1906 catalog (Bomm 297)
E48	-10" vase	1906 catalog (Bomm 297)
E49	-10" vase	1906 catalog (Bomm 297)
E50	-12" vase	1905 and 1906 catalogs (Bomm 299, 296)
E51	-12.25" ewer	1905 and 1906 catalogs (Bomm 299, 297)
E52	-8" vase	1906 catalog (Bomm 297)
E53	-7.5" vase	1906 catalog (Bomm 297)
E56	-4.5" vase	1906 catalog (Bomm 297)
E57	-3.5" vase	1906 catalog (Bomm 297)
E58	-14.5" basket	1906 catalog (Bomm 297)
E59	-15.5" basket	1906 catalog (Bomm 297)
E60	-3.75" candlestick	Shown on Offinger "wallet card"
E68	-16.25" vase	1906 catalog (Bomm 297)

Egypto. E58-14.5" basket, Egypto wafer; 10" vase, Egypto wafer. *Hoppe collection.* **$1200–1500, $750–950.** In a version with handles, this 10" vase is shape E48 (shown in 1906 catalog).

Egypto. E60-3.75" candlestick, Egypto wafer. *Merritt collection.* **$500–600.** See the Creamware section for a gilt creamware version of this shape.

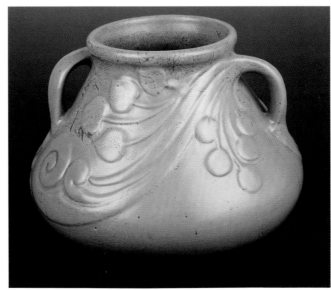

Egypto. E44-6"
vase; E35-5.25" oil
lamp, two spouts,
both marked with
Egypto wafer.
Wagner collection.
**$700–800, $650–
750**

Left:
Egypto. E17-6"
vase, cherries,
Egypto wafer.
Merritt collection.
$500–600. The
obverse of this
vase is decorated
with pears.

Egypto. E68-16.25"
vase, birds roosting
in tall tree, Egypto
wafer. *Hoppe
collection.* **$1800–
2200**

Egypto. 3.25" x 5"
inkwell, Egypto wafer.
Scheytt collection.
$500–600. The stains
inside this inkwell
indicate that it had no
glass insert. The
decorations are a
mixture of the
legalistic, patriotic,
and religious. To slow
evaporation, this piece
may originally have
had a lid.

Another view of Egypto inkwell.

FALLINE

A Middle Period Line, introduced in 1933

Factory Name(s): Falline
Standard Color(s): Blue, or brown
Style: Art Deco
Typical Marks: Foil labels. (These could be lost, leaving the piece unmarked.) Some have hand-written (crayon) shape numbers.

Falline is one of Roseville's more elegant Middle Period designs. An early trade notice called it a "new fancy line ... of much artistic merit and up to date in character" (*Pottery, Glass and Brass Salesman,* August 17, 1933: 9). Another commentator described Falline as having "shaded effects with a 'Pea-in-the-Pod' design in a fine green around the center—a very pleasing color harmony, and in good, practical shapes, to retail for $1.00 to $3.50" (trade notice, *Crockery and Glass Journal,* September 1933: 21).

Such prices are history! In the blue-green variety, a medium to tall example of Falline today can retail for $1000 or more.

The highest values can be obtained for pieces with particularly clear "peas" and other details, and of course lots of blue. Brown Falline has its collectors too, but prices are perhaps one third lower.

The only known factory stock page shows 16 items in Falline (whose name is said to be a contraction of the phrase "fall line"). Most collectors use the pronunciation "fay-leen."

FALLINE

Shape No.	Description	Shape No.	Description
244	-8" bowl	649	-8" vase
642	-6" vase	650	-6" vase
643	-6" vase	651	-8" vase
644	-6" vase	652	-9" vase
645	-6.5" vase	653	-12" vase
646	-8" vase	654	-13.5" vase
647	-7" vase	655	-15" vase
648	-7" vase	1092	-3.5" candlestick

Falline. 649-8" vase, blue; 652-9" vase, blue; 648-7" vase, blue. *Auclair collection.* **$1200–1500, $1500–2000, $950–1200**

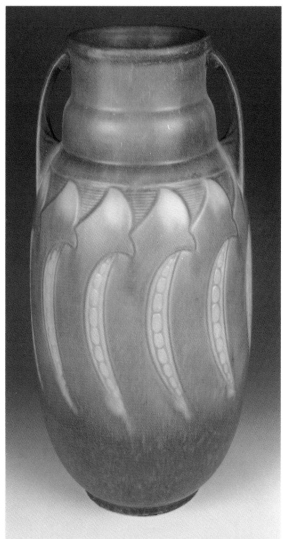

Falline. 655-15" floor vase, blue. *Auclair collection.* **$2500–3000**

Left:
Falline. 645-6.5" vase, brown; 244-8" bowl, brown; 651-8" vase, brown; 642-6" vase, brown. *Auclair collection.* **$600–700, $400–500, $950–1200, $475–550**

Falline. 643-6" vase, blue; 644-6" vase, brown. *Shannon collection.* **$600–700 (each)**

FERELLA

A Middle Period Line, introduced in 1930

Factory Name(s): Ferella
Alternate Spelling(s): Ferrella (see Clifford, 1968)
Standard Color(s): Tan ("brown"), or Rose ("red" or "raspberry")
Style: Art Deco
Typical Marks: Paper labels. (These could be lost, leaving the piece unmarked.) Some examples have a hand-written (crayon) shape number.

In 1930, Ferella was called a "a fascinating group of art pieces in open work pottery" (trade notice, *Crockery and Glass Journal,* August 1930: 71). The commentator predicted that bowl 87, which has an attached flower frog, would make "a most desirable item for Holiday selling."

Named after art director Frank Ferrell, this line was inspired by a wheel-thrown, hand-carved porcelain coupe, the work of *Keramic Studio* editor Adelaide Alsop Robineau (1865–1929). Now owned by the Metropolitan Museum of Art, the eggshell porcelain toured the U.S. in a 1929 Memorial Exhibition. In addition to the many published photographs (see, for example, *Art Digest,* December 1, 1929: 21), Ferrell probably saw the piece in person in either New York or Cleveland.

As early as 1922, Robineau began to envision the delicate design. She wrote to Metropolitan curator Joseph Breck:

As I couldn't sleep last night I spent the time making a few sketches which I send you herewith, of a little bowl which I can see, so to speak, in my mind's eye, as being made of paper-thin white porcelain with a narrow border carved in low relief on the inside, and possibly pierced here and there so that the light would shine through the glaze" (quoted in Ethel Brand Wise, "Adelaide Alsop Robineau—American Ceramist, *American Magazine of Art,* December 1929: 687–691).

After Robineau's death, Breck wrote in the *Bulletin* that the finished piece "—as imponderous as an apple blossom, with its lacy open work and delicate relief carving—is a masterpiece" (see *Pottery, Glass and Brass Salesman,* November 28, 1929: 11).

At Roseville, Ferrell eliminated the carved lotus inside and simplified the reticulated details. Matte mottled glazes were developed to complement the hand-colored yellow and green shell-like motifs. Ferrell's adaptations for mass production illustrated the philosophy of leading American art museums then—namely, that emulating objects of fine art (or of antiquity) could raise artistic standards in American industrial design.

Roseville collectors agree that Ferella is a remarkable achievement. The line remains high on the want list of many Art Deco lovers. Only one factory stock page is known, and it shows 24 Ferella shapes:

FERELLA

Shape No.	Description	Shape No.	Description
15	-2.5" flower block	503	-5" vase
15	-3.5" flower block	504	-5.5" vase
87	-8" bowl (with attached flower frog)	505	-6" vase
		506	-8" vase
210	-4" comport	507	-9" vase
211	-8" bowl	508	-8" vase
212	-12" x 7" bowl	509	-8" vase
497	-4" bud vase	510	-9" vase
498	-4" vase	511	-10" vase
499	-6" bud vase	620	-5" flower pot (with attached saucer)
500	-5" vase		
501	-6" vase	1078	-4" candlestick
502	-6" vase	1266	-6.5" wall pocket

Ferella. 500-5" vase, brown; 507-9" vase, brown; 506-8" vase, brown. *Hoppe photograph.* **$500–600, $700–800, $700–800**

Ferella. 505-6" vase, red; 497-4" vase, red; 509-8" vase, red. *Courtesy of McAllister Auctions.* **$600–700, $400–500, $800–900**

Ferella. 511-10" vase, brown; 1266-6.5" wall pocket, raspberry. *Courtesy of McAllister Auctions.* **$950–1200, $1200–1500**

Ferella. 499-6" vase, red; 501-6" vase, red. *Shannon collection.* **$600–700, $700–800**

FLORANE

A Late Line, introduced ca. 1949

Factory Name(s): Florane

Collector Nickname(s): Commercial line (see Huxford, 1976); Nova (see Buxton, 1977); Etruscan (see Buxton, 1977); Florane II (see Buxton, 1977)

Style: Mid-Century Modern

Standard Color(s): Blue, green, or tan (these matte glazes are usually lined in tan, although sometimes the tan color is lined in green)

Typical Marks: Molded (raised-relief) marks, including "Roseville" (script), shape number, and size

With increasing interest in the Mid-Century Modern style, Florane can be expected to go up in value over the next few years. At this time, collectors seem to show only a mild interest in the line—perhaps due partly to confusion about the name.

Some Florane shapes are fairly traditional. Most have a stylized design, and many of these are biomorphic, making them appropriate for any "Fabulous Fifties" interior. Several planters feature an impressed spiraling "nova" motif. Three vases in the shape of a flower pot have a stepped contour roughly comparable to a heartbeat or brainwave pattern.

There are no known factory stock pages. The Florane brochure shows 24 items in the line:

Shape No.	Description	Reference/Notes
50	-8" jardiniere	
51	-10" jardiniere	
52	-12" jardiniere	
60	-6" bowl	
61	-9" planter	
62	-8" bowl	
63	-10" bowl	
64	-12" bowl	
71	-4" vase, flower pot shape	
72	-5" vase, flower pot shape	
73	-6" vase, flower pot shape	
79	-7" bud vase	
80	-6" vase	
81	-7" vase	
82	-9" vase	
83	-11" vase	
84	-14" vase	
90	-4" planter	Bomm 242
91	-6" window box	Bomm 242
92	-6" planter	Bomm 242
93	-7" square bowl	Bomm 242
94	-8" window box	Bomm 242
95	-10" rectangular bowl	
96	-10" window box	Bomm 242

Florane. 80-6" vase, tan; 81-7" vase, tan; 71-4" vase, flowerpot shape, tan. *Hoppe photograph.* **$60–75, $75–95, $60–75**

Florane. 71-4" vase, flower pot shape, blue; 92-6" planter, square, blue. *Fairfield collection.* **$75–95, $60–75**

Florane. 51-10" sand jar, medium matte green. *Bassett collection.* **$150–200.** Perhaps this unusual coloring was a short-lived and early glaze treatment for Florane.

Florane. 96-10" window box, green; 90-4" planter, green. *Hoppe photograph.* **$60–75 (each)**

LORENTINE

A Middle Period Line, introduced in 1924

Factory Name(s): Florentine

Collector Nickname(s): Florentine II (see Huxford, 1976); Ivory Florentine (see Huxford, 1980); Florentine I and II (see Bomm, 1998)

Style: Italianate

Standard Color(s): Brown, and blonde

Typical Marks: Some examples are unmarked. Others have a blue inkstamp Rv logo.

When introduced to the trade, Florentine was said to make "a very fine appearance. As might be imagined from the name, the effect is that of Italian renaissance, with all its rich ornamentation. The ware shows a brown and tan ground with green and touches of rose" (trade notice, *Pottery, Glass and Brass Salesman,* May 8, 1924: 17). Along the shoulder are sculptural clusters of fruit and leaves, hand decorated in natural colors.

Florentine remained a popular Roseville product for many years; new shapes were undoubtedly added from time to time. The blonde coloring was probably introduced between 1933 and 1935. (Compare the lettering of "Florentine" on the only "blonde Florentine" stock page to the lettering used on the Morning Glory, Orian, and Tourmaline pages.) Both colors have a following, although prices for Florentine remain relatively moderate.

There are 55 Florentine shapes in the various factory stock pages:

FLORENTINE

Shape No.	Description	Reference/Notes
	-4" comport	
	comport	
	-2.5" flower block	
	-3.5" flower block	
	-3" ashtray	
	-8" comport	
	-4.5" double bud vase, gate shape	
	-6" double bud vase, gate shape	
5	-4" bowl	
5	-5" bowl	
5	-6" bowl	
5	-7" bowl	
6	-4" bowl	
6	-5" bowl	
6	-6" bowl	
6	-7" bowl	
0	-4" vase	
3	-6" vase	

Shape No.	Description	Reference/Notes
229	-6" vase	
230	-8" vase	
231	-8" vase	
232	-10" vase	
233	-10" vase	
234	-12" vase	
252	-6" vase	
253	-6" vase	
254	-7" vase	
255	-8" vase	
257	-5" ferner	
257	-6" ferner	
258	-5" ferner	
258	-6" ferner	
320	-6" basket	
321	-7" basket	
322	-8" basket	
337	-6" hanging basket	
337	-7" hanging basket	
339	-5" hanging basket	
602	-5" jardiniere	
602	-6" jardiniere	
602	-7" jardiniere	
602	-8" jardiniere	
602	-9" jardiniere	
602	-9" jardiniere & pedestal	
602	-10" jardiniere & pedestal	
763	-20" umbrella stand	
764	-14" x 11" sand jar	Bomm 383
1049	-8" candlestick	
1050	-10" candlestick	
1062	-4" candlestick	
1230	-10" wall pocket	
1231	-12" wall pocket	
1238	-7" wall pocket	
1238	-8" wall pocket	
1239	-7" wall pocket	

Florentine. 602-6" jardiniere, blonde; 233-10" vase, blonde. *Hoppe photograph.* **$150–200, $250–300**

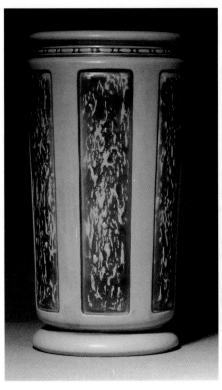

Florentine. 253-6" vase, brown; 234-12" vase, brown; 232-10" vase, blonde. *Shannon collection.* **$125–150, $325–375, $275–325**

Florentine. 125-4" bowl, two open square handles; 231-8" vase; 229-6" vase; 232-10" vase; 17-3" ashtray; 1049-8" candlestick; 1050-10" candlestick; 6-4.25" comport; 255-8" vase. *Fairfield collection.* **$75–95, $250–300, $125–175, $275–325, $95–125, $125–150, $150–175, $125–150, $200–250.** Note the different shades possible in the brown coloring of Florentine.

Florentine. 298-18.5" umbrella stand, blonde. *Hoppe photograph.* **$500–600.** Note: this example of Florentine is unusual in having no fruit cascades.

FOXGLOVE

A Late Line, introduced in 1942

Factory Name(s): Foxglove
Style: Realistic, many shapes have angular handles or other details
Standard Color(s): Blue, Petal Green ("green"), or Red ("pink")
Typical Marks: Molded (raised-relief) marks, including "Roseville" (script), shape number, and size

Roseville advertised their "delicate" Foxglove pattern as having "fragile" or an "enchanting wilderness beauty," the floral designs being "gently sculptured on smooth new shapes" (*Gift and Art Buyer,* December 1941: 2; and January 1942: 2). The flowers were colored pink on the Red pieces, and either white, pink, or yellow on the Blue or Petal Green pieces. Some shapes have distinctly Art Deco touches.

Foxglove is a popular but moderately priced pattern today, with higher prices going to the pink and blue colors. Although Roseville advertised that there were 55 Foxglove shapes, only 53 are shown in the factory stock pages:

Foxglove. 373-8" basket, green; 375-12" basket, pink; 374-10" basket, blue. *Shannon collection.* **$225–275, $400–500, $350–400**

FOXGLOVE

Shape No.	Description	Shape No.	Description
2	-10" comport	164	-8" cornucopia
4	-6.5" ewer	165	-5" flower holder
5	-10" ewer	166	-6" cornucopia
6	-15" ewer	373	-8" basket
10	-5.5" bookend	374	-10" basket
42	-4" vase	375	-12" basket
43	-6" vase	418	-4" vase
44	-6" vase	418	-6" rose bowl
45	-7" vase	419	-6" tray
46	flower frog	420	-10" tray
46	-7" vase	421	-10" bowl
47	-8" vase	422	-10" bowl
48	-8" vase	423	-12" bowl
49	-9" vase	424	-14" tray
50	-9" vase	425	-14" bowl
51	-10" vase	426	-6" conch shell
52	-12" vase	466	-5" hanging basket
53	-14" vase	659	-3" jardiniere
54	-15" vase	659	-4" jardiniere
55	-16" vase	659	-5" jardiniere
56	-18" vase	659	-6" jardiniere
159	-5" candlestick	659	-8" jardiniere & pedestal
160	-4.5" double bud vase, gate shape	659	-10" jardiniere & pedestal
		660	-5" flower pot and saucer
161	-6" vase	1149	candlestick
162	-8" vase	1150	-4.5" candlestick
163	-6" cornucopia	1292	-8" wall pocket

Foxglove. 47-8" divided vase, green; 53-14" vase, pink. *Fairfield collection.* **$200–250, $600–700**

Foxglove. 44-6" vase, blue; 45-7" vase, blue; 161-6" vase, blue. *Hoppe photograph.* **$150–175, $175–200, $150–175**

Foxglove. 55-16" vase, green.
Courtesy of McAllister Auctions.
$800–900

FREESIA

A Late Line, introduced in 1945

Factory Name(s): Freesia; Freesia Assortment
Style: Realistic
Standard Color(s): Delft Blue ("blue"), Tangerine ("brown"), or Tropical Green ("green")
Typical Marks: Molded (raised-relief) marks, including "Roseville" (script), shape number, and size

Even though wartime conditions delayed the first deliveries until after June 1945, that year Roseville advertised the new Freesia line in every issue of *Gift and Art Buyer.* The factory's survival depended heavily then upon keeping the Roseville name in the mind of buyers. "Freesia, so new, so lovely. A bit different, too," one advertisement read. "The striking Freesia motif tends toward the modern, while the three basic colors … display new depth and richness" (*Gift and Art Buyer,* March 1945: 2).

Fortunately, the factory had again offered a line that would sell. Just as Clematis was the only new product line Roseville was able to introduce in 1944, Freesia would be the only new offering of 1945. Moderately priced for today's collectors, Freesia has a textured background beneath the spray of freesia blossoms and has admirers for all three colors.

Although Roseville advertised that there were 48 Freesia shapes, only 47 appear in the factory stock pages:

FREESIA

Shape No.	Description	Shape No.	Description
4	-8" cookie jar	197	-6" cornucopia
6	-C creamer	198	-8" cornucopia
6	-S sugar	199	-6" fan vase
6	-T teapot	200	-7" fan vase
7	-10" comport	390	-7" basket
15	bookend	391	-8" basket
19	-6" ewer	392	-10" basket
20	-10" ewer	463	-5" vase
21	-15" ewer	464	-6" bowl
117	-6" vase	465	-8" bowl
118	-6" vase	466	-10" bowl
119	-7" vase	467	-10" bowl
120	-7" vase	468	-12" bowl
121	-8" vase	469	-14" bowl
122	-8" vase	471	-5" hanging basket
123	-9" vase	669	-4" jardiniere
124	-9" vase	669	-6" jardiniere
125	-10" vase	669	-8" jardiniere & pedestal
126	-10" vase	670	-5" flower pot and saucer
127	-12" vase	1160	-2" candlestick
128	-15" vase	1161	-4.5" candlestick
129	-18" vase	1296	-8" wall pocket
195	-7" bud vase	1392	-8" window box
196	-8" vase		

Freesia. 126-10" vase, brown; 128-15" vase, brown. *Hoppe collection.* **$200–250, $700–800**

Freesia. 121-8" vase, green; pair, 1160-2" candlesticks, blue; 390-7" basket, blue; 123-9" vase, green. *Courtesy of McAllister Auctions.* **$175–225, $95–125 (pair), $175–225, $225–275**

Freesia. 118-6" vase, brown; 200-7" fan vase, brown; 199-6" pillow vase, brown. *Hoppe collection.* **$125–175 (each)**

Freesia. 670-5" flower pot, separate saucer, green; 119-7" vase, blue. *Shannon collection.* **$175–225, $125–175**

FUCHSIA
A Middle Period Line, introduced in 1938

Factory Name(s): Fuchsia
Alternate Spelling(s): Fushia (see Clifford, 1968); Fuschia (see Alexander, 1970); Fuchia (see Buxton, 1977)
Style: Realistic, with an Art Deco feel
Standard Color(s): Blue, Brown, and Green
Typical Marks: Die-impressed marks, including "Roseville" (script), shape number, and size

The "brilliant colors" of Fuchsia continue to appeal to present-day collectors, who value all three variations. The bright red and white flowers make a pleasant contrast to the background colors chosen for this lovely pattern. Fuchsia shapes can have traditional rims, or these can have an occasional pleat or notch. A few bowl designs allow the Fuchsia leaves to rise slightly above the rest of the shape. Backgrounds have been textured in a very low relief.

For the summer of 1939, an ice-lip pitcher was added to the line (advertisement, *Gift and Art Buyer*, April 1939: 2), too late to make its way into the factory stock pages. Although the earliest Fuchsia advertisements mention 40 shapes, the stock pages show only 38:

FUCHSIA

Shape No.	Description	Shape No.	Description
37	flower frog	646	-5" vase
129	-6" cornucopia	891	-6" vase
346	-4" vase	892	-6" vase
347	-6" vase	893	-6" vase
348	-5" bowl	894	-7" vase
349	-8" bowl	895	-7" vase
350	-8" bowl	896	-8" pillow vase
350	-8" basket with built-in flower frog	897	-8" vase
		898	-8" vase
351	-10" basket	899	-9" vase
351	-10" bowl	900	-9" vase
352	-12" bowl	902	-10" ewer
353	-14" bowl	901	-10" vase
359	-5" hanging basket	903	-12" vase
645	-3" jardiniere	904	-15" vase
645	-4" jardiniere	905	-18" floor vase
645	-5" jardiniere	1132	-candlestick
645	-6" jardiniere	1133	-5" candlestick
645	-8" jardiniere & pedestal	1282	-8" wall pocket
645	-10" jardiniere & pedestal		

Fuchsia. 894-7" vase, brown; 902-10" ewer, blue. *Shannon collection.* **$200–250, $400–500**

Fuchsia. 645-4" jardiniere, green; 645-3" jardiniere, green. *Hoppe photograph.* **$175–225, $125–175**

Fuchsia. 900-9" vase, blue; 895-7" vase, brown; 899-9" vase, blue. *Auclair collection.* **$400–500, $200–250, $400–500**

Fuchsia. Three 1322 ice-lip pitchers, in blue, brown, and green. *Auclair collection.* **$600–700 (each)**

FUDJI

An Early Line, introduced by 1906

Factory Name(s): Rozane Fudji
Alternate Spelling(s): Fugi (see Clifford, 1968)
Style: Japonisme, or Art Nouveau
Standard Color(s): Various, as described below
Typical Marks: Unmarked. Some examples have a Rozane Ware wafer.

The Fudji line began life as a group of Rozane Royal shapes. Starting with Rozane Royal blanks as his "canvas," designer Gazo Foudji—born in Japan—first air-brushed background colors in shades of tan, light blue, and gray. Decorators were taught how to use a fine-tipped brush, and working carefully, to apply drops of thick brightly colored enamel glazes—usually aquamarine, blue, or red—to complete the decorations.

A 1905 trade notice indicates that many of these decorators may have been "native Japanese artists," undoubtedly trained by Foudji personally (*China, Glass and Lamps,* March 18, 1905). This trade notice calls the line "Fujiyama," but (as explained below) Roseville works marked Fujiyama—in contrast to the regular Fudji line—are believed to be the work of Gazo Foudji himself.

There are no known factory stock pages for Fudji. The 1906 Rozane Ware catalog shows 16 shapes, which are located in Bomm under "Rozane–Fudjiyama/Fudgi."

Right:
Fudji. 961-10.5" vase, Rozane Ware wafer, artist monogram EN (or NE), die-impressed 8. *Nickel and Horvath collection.* **$2000–2500**

Below:
Fudji. 971-9" vase, Rozane Ware wafer, artist monogram SG (or GS), die-impressed 8; 961-10.5" vase, artist monogram EN (or NE), die-impressed 7. *Courtesy of McAllister Auctions.* **$1500–1800, $1800–2200**

FUDJI

Shape No.	Description	Shape No.	Description
892	-8.25" vase	975	-6.5" bud vase
893	-12.5" vase	982	-8.75" bud vase
961	-10.5" vase	R3	-10.5" vase
970	-10" bud vase	R5	-10.25" vase
971	-9" vase	R6	-8.25" vase
972	-8" vase	R12	-8" vase
973	-11.5" vase	R14	-8.25" vase
974	-11.5" vase	R15	-10.5" vase

Left:
Fudji. R6-8.75" vase. *Shannon collection.* **$1500–1800**

Right:
Fudji. R5-10.25" vase; 972-8" vase, both decorated as shown in 1906 catalog, both marked with Rozane Ware wafer. *Hoppe collection.* **$1800–2200, $1500–1800**

FUJIYAMA

An Early Line, introduced in 1905

Factory Name(s): Unknown (probably Fujiyama)
Style: Japonisme, or Art Nouveau
Standard Color(s): Same as for Fudji
Typical Marks: This line can be definitively identified only by the presence of a distinctive inkstamp reading "Fujiyama" (in artistic script-like lettering). Unmarked examples can be "attributed" to Fujiyama, but are more likely to be Fudji.

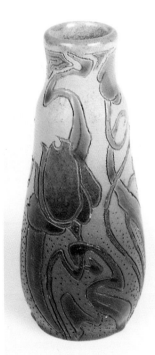

Fujiyama. 980-5.75" vase, inkstamp "Fujiyama." *Nickel and Horvath collection.* **$1200–1500**

Little is known about the rare Roseville pieces marked "Fujiyama." As mentioned above, Japanese-born artist and designer Gazo Foudji is believed to have decorated them himself. As Foudji's 1917 obituary indicates, this artist made many important contributions to American decorative arts. In the United States, his career seems to have begun in about 1904, at Weller Pottery, where Foudji created a line similar to Roseville Fudji, but spelled Fudzi. After leaving Roseville (about 1907), Foudji appears to have studied in Europe, at some time being named "a fellow of the Beaux Arts."

Next Foudji was "associated with the Tiffany Studios in New York and was later chief designer for Duffner & Kimberley" (*Pottery, Glass and Brass Salesman*, January 4, 1917: 9). At the time of his death from heart failure, Foudji was chief designer and decorator for the Jefferson Glass Company of Follansbee, West Virginia. The obituary reassured the trade that, at Jefferson Glass Co., Foudji had "gathered around him a force of nearly a score of Japanese artists who worked under him and who will of course, now carry on the work which he so ably started."

There are no known factory stock pages for Fujiyama. Count yourself lucky to find an example you can afford.

Fujiyama. 969-12" vase, inkstamp "Fujiyama." *Nickel and Horvath collection.* **$1800–2200**

FUTURA

A Middle Period Line, introduced in 1928

Factory Name(s): Futura

Style: Art Deco

Standard Color(s): Various, usually a single standard coloring for each shape. Some are matte glazes, others glossy.

Typical Marks: Paper labels. (These could be lost, leaving the piece unmarked.) Some examples have a hand-written (crayon) shape number.

Monsen (1995) offers collectors the most thorough discussion of Futura anyone could want. Introduced in 1928, the Futura line is widely viewed as incorporating several of the chief archetypes of Art Deco in American ceramics. "Done in the modern manner, they exhibit the vogue of today and breathe the spirit of tomorrow ... all with the youthful verve and daring of these our times," reads the November 1928 advertisement in *House Beautiful*. In the months to come, Roseville called Futura "fascinating," "dashing," "happily distinctive," "exquisite," "intriguing"—language that still rings true to every Futura lover.

It is not difficult to see why collectors are enamored with this line. There is a Futura piece for almost every color scheme—in various shades of blue, brown, gray, green, pink, purple, tan, and yellow. Some pieces feature stylized low-relief floral motifs; others are purely geometrical.

After the October 1929 stock market crash, buyers worried about the long-term "livability" of new purchases. By early 1930, Futura had lost its appeal. Today, Futura has such a following that collectors have developed nicknames for most designs. The factory stock pages show 78 different Futura shapes:

FUTURA

Shape No.	Description
5	-2.5" flower block ("Little Round Frog")
5	-3.5" flower block ("Big Round Frog")
81	-5" x 1.5" x 5" pillow vase ("Blue Sunray")
82	-6" fan vase ("Blue Fan")
85	-4" pillow vase ("2-Pole Pink Pillow Vase")
187	-8" bowl ("Balloons Bowl")
188	-8" bowl ("Aztec Bowl")
189	4" x 6" vase ("Sand Toy")
190	-3.5" x 6" vase ("Blue Box")
191	-8" planter ("Square Box")
194	-5" bowl ("Little Flying Saucer," or "Ashtray")
195	-10" bowl ("Flying Saucer")
196	-12" x 5" x 3.5" bowl with separate flower frog ("Sailboat")
197	-6" planter ("Half-Egg")
198	-5" planter ("Hibachi")
344	-5" hanging basket ("Little Hanging Basket")
344	-6" hanging basket ("Big Hanging Basket")
376	-15" x 4" x 6" window box ("Window Box")
380	-6" vase ("Torch")
381	-6" vase ("Beer Mug")
382	-7" vase ("Telescope")
383	-8" vase ("Little Blue Triangle")
384	-8" vase ("Ball Bottle")
385	-8" vase ("Pleated Star")
386	-8" vase ("Jukebox")

Shape No.	Description
387	-7" vase ("Bamboo Leaf Ball")
388	-9" vase ("Big Blue Triangle")
389	-9" vase ("Emerald Urn")
390	-10" bud vase ("Christmas Tree")
391	-10" vase ("Black Flame")
392	-10" vase ("Shooting Star")
393	-12" vase ("Four Ball Vase")
394	-12" vase ("Bomb")
395	-10" vase ("Stepped Urn")
396	-5.5" vase ("Chalice")
397	-6" vase ("Square Cone")
398	-6.5" vase ("Green Twist")
399	-7" vase ("Red Vee")
400	-7" vase ("Ostrich Egg")
401	-8" vase ("Cone")
402	-8" vase ("Milk Carton")
403	-7" vase ("Spittoon")
404	-8" vase ("Balloons Globe")
405	-7.5" vase ("Spaceship")
406	-8" vase ("Beehive")
407	-9" vase ("Green Fan")
408	-10" vase ("Seagull")
409	-9" vase ("Football Urn")
410	-12" vase ("Table Leg")
411	-14" vase ("Arches")
412	-9" vase ("Tank")
421	-5" vase ("Brown Stump")
422	-6" bud vase ("Two-Pole Bud Vase")
423	-6" pillow vase ("Tombstone")
424	-7" vase ("Stepped Egg")
425	-8" vase ("Hexagon Twist")
426	-8" vase ("Winged Vase")
427	-8" vase ("Mauve Thistle")
428	-8" vase ("Egg with Leaves")
429	-9" vase ("Purple Crocus")
430	-9" vase ("Chinese Pillow")
431	-10" vase ("Falling Bullet")
432	-10" vase ("Space Capsule")
433	-10" vase ("Pine Cone")
434	-10" vase ("Michelin Man")
435	-10" vase ("Elephant Leg")
436	-12" vase ("Chinese Bronze")
437	-12" vase ("Weeping Tulip")
438	-15" vase ("Tall Teasel")
616	-6" jardiniere
616	-7" jardiniere
616	-8" jardiniere
616	-9" jardiniere
616	-10" jardiniere & pedestal
1072	-4" candlestick ("Aztec Ladies")
1073	-4" candlestick ("Candlesticks with Leaves")
1075	-4" candlestick ("Flying Saucer Candlesticks")
1261	-8" wall pocket

Futura. 403-7" vase; 400-7" vase.
Hoppe photograph. **$800–900,**
$600–700

Futura. 616-9" jardiniere, brown; 616-6" jardiniere, gray. *Courtesy of McAllister Auctions.* **$600–700, $400–500.**

Futura. 85-4" pillow vase; 382-7" vase. *Shannon collection.* **$300–400, $375–450**

Futura. 423-6" pillow vase; 429-9" vase. *Hoppe photograph.* **$375–450, $950–1200**

Futura. 384-8" vase, bottle shape; 389-9" vase; 385-8" vase, star shape. *Shannon collection.* **$500–600, $800–900, $500–600**

Futura. 402-8" vase; 408-10" vase; 401-8" vase. *Hoppe photograph.* **$550–650, $950–1200, $700–800**

GARDEN POTTERY

A Middle Period Line, introduced in 1927

Factory Name(s): Garden Pottery
Collector Nickname(s): Garden Line (see Bomm, 1998)
Style: Italianate
Standard Color(s): Gray bisque
Typical Marks: Unknown

Roseville's line of Garden Pottery may not have been marked. No pieces could be located for photography, nor any collector claiming to own an example. According to the factory's New York office directory listings in *Crockery and Glass Journal,* the line was available from 1927 through 1930 or later.

The factory stock pages show 17 shapes. (The page showing bird baths and sand jars is dated January 31, 1929.) The wares have an Italianate look and appear to have been glazed in gray bisque. Perhaps winter was too harsh for them to survive. With no market history, distrust any price guide that speculates about their value!

GARDEN POTTERY

Shape No.	Description	Shape No.	Description
1	-23" bird bath and pedestal	610	-12" jardiniere
2	-26" bird bath and pedestal	610	-14" jardiniere
2	-26" bird bath and pedestal	611	-8" jardiniere
3	-31" bird bath and pedestal	611	-10" jardiniere
3	-31" bird bath and pedestal	611	-12" jardiniere
10	-14" x 12" jardiniere	611	-14" jardiniere
11	-18" x 12" sand jar	612	-8" jardiniere
610	-8" jardiniere	612	-10" jardiniere
610	-10" jardiniere	612	-12" jardiniere
		612	-14" jardiniere

GARDENIA

A Late Line, introduced in 1950

Factory Name(s): Gardenia
Style: Realistic, with some shapes having Art Deco features
Standard Color(s): Golden Tan ("brown"), Sea Foam Green ("green"), or Silver Haze Grey ("gray")
Typical Marks: Molded (raised-relief) marks, including "Roseville" (script), shape number, and size

In 1950, Roseville described Gardenia as "a new design of truly thrilling beauty ... large, white gardenias and green leaves on three softly blended background colors" (advertisement, *Gift and Art Buyer,* January 1950:). Most shapes are symmetrical, and there are few design surprises in the line. The 630-12" bowl is exceptional, having a rim that is upswept into a sculptural feather-like shape at each end.

Collectors tend to prefer the brown colors, although gray is a more typically 1950s color choice. Although the original advertising mentions 40 shapes, only 39 are shown in the factory brochure:

Gardenia. Pair, 651-2" candlesticks, green; 626-6" bowl, green. *Hoppe collection.* **$75–95 (pair), $125–150**

GARDENIA

Shape No.	Description	Shape No.	Description
600	-4" vase	652	-4.5" candlestick
601	-6" vase	656	-3" planter
605	-8" jardiniere & pedestal	657	-3.5" rose bowl
608	-8" basket	658	-8" window box
609	-10" basket	659	bookend
610	-12" basket	661	-5" hanging basket
616	-6" ewer	666	-8" wall pocket
617	-10" ewer	668	-8" window box
618	-15" ewer	669	-12" window box
621	-6" cornucopia	681	-6" vase
622	-8" double cornucopia	682	-6" vase
626	-6" bowl	683	-8" vase
627	-8" bowl	684	-8" vase
628	-10" bowl	685	-10" vase
629	-10" bowl	686	-10" vase
630	-12" bowl	687	-12" vase
631	-14" tray	688	-12" vase
632	-14" bowl	689	-14" vase
641	-5" bowl	690	-16" vase
651	candlestick		

Gardenia. 685-10" vase, gray; 683-8" vase, brown. *Fairfield collection.* **$175–225, $150–200**

Gardenia. 684-8" vase, tan; 656-3" vase, gray; 630-12" window box, gray. *Shannon collection.* **$125–150, $75–95, $175–225**

Gardenia. 682-6" vase, green; 657-3.5" vase, green; 681-6" vase, green. *Hoppe collection.* **$95–125, $75–95, $95–125**

HEXAGON

A Middle Period Line, introduced in 1925

Factory Name(s): Rosecraft Hexagon
Collector Nickname(s): Hexagon (see Monsen, 1995)
Standard Color(s): Antique Green with Grey lining ("green"), Brown with Tangerine lining ("brown"), or Royal Blue ("blue")
Typical Marks: Most examples have a blue inkstamp Rv logo, although some are unmarked. (In other cases, the inkstamp mark may be obscured by a thick glaze.)

In 1925, the 16-piece Hexagon "showing of gift articles" was said to have "a unique character for the Roseville concern, as it never before has ever put on such a popular price line of merchandise" (trade notice, *Pottery, Glass and Brass Salesman*, August 20, 1925: 17). As the name suggests, Hexagon pieces are "hexagonal in shape with sharp edges." Each piece has an impressed design that may be a stylized representation of a torch and flame.

Today, the glossy blue pieces are extremely hard to find and therefore slightly more expensive. Brown is more plentiful than green, and perhaps is in somewhat less demand as a result.

The only known factory stock page shows 15 Hexagon shapes. In Bomm, they are located under "Rosecraft–Hexagon."

Hexagon. 272-10" vase, green. *Auclair collection.* **$500–600**

Shape No.	Description	Shape No.	Description
3	-7" vase	266	-4" vase
47	-5" double bud vase, gate shape	267	-5" vase
		268	-6" vase
134	-4" bowl	269	-6" vase
135	-4" bowl	270	-8" vase
136	-5" bowl	271	-8" vase
137	-6" bowl	272	-10" vase
138	-4" rose bowl	1240	-8" wall pocket

Hexagon. 271-8" vase, green; 267-5" vase, brown. *Shannon collection.* **$300–400, $200–250**

Hexagon. Three examples of 269-6" vase, in glossy blue; brown; green. *Fairfield collection.* **$375–450, $225–275, $250–300**

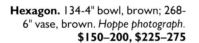

Hexagon. 134-4" bowl, brown; 268-6" vase, brown. *Hoppe photograph.* **$150–200, $225–275**

IMPERIAL (Glazes)
A Middle Period Line, introduced in 1930

Factory Name(s): Imperial

Collector Nickname(s): Imperial Second (see Clifford, 1968); Imperial II (see Purviance and Schneider, 1970)

Style: Art Deco, or Arts and Crafts

Standard Color(s): Several standard matte or semigloss glazes, as shown in the illustrations

Typical Marks: Paper labels. (These could be lost, leaving the piece unmarked.) Some examples have a hand-written (crayon) shape number.

The multicolor palette and attractive textures of Imperial (Glazes) have won over many collectors. In 1930, Roseville emphasized this line's less tangible qualities:

Charm … is in many things … gay sunlight on southern seas … irresistible strains of a Wagnerian symphony … cozy nook by the fireside when the wind is blustering…. In Roseville Pottery there is a charm that endures … permanently wrought by artists who love their craft. Glorious shapes, soft blending of twilight tints, subtle

beauty of heirlooms … (ellipses in original advertisement, *House and Garden,* March 1930: 124).

Many devotees of the Arts and Crafts movement appreciate Roseville's achievement in Imperial (Glazes). Yet the line's generally bright colors and strong tonal contrasts are more typical of the Art Deco style. Another factory advertisement acknowledges these twin influences: "We like to possess things that are smart … voguish … correct … beautiful. We like to enjoy them. The recent Roseville Pottery designs meet these ideals, with classic and Early American distinctiveness" (*Good Housekeeping,* April 1930).

Some shapes have low-relief carvings representing stylized flora. Others are adorned only by their glazes, or by impressed lines intended to represent the finger marks left from throwing pottery on a wheel. A few pieces—notably the 478-8" vase—were sometimes in fact thrown, not molded!

Caution: Do not confuse the Imperial (Glazes) and the Earlam versions of the 1263 wall pocket, a mistake that occurs in Huxford (1976).

The factory stock pages show 34 shapes in the Imperial (Glazes) line.

IMPERIAL (GLAZES)

Shape No.	Description	Shape No.	Description
20	ashtray	473	-7.5" vase
199	-4.5" vase	474	-7" vase
200	-4.5" vase	475	-9" vase
201	-4.5" vase	476	-8" vase
202	-6" planter	477	-9.5" vase
203	-5" vase	478	-8" vase
204	-8" bowl	479	-8" vase
205	-8" bowl	480	-8" vase
206	-8" planter	481	-8.5" vase
207	-12" x 8" bowl	482	-11" vase
466	-4" vase	483	-10" vase
467	-5" vase	484	-11" vase
468	-5" vase	1076	-2.5" candlestick
469	-8" vase	1077	-4" candlestick
470	-5.5" vase	1262	wall pocket
471	-7" vase	1263	wall pocket
472	-7" vase	1264	wall pocket

Imperial (Glazes). 481-8.5" vase, pink and green; 479-8" vase, turquoise and yellow. *Hoppe photograph.* **$500–600, $400–500**

Imperial (Glazes). 9.5" ashtray, blue and yellow. *Hoppe photograph.* **$225–275**

Imperial (Glazes). 201-4" urn, turquoise; 477-9.5" vase, dark blue; 468-5" vase, olive green and turquoise. *Hoppe photograph.* **$275–325, $500–600, $225–275**

Top left:
Imperial (Glazes). 202-6" bowl, pink and green; 206-8" bowl, pink and green. *Hoppe photograph.* **$950–1200, $325–375**

Center left:
Imperial (Glazes). 482-11" vase, blue and yellow; 484-11" vase, blue and yellow. *Hoppe photograph.* **$750–950 (each)**

Left:
Imperial (Glazes). 478-8" vase, brown and gold; 471-7" vase, green and maroon. *Hoppe photograph.* **$500–600, $400–500**

142

IMPERIAL (Textured)
A Middle Period Line, introduced in 1921

Factory Name(s): Imperial

Collector Nickname(s): Imperial First (see Clifford, 1968); Imperial I (see Purviance and Schneider, 1970)

Style: Rustic

Standard Color(s): One standard coloring, as described below

Typical Marks: Unmarked. Some have a blue inkstamp mark giving the shape number and size (only).

Like Blackberry, Imperial (Textured) has an irregularly modeled background—which may represent bark—glazed in semigloss shades of green and brown. Here the low-relief decoration is a stylized knot of vine, with a single green leaf, brown vine, and purple berries (or grapes).

Neither the name nor the decoration of this line is easily interpreted. Perhaps for this reason, Imperial (Textured) has made relatively fewer converts than Blackberry, Dogwood (Textured), or other comparable Middle Period lines. Yet this pattern is innovative and intriguing. Certain rather bizarre shapes foreshadow the Mid-Century Modern style of the years after World War II. Give this line another look, and allow it time to grow on you.

IMPERIAL (TEXTURED)

Shape No.	Description	Shape No.	Description
29	-8" triple bud vase	333	-6" hanging basket
30	-8.5" triple bud vase	333	-7" hanging basket
31	-9" bud vase	370	-10" window box
71	-7" bowl	370	-12" window box
71	-8" bowl	591	-6" jardiniere
150	-8" vase	591	-7" jardiniere
151	-8" vase	591	-8" jardiniere
152	-8" vase	591	-9" jardiniere
156	-12" vase	591	-10" jardiniere
162	-18" floor vase	591	-10" jardiniere & pedestal
163	-18" floor vase	591	-12" jardiniere
251	-6" ferner	759	-20" umbrella stand
251	-7" ferner	1221	-7" wall pocket
252	-7" footed ferner	1222	-9" wall pocket
291	-7" basket	1223	-10" wall pocket

Right:
Imperial (Textured). 14" floor vase; 12" lamp. *Shannon collection.*
$400–500, $250–300

Imperial (Textured). 12.25" basket, unmarked. *Courtesy of Treadway Gallery.*
$300–400

Right:
Imperial (Textured). 8" basket; 12.5" basket; 291-7" basket. *Shannon collection.*
$200–250, $275–325, $175–225

Imperial (Textured). 29-8" triple bud vase; 10.75" basket; 71-8" bowl. *Shannon collection.* **$175–225, $225–275, $125–150**

IRIS

A Late Line, introduced in 1939

Factory Name(s): Iris
Style: Realistic, with some shapes having Art Deco features
Standard Color(s): Blue, Brown, and Coral ("pink")
Typical Marks: Die-impressed marks, including "Roseville" (script), shape number, and size

According to the factory, Iris captured "the rare natural beauty of this graceful flower" so well "that it [was] acclaimed as one of the most successful decorative motifs introduced by ROSEVILLE in years" (advertisements, *Gift and Art Buyer,* January 1939: 2; and February 1939: 2). Part of this popularity may stem from the popularity of the flower itself among gardeners.

Today, the pink and blue colors are usually valued more highly than the brown. Of particular interest—from the viewpoint of design—is the floriform Iris candlestick (shape 1134). As usual, there are collectors avidly seeking the baskets and the wall pocket too.

Although Iris was advertised as a line of 45 shapes, the factory stock pages show only 43:

IRIS

Shape No.	Description	Shape No.	Description
2	wall shelf	647	-10" jardiniere & pedestal
5	bookend	648	-5" flower pot and saucer
38	flower frog	914	-4" vase
130	-4" vase	915	-5" vase
131	-6" cornucopia	916	-6" vase
132	-8" cornucopia	917	-6" vase
354	-8" basket	918	-7" bud vase
355	-10" basket	919	-7" vase
357	-4" vase	920	-7" vase
358	-6" vase	921	-8" vase
359	-5" bowl	922	-8" pillow vase
360	-5" hanging basket	923	-8" vase
360	-6" bowl	924	-9" vase
361	-8" bowl	925	-9" vase
362	-10" bowl	926	-10" ewer
363	-12" bowl	927	-10" vase
364	-14" bowl	928	-12" vase
647	-3" jardiniere	929	-15" vase
647	-4" jardiniere	1134	candlestick
647	-5" jardiniere	1135	-4.5" candlestick
647	-6" jardiniere	1284	-8" wall pocket
647	-8" jardiniere & pedestal		

Iris. 926-10" ewer, pink; 919-7" vase, pink; 924-9" vase, pink. *Shannon collection.* **$275–350, $175–225, $250–300**

Iris. 914-4" vase, blue; 927-10" vase, blue; 916-6" vase, blue. *Hoppe photograph.* **$95–125, $325–375, $150–200**

Iris. 354-8" basket, tan; 130-4" vase, pink; 917-6" vase, tan. *Shannon collection.* **$275–350, $95–125, $150–200**

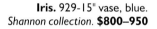

Iris. 929-15" vase, blue. *Shannon collection.* **$800–950**

IVORY

A Middle Period Line, introduced in 1932

Factory Name(s): Ivory

Collector Nickname(s): Ivory (New) [see Alexander, 1970]; Ivory II (see Huxford, 1976); Ivory, Second Line (see Huxford, 1976)

Style: Classical, or Art Deco

Standard Color(s): Matt ivory

Typical Marks: The earliest examples have paper or foil labels. (These could be lost, leaving the piece unmarked.) Some examples have a hand-written (crayon) shape number. Pieces made in 1936 or later have die-impressed marks, including "Roseville" (script), shape number, and size.

Few Roseville products earned higher praise than was given to Ivory in 1932:

> Roseville Pottery Co. has been noted for picking winners and they have turned to production on a new line of art pottery in white which already is proving its selling quality. Utter absence of color in pottery demands good shapes and Roseville has taken for this new line a number of models which proved successful in other years. Simplicity is the keynote to the new Roseville ware. The vases, jugs, bowls, console sets, pots and saucers which make up this line are all of them simple verging on classical design with the result that each piece in the series has individual beauty. In case you fear your customers might refuse to take anything but new shapes do not deceive yourself. As [industrial arts educator] Richard F. Bach [of the Metropolitan Museum of Art] says, it is effect madam is after. And it's effect she will get with this new line. Incidentally the pieces retail from 50 cents to $10, so that whether you are in the low or high price market you can find your level (trade notice, *Crockery and Glass Journal*, April 1932: 20).

New shapes were added from season to season. In the fall of 1934, some Volpato and Savona shapes were produced in Ivory. One reviewer commented, "Flutes that are highly suggestive of Doric columns play a considerable part in the embossment, which is completed by what might be described as an Adam interpretation of a Greek frieze motif" (trade notice, *Pottery, Glass and Brass Salesman*, October 18, 1934: 9). There followed a hanging basket (probably Matt Green shape 3645), said to be "noteworthy for the classic purity of its lines ... It has about it the appeal of a bit of Greek sculpture" (trade notice, *PGBS*, November 29, 1934: 8). Sometimes entirely new shapes were designed for the Ivory line, such as "an attractive little line of shell-shaped dishes set on tiny feet ... intended for ash receivers and candy and nut dishes." (These were soon produced in colored glazes too.)

In the fall of 1935, many new shapes were added to the Ivory line, including most (or all) of the Russco line. One reviewer noted, "For the modern demands that lovely Russco line that has such pleasing shapes is being offered in a plain white and a white with yellow and blue linings" (trade notices, *PGBS*, August 15, 1935: 7; and September 1935: 27; quotation from the latter).

For 1936 buyers, among the "outstanding new shapes" in Ivory were a 303-12.5" centerpiece, "an almost Pompeiian type of bowl, with a candle-stick inset at either end, thereby creating what is to all intents and purposes a one-piece console set" (*PGBS*, September 1936: 20). Other new offerings that fall included the dog figure, the lady flower frog, the first of the so-called "Crystal Green" shapes, and an Art Deco dealer sign.

In the fall of 1939, the rest of the so-called "Crystal Green" shapes were introduced, along with another group—based in part on Orian—that "have a smooth surface and are distinctive for their outstanding architectural form" (quotation from advertisement, *Gift and Art Buyer*, August 1939: 2; see also trade notice, page 20).

As Roseville pointed out in 1939, "IVORY will lend dignity and beauty to any interior. It will harmonize with all colors." Ivory's classic neutral color, abundant variety, sculptural shapes, moderate prices, and relative availability are bound to inspire new collector interest soon. A word to the wise: Buy low!

Altogether, the factory stock pages show 179 shapes in the Ivory line, not including 23 Luffa shapes that may also have been offered in Ivory. (The Luffa stock pages are not hand-tinted, like the rest.)

IVORY

Shape No.	Description	Reference/Notes
1	dog	
2	-4.75" bookend	
5	-7" vase (Volpato shape)	
12	-8" x 4.5" bowl (Volpato shape)	
14	-2.5" flower block (Donatello shape)	Bomm 126
14	-3.5" flower block (Donatello shape)	Bomm 126
14	-4" comport (Volpato shape)	
15	-3.5" flower block (Mostique shape, or older)	
17	-3" ashtray (Florentine shape)	
17	-4.5" flower block (Carnelian shape)	
24	-3.5" shell	
24	-5.5" shell	
24	-7.5" shell	
28	-9" lady flower frog	
44	-8" vase (Rosecraft shape)	
60	-6" bowl (Donatello shape)	Bomm 126
60	-8" bowl (Donatello shape)	Bomm 126
60	-10" bowl (Donatello shape)	Bomm 126
60	-12" bowl (Donatello shape)	Bomm 126
61	-6" bowl (Donatello shape)	Bomm 126
61	-8" bowl (Donatello shape)	Bomm 126
97	-3.5" x 5" vase (Volpato shape)	
99	-5" bowl (Volpato shape)	
103	-6" ginger jar	
105	-8" vase	
105	-12" x 9" bowl (Volpato shape)	
105	-14" x 9" bowl (Volpato shape)	
106	-7" cornucopia	
106	-9" cornucopia	
108	-6" vase (Russco shape)	
109	-8" vase (Russco shape)	
110	-7" cornucopia (Russco shape)	
111	triple cornucopia (Russco shape)	
113	-8" vase	Bomm 126
113	-10" vase	Bomm 126
113	-12" vase	Bomm 126
113	-15" vase	Bomm 126
115	-7" vase (Velmoss shape)	
115	-10" vase (Donatello shape)	Bomm 126
116	-6" vase (Donatello shape)	Bomm 126
119	-6" comport (Volpato shape)	
120	-8" x 5.5" vase (Volpato shape)	
126	-6" cornucopia (Pine Cone shape)	
152	-6" bowl (Carnelian shape)	
158	-5" vase (Rosecraft shape)	
159	-6" bowl (Carnelian shape)	
161	-7" bowl (Carnelian shape)	
167	-12" bowl (Carnelian shape)	
168	-10" bowl (Carnelian shape)	
183	-10" x 9" x 4" bowl (Savona shape)	

Shape No.	Description	Reference/Notes
191	-10" vase (Volpato shape)	
196	-12" x 5" x 3.5" bowl (Futura shape)	
207	-8" x 12" bowl (Imperial Glazes shape)	Misprinted as 277 in Ivory stock pages
209	-10" vase (Volpato shape)	
222	-12" vase (Savona shape)	
231	-4" comport	Bomm 126
231	-5" comport	Bomm 126
231	-6" comport	Bomm 126
232	-8" footed comport	Bomm 126
233	-8" basket (Donatello shape)	Bomm 126
236	-3" vase (Solid Colors shape)	
238	-5" vase (Solid Colors shape)	
249	-12" bowl (Topeo shape)	
259	-6" vase (Russco shape)	
260	-8" vase (Russco shape)	
266	-8" bowl (Velmoss shape)	
266	-12" bowl (Velmoss shape)	
267	-6" x 12" bowl	
272	-10" bowl (Orian shape)	
273	-12" x 5" x 4" bowl (Orian shape)	
274	-6" vase (Orian shape)	
275	-12" x 8" bowl (Orian shape, but not shown in Orian stock page)	
301	-10" bowl (Moderne shape)	
302	-14" x 6" bowl (Moderne shape)	
303	-13.5" centerpiece	
311	-7" vase (Rosecraft shape)	
314	-14" bowl	
315	-4" vase (Dawn shape)	
316	-10" vase (Rosecraft shape)	
317	-10" vase (Rosecraft shape)	Misprinted in Bomm (271) as shape 319
318	-8" vase (Rosecraft shape)	
327	-8" hanging basket	Bomm 126
335	-8" vase (Rosecraft shape)	
337	-10" basket (Russco shape)	
341	-5" vase (Tuscany shape)	
345	-8" vase (Tuscany shape)	
346	-9" vase (Tuscany shape)	
356	-8" basket	
364	-4.5" x 10.5" window box (Donatello shape)	
365	-6" bowl	
366	-7" bowl	
367	-8" bowl	
368	-10" bowl	
371	-6" vase (Savona shape)	
372	-6" vase (Savona shape)	
373	-8" vase (Savona shape)	
374	-8" vase (Savona shape)	
378	-3.5" x 10" window box	
467	-5" vase (Imperial Glazes shape)	
548	-4" planter (Matt Green shape)	
549	-4" planter (Matt Green shape)	
550	-4" jardiniere (Antique Matt Green shape)	
575	-4" jardiniere (Donatello shape)	
575	-5" jardiniere (Donatello shape)	
575	-6" jardiniere (Donatello shape)	
575	-8" jardiniere (Donatello shape)	
579	-6" vase (Donatello shape)	Bomm 126
579	-8" vase (Donatello shape)	Bomm 126
579	-10" vase (Donatello shape)	Bomm 126
580	-4" flower pot and saucer (Donatello shape)	

Shape No.	Description	Reference/Notes
580	-5" flower pot and saucer (Donatello shape)	
580	-6" flower pot and saucer (Donatello shape)	
585	-4" vase	
586	-8" vase	
617	-10" jardiniere & pedestal (Donatello shape)	
630	-4" planter	
630	-5" planter	
679	-6" vase	
694	-7" vase (Russco shape)	
695	-8" vase (Russco shape)	
696	-8" vase (Russco shape)	
697	-8" vase (Russco shape)	
698	-9" vase (Russco shape)	
699	-9" vase (Russco shape)	
701	-10" vase (Russco shape)	
702	-12" vase (Russco shape)	
703	-15" vase (Russco shape)	
722	-14" vase (Velmoss shape)	
733	-6" vase (Orian shape)	
734	-7" vase (Orian shape)	
735	-7" vase (Orian shape)	
736	-8" vase (Orian shape)	
737	-7" vase (Orian shape)	
738	-9" vase (Orian shape)	
739	-9" vase (Orian shape)	
740	-10" vase (Orian shape)	
741	-10" vase (Orian shape)	
742	-12" vase (Orian shape)	
743	-14" vase (Orian shape)	
836	-12" vase	
837	-14" vase	
930	-6" vase	
931	-6" vase	
932	-7" vase	
933	-7" vase	
934	-8" vase	
935	-8" vase	
936	-8" vase	
937	-9" vase	

Shape No.	Description	Reference/Notes
938	-9" vase	
939	-10" vase	
940	-10" vase	
941	-10" vase	
942	-8" vase	
943	-10" vase	
1011	candlestick	Bomm 126
1063	-3" candlestick (Carnelian shape)	
1065	-4" candlestick (Carnelian shape)	
1070	-3.5" candlestick (Savona shape)	
1093	-4" candlestick (Topeo shape)	
1095	4.5" double candelabra	
1096	-4" double candelabra	
1098	-4.5" candlestick (Russco shape)	
1101	-4.5" candlestick (Russco shape)	
1108	-4.5" candlestick (Orian shape)	Misprinted as 1103 in Ivory pages
1111	-4.5" candlestick (Moderne shape)	
1112	-5.5" triple candelabra (Moderne shape)	
1114	-2" candlestick	
1115	-6.5" triple candelabra	
1116	-6.25" quintuple candelabra	
1122	5.5" candlestick	
1212	-12" wall pocket (Donatello shape)	Bomm 126
1273	-8" wall pocket (Pine Cone shape)	
1307	pitcher (Donatello shape)	Bomm 126
1315	-15" ewer (Carnelian shape)	
3645	-5" hanging basket (Matt Green shape)	
A602	-8" jardiniere & pedestal (Florentine shape)	
A602	-10" jardiniere & pedestal (Florentine shape)	
A764	-10" x 14" sand jar (Florentine shape)	

Ivory. 115-7" bud vase, Velmoss shape; 158-5" urn, Rosecraft shape; 345-8" basket, Dawn shape. *Hoppe photograph.* **$75–95, $95–125, $125–150**

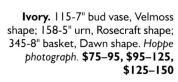

Ivory. 679-6" vase (also a Tourmaline shape); 378-3.5" x 9" window box. *Hoppe photograph.* **$75–95, $150–175**

Ivory. 1-6.5" figurine, reclining dog. *Shannon collection.* **$400–500.** This charming design is one of Roseville's very few true sculptures—having a decorative, but not a utilitarian, function.

Ivory. 575-4" jardiniere, Donatello shape; 346-9" vase, Tuscany shape. *Hoppe photograph.* **$75–95, $95–125**

Ivory. 371-6" vase, Volpato shape; 7.5" basket (shape number illegible), Crystal Green shape; 236-3" bowl, Solid Colors shape. *Private collection.* **$75–95, $125–150, $75–95**

Left:
Ivory (Blue Lined). 111 triple cornucopia, Russco shape. *Courtesy of McAllister Auctions.* **$200–250**

Ivory. 28-9" flower holder (or "flower frog"), depicting a draped female figure. *Scheytt collection.* **$750–950**

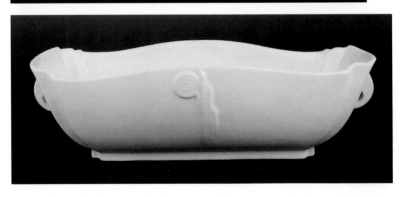

Ivory. 302-14" window box, Moderne shape. *Merritt collection.* **$150–175**

IXIA

A Middle Period Line, introduced in 1937

Factory Name(s): Ixia
Style: Art Deco
Standard Color(s): Coral ("pink"), green, and yellow
Typical Marks: Die-impressed marks, including "Roseville" (script), shape number, and size

By October 1937, when Ixia was introduced, Roseville had dubbed its products "The Fastest Selling Pottery in America." (Similar comments were made about Roseville in the trade notices reporting on the company's 1930s lines, particularly Ivory.)

The flowers of Ixia appear realistic enough, but there may be no real-life counterpart to the dainty bell-shaped blooms. Although many shapes feature a smooth, round rim, many Ixia shapes have angular elements. Buttress-like handles abound; or handles may suggest a pair of wings held poised before a flight.

Most collectors are happy with a few choice examples of Ixia. Prices are moderate enough that one might attempt reassembling the entire line!

Forty shapes were introduced for the Ixia line, but the factory stock pages show only 38:

Ixia. 853-6" vase, yellow; 864-12" vase, yellow; 325-5" bowl, yellow. *Hoppe photograph.* **$125–150, $275–350, $75–95**

XIA

Shape No.	Description	Shape No.	Description
34	flower frog	641	-5" flower pot and saucer
325	-5" planter	852	-6" vase
326	-4" rose bowl	853	-6" vase
327	-6" rose bowl	854	-7" vase
328	-11.5" centerpiece	855	-7" vase
329	-7" bowl	856	-8" vase
330	-9" bowl	857	-8" vase
331	-9" bowl	858	-8" pillow vase
332	-12" bowl	859	-9" vase
333	-14" bowl	860	-9" vase
346	-10" basket	861	-10" vase
357	-5" hanging basket	862	-10" vase
640	-4" jardiniere	863	-10" fan vase
640	-5" jardiniere	864	-12" vase
640	-6" jardiniere	865	-15" vase
640	-7" jardiniere	1125	candlestick
640	-8" jardiniere & pedestal	1126	-4.5" candlestick
640	-9" jardiniere (misprinted as 610)	1127	-4" double candelabra
640	-10" jardiniere & pedestal	1128	-triple candelabra

Ixia. 327-6" rose bowl, green; 328 centerpiece (combination vase and candelabra), pink; 1128 triple candlestick, yellow. *Fairfield collection.* **$175–225, $275–350, $95–125**

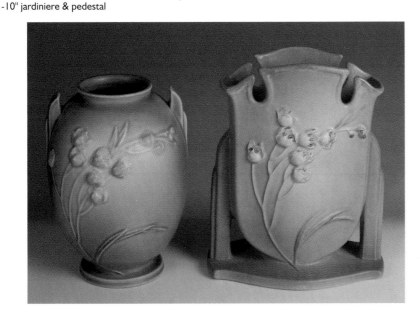

Ixia. 855-7" vase, green; 858-8" pillow vase, pink. *Shannon collection.* **$150–200, $225–275**

Ixia. 852-6" vase, yellow; 861-10" vase, yellow. *Hoppe collection.* **$125–150, $200–250**

JONQUIL
A Middle Period Line, introduced ca. 1931

Factory Name(s): Jonquil; Jonquil Ware
Style: Realistic
Standard Color(s): One standard coloring, as described below
Typical Marks: Early examples had paper labels. Pieces made in 1933 or later would have foil labels. (These could be lost, leaving the piece unmarked.) Some examples have a hand-written (crayon) shape number.

Most collectors think Jonquil is a particularly attractive line. Because it depicts one of spring's first flowers, the line can also symbolize optimism. Like Blackberry, Imperial (Textured), and Sunflower, Jonquil is one of Roseville's "rustic" lines, setting low-relief floral designs against a bark-like textured background. The blossoms are arranged in balanced clusters of three, and stems gently curved into a C shape. Rhythm and harmony reign.

The strawberry jars and related shapes add variety, as do the remarkable basket designs. Beyond any doubt, these are the most highly valued Jonquil shapes today.

The factory stock pages show 41 Jonquil shapes:

JONQUIL

Shape No.	Description	Shape No.	Description
15	-2.5" flower block	526	-6.5" vase
15	-3.5" flower block	527	-7" vase
93	-4.5" fan vase	528	-8" vase
94	-5.5" vase, flower pot shape	529	-8" vase
95	-6.5" ivy jar	530	-10" vase
96	-7" crocus pot with attached saucer	531	-12" vase
		538	-4" vase
97	-6" strawberry jar with attached saucer	539	-4" vase
		540	-6" vase
98	-10" bowl with built-in flower frog	541	-7" vase
219	-8" x 6" x 3.5" bowl	542	-5.5" vase
220	-10" x 6" x 3.5" bowl	543	-6.5" vase
223	-6" bowl	544	-9" vase
323	-7" basket	621	-4" jardiniere
324	-8" basket	621	-5" jardiniere
325	-6" basket	621	-6" jardiniere
326	-8" basket	621	-7" jardiniere
327	-8" basket	621	-8" jardiniere
328	-9" basket	621	-9" jardiniere
523	-3" vase	621	-10" jardiniere & pedestal
524	-4" vase	1082	-4" candlestick
525	-5" vase		

Jonquil. 530-10" vase; 95-6.5" ivy jar. *Hoppe collection.* **$400–500 (each)**

Jonquil. 98-10" console bowl with built-in flower frog. *Hoppe photograph.* **$350–400**

Jonquil. 223-6" bowl; 540-6" vase; 5" hanging basket (upside down). *Hoppe collection.* **$200–250, $225–275, $500–600**

Jonquil. 97-6" strawberry pot, attached underplate; 96-7" crocus pot, attached underplate. *Hoppe photograph.* **$700–800, $600–700**

Jonquil. 323-7" basket; 326-8" basket. *Hoppe photograph.* **$300–375, $400–500**

KEYNOTE
A Late Line, introduced ca. 1954

Factory Name(s): Keynote; Keynote Group
Style: Mid-Century Modern
Standard Color(s): Black Earth ("black"), Laurel Pink ("pink"), Lime Rock ("green"), Nutmeg ("brown"), Red Earth ("red"), Tunxis Blue ("blue"), and White Earth ("white")
Typical Marks: Molded (raised-relief) marks, including "Roseville" (script), shape number, and size

In 1954, when Roseville decided to sell its Zanesville property to Mosaic Tile Company, the factory's trademark, patents, business goodwill, molds, and other supplies were sold to a group of businessmen in Torrington, Connecticut. "Connecticut Roseville" (like "Mississippi Rookwood") was a short-lived venture whose products are similar to (but also decidedly different from) the original company's products.

The new Roseville company located its general sales office and showroom at Bernard Lipman, in New York, and at the Merchandise Mart, in Chicago. According to Richard A. Clifford, author of *Roseville Art Pottery* (1968), the New England Ceramics Company, Inc. (of Torrington) was hired to manufacture the "Connecticut Roseville" items.

The first "Connecticut Roseville" products were made with original Mock Orange and Bittersweet molds (but using different glazes and manufacturing methods). Some of these pieces are hand decorated; others were given only a solid-colored glaze. The clay body is white, and relatively fragile.

Perhaps as early as the fall of 1954, a new line was introduced—called Keynote, designed by the New York-based artist Belle Kogan. Starting in the 1930s, Kogan had previously done freelance design work for the Red Wing Pottery Company (of Red Wing, Minnesota). For the "Connecticut Roseville" group, Kogan's shape repertoire included three vases influenced by the Danish Modern style (the "Scandia Trio"), several biomorphic (or "free form") bowls and ashtrays, and classical round forms. Colors were semi-matte, often having a speckled shading or drippy overglaze to highlight a shape's contours.

A factory brochure (in the collection of the artist's nephew, Bernard Banet) shows 38 Keynote shapes. Because this document has not previously been available to Roseville researchers, Keynote shapes are easily overlooked in shops and shows, and have not usually been shown (or mentioned) in previous books on Roseville.

KEYNOTE

Shape No.	Description
101	-7" ashtray
102	-8" combination cigarette box and ashtray
103	-8" ashtray
104	-10" divided ashtray
105	-10" ashtray
201	-7" seafood dish (or combination cigarette/ashtray service)
202	-10" divided tray, three round sections
203	-12" divided tray, three oval sections
204	-13" compartment tray, two sections
205	-14" compartment tray, three sections
301	-7" x 5.5" bowl
302	-8" bowl, paneled square
303	-9" x 4" bowl
304	-10" x 2" bowl
305	-12" freeform bowl
306	-12" bowl, boat shape
307	-10" freeform double planter
308	-9" bowl, flared oval
401	-4.5" candlestick
402	-4.25" candlestick
501	-7" x 9.75" comport
503	-9" x 8.25" comport
505	-10" x 6.25" comport
601	-6" vase, paneled square
602	-8" vase, paneled square
603	-8" bud vase
604	-8" bud vase
605	-8" fan vase
606	-8" vase, fin handles
607	-8" vase, flared oval
608	-10" vase, flared oval
609	-10" vase, paneled square
610	-10" vase
611	-12" fan vase
612	-12" vase, flared oval
613	-14" vase, one of the "Scandia Trio"
614	-10" vase, one of the "Scandia Trio"
615	-6" vase, one of the "Scandia Trio"

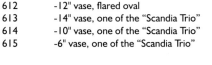

Keynote. 614-10" vase, black. *Photograph courtesy of Bernard A. Banet.* **$95–125**

Keynote. 601-6" vase, mottled green. *Courtesy of John Ross Dougar.* **$40–50**

Keynote. 615-6" vase, white. *Photograph courtesy of Bernard A. Banet.* **$75–95**

Keynote. 102-8" combination cigarette box and ashtray, blue. *Hoppe photograph.* **$30–40**

LA ROSE

A Middle Period Line, introduced in 1924

Factory Name(s): La Rose

Collector Nickname(s): La Rose (Garland) [see Monsen, 1997]

Alternate Spelling(s): La Rosa (see Mollring, 1995); LaRose (see Bomm, 1998)

Style: Edwardian

Standard Color(s): One standard coloring, as described below

Typical Marks: Some examples are unmarked. Others have a blue inkstamp Rv logo.

La Rose is characterized by its "egg-shell body adorned with raised garlands of green leaves and pink roses ... finished with a Greek fret border" (trade notice, *Pottery, Glass and Brass Salesman,* July 3, 1924: 15). The so-called "egg-shell" glaze closely resembles that used on Creamware or Old Ivory, but is here applied to a textured surface.

Today, apart from the wall pockets, La Rose pieces hold only a moderate interest for most collectors. The factory stock pages show 35 different shapes:

LA ROSE

Shape No.	Description	Shape No.	Description
14	-2.5" flower frog (same as Corinthian)	243	-10" vase
14	-3.5" flower frog (same as Corinthian)	259	-5" ferner
		259	-6" ferner
43	-4.5" double bud vase, gate shape	338	-6" hanging basket
		338	-7" hanging basket
127	-5" bowl	604	-5" jardiniere
127	-6" bowl	604	-6" jardiniere
127	-7" bowl	604	-7" jardiniere
128	-5" bowl	604	-8" jardiniere & pedestal
128	-6" bowl	604	-9" jardiniere
128	-7" bowl	604	-10" jardiniere & pedestal
236	-4" vase	605	-5" flower pot and saucer
237	-5" vase	605	-6" flower pot and saucer
238	-6" vase	761	-20" umbrella stand
239	-6" vase	1051	-4" candlestick
240	-7" vase	1052	-8" candlestick
241	-8" vase	1233	-7" wall pocket
242	-9" vase	1234	-8" wall pocket
		1235	-11" wall pocket

La Rose. 14-3.5" flower block; 127-7" bowl; pair, 1051-4" candlesticks. *Hoppe photograph.* **$40–50, $125–175, $150–200 (pair)**

La Rose. 238-6" vase; 241-8" vase. *Shannon collection.* **$175–225, $225–275**

La Rose. 43-4.5" double bud vase; 236-4" vase. *Hoppe photograph.* **$125–175 (each)**

La Rose. 604-5" jardiniere; 1052-8" candlestick; 605-6" vase, flowerpot shape (no hole in base). *Hoppe photograph.* **$125–175, $95–125, $175–225**

LAMPS

Lamps. Sunflower 6" factory lamp, derived from 488-6" vase, standard coloring; Luffa 10" factory lamp, derived from 689-9" vase, non-standard coloring of green and burgundy; Cherry Blossom 8.5" factory lamp, derived from 625-8" vase, standard coloring. *Schultz collection.* **$2500–3000, $800–950, $1200–1500.** When measuring lamps, measure only the pottery portion.

Detail of Cord Hole on Factory Lamp. To identify an original factory lamp, inspect the cord hole. If the cord hole was added at Roseville Pottery during manufacture, the interior of the hole will be smooth and at least partly glazed (as shown here). Any lamp shop can also convert a vase into a lamp by drilling a cord hole through a vase and adding a vase cap and other parts. The resulting cord hole is always unglazed inside and usually a bit rough, instead of perfectly round. Most Roseville collectors consider "lamp conversions" to be nothing more than "damaged vases," although such lamps may still have both decorative and utilitarian value.

Lamps. Tuscany 8.5" factory lamp, derived from 345-8" vase; 6.25" factory lamp, derived from Ivory 679-6" vase; 9.5" factory lamp, derived from Rozane Royal 814-9.25" vase; 9.5" factory lamp, ginger jar shape. *Hoppe collection.* **$300–400, $200–250, $275–350, $400–500.** These four lamps have the same glaze—a semigloss or glossy mottled golden brown blended with dark greenish blue. These lamps all have factory drill holes for the cords (the holes are glazed inside). The works appear to be original—whether brass or teak.

Lamps. 9" factory lamp (24" with hardware), matte mottled ~~re~~ddish brown (a Windsor glaze), *courtesy of Bill Bilsland;* ~~1~~0.25" factory lamp, Baneda-style foliage and star-shaped ~~flo~~wers, hand decorated, semigloss speckled brown and ~~w~~hite background; 11.5" factory lamp, glossy bright and dark ~~re~~d (a Topeo glaze), silver foil label, *both courtesy of Robert* ~~O~~*ttinger.* **$500–600, $950–1200, $600–700**

Left:
Lamps. Pair, Wisteria 641-15" vases, blue, drilled for conversion into lamps, mounted with brass filigree and pink marble bases. *Schultz collection; courtesy of Jeanette Stofft.* **$2000–2500 (each).** Despite their "conversion" status, these tall vases retain most of their value (because of their rarity, size, and the high demand for blue Wisteria among collectors). The lamps are also quite decorative and were purchased to use in the home.

Lamps. Panel 10" factory lamp, derived from a 9" vase, light green and blue. *Ross collection.* **$1500–1800**

Right:
An Original Roseville Lamp Finial. This metal finial appears on several Roseville lamps in stock pages from the Flexo Product Corporation. Flexo may have made the finials. Certainly, they are not a Roseville product, since potteries work with clay, not metal. (Likewise, original Roseville lamp shades were manufactured outside the pottery.)

LATE CAPRI
A Late Line, introduced ca. 1954

Factory Name(s): Unknown

Collector Nickname(s): Late unnamed line (see Purviance and Schneider, 1970); Pasadena, or Unnamed line (see Huxford, 1976); Capri (see Bomm, 1998)

Style: Mid-Century Modern

Standard Color(s): Black (semigloss Burmese-type black, with glossy speckled white drip overglaze), blue (a matte mottled blue-green, perhaps sponge applied), pink (a semigloss speckled pink), and white (a crystalline glaze)

Typical Mark(s): Molded (raised-relief) marks, including "Roseville" (script), shape number, and size

Little is known about Late Capri, other than a factory brochure (formerly in the George Krause collection) that shows 41 Late Capri shapes. Some were originally part of an earlier line. Others appear to have been introduced for use with these new glazes. Designs tend to be biomorphic—often vaguely floriform. The pink glaze is the most scarce, and may not have been intended for regular production.

Until the publication of Jack and Nancy Bomm's *Roseville in All Its Splendor* (1998), most collectors did not realize that these pieces formed a distinct line. Early books tend to classify it (when included at all) as a variety of either Capri, Florane, and Pasadena. Perhaps because of this "identity crisis," Late Capri values have remained affordable.

In Bomm, Late Capri is located under "Capri," just before the small black-and-white reprinting of the Capri brochure.

Shape No.	Description
508	-7" basket (Capri shape)
522	-4" rectangular bowl
525	-5" bowl
526	-7" bowl (Capri shape)
527	-7" bowl (Capri shape)
528	-9" bowl (same as Florane 61-9" bowl)
529	-9" bowl (Capri shape)
530	-12" bowl (same as Florane 64-12" bowl)
531	-14" bowl (Capri shape)
532	-15" bowl (Capri shape)
533	-10" bowl
534	-16" bowl
553	-4" planter
554	-6" planter
555	-7" planter (Capri shape)
556	-6" cornucopia (Capri shape)
557	-7" vase (Capri shape)
563	-10" conch shell (same as Rozane Pattern 410 conch shell?)
569	-10" window box (Capri shape)
570	-12" window box
578	-7" bud vase
579	-8" bud vase
580	-6" vase (Capri shape)
581	-9" vase
583	-9" vase
586	-12" vase (Capri shape)
593	-12" vase
597	-7" ashtray (Capri shape)
598	-9" ashtray (Capri shape)
599	-13" ashtray (Capri shape)
C1009	-8" bowl (Mayfair shape)
C1010	-10" planter (Mayfair shape)
C1012	-10" basket (Mayfair shape)

Late Capri. 580-6" vase, biomorphic Capri shape, black; 555-7" planter, oval Capri shape, one side folded down, black; 578-7" bud vase, identical to Florane shape 79-7" but renumbered, black; 579-8" bud vase, black; 553-4" planter, square, black; 556-6" cornucopia, Capri shape, black. *Fairfield collection.* **$125–175, $50–60, $60–75, $75–95, $50–60, $95–125**

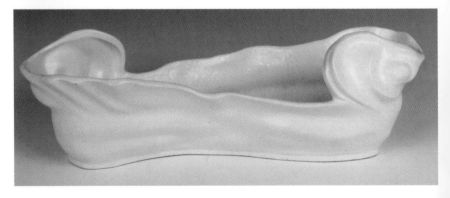

Late Capri. 530-12" planter, biomorphic Florane shape, white. *Fairfield collection.* **$150–200**

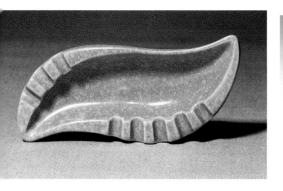

ate Capri. 597-7" ashtray, pink. *Hoppe photograph.*
40–50. This glaze is harder to find than the other Late
apri glazes.

Late Capri. 533-10" bowl, blue; 508-7" basket, Capri shape, blue. *Auclair collection.*
$60–75, $125–175

AUREL

A Middle Period Line, introduced in 1934

ctory Name(s): Laurel
yle: Realistic, with angular, stepped handles; glazes tend to be
   either Arts and Crafts (green) or Art Deco (red or yellow)
andard Color(s): Autumn Red ("red"), Green, or Yellow and Black
   ("yellow")
pical Marks: Foil labels. (These could be lost, leaving the piece
   unmarked.) Some have hand-written (crayon) shape numbers.

In 1934, reviewers thought Laurel attractive, up to date, and
asonably priced. One observer called it "a Mountain Laurel design
three finishes: autumn red, a finish you all know; green, the shade
hich takes very well to this motif; and finally—quite a slick idea—
yellow and black finish, a yellow (bright and gay) with a black
side and black tints to the florals" (trade notice, *Crockery and
ass Journal,* February 1934: 29). Another reviewer thought the
d coloring to be "really a strawberry," and also commented, "The

raised leaf is done in brown on the red, multi-colors on the green
and orange on the yellow–black" (trade notice, *Pottery, Glass and
Brass Salesman,* February 22, 1934: 26).

Today, some pottery dealers predict that the prices paid by
collectors for green Laurel—because of its Arts and Crafts look—
may soon rival those of Baneda. The only known factory stock
page shows only 13 Laurel shapes.

LAUREL

Shape No.	Description	Shape No.	Description
250	-6.25" vase	673	-8" vase
667	-6" vase	674	-9.25" vase
668	-6" vase	675	-9" vase
669	-6.5" vase	676	-10" vase
670	-7.25" vase	677	-12.25" vase
671	-7.25" vase	678	-14.25" vase
672	-8" vase		

Laurel. 668-6" vase, rust; 671-
7.25" vase, yellow. *Shannon
collection.* **$275–325, $325–375**

Laurel. Pair, 1094-4.5" candlesticks, green; 250-6.25" bowl, green. *Hoppe photograph.* **$375–450 (pair), $275–325**

Laurel. 677-12.25" vase, rust; 674-9.25" vase, yellow. *Courtesy of Cincinnati Art Galleries.* **$600–700, $400–500.** Both examples have silver foil labels.

Laurel. 8.5" bowl, green. *Courtesy of Mark Bassett Antiques.* **$375–450.** According to Randall B. Monsen, *Collectors' Compendium of Roseville Pottery, Volume II,* this is a 253-8.5" bowl.

LOMBARDY
A Middle Period Line, introduced ca. 1926

Factory Name(s): Lombardy
Style: Italianate
Standard Color(s): Semimatte green or turquoise
Typical Marks: Most examples are unmarked. Some may have paper labels.

This classical line was made in two very similar colorings and a limited repertoire of shapes. The rounded vessels are vertically scored at regular intervals. Bowls, jardinieres, and vases all have three "squarish" feet. Prices tend to be moderate (or even affordable), perhaps due to the predictability of Lombardy. Most collectors would like to own an example, but few are compelled to seek the entire line. A total of 18 shapes appear in the factory stock pages.

Without contemporary published references, Lombardy is difficult to date. The handwriting used for shape numbers on factory stock pages most closely resembles that of Carnelian, Cremona, Dahlrose, and Dogwood (Textured), suggesting a date of about 1926.

Caution: There is a 6" RumRill Pottery (by Red Wing) vase of the same shape as Lombardy. Don't let the unfamiliar glazes fool you, as they once did Buxton (1977).

Lombardy. 613-9" jardiniere. *Hoppe photograph.* **$400–500**

LOMBARDY

Shape No.	Description	Shape No.	Description
15	-2.5" flower block	350	-10" vase
15	-3.5" flower block	613	-6" jardiniere
175	-5" bowl	613	-7" jardiniere
175	-6" bowl	613	-8" jardiniere
175	-7" bowl	613	-9" jardiniere
342	-5" hanging basket	613	-10" jardiniere
342	-6" hanging basket	613	-12" jardiniere
350	-6" vase	1256	-8" wall pocket
350	-8" vase	1257	-8" wall pocket

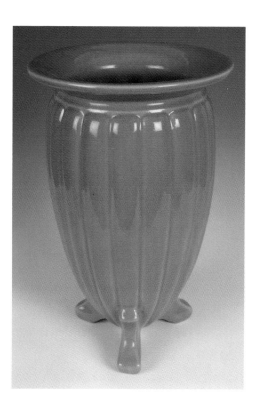

Left:
Lombardy. 175-7"
bowl; 350-8" vase.
Hoppe photograph.
$125–150, $275–325

Right:
Lombardy. 350-10"
vase. *Shannon collection.*
$325–375

Lombardy. 613-6" jardiniere,
semigloss aqua; 1256-8" wall pocket,
dark semimatte teal green. *Fairfield
collection.* **$150–200, $275–325**

OTUS

A Late Line, introduced in 1952

Factory Name(s): Lotus
Designer: Smith-Scheer
Style: Egyptian Revival
Standard Color(s): Cocoa Brown and Yellow ("brown"); Forest
   Green and Chartreuse ("green"); Mulberry and Pink ("red");
   and Powder Blue and Beige ("blue")
Typical Marks: Molded (raised-relief) marks, including "Lotus"
   (script), shape number, and size

For the short-lived Lotus line, Roseville commissioned the freelance design firm of Smith and Scheer. This was the first of several lines designed for Roseville by artists who were *not* working under the direct supervision of art director Frank Ferrell. In 1952, a factory advertisement for Lotus observed, "The charm of the Nile and old Egypt is symbolized in this new, unusual and intriguing art pottery motif" (*Gift and Art Buyer,* January 1952: 2).

Like Lombardy, Lotus had a limited shape repertoire and a consistent look, despite four color combinations. Today most collectors are happy to add a Lotus example to their Roseville collection.

There are no known factory stock pages. The advertisement for Lotus shows just 7 shapes:

LOTUS

Shape No.	Description	Shape No.	Description
L3	-10" vase	L7	-10" window box
L4	-10" x 8" pillow vase		
L5	-3" candlestick	L8	-7" wall pocket
L6	-9" bowl	L9	-4" planter

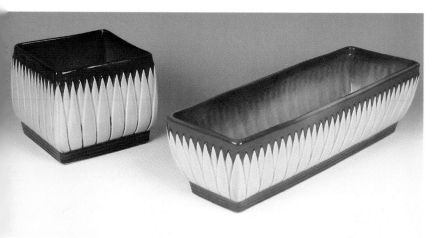

Lotus. L9-4" square planter, brown; L7-10" window
box, green. *Auclair collection.* **$75–95, $125–150**

Lotus. Two L4-10" pillow vases, one in red and pink, the other in blue and celadon green. *Fairfield collection.* **$200–250 (each)**

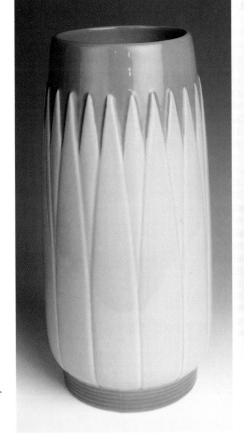

Lotus. L3-10" vase, blue. *Courtesy of Treadway Gallery.* **$175–225**

LUFFA

A Middle Period Line, introduced in 1934

Factory Name(s): Luffa
Style: Realistic
Standard Color(s): Green or brown
Typical Marks: Foil labels. (These could be lost, leaving the piece unmarked.) Some have hand-written (crayon) shape numbers.

Luffa features "a tropical flower that is used as decor and has been copied exactly as it is in actual life"—namely, the *Luffa aegyptica,* whose seed pods are dried for use as "loofah" sponges. The 1934 reviewers noted that "Luffa uses the floral and leaf effects about the top of each piece, while the entire surface is covered with terrace-like effects that are smartly decorative" (trade notice, *Crockery and Glass Journal,* September 1934: 23).

There are "two color treatments, in one of which green predominates mixed with brown, and in the other the brown predominates mixed with green. In the green numbers the flower centers are in white, and in the brown in a yellowish brown shade" (trade notice, *Pottery, Glass and Brass Salesman,* September 6, 1934: 8). Today's collectors seem to like both varieties of this moderately priced line equally well.

The factory stock pages show 25 Luffa shapes. For some reason, the Luffa pages were not hand-tinted like most were. Perhaps many (or all) of the Luffa shapes were also produced as Ivory.

Luffa. 258-12" bowl, brown, molded (raised relief) markings, gold foil label. *Shannon collection.* **$200–250.** The marks appear to indicate that this example of Luffa was made in 1940 or later.

Shape No.	Description
7	-4.5" flower block
55	-6" urn
57	bowl
58	bowl
631	-4" jardiniere
631	-5" jardiniere
631	-6" jardiniere
631	-7" jardiniere
631	-8" jardiniere & pedestal
631	-9" jardiniere
631	-10" jardiniere & pedestal
683	-6" vase
684	-6" vase
685	-7" vase
686	-7" vase
687	-8" vase
688	-8" vase
689	-8" vase
690	-9" vase
691	-12" vase
692	-14" vase
693	-15" vase
771	-15" x 10" sand jar
1097	-4.5" candlestick
1272	-8" wall pocket

Luffa. 689-8" vase, green; 684-6" vase, green. *Auclair collection.* **$325–375, $200–250**

Luffa. 257-8" bowl, brown; 685-7" vase, brown. *Auclair collection.* **$125–175, $200–250**

Luffa. 687-8" vase, green; 688-8" vase, green. *Hoppe photograph.* **$275–325, $300–350c**

LUSTRE

A Middle Period Line, introduced in 1922

Factory Name(s): Lustre
Alternate Spelling(s): Luster (see Alexander, 1970)
Style: Art Deco or Classical
Standard Color(s): Blue, gray, green, orange, pink, and yellow
Typical Marks: Early examples were unmarked. About 1922, some were marked with a die-impressed Rv logo. Starting about 1923, paper labels were used. (These could be lost, leaving the pieces unmarked.)

Lustre products were mentioned in Roseville directory listings through 1926. Shapes tend to be classical, although the delicate handles and bright colors give this line an Art Deco look. In their day, these pieces were considered fashionable and were extremely popular. Today, collectors do not usually value them as highly as the floral lines.

Lustre's solid colors and reflective mirror surface can make attractive accents in any room setting. While prices remain moderate to affordable, don't overlook the possibility of building a beautiful (and useful) collection of Roseville Lustre!

Caution: Other Ohio companies made Lustre too, in similar shapes and colors, including Cowan, Fraunfelter, and Weller. Like these other companies, Roseville used a white clay body with this line (and a relatively thin body), in order to keep colors pure and to imitate porcelain.

The factory stock pages show 60 shapes in the Lustre line.

LUSTRE

Shape No.	Description	Reference/Notes
5	-8" comport	
6	-10" comport	
7	-10" bowl	
8	-6" comport	
15	-2.5" flower block	
15	-3.5" flower block	
34	-8" bud vase	
35	-10" bud vase	
76	-5" bowl	
77	-5" bowl	
78	-6" bowl	
79	-6" bowl	
80	-7" bowl	

Shape No.	Description	Reference/Notes
81	-7" bowl	
82	-4" rose bowl	
83	-5" urn	
	(also a Rosecraft shape)	
84	-6" bowl	
84	-7" bowl	
84	-8" bowl	
84	-10" bowl	
85	-10" bowl	
85	-12" bowl	
86	-8" bowl	
86	-10" bowl	
86	-12" bowl	
87	-7" vase	
169	-6" vase	
170	-12" vase	
171	-8" vase	
172	-9" vase	
173	-10" vase	
175	-6" vase	
175	-8" vase	
	(also a Rosecraft shape)	
176	-12" vase	
177	-12" vase	
178	-14" vase	
179	-14" vase	
294	-6" basket	
295	-6" basket	
296	-6" basket	
297	-7.5" basket	
298	-8" basket	
299	-9" basket	
300	-14" basket	
307	-9" basket	
308	-9" basket	
309	-9" basket	
310	-9" basket	
	(also a Rosecraft shape)	
311	-9.5" basket	
312	-13" basket	
1019	-8" candlestick	
1020	-10" candlestick	
1021	-12" candlestick	
1023	-4.75" candlestick	
1024	-6" candlestick	
1025	-8" candlestick	
1026	-10" candlestick	
1027	-10" candlestick	
1028	-12" candlestick	
	12" vase	Bomm 214, bottom right

Lustre. 8-6" comport, pink; 86-12" shallow bowl with 15-3.5" flower block, both pink; 227-12" vase, gray; 10" bud vase (or candlestick), blue, attributed to Roseville; 1020-10" candlestick, orange. *Fairfield collection.* **$125–175, $150–200 (bowl), $25–30 (flower block), $200–250, $125–150, $95–125**

Lustre. 15-2.5" flower block, orange; 82-4" vase, orange; 15-3.5" flower block, gray; 1020-10" bud vase (or candlestick), yellow; 295-6" basket, yellow. *Shannon collection.*
$20–25, $75–95, $25–30, $75–95, $125–175

..ustre. 310-9" basket, pink, die-impressed Rv logo; 298-8" basket, pink, ..ack paper label. *Shannon collection.* **$250–300, $200–250**

Lustre. 5-8" comport (9.5" diameter), green. *Courtesy of McAllister Auctions.* **$125–150**

AGNOLIA

A Late Line, introduced in 1943

ctory Name(s): Magnolia
andard Color(s): Blue, brown, or green
yle: Realistic, with some shapes having a Mid-Century Modern feel
bical Marks: Molded (raised-relief) marks, including "Roseville" (script), shape number, and size

Roseville's advertisements describe Magnolia well: "We believe ..agnolia to be one of the loveliest and most gracious floral motifs

our potters have ever designed. Delicate pink and white blossoms are brought into pleasing contrast with the characteristic sturdy stems of the Magnolia tree. And, adding to the pleasing effectiveness of this charming pattern, is the soft wood-bark background accented by blended color tones" (*Gift and Art Buyer,* June 1943: 2).

Angular handles are the rule, and some shapes have Mid-Century Modern touches—odd combinations of curves and angles, exaggerated proportions, and the like. Today's collector prefers the blue color over the green or brown.

Although 1943 advertising mentions 65 Magnolia shapes, only 62 are shown in the factory stock pages:

MAGNOLIA

Shape No.	Description	Shape No.	Description
2	-8" cookie jar	184	-6" cornucopia
3	-3" cider mug	185	-8" cornucopia
4	teapot	186	-4.5" double bud vase,
4	-C creamer		gate shape
4	-S sugar	383	-7" basket
5	-10" bowl	384	-8" basket
13	bookend	385	-10" basket
13	-6" ewer	386	-12" basket
14	-10" ewer	388	-6" window box
15	-15" ewer	389	-8" window box
28	ashtray	446	-4" rose bowl
49	flower frog	446	-6" rose bowl
86	-4" vase	447	-6" bowl
87	-6" vase	448	-8" bowl
88	-6" vase	449	-10" bowl
89	-7" vase	450	-10" bowl
90	-7" vase	451	-12" bowl
91	-8" vase	452	-14" bowl
92	-8" vase	453	-6" conch shell
93	-9" vase	454	-8" conch shell
94	-9" vase	469	-5" hanging basket
95	-10" vase	665	-3" jardiniere
96	-12" vase	665	-4" jardiniere
97	-14" vase	665	-5" jardiniere
98	-15" vase	665	-8" jardiniere & pedestal
99	-16" vase	665	-10" jardiniere & pedestal
100	-18" floor vase	666	-5" flower pot and saucer
179	-7" bud vase	1156	-2.5" candlestick
180	-6" vase	1157	-4.5" candlestick
181	-8" vase	1294	-8" wall pocket
182	-5" flower arranger	1327	ice-lip pitcher
183	-6" planter		

Magnolia. 179-7" bud vase, blue; 93-9" vase, brown. *Shannon collection.* **$125–150, $175–225**

Right:
Magnolia. 14-10" ewer, brown; 15-15" ewer, blue; 13-6" ewer, green. *Shannon collection.* **$200–250, $650–750, $125–175**

Magnolia. 97-14" vase, brown; 96-12" vase, blue. *Shannon collection.* **$375–450, $350–400**

Magnolia. 665-4" jardiniere, brown; 98-15" floor vase, green; 446-4" rose bowl, green. *Courtesy of McAllister Auctions.* **$75–95, $600–700, $95–125**

MAJOLICA

An Early Glaze Family, introduced by 1901

Factory Name(s): Blended; Colored Glazes; Glaze; perhaps others
Collector Nickname(s): Cornelian (see Purviance and Schneider, 1970);
    Banks and Novelties (see Buxton, 1977); Blended Glazed, and
    Mahogany (see Huxford, 1980); Brown, Stork, Submarine (see
    Buxton, rev); Fleur de Lis, Iris, and Special (see Bomm, 1998)
Style: Late Victorian
Standard Color(s): Variety of glossy blended, hand-decorated, and solid
    colors. Palette included brown, cream, gray, green, red, and slate
    blue.
Typical Marks: Unmarked. Some examples have a die-impressed shape
    number.

Majolica has become a generic "farm auction" term for these ca.
1900 utilitarian products—regardless of maker. Even at the Roseville,
Ohio, location the Roseville Pottery had begun to manufacture Majolica.
By 1901 Roseville's "majolica" was the most important finish in the
company's line of "art goods, such as jardinieres, pedestals, cuspidors,
umbrella stands, vases, novelties, etc." The term "novelties" appears
to refer to a group of at least 12 figural banks, which were also glazed
as Cornelian. To describe the Majolica finish, factory advertisements
and records used descriptive phrases such as "colored glazes,"
"blended," "glaze," and the like.

In 1906, Roseville's hand-decorated "landscape" jardiniere (shape
575) was described as having "one of the handsomest and best executed
pieces of decoration one could possibly imagine" (trade notice, *China,
Glass and Lamps,* January 13, 1906: 17). Other noteworthy motifs
include Art Nouveau ladies, dolphins, fish, grape clusters, herons, irises,
jeweled swags, lions, pine cones, poppies, rams, rose garlands, seashells,
teddy bears, violins, and water lilies. Even as late as 1920, Majolica was
an important staple of the Roseville line (advertisement, *Crockery and
Glass Journal,* December 18, 1919: 86).

Caution: Other American (and European) companies produced
products similar to Roseville's Majolica. If you cannot find a shape
decorated as "Majolica" in the factory stock pages, try looking for it as
"Decorated Artware," "Matt Green," or "Old Ivory." If the shape does
not appear in the Roseville factory stock pages, use the phrase
"attributed to Roseville Pottery" or "maker unknown."

Counting only those items appearing as Majolica in the factory stock
pages or mentioned in the 1916 price list as being available in Majolica
glazes, we can identify 232 shapes that were produced in such a finish.

Majolica (Blended Colors). 612-7.5" x 5.5" cuspidor. *Merritt
collection.* **$125–150**

Majolica (Blended Colors). 20" umbrella stand, iris motifs, die-
impressed shape number, nearly illegible (perhaps 609). *Fairfield
collection.* **$350–400**

Majolica (Blended Colors). Pair,
313-8" fern dishes (liners missing).
Hoppe photograph. **$95–125 (each)**

Shape No.	Description	Reference/Notes
200	-11" bud vase (same as Rozane Royal shape 916)	Bomm 353
201	-12.5" bud vase (same as Rozane Royal shape 917)	Bomm 353
203	-8" bud vase (same as Rozane Royal shape 919)	Bomm 353
204	-7" bud vase (same as Rozane Royal shape 918)	Bomm 353
205	-6" bud vase (same as Rozane Royal shape 914)	Bomm 353
206	-7" bud vase (same as Rozane Royal shape 915)	Bomm 353
313	-6" fern dish	Bomm 138
313	-7" fern dish	Bomm 138
313	-8" fern dish	Bomm 138
313	-9" fern dish	Bomm 138
403	-7" jardiniere	Bomm 167
403	-8" jardiniere	Bomm 167
403	-9" jardiniere	Bomm 167
403	-10" jardiniere	Bomm 167
403	-10" x 26" jardiniere & pedestal	Bomm 167
404	-8" jardiniere	Bomm 71
404	-10" jardiniere	Bomm 71
404	-12" jardiniere	Bomm 71
404	-12" x 27.5" jardiniere & pedestal	Bomm 71
405	jardiniere	Bomm 72
405	-15" x 34" jardiniere & pedestal	Bomm 390
405	-15" x 35" jardiniere & pedestal	Bomm 114
406	jardiniere	Bomm 72
406	-30" jardiniere & pedestal	Bomm 68
407	-6" jardiniere	Bomm 166
407	-7" jardiniere	Bomm 166
407	-8" jardiniere	Bomm 166
407	-9" jardiniere	Bomm 166
407	-10" jardiniere	Bomm 166
407	-11" jardiniere	Bomm 166
407	-12" x 30" jardiniere & pedestal	Bomm 167
407	-14" jardiniere	Bomm 167
407	-14" x 33" jardiniere & pedestal	Bomm 166
407	-19" jardiniere	Bomm 167
407	-19" x 48" jardiniere & pedestal	Bomm 167
409	jardiniere	Bomm 66
410	-8" jardiniere	Bomm 167
410	-10" jardiniere	Bomm 167
410	-11" jardiniere	Bomm 167
410	-12" jardiniere	Bomm 167
410	-12" x 22" jardiniere & pedestal	Bomm 167
410	-37" jardiniere & pedestal	Bomm 71
411	-22" jardiniere & pedestal	Bomm 386
411	-37" jardiniere & pedestal	Bomm 386
412	-8" x 20" jardiniere & pedestal	Bomm 139
413	jardiniere	Bomm 66
414	-12" x 27" jardiniere & pedestal	Bomm 386
414	-14" x 33" jardiniere & pedestal	Bomm 71
417	jardiniere	Bomm 66
418	jardiniere	Bomm 66
419	-6" jardiniere	Bomm 372
419	-7" jardiniere	Bomm 64
419	-8" jardiniere	Bomm 64
419	-9" jardiniere	Bomm 72
419	-10" jardiniere	Bomm 64
420	-6" x 13" jardiniere & pedestal	Bomm 385
420	-7" jardiniere	Bomm 64
420	-9" jardiniere	Bomm 64
420	-10" jardiniere	Bomm 64
421	-8" jardiniere	Bomm 64
421	-9" jardiniere	Bomm 64
421	-10" jardiniere	Bomm 64
421	-10" x 25" jardiniere & pedestal	Bomm 388
422	-7" jardiniere	Bomm 64
422	-8" jardiniere	Bomm 64
422	-9" jardiniere	Bomm 64
422	-10" jardiniere	Bomm 71
422	-10" x 24" jardiniere & pedestal	Bomm 71
422	-11" jardiniere	Bomm 71
422	-12" jardiniere	Bomm 71
422	-12" x 29" jardiniere & pedestal	Bomm 71
423	jardiniere	Bomm 65
423	-12" x 32" jardiniere & pedestal	Bomm 390
425	-15" x 44" jardiniere & pedestal	Bomm 394
426	jardiniere	Bomm 65
426	-11" x 26" jardiniere & pedestal	Bomm 388
427	-9" x 23" jardiniere & pedestal	Bomm 388
430	jardiniere	Bomm 65
430	-10" x 25" jardiniere & pedestal	Bomm 69
431	-10" x 25" jardiniere & pedestal	Bomm 69
432	-13" x 29" jardiniere & pedestal	Bomm 390
433	-13" x 39" jardiniere & pedestal	Bomm 394
437	-12" jardiniere	Bomm 71
437	-13" jardiniere	Bomm 71
437	-13" x 27" jardiniere & pedestal	Bomm 71
439	-13" x 34" jardiniere & pedestal	Bomm 386
440	-15" x 12" x 45" jardiniere & pedestal	Bomm 387
441	-9" x 12" x 37" jardiniere & pedestal	Bomm 393
442	-7.5" jardiniere	Bomm 385
442	-8.5" jardiniere	Bomm 385
442	-9.5" jardiniere	Bomm 385
442	-10.5" jardiniere	Bomm 385
442	-12" x 28" jardiniere & pedestal	Bomm 70
442	-14" x 30" jardiniere & pedestal	Bomm 385
446	-8" jardiniere	Bomm 373
446	-9" jardiniere	Bomm 373
446	-10" jardiniere	Bomm 373
446	-12" jardiniere	Bomm 373
447	-8" jardiniere	Bomm 373
447	-9" jardiniere	Bomm 373
447	-10" jardiniere	Bomm 373
447	-12" jardiniere	Bomm 373
448	-8" jardiniere	Bomm 373
448	-9" jardiniere	Bomm 373
448	-10" jardiniere	Bomm 373
448	-12" jardiniere	Bomm 373
450	-7" jardiniere	Bomm 185
450	-8" jardiniere	Bomm 185
450	-9" jardiniere	Bomm 185
450	-10" jardiniere	Bomm 185
450	-12" jardiniere	Bomm 185
450	-12" x 36" jardiniere & pedestal	Bomm 185
451	-8" jardiniere	Bomm 373
451	-9" jardiniere	Bomm 373
451	-10" jardiniere	Bomm 373
451	-12" jardiniere	Bomm 373
452	-14" jardiniere	See July 1916 price list
452	-14" x 33" jardiniere & pedestal	Bomm 70; also in July 1916 price list
454	-4" jardiniere	Bomm 70
454	-5" jardiniere	Bomm 70
454	-6" jardiniere	Bomm 70
458	-7" jardiniere	Bomm 66
458	-8" jardiniere	Bomm 66
458	-9" jardiniere	Bomm 66
458	-10" jardiniere	Bomm 66
458	-10" x 25" jardiniere & pedestal	Bomm 70
459	-8" jardiniere	Bomm 72
459	-10" jardiniere	Bomm 72
459	-10" x 25" jardiniere & pedestal	Bomm 70
460	-8" jardiniere	Bomm 72
460	-10" jardiniere	Bomm 72
460	-10" x 25" jardiniere & pedestal	Bomm 70

Shape No.	Description	Reference/Notes	Shape No.	Description	Reference/Notes
464	-7" jardiniere	Bomm 72	564	-9" jardiniere	See July 1916 price list
464	-9" jardiniere	Bomm 72	564	-10" jardiniere	See July 1916 price list
464	-10" x 25" jardiniere & pedestal	Bomm 70	564	-10" x 28" jardiniere & pedestal	See July 1916 price list
468	-16" jardiniere & pedestal	Huxford, 1977 (page 10, row 1, item 4)	571	-7" jardiniere	See July 1916 price list
475	-6" x 14.25" jardiniere & pedestal	Bomm 388	571	-8" jardiniere	See July 1916 price list
475	-7" x 18.25" jardiniere & pedestal	Bomm 388	571	-9" jardiniere	See July 1916 price list
475	-8" x 21.5" jardiniere & pedestal	Bomm 388			
475	-9" x 25.75" jardiniere & pedestal	Bomm 388	571	-10" jardiniere	See July 1916 price list
475	-10" x 30" jardiniere & pedestal	Bomm 392	571	-10" x 28" jardiniere & pedestal	See July 1916 price list
477	-6" x 12" jardiniere & pedestal	Bomm 388	576	-7" jardiniere	See July 1916 price list
477	-7" x 18" jardiniere & pedestal	Bomm 388	576	-8" jardiniere	See July 1916 price list
477	-10" x 30" jardiniere & pedestal	Bomm 392	576	-9" jardiniere	See July 1916 price list
478	-10" x 30" jardiniere & pedestal	Bomm 392	576	-10" jardiniere	See July 1916 price list
479	-6" jardiniere	Bomm 372	576	-10" x 29" jardiniere & pedestal	See July 1916 price list
479	-8" jardiniere	Bomm 372	582	-4" flower pot and saucer	See July 1916 price list
479	-8" x 24.5" jardiniere & pedestal	Bomm 388	582	-5" flower pot and saucer	See July 1916 price list
479	-10" x 30" jardiniere & pedestal	Bomm 70	582	-6" flower pot and saucer	See July 1916 price list
495	-6" x 12" jardiniere & pedestal	Bomm 390	601	cuspidor	Bomm 110; also in July 1916 price list (as "Blend" or "Porcelain Lined")
495	-10" x 30" jardiniere & pedestal	Bomm 390	602	cuspidor	Bomm 110
496	-6" x 12" jardiniere & pedestal	Bomm 390	603	cuspidor	Bomm 110
506	-8" jardiniere	Bomm 67	604	cuspidor	Bomm 110
506	-8" jardiniere	Bomm 67	606	cuspidor	Bomm 110
506	-10" jardiniere	Bomm 67	607	cuspidor	Bomm 110; also in July 1916 price list (as "Blend")
506	-12" jardiniere	Bomm 67; also in July 1916 price list			
508	-7" jardiniere	Bomm 67	608	cuspidor	Bomm 110
508	-8" jardiniere	Bomm 67	611	cuspidor	Bomm 110
508	-10" jardiniere	Bomm 67	612	cuspidor	Bomm 110
508	-10" x 27" or 34" jardiniere & pedestal	Bomm 391; also in July 1916 price list	613	cuspidor	Bomm 110
531	-7" jardiniere	See July 1916 price list	614	cuspidor	Bomm 110
531	-8" jardiniere	See July 1916 price list	615	cuspidor	Bomm 111; also in July 1916 price list (as "Gold Lines")
531	-9" jardiniere	See July 1916 price list			
531	-10" jardiniere	See July 1916 price list	627	cuspidor	Bomm 111; also in July 1916 price list (as "Gold Lines")
531	-10" x 28" jardiniere & pedestal	See July 1916 price list			
533	-4" jardiniere	Bomm 372	701	-21" x 10" floor vase	Bomm 68
533	-10" x 28" jardiniere & pedestal	See July 1916 price list	703	-22" x 9" umbrella stand	Bomm 381
534	-10" x 29" or 30" jardiniere & pedestal	Bomm 392; also in July 1916 price list	705	-18" x 8" floor vase	Bomm 67
			706	-21" x 8" floor vase	Bomm 67
537	-5" jardiniere	Bomm 372	707	-23" x 9.5" umbrella stand	Bomm 380
537	-7" jardiniere	Bomm 372	708	-19.5" x 8" floor vase	Bomm 67
537	-10" x 28" jardiniere & pedestal	See July 1916 price list	709	-23" x 11" umbrella stand	Bomm 380
547	-6" jardiniere	See July 1916 price list	710	-22" x 10.5" umbrella stand	Bomm 380
547	-7" jardiniere	Bomm 372; also in July 1916 price list	711	-26" x 11" x 8.5" umbrella stand	Bomm 170
547	-8" jardiniere	See July 1916 price list	712	-22.5" x 9.5" umbrella stand	Bomm 171
547	-9" jardiniere	See July 1916 price list	713	-23" x 9" umbrella stand	Bomm 378
547	-10" jardiniere	See July 1916 price list	714	-23" x 8.5" umbrella stand	Bomm 382
547	-10" x 28" jardiniere & pedestal	See July 1916 price list	716	-23" x 8.5" umbrella stand	Bomm 378
564	-7" jardiniere	See July 1916 price list	717	-24" x 10" umbrella stand	Bomm 170
564	-8" jardiniere	See July 1916 price list	718	-21.5" x 9" umbrella stand	Bomm 338
			719	-21.5" or 22" x 9" umbrella stand	Bomm 338; also in July 1916 price list
			720	-22.5" x 9.5" (or 24" x 10") umbrella stand	Bomm 380; also in July 1916 price list
			721	-21.5" x 8" umbrella stand	Bomm 381
			727	-21" x 10" umbrella stand	Bomm 383; also in July 1916 price list
			729	umbrella stand	Bomm 383
			734	-21" x 10" umbrella stand	See July 1916 price list
			739	-19" x 10" umbrella stand	See July 1916 price list
			1201	-25" jardiniere & pedestal	Bomm 69
			1203	-10" x 25" jardiniere & pedestal	Bomm 69

Majolica (Blended Colors). 506-12" jardiniere, green, rose, and dark brown. *Fairfield collection.* **$250–300**

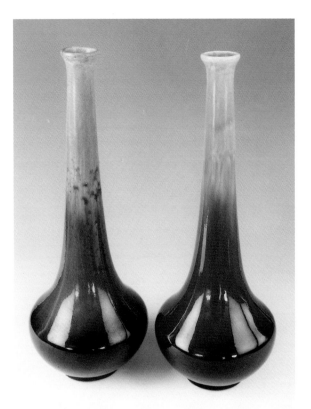

Majolica (Blended Colors). Pair, 201-12" bud vases. *Hoppe collection.* **$150–200 (each)**

Majolica (Blended Colors). 710-10.5" x 22" umbrella stand, scrolls and frieze work, green, yellow, and pink. *Courtesy of Joseph Davis Antiques.* **$300–350**

Left:
Majolica (Hand Decorated). 711-26" x 8.5" x 11" umbrella stand, Art Nouveau ladies. *Courtesy of Jane Langol Antiques.* **$1800–2200**

Right:
Majolica (Hand Decorated). 475-8" jardiniere and 18" pedestal, castle and forest scene, glossy colors in brown, yellow, green, and red. *Hoppe collection.* **$750–950 (or $950–1200, with 9" jardiniere).** This pedestal was intended to fit the 9" jardiniere.

Majolica (Hand Decorated). 414-14" x 33" jardiniere and pedestal, lionhead handles, paw feet, unmarked. *Fairfield collection.* **$1200–1500.** In this case, some details were hand decorated; other sections were glazed in blended colors.

Majolica (Hand Decorated). 412-8" jardiniere, fleur de lis. *Courtesy of Mark Bassett Antiques.* **$175–225**

Majolica (Solid Colors). Pair, 468-6" jardinieres, storks. *Hoppe photograph.* **125–175 (each).** A similar design was made by Brush McCoy.

Majolica (Solid Colors). 4.5" Uncle Sam bank, green. *Hoppe photograph.* **$175–225**

MARA

An Early Line, introduced in 1905

Factory Name(s): Rozane Mara
Collector Nickname(s): Mara (see Huxford, 1976)
Style: Art Nouveau, or Arts and Crafts
Standard Color(s): Iridescent lustre glazes, usually red blended with other colors, like blue, green, and yellow
Typical Marks: Most examples have a Mara wafer. Some are unmarked.

In the 1905 Rozane Ware catalog, Roseville described the name, inspiration, and distinctive look of Mara:

As changing as the sea, from which it derives its name, and from which, like an opalesque and dainty shell, it seems to have caught every morning hue of iridescence when the sunbeam kissed the spray, Rozane Mara is one of the most decorative as well as one of the most pleasing results yet obtained at the Roseville Potteries. Studying to obtain the exquisite rainbow tints seen in rarest pieces of old Italian glass, our artist chemist evolved this oddity. The surface, in texture much resembling the lining of the ocean's rarest shells, is somewhat irregular, presenting surfaces most favorable for catching every ray of light, throwing it back in all lustrous shades imaginable.

Most researchers believe Mara was intended to compete with Weller's Sicard line, introduced by 1903 and admired by Louis Comfort Tiffany. That year J.B. Owens inaugurated his factory's attempt to duplicate Sicard, with a line named Venetian. Today, Mara is extremely rare, making prices high when a piece does manage to surface in the market. The glaze was undoubtedly difficult to produce, limiting the factory's output.

In the 1905 catalog, 7 examples of Mara are shown. There are no known factory stock pages. In Bomm, Mara is located under "Rozane–Mara."

MARA

Shape No.	Description
K11	-8.75" vase (Rozane Royal shape R17)
K12	-11.5" vase (Rozane Royal shape R15)
K14	-8.5" vase (Chloron shape C14)
K15	-8.25" vase (Rozane Royal shape R14)
K21	-6.5" vase (Rozane Royal shape R13)
K22	-8" vase (Rozane Royal shape R12)
K24	-4.5" vase (Chloron shape C24)

Mara. 11-8.5" vase, hand-painted with stylized scroll-like motifs. *Hoppe photograph.* **$1500–2000**

Mara. 8.5" jug, Mara wafer. *Fairfield collection.* **$2500–3000**

MATT GREEN

An Early Glaze Family, introduced by 1907

Factory Name(s): Mat Green; Matt Green
Collector Nickname(s): Some shapes called Chloron (see Purviance and Schneider, 1970) or Egypto (see Huxford, 1980); some called Ceramic Design (see Bomm, 1998)
Style: Arts and Crafts, or Art Nouveau
Standard Color(s): Matte green, sometimes mottled
Typical Marks: Unmarked. Some examples have a die-impressed shape number.

At both the 1900 Paris Exposition and the 1904 World's Fair in St. Louis, Grueby Pottery won major awards for wheel-thrown and hand-modeled matte green wares. At the time, in furniture and lighting too, the Arts and Crafts style was extremely popular. Like Owens, Rookwood, and Weller, Roseville soon introduced mass-produced matte green wares as an affordable alternative to Grueby.

The first matte green glazes at Roseville may have been introduced before 1905, intended to provide another choice of finish for jardinieres and other wares, along with Majolica and Old Ivory (Tinted). In early 1905 came Roseville's short-lived Chloron line, which used a matte green glaze on Art Nouveau floral shapes. Later that year and in 1906, Roseville promoted a Rozane Ware line called Egypto, which borrowed many shapes from the Chloron repertoire. (See Chloron and Egypto entries.) At least by 1907, Roseville was marketing products in "Matt" (or "Mat") Green. Sometimes the term "Egypto" appears to have been used as a synonym for Matt Green.

At the 1907 Pittsburgh glass and china show, one reviewer remarked that Roseville's "matte green finish with clouded effect is still my choice. The subdued tone of this finish must appeal strongly to everyone. There are some new creations in this, also a box-shaped jardiniere which is unique and original. Lamp bases are in the shape of an elephant, and window boxes, complete a most attractive exhibit" (trade notice, *China, Glass and Lamps*, January 12, 1907: 8).

New shapes were introduced in 1908: "The first thing that greets the eye of the buyer when he enters the room is the gorgeous Egypto matt green ware, made in many beautiful designs and shapes representing foreign ware of long ago. In many different sizes are made gondola boats and boxes. In this ware there is a novel idea of wall pockets exclusively made by the Roseville pottery which are not only very artistic but also very useful" (trade show review, *China, Glass and Lamps*, January 11, 1908: 11).

Some otherwise unknown "Mat Green" shapes are shown in a full-page color advertisement (publication information not known, collection of Moses Mesre, formerly in the collection of C.E. Offinger). A number of Matt Green items are mentioned in a typewritten price list dated July 1916 (collection of Ohio Historical Society). In 1921 or even later, the glaze was still part of the Roseville repertoire (advertisement, *Crockery and Glass Journal*, December 16, 1920: 164). Clearly, the many variations on this glaze were an important offering of the Roseville factory.

Today's collectors have spent considerable energy trying to devise a means to distinguish Chloron from Egypto, and vice versa. Earlier books on Roseville have added to the confusion by terming various Matt Green wares Chloron, even where the factory does not appear to have used that name. Perhaps it would be wiser to judge Roseville's various matte green wares by the quality of their glazes and the interest of a particular shape. Value can be added when a fine example also happens to have the seldom encountered Chloron inkstamp or Egypto wafer.

Caution: Other American (and European) companies produced products similar to Roseville's Matt Green. If you cannot find a shape in Matt Green in the factory stock pages, try looking for it as "Decorated Artware," "Majolica," or "Old Ivory (Tinted)." If the shape does *not* appear in the Roseville factory stock pages, use the phrase "attributed to Roseville Pottery" or "maker unknown."

Counting only the items that appear as Matt Green (not Chloron or Egypto) in the factory stock pages, are mentioned in the 1916 price list, or are shown in the ca. 1907 "Mat Green" advertisement, we know that 302 shapes were produced in some variation of this glaze.

MATT GREEN

Shape No.	Description	Reference/Notes
1	-3" bouquet holder (covered)	See July 1916 price list
1	-4" bouquet holder (covered)	See July 1916 price list
1	-6" bouquet holder (covered)	See July 1916 price list
1	-10" cemetery vase	See July 1916 price list
1	-12" vase	
1	-16" vase	
1	-18" vase	
1	-24" floor vase	
1	tobacco jar	See July 1916 price list
1	vase or kerosene lamp base	See "Mat Green" advertisement
2	-3" bouquet holder (covered)	See July 1916 price list
2	-4" bouquet holder (covered)	See July 1916 price list
2	-12" cemetery vase	See July 1916 price list
2	-12" vase	
2	-16" vase	
2	-18" vase	

Shape No.	Description	Reference/Notes
2	-24" floor vase	
2	vase or kerosene lamp base	See "Mat Green" advertisement
3	-12" "florist" vase	Also in July 1916 price list
3	-16" "florist" vase	Also in July 1916 price list
3	-18" "florist" vase	Also in July 1916 price list
3	-24" "florist" floor vase	Also in July 1916 price list
3	combination smoker set	Bomm 332
3	double bud vase, gate shape	See July 1916 price list
4	-2" match holder	See July 1916 price list
4	-3" bouquet holder	See July 1916 price list
4	-12" vase	
4	-16" vase	
4	-18" vase	
4	-24" floor vase	
4	combination smoker set	Bomm 332
4	vase or kerosene lamp base	See "Mat Green" advertisement
5	-6" bouquet holder	See July 1916 price list
5	-6" x 4" "florist" vase	Also in July 1916 price list
5	-8" x 5" "florist" vase	Also in July 1916 price list
5	-9" x 6" "florist" vase	Also in July 1916 price list
5	-12" x 7" "florist" vase	Also in July 1916 price list
5	-15" x 8" (or 9") "florist" vase	Also in July 1916 price list
5	-18" x 10" "florist" vase	Also in July 1916 price list
5	vase or kerosene lamp base	See "Mat Green" advertisement
6	-4" bouquet holder	See July 1916 price list
6	vase or kerosene lamp base	See "Mat Green" advertisement
7	-16" vase	Bomm 93
7	double bud vase, gate shape	Also in July 1916 price list
7	vase or kerosene lamp base	See "Mat Green" advertisement
10	double bud vase, gate shape	See July 1916 price list
10	vase or kerosene lamp base	See "Mat Green" advertisement
18	combination ashtray	See July 1916 price list
19	combination ashtray	See July 1916 price list
20	combination ashtray	See July 1916 price list
47	-10" bowl, round, footed	See July 1916 price list
48	-12" bowl, round, footed	See July 1916 price list
49	-14" bowl, round, footed	See July 1916 price list
50	-10" bowl, round	See July 1916 price list
51	-12" bowl, round	See July 1916 price list
52	-14" bowl, round	See July 1916 price list
102	-4" hanging basket	
102	-5" hanging basket	
102	-6" hanging basket	
102	-7" hanging basket	
201	-4" fern dish	Bomm 90
201	-5" fern dish	Bomm 90
201	-6" fern dish	Bomm 90
201	-7" fern dish	Bomm 90
202	-5" fern dish	See July 1916 price list
203	-4" fern dish	Bomm 90
203	-5" fern dish	Bomm 90; also in July 1916 price list
203	-6" fern dish	Bomm 90
204	-3" fern dish	See July 1916 price list
204	-4" fern dish	See July 1916 price list
204	-5" fern dish	See July 1916 price list
205	-3" fern dish	See July 1916 price list
205	-5" fern dish	See July 1916 price list
207	-6" fern dish	Bomm 138
208	-7" fern dish	See July 1916 price list
209	-6" fern dish	See July 1916 price list
210	-8" x 4" combination window box	Bomm 90; also in July 1916 price list
211	-6" x 3.5" combination window box	See July 1916 price list
212	-10.5" combination planter	See July 1916 price list
213	-3.5" combination planter	Bomm 90; also in July 1916 price list
213	-4.25" combination planter	Bomm 90; also in July 1916 price list
213	-5.25" combination planter	Bomm 90; also in July 1916 price list
214	-4" combination planter	Bomm 90
214	-5" combination planter	Bomm 90; also in July 1916 price list
215	-4" combination planter	Bomm 90; also in July 1916 price list
215	-5" combination planter	Bomm 90; also in July 1916 price list

Shape No.	Description	Reference/Notes
216	-4" combination planter	Bomm 90; also in July 1916 price list
217	-5" combination planter	Bomm 90; also in July 1916 price list
218	-3" (or -3.5") combination planter	Bomm 90; also in July 1916 price list
218	-4" combination planter	Bomm 90; also in July 1916 price list
218	-5" combination planter	Bomm 90; also in July 1916 price list
313	-8" fern dish	
314	-6" fern dish	Also in "Mat Green" advertisement
314	-7" fern dish	Also in "Mat Green" advertisement
314	-8" fern dish	Also in "Mat Green" advertisement
314	-9" fern dish	Also in "Mat Green" advertisement
315	-4" hanging basket	See "Mat Green" advertisement and July 1916 price list
315	-5" hanging basket	See "Mat Green" advertisement and July 1916 price list
315	-6" hanging basket	See "Mat Green" advertisement and July 1916 price list
315	-7" hanging basket	Also in "Mat Green" advertisement and July 1916 price list
315	-7" jardiniere	
315	-8" hanging basket	See "Mat Green" advertisement and July 1916 price list
315	-9" hanging basket	See "Mat Green" advertisement and July 1916 price list
315	-10" hanging basket	See "Mat Green" advertisement and July 1916 price list
316	-6" fern dish	See July 1916 price list (mentioned as "Decorated Ceramic")
316	-7" fern dish	See July 1916 price list (mentioned as "Decorated Ceramic")
316	-8" fern dish	Also in July 1916 price list (mentioned as "Decorated Ceramic")
317	-8" fern dish	
318	-8" fern dish	
319	-7" fern dish	
320	-8" fern dish	
321	-8" fern dish	
322	-21" window box, ship shape	Bomm 94
323	-19" window box	Bomm 94
324	wall pocket	Bomm 94
325	wall pocket	Bomm 94
326	-10" wall pocket	Bomm 94; also in July 1916 price list
327	-10" wall pocket	Bomm 94
328	-10" (or -11") wall pocket	Bomm 94; also in July 1916 price list
329	wall pocket	Bomm 94
330	-11.5" wall pocket	Bomm 93
331	-11" wall pocket	Bomm 94
332	wall pocket, fan shape	Bomm 94
333	wall pocket	Bomm 94
334	wall pocket	Bomm 94
335	-13" wall pocket	Bomm 94
336	-18" wall pocket	Bomm 93
338	-17.5" wall pocket	Bomm 93
341	-7" bedside candlestick	Bomm 93
342	-9" x 2.5" bedside candlestick	Bomm 93; also in July 1916 price list
344	-12" corner wall sconce	Bomm 93
345	-9.25" wall mask	Bomm 93
346	-9.5" wall mask	Bomm 93
358	-8.5" wall mask	Bomm 93
444	-7" jardiniere	See "Mat Green" advertisement
444	-8" jardiniere	See "Mat Green" advertisement
444	-9" jardiniere	See "Mat Green" advertisement
444	-10" jardiniere	See "Mat Green" advertisement
444	-12" jardiniere	See "Mat Green" advertisement
445	-7" jardiniere	See "Mat Green" advertisement
445	-8" jardiniere	See "Mat Green" advertisement
445	-9" jardiniere	See "Mat Green" advertisement
445	-10" jardiniere	See "Mat Green" advertisement
445	-12" jardiniere	See "Mat Green" advertisement
448	-7" jardiniere	See "Mat Green" advertisement
448	-8" jardiniere	See "Mat Green" advertisement

Shape No.	Description	Reference/Notes
448	-9" jardiniere	See "Mat Green" advertisement
448	-10" jardiniere	See "Mat Green" advertisement
448	-12" jardiniere	See "Mat Green" advertisement
450	-7" jardiniere	See "Mat Green" advertisement
450	-8" jardiniere	See "Mat Green" advertisement
450	-9" jardiniere	See "Mat Green" advertisement
450	-10" jardiniere	See "Mat Green" advertisement
450	-12" jardiniere	See "Mat Green" advertisement
452	-14" x 33" jardiniere & pedestal	See "Mat Green" advertisement
456	-4" jardiniere	See "Mat Green" advertisement
456	-5" jardiniere	Also in "Mat Green" advertisement and July 1916 price list
456	-6" jardiniere	Also in "Mat Green" advertisement and July 1916 price list
456	-7" jardiniere	Also in "Mat Green" advertisement and July 1916 price list
456	-8" jardiniere	Also in "Mat Green" advertisement and July 1916 price list
456	-9" jardiniere	Also in "Mat Green" advertisement and July 1916 price list
456	-10" jardiniere	Also in "Mat Green" advertisement and July 1916 price list
456	-10" x 27" or 28" jardiniere & pedestal	Also in "Mat Green" advertisement and July 1916 price list
456	-12" jardiniere	Also in "Mat Green" advertisement and July 1916 price list
456	-12" x 31" or 32" jardiniere & pedestal	Also in "Mat Green" advertisement and July 1916 price list
456	-14" jardiniere	Also in "Mat Green" advertisement and July 1916 price list
456	-14" x 44" jardiniere & pedestal	See "Mat Green" advertisement and July 1916 price list
457	-4" jardiniere	Also in "Mat Green" advertisement
457	-5" jardiniere	Also in "Mat Green" advertisement
457	-6" jardiniere	Also in "Mat Green" advertisement
457	-7" jardiniere	Also in "Mat Green" advertisement
457	-8" jardiniere	Also in "Mat Green" advertisement
457	-9" jardiniere	Also in "Mat Green" advertisement
457	-10" jardiniere	Also in "Mat Green" advertisement
457	-10" x 32" jardiniere & pedestal	See "Mat Green" advertisement
457	-12" jardiniere	Also in "Mat Green" advertisement
457	-12" x 38" jardiniere & pedestal	See "Mat Green" advertisement
461	-10" x 12" jardiniere & pedestal	See "Mat Green" advertisement
461	-11" x 13" jardiniere & pedestal	See "Mat Green" advertisement
461	-12" x 14" jardiniere & pedestal	See "Mat Green" advertisement
461	-13" x 15" jardiniere & pedestal	See "Mat Green" advertisement
462	-3" jardiniere	Also in July 1916 price list
462	-4" jardiniere	Also in "Mat Green" advertisement and July 1916 price list
462	-5" jardiniere	Also in "Mat Green" advertisement and July 1916 price list
462	-6" jardiniere	Also in "Mat Green" advertisement and July 1916 price list
462	-7" jardiniere	Also in "Mat Green" advertisement and July 1916 price list
462	-8" jardiniere	Also in "Mat Green" advertisement and July 1916 price list
462	-9" jardiniere	Also in "Mat Green" advertisement and July 1916 price list
462	-10" jardiniere	Also in "Mat Green" advertisement and July 1916 price list

Shape No.	Description	Reference/Notes
462	-10" x 27" or 28" jardiniere & pedestal	See "Mat Green" advertisement and July 1916 price list
462	-12" jardiniere	Also in "Mat Green" advertisement and July 1916 price list
462	-12" x 33" jardiniere & pedestal	See "Mat Green" advertisement and July 1916 price list
463	-4" jardiniere	Also in July 1916 price list
463	-5" jardiniere	Also in July 1916 price list
463	-6" jardiniere	Also in July 1916 price list
463	-7" jardiniere	Also in July 1916 price list
463	-8" jardiniere	Also in July 1916 price list
463	-9" jardiniere	Also in July 1916 price list
463	-10" jardiniere	Also in July 1916 price list
463	-12" jardiniere	Also in July 1916 price list
466	-14" x 34" jardiniere & pedestal	See "Mat Green" advertisement
466	-20" jardiniere	See July 1916 price list
468	-5" jardiniere	Also in July 1916 price list
468	-6" jardiniere	Also in July 1916 price list
468	-7" jardiniere	Also in July 1916 price list
468	-8" jardiniere	Also in July 1916 price list
468	-9" jardiniere	Also in July 1916 price list
468	-10" jardiniere	Also in July 1916 price list
468	-10" x 29" jardiniere & pedestal	See July 1916 price list
468	-12" jardiniere	Also in July 1916 price list
468	-12" x 35" jardiniere & pedestal	See July 1916 price list
501	-4" jardiniere	Also in July 1916 price list
501	-5" jardiniere	Also in July 1916 price list
501	-6" jardiniere	Also in July 1916 price list
501	-7" jardiniere	Also in July 1916 price list
501	-8" jardiniere	Also in July 1916 price list
501	-9" jardiniere	Also in July 1916 price list
501	-10" jardiniere	Also in July 1916 price list
502	-6" jardiniere	
502	-8" jardiniere	
502	-10" jardiniere	
503	-8" jardiniere	
503	-9" jardiniere	
503	-10" jardiniere	
504	-7" jardiniere	
504	-9" jardiniere	
504	-10" jardiniere	
505	-7" jardiniere	
505	-8" jardiniere	
505	-10" jardiniere	
506	-8" jardiniere	
506	-9" jardiniere	
506	-10" jardiniere	
506	-12" jardiniere	
507	-7" jardiniere	
507	-8" jardiniere	
507	-9" jardiniere	
508	-7" jardiniere	
508	-8" jardiniere	
508	-10" jardiniere	
508	-10" x 34" jardiniere & pedestal	Bomm 391
531	-10" x 28" jardiniere & pedestal	See July 1916 price list
534	-10" x 29" (or 30") jardiniere & pedestal	Bomm 392; also in July 1916 price list
546	-8" jardiniere	See July 1916 price list
547	-10" x 28" jardiniere & pedestal	See July 1916 price list
548	-3" planter	Also in July 1916 price list
548	-4" planter	Also in July 1916 price list
549	-4" planter	Also in July 1916 price list
550	-4" jardiniere	See July 1916 price list
550	-6" jardiniere	See July 1916 price list
550	-7" jardiniere	See July 1916 price list
550	-8" jardiniere	See July 1916 price list
550	-9" jardiniere	See July 1916 price list
550	-10" jardiniere	See July 1916 price list
550	-10" x 28" jardiniere & pedestal	See July 1916 price list
550	-12" jardiniere	See July 1916 price list
550	-12" x 33" jardiniere & pedestal	See July 1916 price list
550	-14" jardiniere	See July 1916 price list
558	-6" jardiniere	See July 1916 price list
558	-8" jardiniere	See July 1916 price list
558	-10" jardiniere	See July 1916 price list
558	-10" x 28" jardiniere & pedestal	See July 1916 price list
558	-12" jardiniere	See July 1916 price list
558	-12" x 33" (or 34") jardiniere & pedestal	Bomm 389; also in July 1916 price list
559	-8" jardiniere	See July 1916 price list
559	-10" jardiniere	See July 1916 price list
626	cuspidor	Bomm 111; also in July 1916 price list
627	cuspidor	Bomm 111; also in July 1916 price list
708	-20" x 8" umbrella stand	See "Mat Green" advertisement
713	-23" x 10" umbrella stand	See "Mat Green" advertisement
718	-22" x 9" umbrella stand	See "Mat Green" advertisement
720	-22" x 10" umbrella stand	See "Mat Green" advertisement
728	-20" x 10" umbrella stand	See July 1916 price list
739	-19" x 10" umbrella stand	See July 1916 price list
740	-22" umbrella stand	Bomm 382
741	-21" x 10" umbrella stand	See July 1916 price list
909	cuspidor	Bomm 111; also in July 1916 price list
963	-4" x 9.5" jardiniere & pedestal	
1004	bedside candlestick	See July 1916 price list
1005	candlestick	See July 1916 price list
1006	candlestick	See July 1916 price list
1010	candlestick	See July 1916 price list
1201	-14.5" or 15" wall pocket	Bomm 88; also in July 1916 price list
1202	-15" wall pocket	See July 1916 price list
1203	-10" wall pocket	See July 1916 price list
1203	-12" wall pocket	See July 1916 price list
1204	-10" wall pocket	See July 1916 price list
1204	-12" wall pocket	See July 1916 price list
1205	wall pocket	See July 1916 price list
1206	wall pocket	See July 1916 price list
1207	wall pocket	See July 1916 price list
3645	-5" hanging basket	Also in July 1916 price list
3656	-5" hanging basket	Also in July 1916 price list
3676	-5" hanging basket	Also in July 1916 price list
3684	-5" hanging basket	Also in July 1916 price list
3694	hanging basket	See July 1916 price list
3704	hanging basket	See July 1916 price list
E11	footed fern dish (Egypto shape)	Bomm 138; also in July 1916 price list
E61	wall sconce	Bomm 94
E62	wall sconce	Bomm 94
E68	-16.25" vase, "birds in foliage" (Egypto shape)	See Bomm 297; mentioned in July 1916 price list

Matt Green. 549-4" vase, flowerpot shape; 1-3" bouquet holder, hexagonal base with round flower-frog lid; 3" ashtray. *Hoppe photograph.* **$75–95 (each)**

Matt Green. 1204-10" wall pocket, geometrical design. *Courtesy of Cincinnati Art Galleries.* **$250–300**

Matt Green. 3676-6" hanging basket, Art Nouveau shield-like motifs; 4-2" match holder. *Courtesy of Mark Bassett Antiques.* **$200–250, $50–60.** Like the Creamware (Dutch) version, the complete Matt Green smoking set includes a humidor, ashtray, and round tray.

Matt Green. Pair, 3656-5" hanging baskets, unmarked. *Courtesy of McAllister Auctions.* **$150–175 (each).** These examples have two very different Matt Green glazes.

Matt Green. 1-12" vase, three buttress-like feet, unmarked. *Courtesy of Treadway Gallery.* **$950–1200**

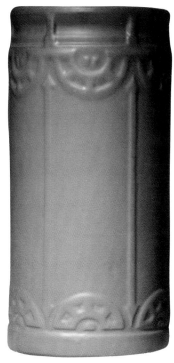

Matt Green. 508-10"
x 34" jardiniere and
pedestal. *Hoppe
collection.* **$1200–
1500**

Matt Green. 568-10" x 31"
rdiniere and pedestal.
otograph by Jeremy J. Caddigan.
800–2200

Matt Green. 727-20" umbrella
stand. *Hoppe photograph.* **$950–
1200**

AYFAIR

A Late Line, introduced in 1952

ctory Name(s): Mayfair

ollector Nickname(s): Acanthus (see Buxton, 1977); Mayfair/Capri
(see Monsen, 1995); Capri/Mayfair (see Monsen, 1997)

yle: Mid-Century Modern, and various Revival styles

andard Color(s): Cocoa Brown with Pink lining ("brown"); Forest
Green with Chartreuse lining ("green"); "Greige," combining
Gray and Beige ("gray")

pical Marks: Molded (raised-relief) marks, including "Roseville"
(script), shape number, and size

In a factory advertisement, Roseville explained that Mayfair was
nspired by the important decorator periods, past and present.
orgeous *new* colors—distinctive *new* textures and glazes of rare

beauty" (*Gift and Art Buyer,* December 1951: 2). It was "an entirely
different Roseville!" Mayfair may have been the work of a freelance
designer, instead of art director Frank Ferrell, whose distinctive design
traits have been analyzed by Randall B. Monsen (1995; 1997).

As a contemporary reviewer noted, Mayfair "incorporates Free
Form Modern, Functional, and Corinthian vases, Modern and
Contemporary bowls and planters, and Early American and
Provincial pitchers" (trade notice, *Gift and Art Buyer,* January 1952:
107). Mayfair's variety of styles have confused earlier Roseville
authors about the line's identity. Perhaps this identity crisis is partly
responsible for the affordable prices that Mayfair brings at auction
today. Brown and green pieces seem to be more highly prized than
the "greige."

There are no known factory stock pages for Mayfair. Although
factory advertising mentions 39 shapes, only 37 are shown in the
Mayfair brochure:

Mayfair. 1101-5" pitcher, brown;
1114-8" window box, gray. *Courtesy
of McAllister Auctions.* **$75–95 (each)**

Shape No.	Description	Shape No.	Description
71	-4" vase (Florane shape)	1105	-8" pitcher
72	-5" vase (Florane shape)	1106	-10" pitcher
72	-6" vase (Florane shape)	1107	-12" tankard
90	-4" planter (Florane shape)	1109	-4" vase
1003	-8" vase	1110	-4" vase
1004	-9" vase	1111	-5" planter
1006	-12" vase	1112	-8" window box
1009	-8" bowl	1113	-8" window box
1010	-10" bowl	1114	-8" window box
1011	-12" bowl	1115	-10" bowl
1012	-10" basket	1116	-10" window box
1014	-8" wall pocket	1117	-5" flower pot and
1016	-10" vase		separate saucer
1017	-12" vase	1118	shell
1018	-6" cornucopia	1119	shell
1101	-5" pitcher	1120	shell
1102	-5" pitcher	1121	coffee pot
1103	-6" pitcher	1122	teapot
1104	-7" lemonade pitcher	1151	shell candlestick

Mayfair. 1117-5" flower pot, separate saucer, brown; 1018-6" cornucopia, green, *Fairfield collection*; 72-5" vase, flower pot shape, brown; 1110-4" vase, stylized leaf and bud designs, grayish tan, *Fairfield collection. Other pieces are courtesy of Mark Bassett Antiques.* **$95–125, $60–75, $50–60, $50–60**

Mayfair. 1104-7" pitcher, green; 1107-12" tankard, fern designs, green; 1103-6" pitcher, green. *Shannon collection.* **$95–125, $125–175, $60–75**

Mayfair. 1121-5" teapot, greige; 1106-10" pitcher, greige; 1018-6" cornucopia, greige. *Courtesy of McAllister Auctions.* **$125–150, $125–175, $60–75**

MING TREE
A Late Line, introduced in 1949

Factory Name(s): Ming Tree
Collector Nickname(s): Unnamed line (see Huxford, 1976)
Style: Chinese Modern
Standard Color(s): Celestial Blue ("blue"), Jade Green ("green"), or Temple White ("white")
Typical Marks: Molded (raised-relief) marks, including "Roseville" (script), shape number, and size

Roseville advertising called Ming Tree "a bold pattern of Oriental influence" that "combines the sensitive art of a Chinese print with the dramatic contours of modern sculpture" (*Gift and Art Buyer*, June 1949: 2). Consciously developed as a group of "Chinese Modern" accessories (see advertisement, *GAB*, September 1949: 2), Ming Tree has gnarled, branch-like handles, often on biomorphic (or freeform) shapes.

Collectors tend to prefer blue or green over white examples, but values today are moderate to affordable.

There are no known factory stock pages. The Ming Tree factory brochure shows 22 shapes:

MING TREE

Shape No.	Description	Shape No.	Description
508	-8" basket	566	-8" wall pocket
509	-12" basket	568	-8" planter
510	-14" basket	569	-10" window box
516	-10" ewer	572	-6" vase
526	-9" planter	581	-6" vase
527	-9" bowl	582	-8" vase
528	-10" bowl	583	-10" vase
551	candlestick	584	-12" vase
559	bookend	585	-14" vase
561	-5" hanging basket	586	-15" vase
563	-8" conch shell	599	ashtray

Ming Tree. 584-12" vase, white; 586-15" vase, white. *Hoppe collection.* **$250–300, $500–600**

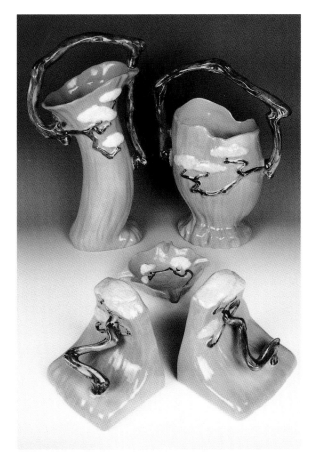

Ming Tree. 510-14" basket, blue; pair, 559 bookends, green; 599 ashtray, blue; 509-12" basket, green. *Auclair collection.* **$275–325, $150–200 (pair), $95–125, $225–275**

Ming Tree. 508-8" basket, green; 583-10" vase, blue. *Shannon collection.* **$150–200, $225–275**

Ming Tree. 563-7.5" conch, white; 527-9" bowl, white. *Hoppe collection.* **$95–125, $150–200**

MOCK ORANGE
A Late Line, introduced ca. 1950

Factory Name(s): Mock Orange
Style: Realistic, often with Mid-Century Modern shapes
Standard Color(s): Green, pink, or yellow
Typical Marks: Molded (raised-relief) marks, including "Roseville" (script), shape number, and size. Many examples also say "MOCK ORANGE."

Mock Orange is one of the most restrained of Roseville's realistic florals. Until contemporary published references can be located, the age of Mock Orange can only be approximated. Many pieces are certainly Mid-Century Modern in style. Some shapes are traditional and symmetrical, but many are biomorphic, attenuated, or oddly off-center.

Values remain moderate to affordable in today's market. All three colors seem to have roughly equal appeal to collectors.

No factory stock pages are known. The (black-and-white) factory brochure shows 42 Mock Orange shapes:

Mock Orange. 903-10" jardiniere, pink. *Courtesy of McAllister Auctions.* **$600–700**

MOCK ORANGE

Shape No.	Description	Shape No.	Description
900	-4" urn	953	-6" planter
901	-6" jardiniere	954	-7" planter
908	-6" basket	956	-8" window box
909	-8" basket	957	-8" bowl
910	-10" basket	961	-5" hanging basket
911	-10" basket	968	-8" window box
916	-6" ewer	969	-12" window box
918	-16" ewer	971	-C covered creamer
921	-6" cornucopia	971	-P teapot
926	-6" bowl	971	-S sugar bowl
927	-6" bowl	972	-7" vase
929	-10" window box	973	-8" ewer
930	-8" vase	974	-8" vase
931	-8" planter	979	-7" bud vase
932	-8" cornucopia	980	-6" vase
932	-10" planter	981	-7" pillow vase
933	-11" planter	982	-8" vase
934	-10" bowl	983	-7" vase
941	-5" vase	984	-10" vase
951	-2" candlestick	985	-12" vase
952	-5" planter	986	-18" floor vase

Mock Orange. 927-6" planter, green, die-impressed 927 and U.S.A.; 984-10" vase, yellow, molded (raised-relief) marks. *Fairfield collection.* **$95–125, $150–200**

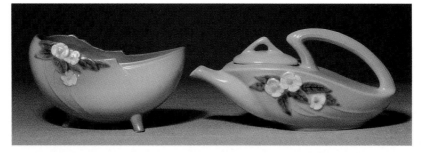

Mock Orange. 957-8" planter, yellow; 971-7" teapot, yellow. *Hoppe photograph.*
$95–125, $150–200

Mock Orange. 910-10" basket, pink; 921-6" cornucopia, green. *Shannon collection.* $200–250, $95–125

Mock Orange. 974-8" vase, green. *Merritt collection.* **$150–200**

MODERN ART
An Early Line, introduced in 1904

Factory Name(s): Modern Art

Collector Nickname(s): Decorated Art (see Huxford, 1980); Modern Art/Gold (see Bomm, 1998)

Style: Art Nouveau; or Japonisme

Standard Color(s): Hand decorated florals, often with a bright green or red background

Typical Marks: Unmarked. Many examples have a die-impressed shape number (only). Some also have an inkstamp TRPCo logo.

In 1904, a reviewer who saw the Roseville display at the annual Pittsburgh glass and china show called Modern Art "a better grade of goods … sort of Japanesque in appearance and … most interesting"

(*China, Glass and Lamps,* January 9, 1904: 34). In March, the company was said to have introduced a "Modern Art" pattern in toilet ware, but this design does not appear in the factory stock pages.

Judging by its method of manufacture, Modern Art could be classified as a sub-category of Decorated Artware. Like the wares sometimes called Special, Modern Art usually has a cream lining and some gilt trim on rims and handles. The primary decorations are hand-painted florals, the leaves usually arranged in whiplash curves.

Few of the earlier Roseville researchers have acknowledged the existence of this line. Values are therefore difficult to assess. Any collector of early Roseville should be proud to acquire an example of this attractive and rare line.

In the factory stock pages, 32 shapes are shown with decoration as Modern Art:

Modern Art. 447-9" jardiniere, poppies; 457-9" jardiniere, thistles. *Hoppe photograph.* **$400–500 (each)**

Modern Art. 457-10" jardiniere, tulips. *Hoppe photograph.* **$500–600**

Shape No.	Description	Reference/Notes	Shape No.	Description	Reference/Notes
429	-10.5" x 26" jardiniere & pedestal	Bomm 229 (row 1)	448	-8" jardiniere	Bomm 373 (row 4, item 3)
444	-8" jardiniere	Bomm 372 (row 6)	448	-9" jardiniere	Bomm 373 (row 4, item 3)
444	-9" jardiniere	Bomm 372 (row 6)	448	-10" jardiniere	Bomm 373 (row 4, item 3)
444	-10" jardiniere	Bomm 372 (row 6)	448	-12" jardiniere	Bomm 373 (row 4, item 3)
444	-12" jardiniere	Bomm 372 (row 6)	457	-5" jardiniere	Bomm 384 (row 1, items 1 and 4)
445	-8" jardiniere	Bomm 373 (row 2)	457	-6" jardiniere	Bomm 384 (row 1, items 2 and 3)
445	-9" jardiniere	Bomm 373 (row 2)	457	-7" jardiniere	Bomm 384 (row 2, items 1 and 2)
445	-10" jardiniere	Bomm 373 (row 2)	457	-8" jardiniere	Bomm 384 (row 3, items 1 and 2)
445	-12" jardiniere	Bomm 373 (row 2)	457	-9" jardiniere	Bomm 384 (row 4, items 1 and 2)
446	-8" jardiniere	Bomm 372 (row 5)	457	-10" x 31" jardiniere & pedestal	Bomm 384 (row 4, items 2 and 3)
446	-9" jardiniere	Bomm 372 (row 5)	457	-12" x 38" jardiniere & pedestal	Bomm 394 (row 2, items 3 and 4)
446	-10" jardiniere	Bomm 372 (row 5)	498	-14" x 32.5" jardiniere & pedestal	Bomm 116 (row 1, item 2)
446	-12" jardiniere	Bomm 372 (row 5)	715	-23" umbrella stand	Bomm 377 (items 1 and 2)
447	-8" jardiniere	Bomm 373 (row 1)	725	-23.5" umbrella stand	Bomm 377 (items 3 and 4)
447	-9" jardiniere	Bomm 373 (row 1)	910	-22" x 10" umbrella stand	Bomm 142 (row 1, item 3)
447	-10" jardiniere	Bomm 373 (row 1)			
447	-12" jardiniere	Bomm 373 (row 1)			

Modern Art. 457-5" jardiniere, florals; 457-8" jardiniere, carnations. *Hoppe photograph.* **$175–225, $300–400**

Modern Art. 448-10" jardiniere, berries and flowers on thorny vine, inkstamp TRPCo monogram. *Hoppe photograph.* **$500–600**

MODERNE
A Middle Period Line, introduced in 1936

Factory Name(s): Moderne
Style: Art Deco
Standard Color(s): Azurine ("blue"), Faience ("turquoise"), or Patina ("pink")
Typical Marks: Die-impressed marks, including "Roseville" (script), shape number, and size

Called "classically simple" by *Crockery and Glass Journal* (trade notice, September 1936: 20), Moderne earned a detailed review from the *Pottery, Glass and Brass Salesman:*

> The modern touch is given, not so much in the forms themselves, which are quite plain, as in the handles and other excrescences which adorn them. These are quite in the modern mode and somewhat suggest the art of the aborigines of the southwest, though handled with restraint and in modified manner. The pillar form is much used—and as every one knows who is familiar with this early American culture—is radically different from the pillar forms of ancient Greece, the chief exemplars of which are the Ionic and the Corinthian. In the majority of pieces, the handles or other ornaments are strikingly different in size on the opposite sides. One will be tall and stately; the other almost squat. The effect is artistic and unusual (trade notice, September 1936: 20).

Moderne's three colors also add variety to the line. Faience is a semigloss glaze of cream, with highlights in reddish pink. Patina is a matte glaze, with highlights in an almost metallic gold. Azurine is a glossy slate blue. Collectors seem equally divided in their preferences, but Art Deco lovers agree: Moderne is second only to Futura with them!

In the factory stock pages, 30 examples of Moderne are shown:

Shape No.	Description	Shape No.	Description
26	-7" flower frog	792	-7" triple bud vase
27	flower frog	793	-7" vase
295	-6" comport	794	-7" vase
296	-6" bowl	795	-8" vase
297	-6" comport	796	-8" vase
298	-6" vase	797	-8" vase
299	-6" rose bowl	798	-9" vase
300	-9" bowl	799	-9" vase
301	-10" bowl	800	-10" vase
302	-14" window box	801	-10" vase
787	-6" vase	802	-12" vase
788	-6" vase	803	-14" vase
789	-6" vase	1110	candlestick
790	-7" bud vase	1111	-4.5" candlestick
791	-8" bud vase	1112	-5.5" triple candelabra

Moderne. 789-6" vase, pink; 791-8" bud vase, turquoise. *Shannon collection.* **$125–175, $175–225**

Moderne. 800-10" vase, turquoise; 801-10" vase, pink; 787-6" vase, turquoise. *Courtesy of McAllister Auctions.* **$225–275, $200–250, $125–150**

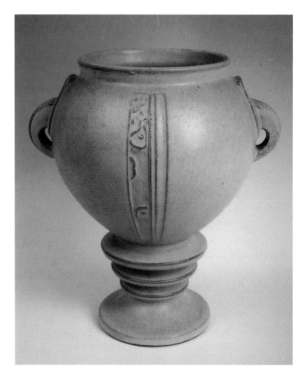

Moderne. 799-9" vase, turquoise. *Cedar Hill collection.* **$300–400**

Moderne. 792-7" triple bud vase, turquoise; 797-8" vase, blue. *Hoppe photograph.* **$200–250, $175–225**

MONGOL
An Early Line, introduced in 1906

Factory Name(s): Rozane Mongol
Collector Nickname(s): Mongol (see Huxford, 1976)
Alternate Spelling(s): Mogul (see Clifford, 1968)
Style: Arts and Crafts
Standard Color(s): Red, sometimes with mottling in black, or pink
Typical Marks: Most examples have a Mongol wafer. Some are unmarked. Huxford (1980) reports that some Mongol pieces turned green when fired too hot.

According to the 1905 Rozane Ware catalog,

Rozane Mongol is the name found upon all pieces of Rozane decorated in the rich, beautiful red, known as "Sang de Boeuf" [oxblood] and which, until very lately, was produced only by the ancient Chinese. For centuries, potters have endeavored to reproduce it, and only in the present generation has this been done. In honor of the famous Mongolian potters who first produced, in pottery, this color of wonderful richness and permanence, the name Mongol was given to this variety of Rozane.

Mongol is said to have won a Gold Medal at the St. Louis World Fair in 1904. Yet oral history has it that the line was not particularly popular among Roseville buyers. Today, most collectors yearn to own just one example of this rare line.

There are no known factory stock pages. In the 1905 catalog, 10 examples of Mongol are shown. In Bomm, Mongol is located under "Rozane–Mongol."

Mongol. 14" vase, trumpet shape, Mongol wafer. *Fairfield collection.* **$1800–2200.** This vase has a thin body, of the sort used for Lustre. Most Mongol pieces have a weight comparable to that of Rozane Royal.

Mongol. R16-7.5" ewer, Mongol wafer, die-impressed number (16?). *Merritt collection.* **$600–750**

MONGOL

Shape No.	Description	Shape No.	Description
M814	-10" vase (Rozane Royal shape 814)	M957	-15" vase (Rozane Royal shape 957)
M821	-9" vase (Rozane Royal shape 821)	M959	-7" vase (Rozane Royal shape 959)
M893	-13" vase (Rozane Royal shape 893)	M960	vase
M900	-6" tyge or 3-handled drinking cup (Rozane Royal shape 900)	M961	-10.5" vase (Rozane Royal shape 961)
		M962	-13.5" vase (Rozane Royal shape 962A)
M956	-8.5" vase (Rozane Royal shape 956)		

Mongol. M900-6" tyge (3-handled drinking cup), Mongol wafer. *Creighton collection.* **$750–950**

Mongol. 989-5" pillow vase, Rozane Ware wafer; 234-8" basket, unmarked. *Hoppe photograph.* **$750–950, $950–1200**

MONTACELLO

A Middle Period Line, introduced in 1931

Factory Name(s): Montacello; Montacello Ware
Alternate Spelling(s): Monticello (Alexander, 1970)
Style: Arts and Crafts
Standard Color(s): Aqua or tan
Typical Marks: Paper labels. (These could be lost, leaving the piece unmarked.) Some examples have a hand-written (crayon) shape number.

"Both in contour and color effects," reads a 1931 Roseville advertisement, Montacello "is strongly suggestive of the Aztec" (*House and Garden*, November 1931: 29). The name Montacello may have been derived from the Italian mineralogist Montacelli (1758–1846), after whom the mineral monticellite was named. This stone is described in the *Oxford English Dictionary* as "a yellowish chrysolitic silicate of magnesium, calcium and iron."

The tan coloring of Montacello often has delicate grayish white mottling. Both aqua and tan variations feature hand-painted motifs reminiscent of the American Indians. The colors used there are rust, green, black, and ivory, with some of the floral shapes having a yellow center.

Most collectors prefer the tan Montacello over the aqua, but both are in high demand today, particularly for use with Arts and Crafts furnishings. The only known Montacello factory stock page shows 15 shapes:

MONTACELLO

Shape No.	Description
225	-9" bowl
332	-6" basket
333	-6" basket
555	-4" vase
556	-5" vase
557	-5" vase
558	-5" vase
559	-5" jardiniere
560	-6" vase
561	-7" vase
562	-7" vase
563	-8" vase
564	-9" vase
565	-10" vase
1085	-4.5" candlestick

Montacello. 558-5" vase, aqua; 559-5" jardiniere. *Hoppe collection.* **$325–375, $375–450**

Montacello. 561-7" vase, tan; 333-6" basket, tan; 560-6" vase, tan. *Shannon collection.* **$400–500, $500–600, $375–450**

Montacello. Pair, 1085-4.5" candlesticks, aqua; 225-9" bowl, aqua. *Hoppe collection.* **$500–600 (pair), $375–450**

Montacello. 556-5" vase, tan; 562-7" vase, aqua. *Shannon collection.* **$300–350, $500–600**

MORNING GLORY
A Middle Period Line, introduced in 1935

Factory Name(s): Morning Glory
Style: Realistic, but arranged into Art Deco-style geometrical designs
Standard Color(s): Green or white
Typical Marks: Early examples had foil labels. (These could be lost, leaving the piece unmarked.) Some have hand-written (crayon) shape numbers. Pieces made in 1936 or later have die-impressed marks, including "Roseville" (script), shape number, and size.

A 1935 reviewer said of Morning Glory that it "uses antique ivory and green as the background with Morning Glories as an all over patterning done in orchid, yellow and pale shades" (trade notice, *Crockery and Glass Journal,* September 1935: 26–27). The glazes are semigloss, and the details outlined in dark brown. Each piece has at least one vine twisted into a heart-like shape.

Art Deco lovers choose Morning Glory for its geometrical patterns, angular handles, and bright colors. Green pieces are usually priced higher than white.

The only known Morning Glory factory stock page shows 18 shapes:

MORNING GLORY

Shape No.	Description	Shape No.	Description
120	-7" pillow vase	726	-8" vase
268	-4" vase	727	-8" vase
269	-6" jardiniere	728	-9" vase
270	-8" x 6" x 4.5" bowl	729	-9" vase
271	-10" x 5" x 5" bowl	730	-10" vase
340	-10" basket	731	-12" vase
723	-5" vase, flower pot shape	732	-14" vase
724	-6" vase	1102	-4.5" candlestick
725	-7" fan vase	1275	-8" wall pocket

Morning Glory. 723-5" vase, flower pot shape, white; 729-9" vase, white. *Shannon collection.* **$375–450, $650–750**

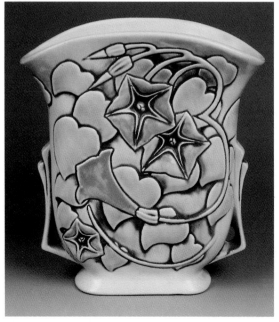

Morning Glory. 120-7" pillow vase, white. *Krause Family collection.* **$475–550**

Morning Glory. 724-6" vase, green; 726-8.5" vase, green; 725-7" vase, green. *Hoppe photograph.* **$400–500, $600–700, $450–550**

Morning Glory. 732-14" vase, green. *Hoppe photograph.* **$1800–2200**

MOSS

A Middle Period Line, introduced in 1936

Factory Name(s): Moss (perhaps also Florida Moss, and/or Southern Moss)

Style: Realistic

Standard Color(s): Coral ("tan" or "peach"), Russet ("pink"), or Sapphire ("blue")

Typical Marks: Die-impressed marks, including "Roseville" (script), shape number, and size

Of Roseville's Moss, a reviewer observed in 1936, "its outstanding feature a raised reproduction of this celebrated growth, that abounds in the Southlands and particularly in the Peninsular State … a nice ornament" (trade notice, *Crockery and Glass Journal,* September 1936: 20). Symmetrical shapes abound in Moss. Most examples have slightly stepped handles.

In comparison to other Middle Period lines, Moss has a moderate price range in today's market. The preferred color for most collectors is blue. In the factory stock pages, 38 examples of Moss are shown:

MOSS

Shape No.	Description	Shape No.	Description
24	flower frog	773	-5" vase
25	flower frog	774	-6" vase
289	-4" planter	775	-6" vase
290	-6" rose bowl	776	-7" vase
291	-5" bowl	777	-7" vase
291	-6" bowl	778	-7" fan vase
291	-7" bowl	779	-8" vase
292	-8" bowl	780	-8" vase
293	-10" bowl	781	-8" pillow vase
294	-12" bowl	782	-9" vase
353	-5" hanging basket	783	-9" vase
635	-4" jardiniere	784	-10" vase
635	-5" jardiniere	785	-12" vase
635	-6" jardiniere	786	-14" vase
635	-7" jardiniere	1107	candlestick
635	-8" jardiniere & pedestal	1108	triple candelabra
635	-9" jardiniere	1109	-2" candlestick
635	-10" jardiniere & pedestal	1278	-8" wall pocket
637	-5" flower pot and saucer	1279	-4" wall bucket

Moss. 774-6" vase, peach; 782-9" vase, peach; 780-8" vase, blue. *Shannon collection.* **$175–225, $375–425, $325–375**

Moss. Pair, 1107-4.5" candlesticks, pink; 779-8" vase, pink; 777-7" vase, pink. *Ross collection.* **$200–250 (pair), $275–325, $175–225**

Moss. 635-6" jardiniere, blue; 635-7" jardiniere, blue. *Hoppe photograph.*
$200–250, $225–275

Moss. 786-14" vase, peach. *Ross collection.* **$650–750**

MOSTIQUE

An Early Line, introduced by 1916

Factory Name(s): Mostique
Style: Arts and Crafts
Standard Color(s): Gray, or tan (both in either matte or glossy)
Typical Marks: Early examples are unmarked. Starting about 1923, Mostique was marked with a black inkstamp Rv logo.

Included in a July 1916 factory price list, Mostique may have been introduced somewhat earlier. The line gets a boldface mention in an advertisement for the 1918 season (*Crockery and Glass Journal,* December 20, 1917: 19). Mostique is a relatively heavy-duty grade of artware, characterized by impressed and hand-colored American Indian motifs against a roughly textured tan or gray background.

Bright colors are the rule for the decorations, as are glossy glazes. The background is usually matte. Some collectors value more highly those pieces whose background is also glossy. Oral history accounts (credited to Roseville researcher Norris Schneider) says these glossy wares were designed for sale exclusively in the factory's New York showroom.

The July 1916 price list mentions 13 Mostique shapes not shown in the factory stock pages, which illustrate an additional 81 designs.

MOSTIQUE

Shape No.	Description	Reference/Notes
1	-6" vase	Also in July 1916 price list
2	-6" vase	Also in July 1916 price list
3	-6" vase	Also in July 1916 price list
4	-6" vase	Also in July 1916 price list
5	-6" vase	Also in July 1916 price list
6	-6" vase	Also in July 1916 price list
7	-8" vase	Also in July 1916 price list
8	-8" vase	Also in July 1916 price list
9	-8" vase	Also in July 1916 price list
10	-8" vase	Also in July 1916 price list
11	-8" vase	Also in July 1916 price list
12	-8" vase	Also in July 1916 price list
13	-8" vase	Also in July 1916 price list
14	-8" vase	Also in July 1916 price list
[15]	-2.5" flower block	
[15]	-3.5" flower block	
15	-10" vase	Also in July 1916 price list
16	-10" vase	Also in July 1916 price list
17	-10" vase	Also in July 1916 price list
18	-10" vase	Also in July 1916 price list
19	-10" vase	Also in July 1916 price list
20	-10" vase	Also in July 1916 price list
21	-10" vase	Also in July 1916 price list
22	-10" vase	Also in July 1916 price list

	Description	Reference/Notes
	-10" vase	Also in July 1916 price list
	-10" vase	Also in July 1916 price list
	-12" vase	Also in July 1916 price list
	-12" vase	Also in July 1916 price list
	-12" vase	Also in July 1916 price list
	-12" vase	Also in July 1916 price list
	-12" vase	Bomm 239 (row 2, item 4); also in July 1916 price list
	-12" vase	Also in July 1916 price list
	-5" bowl	
	-6" bowl	
	-7" bowl	
	-8" bowl	
	-6" crocus pot and saucer	
	-10" strawberry jar and saucer	
	-4" bowl	
	-5" bowl	
	-6" bowl	
	-7" bowl	
	-6" vase	
	-8" vase	
	-10" vase	
	-12" vase	
	-15" vase	
	-6" bowl	
	-8" bowl	
	-5" ferner	
	-6" ferner	
	-6" hanging basket	
	-8" hanging basket	
	-6" vase	
	-8" vase	
	-10" vase	
	-12" vase	
	-8" vase	
	-8" vase	
	-8" vase	
	-9" vase	
	-10" vase	
	-7" jardiniere	See July 1916 price list
	-8" jardiniere	See July 1916 price list
	-9" jardiniere	See July 1916 price list
	-10" jardiniere	See July 1916 price list
	-10" x 28" jardiniere & pedestal	See July 1916 price list
	-7" jardiniere	See July 1916 price list

Shape No.	Description	Reference/Notes
573	-8" jardiniere	See July 1916 price list
573	-9" jardiniere	See July 1916 price list
573	-10" jardiniere	See July 1916 price list
571	-10" x 29" jardiniere & pedestal	See July 1916 price list
571	-12" x 33" jardiniere & pedestal	See July 1916 price list
573	-12" jardiniere	See July 1916 price list
592	-6" jardiniere	
592	-8" jardiniere	
592	-10" jardiniere	
593	-7" jardiniere	
593	-9" jardiniere	
593	-12" jardiniere	
606	-6" jardiniere	
606	-7" jardiniere	
606	-8" jardiniere	
606	-9" jardiniere	
606	-10" jardiniere & pedestal	
622	-7" jardiniere	
622	-8" jardiniere	
622	-9" jardiniere	
622	-10" jardiniere & pedestal	
631	cuspidor	
752	-20" x 10" umbrella stand	See July 1916 price list
1083	-4" candlestick	
1224	-10" wall pocket	
1224	-12" wall pocket	

Mostique. 606-7" jardiniere, gray, blue Rv inkstamp; 164-6" vase, gray, die-impressed 164; 7" bowl, tan. *Courtesy of McAllister Auctions.* **$200–250, $125–150, $125–150**

Mostique. 1-6" vase, tan; 4-6" vase, gray; 13-8" vase, gray; 2-6" vase, gray. *Shannon collection.* **$125–150, $150–175, $200–250, $150–175**

Mostique. 532-10" vase, tan, high gloss overall; 1083-4" candlestick, gray, high gloss overall; 536-9" vase, gray, high gloss overall. *Shannon collection.* **$275–350, $150–200, $275–350**

Mostique. 17-10" vase, tan, high gloss overall. *Merritt collection.* **$275–350**

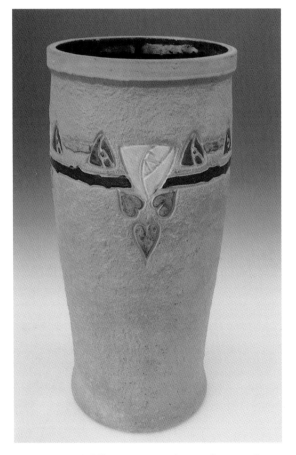

Mostique. 752-20" umbrella stand, gray. *Courtesy of Clarabelle Antiques.* **$750–950**

Mostique. 19-10" vase, tan; 24-10" vase, tan. *Shannon collection.* **$250–300 (each)**

NORMANDY

A Middle Period Line, introduced ca. 1928

Factory Name(s): Unknown

Style: Italianate

Standard Color(s): One standard coloring, described below

Typical Marks: Unmarked.

Little contemporary information is available for the short-lived Normandy line. Its design characteristics make it almost a blend between Corinthian and Imperial (Textured).

Each Normandy piece has a band of decoration at the rim. Here in low relief are stylized knots of vine, alternating with a single green leaf and a cluster of purple berries (or grapes). These are decorated in natural colors, against a brown textured background. The body of each Normandy shape is fluted in green and ivory, in the manner of Corinthian or Donatello.

Today's collectors have only a mild interest in this pattern. Most prefer the more colorful Corinthian, or the more varied Donatello. Yet there are always collectors wanting to locate an example of each Roseville line.

In the factory stock pages, 8 examples of Normandy are shown:

NORMANDY

Shape No.	Description	Reference/Notes
341	-5" hanging basket	
341	-6" hanging basket	
609	-7" jardiniere	
609	-8" jardiniere	
609	-9" jardiniere	
609	-10" jardiniere	
609	-10" jardiniere & pedestal	
760	-14" x 12" sand jar	Bomm 383

Normandy. 609-9" jardiniere; 609-8" jardiniere. *Hoppe photograph.* **$500–600, $475–550**

Normandy. 341-5" hanging basket; 341-6" hanging basket. *Hoppe photograph.* **$325–375, $350–400**

Normandy. 20" umbrella stand. *Merritt collection.* **$950–1200**

OLD IVORY
An Early Line, introduced in 1905

Factory Name(s): Rozane; Aztec; Cremona; perhaps others

Collector Nickname(s): Cameo (see Purviance and Schneider, 1970; Bomm, 1998); Ivory Tint, or Ceramic Design (see Alexander, 1970); Ivory (Ivory Frieze) and Tints (see Huxford, 1976); Green Tint, or Fern Trail (see Buxton, 1977); Old Ivory (see Huxford, 1980); Ivory I (see Mollring, 1995); Ivory (Old) [see Bomm, 1998]

Style: Edwardian, or Italianate

Standard Color(s): Cream, with recessed areas tinted blue, brown, green, or yellow

Typical Marks: Unmarked. Some examples have a die-impressed shape number. In the case of combination jardinieres, this mark can appear only on the liner.

Old Ivory was introduced at the 1905 Pittsburgh glass and china show. At first, it appears that only green tinted items were produced. Later, Old Ivory (Tinted) was also made in pale shades of pink, gold, or blue. The finish requires that each shape have a low-relief sculptural surface design. The molded wares were dipped in the same cream-colored matte glaze used in Creamware. After drying, the decorated portions were sprayed with the selected tint, but the piece was gone over quickly with a cloth or sponge before the second color had time to dry. This procedure removed the pastels from all but the recessed areas of the decoration.

Some examples of Old Ivory—like some Creamware—were banded or otherwise individually decorated. These Old Ivory (Decorated) pieces contrast stronger hand-painted colors with pastel tinted hues.

Some authors claim that Old Ivory pieces were also produced without any tinting or other decoration. Although this possibility is plausible, none have been located for photography or study.

Today, collectors of early Roseville like to own one or more examples of Old Ivory. Even so, values are generally affordable for this line. Current taste has focused many collectors on the brightly colored, Arts and Crafts, or Art Deco lines instead.

Caution: Other American (and European) companies produced products similar to Roseville's Old Ivory (Tinted). If you cannot find a shape glazed as Old Ivory in the factory stock pages, try looking for it as "Decorated Artware," "Majolica," or "Matt Green." If the shape does *not* appear in the Roseville factory stock pages, use the phrase "attributed to Roseville Pottery" or "maker unknown."

Old Ivory (Decorated). 489-7" jardiniere, Bacchantes in the forest, tinted tan, with gilt tracing and hand-painted green trim, die-impressed 489. *Auclair collection.* **$500–600**

Left:
Old Ivory (Tinted). 533-9" jardiniere, wild roses, tinted tan. *Scheytt collection.* **$150–175**

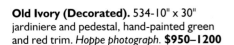

Old Ivory (Decorated). 534-10" x 30" jardiniere and pedestal, hand-painted green and red trim. *Hoppe photograph.* **$950–1200**

190

In the factory stock pages, 79 shapes are shown decorated as
in Old Ivory (Tinted) or Old Ivory (Decorated). An additional 7
shapes are mentioned in the July 1916 shape list:

OLD IVORY

Shape No.	Description	Reference/Notes
3	-5" double bud vase, gate shape	See July 1916 price list
8	combination smoker set	Bomm 332
8S	combination smoker set	Bomm 332
201	-4" planter	Bomm 90; also in July 1916 price list
201	-5" planter	Bomm 90; also in July 1916 price list
201	-6" planter	Bomm 90; also in July 1916 price list
201	-7" planter	Bomm 90; also in July 1916 price list
207	-6" fern dish	Bomm 138
208	-7" combination planter	Bomm 90; also in July 1916 price list
209	-6" combination planter	Bomm 90; also in July 1916 price list
211	-6" x 3.5" combination window box	Bomm 90; also in July 1916 price list
212	-10.5" combination planter	Bomm 90; also in July 1916 price list
260	combination tea set	See July 1916 price list (see also "Utility Ware," as "Romafin")
489	-6" or -6.5" jardiniere	Bomm 79; also in July 1916 price list (as "Ivory Frieze & Green Bands - Gold Lines")
489	-7" or -7.5" jardiniere	Bomm 79; also in July 1916 price list (as "Ivory Frieze & Green Bands - Gold Lines")
489	-8" jardiniere	Bomm 79; also in July 1916 price list (as "Ivory Frieze & Green Bands - Gold Lines")
489	-9" jardiniere	Bomm 79; also in July 1916 price list (as "Ivory Frieze & Green Bands - Gold Lines")
489	-10" jardiniere	Bomm 79; also in July 1916 price list (as "Ivory Frieze & Green Bands - Gold Lines")
489	-10" jardiniere & pedestal	Bomm 79
489	-12" jardiniere	Bomm 89
489	-12" jardiniere & pedestal	Bomm 79
497	-18" x 52" jardiniere & pedestal	Bomm 79
503	-8" jardiniere	Bomm 186
503	-9" jardiniere	Bomm 186
503	-10" jardiniere	Bomm 186
504	-7" jardiniere	Bomm 186
504	-9" jardiniere	Bomm 186
504	-10" jardiniere	Bomm 186
505	-7" jardiniere	Bomm 186
505	-8" jardiniere	Bomm 186
505	-10" jardiniere	Bomm 186
506	-8" jardiniere	Bomm 186
506	-9" jardiniere	Bomm 186
506	-10" jardiniere	Bomm 186
507	-7" jardiniere	Bomm 186
507	-8" jardiniere	Bomm 186
507	-9" jardiniere	Bomm 186
508	-7" jardiniere	Bomm 186
508	-8" jardiniere	Bomm 186
508	-10" jardiniere	Bomm 186
508	-10" x 34" jardiniere & pedestal	Bomm 391
510	-4" combination jardiniere	Bomm 87
510	-6" combination jardiniere	Bomm 87
510	-8" combination jardiniere	Bomm 87
510	-10" combination jardiniere	Bomm 87
513	-4" combination jardiniere	Bomm 87
513	-5" combination jardiniere	Bomm 87
513	-8" combination jardiniere	Bomm 87
513	-9" combination jardiniere	Bomm 87
514	-4" combination jardiniere	Bomm 87
514	-7" combination jardiniere	Bomm 87
514	-8" combination jardiniere	Bomm 87
514	-10" combination jardiniere	Bomm 87
515	-4" combination jardiniere	Bomm 87
515	-6" combination jardiniere	Bomm 87

Shape No.	Description	Reference/Notes
515	-8" combination jardiniere	Bomm 87
515	-10" combination jardiniere	Bomm 87
516	-4" combination jardiniere	Bomm 87
516	-5" combination jardiniere	Bomm 87
516	-7" combination jardiniere	Bomm 87
516	-8" combination jardiniere	Bomm 87
527	-8" combination jardiniere	Bomm 89
532	-8" jardiniere	Bomm 89
532	-9" jardiniere	Bomm 89
532	-10" jardiniere	Bomm 89
532	-12" jardiniere	Bomm 89
532	-14" jardiniere	Bomm 89
532	-16" jardiniere	Bomm 89
533	-5" jardiniere	Bomm 372
533	-6" jardiniere	Bomm 372
533	-7" jardiniere	Bomm 372
533	-8" jardiniere	Bomm 372
534	-10" x 30" jardiniere & pedestal	Bomm 392
537	-4" jardiniere	Bomm 372
621	cuspidor, fern trail design	Bomm 111; also in July 1916 price list
739	-19" x 10" umbrella stand	See July 1916 price list
1201	-14.5" or -15" wall pocket	Bomm 88; also in July 1916 price list
1202	-15" wall pocket	Bomm 88; also in July 1916 price list
1203	-10" wall pocket	Not reprinted, but see Huxford (1980), page 162, bottom left and bottom right; also see July 1916 price list
1203	-12" wall pocket	Not reprinted; see July 1916 price list
1204	-10" wall pocket	Not reprinted; see July 1916 price list
1204	-12" wall pocket	Not reprinted; see July 1916 price list
E11	footed fern dish	Bomm 138
	stein set no. 2 (tankard, 6 steins)	Bomm 193
	sugar and creamer no. 5	Bomm 344
	tea set no. 4 (teapot, creamer, sugar)	Bomm 192

Old Ivory (Tinted). 3-7.25" x 8.5" combination smoker set, separate lid on humidor, other pieces attached to base; 4" powder box; 13.5" tankard; 4.25" stein. *Scheytt collection.* **$275–325, $150–200, $300–350, $95–125.** According to the factory stock pages, the tankard and stein shown here are part of "Stein set #2."

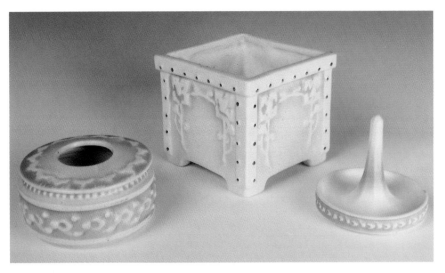

Old Ivory (Tinted). 4" hair receiver, tinted blue; 201-4" planter, tinted tan, red stippled trim; 3" ring holder, tinted blue. *Fairfield collection.* **$150–200, $125–150, $95–125**

Old Ivory (Tinted). 621-5" cuspidor, tinted tan. *Shannon collection.* **$125–175.** The outside diameter of this piece measures 7.75" across. One factory stock page has a penciled-in nickname for this veined motif: "fern trail" (see Bomm 111).

OLYMPIC

An Early Line, introduced ca. 1906

Factory Name(s): Olympic; Rozane Olympic
Collector Nickname(s): Grecian (see Clifford, 1968)
Style: Decorated in the style of Ancient Greek Redware
Standard Color(s): Dark red, black, and ivory
Typical Marks: Most (if not all) examples have black hand-lettered marks, including the line name "OLYMPIC." Many also have hand-written titles.

Introduced while Frederick Hurten Rhead was Roseville's art director, Olympic was probably the work of artist Loiz Whitcomb Rhead, then Rhead's wife. Because Olympic shares several shapes with Crystalis, this rare line appears to date to about 1906. Like several Creamware motifs—notably, Gibson Girls and Tourist—the decorations were applied by means of pouncing. The brick red background color must have been applied very carefully in order

to avoid a "spill" into the decorated areas. Judging from their bottoms, the clay body used for Olympic may be identical to the standard Creamware body.

Olympic is described as follows in Sharon Dale's *Frederick Hurten Rhead: An English Potter in America* (1986):

Featuring narratives from classical mythology, "Olympic" is among the most conservative of [F.H.] Rhead's lines in terms of both design and technique. The pieces were generally produced on shapes reminiscent of Classical wares and were decorated in imitation of Attic pottery using … a calligraphic design of white and black figures. Ultimately paying homage to the Neo-Classical designs that Joseph Flaxman executed for Wedgwood, "Olympic" recalls many similar lines produced by nineteenth century English potteries and usually called "Etruscan" wares (page 46).

Most Roseville collectors would be proud to own an example of the highly valued Olympic line. There are no known factory stock pages for Olympic, nor any known catalog listings.

Olympic. 5" stein, youth seated with libation cup, marked with three-line OLYMPIC mark. *Downey collection.* **$1200–1500**

lympic. 14.25" urn, three-line OLYMPIC mark, titled **"**AMPETIA COMPLAINING TO APOLLO." *Zanesville Art ***C**enter Permanent Collection A5840, Gift of Mr. James A. **R**ansbottom, 1991.* **NPD**

Olympic. 13" vase, two views of Olympic vase with three figures. *Zanesville Art Center Permanent Collection A10504, Gift of Mrs. Robert P. Windisch, 1954; and A16022, Gift of Dr. and Mrs. Lewis M. Nixon, in memory of Simeon S. Senter, 1984. Both marked (black ink, all capitals) "ROZANE POTTERY." **NPD**. Note the minor differences in execution of the border designs.*

ORIAN

A Middle Period Line, introduced in 1935

*F*ctory Name(s): Orian

*St*le: Art Deco

*Sta*ndard Color(s): Blue, red, tan, or yellow

*T*pical Marks: Foil labels. (These could be lost, leaving the piece unmarked.) Some have hand-written (crayon) shape numbers.

In 1935, Orian was called "a solid-color line that is a real **ac**hievement in ceramic art. Its inspiration was either directly or **in**directly the lovely old Chinese vases of the Ming period,

noteworthy at once for the beauty of their contour and the nature of their glaze, the secret of which has defied all efforts of our modern ceramic chemists to discover. It can be said, however, that this new Roseville offering is a most creditable one. Shapes are lovely, but in no way extreme, while the colors are such as one might expect in real porcelain rather than in earthenware" (trade notice, *Pottery, Glass and Brass Salesman,* August 15, 1935: 7–8).

Orian's four glossy color combinations usually include a contrasting lining, and most examples have hand-painted trim at the mouth: a series of short vertical lines. Yellow pieces often (or always) omit the hand-painted details. Handles are colored to contrast with the surface glaze. Most collectors think the look very smart, very Art Deco.

The origin of this line's name is not clear, despite its possible relation to Orion, of Greek mythology, after whom the constellation is named. Values are usually moderate, with the bright colors selling higher than the tan.

The only known Orian factory stock page shows 16 shapes:

ORIAN

Shape No.	Description	Shape No.	Description
272	-10" bowl	738	-9" vase
273	-12" x 5" x 4.5" bowl	739	-9" vase
274	-6" urn	740	-10" vase
733	-6" vase	741	-10" vase
734	-7" vase	742	-12" vase
735	-7" vase	743	-14" vase
736	-8" vase	1108	-4.5" candlestick
737	-7" vase	1276	-8" wall pocket

Orian. 741-10" vase, turquoise; 743-14" vase, turquoise. *Hoppe collection.* **$350–425, $600–700**

Orian. 742-12" vase, yellow, red crayon shape number, no other marks; 733-6" vase, yellow, die-impressed marks. *Auclair collection.* **$400–500, $175–225**

Orian. 272-10" bowl, red, unmarked *Auclair collection.* **$250–300**

Orian. 734-7" vase, tan; 740-10" vase, yellow; 737-7" vase, red. *Shannon collection.* **$200–250, $300–350, $275–325**

PANEL

A Middle Period Line, introduced by 1926

Factory Name(s): Rosecraft Panel

Collector Nickname(s): Panel (see Clifford, 1968)

Style: Realistic florals, or nude figures, often with Art Nouveau touches

Standard Color(s): Brown, or green

Typical Marks: Most examples have a blue inkstamp Rv logo, although some are unmarked. (In other cases, the inkstamp mark may be obscured by a thick glaze.)

Panel is one of the Roseville lines featured in the November 1926 catalog of Butler Brothers, "a large wholesale business with warehouses in New York, Chicago, St. Louis, Minneapolis, and Dallas" (Sigafoose 249). Many Panel designs are influenced by the Art Nouveau style. Floral sprays are shown in Japanesque or whiplash arrangements, modeled in low-relief panels that alternate with a smooth background. The nude or draped figures recall Art Nouveau—a dancer Loïe Fuller.

Matte glazes are used for the background, and semigloss colors decorate the motifs. The brown coloring pairs rust-colored decorations with dark brown. Most collectors today prefer the green variation, in which the decorations include white, lavender, yellow, and other colors against dark matte green. Prices are considerably higher for the nudes.

Only one factory stock page is known for Panel, and it shows just 10 shapes:

PANEL

Shape No.	Description	Shape No.	Description
291	-8" vase	296	-10" vase
292	-8" vase	297	-10" vase
293	-8" vase	298	-11" vase
294	-8" vase	299	-12" vase
295	-9" covered vase	1057	-8" candlestick

Panel. 7" vase, floral, green; 10.5" vase, nude, brown; 6" vase, floral, brown. *Shannon collection.* **$200–250, $950–1200, $125–150**

Panel. 8" fan vase, nude, green; 6" fan vase, nude, green. *Hoppe photograph.* **$750–950, $600–750**

Panel. 10" vase, floral, brown; 12" vase, floral, green. *Shannon collection.* **$275–325, $375–450**

Panel. 4" urn, floral, green; 8" vase, floral, green. *Hoppe photograph.* **$125–175, $225–275**

PASADENA PLANTERS
A Late Line, introduced ca. 1954

Factory Name(s): Pasadena Planters
Collector Nickname(s): Planters (see Purviance and Schneider, 1970); Pasadena Planter (see Alexander, 1970); Pasadena (see Huxford, 1976)
Style: Mid-Century Modern
Standard Color(s): Believed to be chartreuse, dark green, or pink

Little is known about this line, which is mentioned in the Board of Director minutes for September 8, 1954. An unfinished factory brochure (formerly in the collection of George Krause; see Bomm) shows that Pasadena Planters originally came with custom-made metal and rubber stands. Some authors speculate that this line was a corporate commission, like the Borden's sets. The known glazes are glossy, often with a mottled drip along the rim.

Collector interest in the Pasadena Planters is low today, keeping prices quite affordable for those who would like to purchase an example.

The factory brochure mentions or illustrates 29 items in this line:

PASADENA PLANTERS

Shape No.	Description	Shape No.	Description
L10	-8" planter	L25	-6.5" planter
L11	-10" planter	L26	-7" planter
L12	-12" planter	L27	-5" planter
L13	-16" planter	L28	-6" planter
L14	-4" planter	L29	-7" planter
L15	-5" planter	L30	-3" planter
L16	-7" planter	L31	-4" planter
L17	-9" planter	L32	-5" planter
L18	-6.5" planter	L33	-6.5" planter
L19	-8" planter	L34	-8" planter
L20	-10" planter	L35	-10" planter
L21	-12" planter	L36	-4" planter
L22	-4" planter	L37	-5" planter
L23	-5" planter	L38	-6.5" planter
L24	-6" planter		

Pasadena Planters. L-19 oval planter, 8" long, dark green, in custom metal frame; L-33 oval planter, scalloped body, 6.5" long, dark green; L-35 window box, 10.75" long, dark green. *Fairfield collection.* **$50–60, $50–60, $60–75.** The window box has two factory-drilled holes at one end, intended to allow drainage after watering plants.

Pasadena Planters. 4" planter L-14, mottled white on pink, in custom metal frame. *Shannon collection.* **$40–50**

Pasadena Planters. L-21 oval planter, 12" long, pink; L-14 planter, 4" square, lime green; L-17 planter, 9" square, pink. *Fairfield collection.* **$60–75, $30–35, $60–75**

PAULEO

An Early Line, introduced ca. 1914

Factory Name(s): Pauleo; Pauleo Pottery

Collector Nickname(s): Lustre (see Huxford, 1980)

Style: Arts and Crafts

Standard Color(s): Numerous glazes, including lustres, matte mottled colors, and semigloss blends

Typical Marks: Many are unmarked. Some have a distinctive wafer reading PAULEO POTTERY, or a distinctive PAULEO paper label in the shape of a covered vase. Many Pauleo examples have a green-painted bottom, through which has been hand-incised a shape number. According to Buxton (1977), some examples have a die-impressed Rv logo.

In April 1916, Harry W. Rhead wrote the short text for a little-known factory booklet titled "Pauleo Pottery":

The first "Pau-le-o Pottery" was taken from our kilns two and a half years ago. The potters and artists responsible for its appearance had worked many years to attain a combination of rich mellow color with simple and graceful forms. That a general appreciation of good color is being rapidly developed, is shown by the increasing demand for reproductions of ancient Chinese "Peach Blow" and "Flambé" glazes. However, "Pau-le-o" is not an imitation, but a new creation, for the wonderful markings which happen in its glazes, may be said to strike an entirely new note in pottery decoration.

Made for its color alone, "Pau-le-o" rarely has any other ornamentation, as the potters believe the making of beautiful pottery to be much more an art of leaving off, than an art of putting on. No two pieces of this pottery are exactly alike, for while it is possible to duplicate a form, or a general color scheme,

new breaks, veins, or striations appear according to the caprice of the flame.

The designing and making of "Pau-le-o" is in the hands of Harry W. Rhead, Russell T. Young, and Charles E. Offinger,— three ceramists whose chief aim is to help in raising the quality level of the American potters' craft. We may add that the idea of a "Pau-le-o" Pottery Shop at 50th Street and 5th Avenue [New York City], was the inevitable outcome of much enthusiastic comment by those whom we believe to be the most capable judges of pottery in America (*quotation from photocopy of original, courtesy of Ed and June Wagner*).

The unusual spelling indicates the origin of the name "Pauleo." This line was named after George Young's daughter-in-law Pauline (married to son Russell) and his daughter Leota.

Pauleo's variegated glazes intrigued potters and buyers alike. A reviewer for one of the trade journals admired the "rare antique color effects produced in the glaze, no two of which are exactly alike. These include plain and mottled effects and are in elusive color tones of marked beauty. A great variety of vase shapes which, in both form and color, are splendidly adapted for use either as vases or lamp mounts are displayed, and several have been equipped with electrical attachments and fabric shades to show their suitability for this purpose" (trade notice, *Pottery, Glass and Brass Salesman,* December 17, 1914: 109).

Another view of Pauleo (Decorated) Vase.
Fraternal decals are extremely unusual to find on Pauleo.

Pauleo (Decorated). 17" vase, hand-painted grapes on purple lustre background; 19" vase, hand-painted chrysanthemums on airbrushed lustre background, reverse with Loyal Order of Moose decal; 15" vase, hand-painted trees in landscape, matte colors. *Courtesy of Clarabelle Antiques.* **$1800–2200, $2500–3000, $2200–2500**

Another reviewer remarked of Roseville's unusual glazes, "How they can accomplish them is a mystery to other potters. It is possible to get the colors themselves, but how they obtain the combined effects which are the ware's distinctive feature puzzles the most expert decorators" (trade notice, *Crockery and Glass Journal*, December 27, 1917: 15). Pauleo remained in the line until 1922 or later (advertisement, *CGJ* December 15, 1921: 109). Several 1920s Weller glazes appear to be late attempts to compete with this distinctive line—notably, Cloudburst (1921), Frosted Matt (1921), and Bronze Ware (1923).

Although glazes predominate in Pauleo, one should note Rhead's remark that the line was "rarely" given "any other ornamentation." Most collectors view one family of Decorated Artware products as a subcategory of the Pauleo line. These wares use Pauleo shapes and glazes, but also have hand-painted floral decorations.

Both glazed and decorated Pauleo pieces are rare today, and highly coveted by collectors. Values are difficult to pinpoint, partly because higher prices can be paid for particularly attractive glazes, or skillfully applied artwork (and as everyone knows, "Beauty is in the eye of the beholder!")

Caution: Pauleo is not shown in any known factory stock page. (Reminder: "Looks can be deceiving!") Until an example came up at auction, Huxford (1980) misidentified a covered Pauleo vase—shown in a black and white catalog—as "Hexagon" because the shape was hexagonal. The same book mistakes another Pauleo vase for Mara.

Pauleo (Glazes). 13.5" vase, deep red lustre. *Fairfield collection.* **$1200–1500.** The base is marked in orange crayon (illegible; appears to read either 124 or 324).

Pauleo (Glazes). E64-14.75" vase, Crystalis shape, bottom painted green (perhaps to make the piece waterproof), hand-incised 2. *Hoppe collection.* **$1800–2200**

Left:
Pauleo (Glazes). 14.5" lamp, matte tan mottled with fuchsia and ivory. *Nickel and Horvath collection.* **$1200–1500.** This piece was originally a lamp; it has a factory-drilled cord hole in the base.

Right:
Pauleo (Glazes). 14.25" vase, blue and purple; 9.25" vase, green and black; 11.5" vase, green and purple. *Zanesville Art Center Permanent Collection A10509 (first piece) and A10510 (second piece), Gifts of Mrs. Robert P. Windisch, 1954; and A15242 (third piece), Gift of Mrs. Vashti Funk, 1987.* **NPD**

PEONY

A Late Line, introduced in 1942

Factory Name(s): Peony

Style: Realistic

Standard Color(s): Coral ("pink"), Nile Green ("green"), or Sienna Brown ("yellow")

Typical Marks: Molded (raised-relief) marks, including "Roseville" (script), shape number, and size

Here is Roseville's 1942 description of Peony: "Because its beautifully rounded blooms, softly blended colors and deep, rich textures have ever been a joy to garden lovers, we are delighted to present *Peony,* newest and gayest floral design in the Roseville collection. The motif of the brilliant *Peony* is exceptionally pleasing against a smart wood texture background and magnificently toned colors of Sienna Brown and Nile Green" (*Gift and Art Buyer,* May 1942: 2). A month later, Coral pieces were introduced.

Today, Peony is one of the more affordable Roseville lines. Produced after the United States entered World War II, Peony is fairly conservative. Many shapes are traditional, although they often have angular handles. Bowl rims are sometimes irregular, completing a profile of peony petals and leaves.

In the factory stock pages, 62 examples of Peony are shown:

PEONY

Shape No.	Description	Shape No.	Description	Shape No.	Description
2	-3.5" mug	67	-12" vase	429	-8" bowl
3	-teapot	68	-14" vase	430	-10" bowl
3	-10" bowl	69	-15" vase	431	-10" bowl
3	-C cream	70	-18" floor vase	432	-12" bowl
3	-S sugar	167	-4.5" double bud vase,	433	-14" bowl
4	-10" bowl		gate shape	434	-6" tray
7	-6" ewer	168	-6" vase	435	-10" tray
8	-10" ewer	169	-8" vase	436	conch shell
9	-15" ewer	170	-6" cornucopia	467	-5" hanging basket
11	bookend	171	-8" cornucopia	661	-3" jardiniere
27	ashtray	172	double cornucopia	661	-4" jardiniere
57	-4" vase	173	-7" bud vase	661	-5" jardiniere
58	-6" vase	376	-7" basket	661	-6" jardiniere
59	-6" vase	377	-8" basket	661	-8" jardiniere & pedestal
60	-7" vase	378	-10" basket	661	-10" jardiniere & pedestal
61	-7" vase	379	-12" basket	662	-5" flower pot and saucer
62	-8" vase	386	-6" window box	1151	-2" candlestick
63	-8" vase	387	-8" window box	1152	-4.5" candlestick
64	-9" vase	427	-4" rose bowl	1153	double candelabra
65	-9" vase	427	-6" rose bowl	1293	-8" wall pocket
66	-10" vase	428	-6" bowl	1326	-7.5" jug

Peony. 378-10" basket, pink; 58-6" vase, pink; 379-12" basket, pink. *Courtesy of McAllister Auctions.* **$250–300, $125–150, $300–400**

Peony. 66-10" vase, green; 67-12" vase, green; 64-9" vase, green. *Hoppe collection.* **$225–275, $250–300, $175–225**

Peony. 1153 double candlestick, yellow; 171-8" cornucopia, yellow; 47 flower arranger, yellow. *Courtesy of McAllister Auctions.* **$95–125, $125–150, $95–125**

Peony. 61-7" vase, yellow; 173-7" bud vase, yellow; 377-8" basket, pink; 169-8" vase, rust. *Shannon collection.* **$125–150, $95–125, $200–250, $225–275.** Perhaps the unusual rust coloring was a short-lived and early glaze treatment for Peony.

PINE CONE
A Middle Period Line, introduced in 1935

Factory Name(s): Pine Cone
Collector Nickname(s): Pine Cone I (see Purviance and Schneider, 1970); Pine Cone (see Huxford, 1980).
Alternate Spelling(s): Pinecone (First) [see Alexander, 1970]; Pinecone (see Huxford, 1976).
Style: Realistic, often with a Japanese-like restraint
Standard Color(s): Blue, brown, or green
Typical Marks: Early examples had foil labels. (These could be lost, leaving the piece unmarked.) Some have hand-written (crayon) shape numbers. Pieces made during 1936–1939 have die-impressed marks, including "Roseville" (script), shape number, and size. Starting in 1940, Pine Cone marks took the form of molded (raised relief) characters.

In January 1935, Roseville introduced an assortment of Pine Cone "vases, bowls, flower bowls, wall pockets, baskets and novelty boxes." One reviewer thought Pine Cone a "charming and quite original" line, "as pleasing a thing as Roseville has brought out in quite a while" (trade notice, *Pottery, Glass and Brass Salesman,* January 10, 1935: 8). The line depicts pine cones, branches, and needles in low relief, all decorated in natural colors against a smooth

background. By September, the line had been expanded to include tall vases, jardinieres, and pedestals (trade notice, *Crockery and Glass Journal,* September 1935: 26).

Like Ivory, Pine Cone sold well for the rest of that decade. In November 1937, Roseville advertisements promised "Splendid Profits for the Pottery Buyer from Our Dependable Creation Pine Cone," which then consisted of 70 shapes, now bearing a Roseville "trade mark on every piece" (*Gift and Art Buyer,* November 1937: 2). A few new shapes were added in 1938, and for the summer 1939 season, Roseville added a ball-shaped lemonade pitcher with an ice-strainer lip. After September 1939 the line is not mentioned in factory advertising. With a new presidency at the helm of Roseville Pottery, the popular line seems to have run its course by the early 1940s.

Collectors still love Pine Cone, which is thought to be one of Frank Ferrell's personal favorites as a designer. (He had introduced a similar motif in the Moss Aztec line at Peters and Reed, when employed there.) See also Pine Cone Modern (below).

Caution: You are reading the first Roseville book to distinguish clearly between Pine Cone and Pine Cone Modern. An identification tip: Only the 1950s Pine Cone Modern shapes are numbered in the 400s. The 1930s examples used a different series of numbers (and can also be unmarked).

In the factory stock pages, 93 examples of Pine Cone are shown:

PINE CONE

Shape No.	Description	Shape No.	Description	Shape No.	Description	Shape No.	Description
1	-4.75" bookend	379	-9" x 3" x 3.25" window box	843	-8" vase	909	-10" ewer
1	-8" x 5" wall shelf	380	-10" x 5.5" window box	844	-8" vase	910	-10" vase
20	-4" flower frog	632	-3" jardiniere	845	-8" fan vase	911	-12" vase
21	-5" flower frog	632	-4" jardiniere	847	-9" vase	912	-15" vase
25	ashtray	632	-5" jardiniere	848	-9" vase	913	-18" floor vase
32	flower frog	632	-6" jardiniere	848	-10" vase	1099C	-4.5" candlestick
33	flower frog	632	-7" jardiniere	849	-10" vase	1106	-5.5" triple candelabra
112	-7" bud vase	632	-8" jardiniere & pedestal	850	-14" vase	1123	candlestick
113	-8" triple bud vase	632	-9" jardiniere	851	-15" ewer	1124	-4.5" double bud vase
114	-8" pillow vase	632	-10" jardiniere & pedestal	906	-6" vase	1273	-8" wall pocket
121	-7" pillow vase	632	-12" jardiniere & pedestal	907	-7" vase	1283	-4" wall bucket
124	-5" planter	633	-5" flower pot and saucer	908	-8" vase		
126	-6" cornucopia	704	-7" vase				
128	-8" cornucopia	705	-9" bud vase				
261	-6" ferner	706	-8" vase				
261	-6" rose bowl	707	-9" vase				
262	-10" bowl	708	-9" vase				
263	-14" bowl	709	-10" vase				
278	-4" planter	711	-10" vase				
279	-9" x 6" bowl	712	-12" vase				
288	-7" wall plate	713	-14" vase				
320	-5" planter	745	-6" vase				
321	-9" bowl	746	-8" vase				
322	-12" bowl	747	-10" vase				
323	-15" bowl	748	-6" vase				
324	-6" centerpiece	776	-14" sand jar				
338	-10" basket	777	-20" umbrella stand				
339	basket	804	-10" vase				
352	-5" hanging basket	805	-12" vase				
352	-8" basket with built-in flower frog	806	-14" vase				
		807	-15" vase				
353	-12" basket	838	-6" vase				
354	-6" bowl	839	-6" vase				
355	-8" bowl	840	-7" vase				
356	-12.5" x 5" x 3.5" centerpiece	841	-7" vase				
		842	-8" vase				

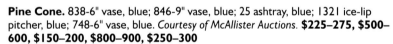

Pine Cone. 848-10" vase, green. *Shannon collection.* **$550–650**

Pine Cone. 838-6" vase, blue; 846-9" vase, blue; 25 ashtray, blue; 1321 ice-lip pitcher, blue; 748-6" vase, blue. *Courtesy of McAllister Auctions.* **$225–275, $500–600, $150–200, $800–900, $250–300**

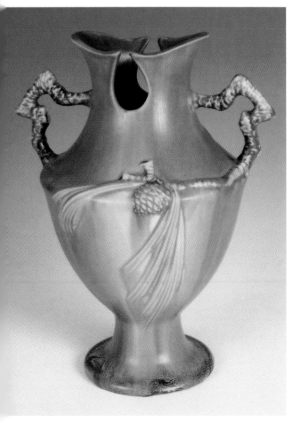

Pine Cone. 709-10" vase, green, orange crayon shape number, gold foil label; 338-10" basket, brown, die-impressed marks, partial silver foil label (shown just below rim). *Cedar Hill collection.* **$400–500 (each)**

Pine Cone. 747-10" vase, brown; 712-12" vase, brown; 711-10" vase, brown. *Hoppe collection.* **$400–500, $600–700, $700–800.** The middle vase has molded (raised) marks; the others have die-impressed marks.

PINE CONE MODERN
A Late Line, introduced in 1953

Factory Name(s): Pine Cone
Collector Nickname(s): Pine Cone II (see Purviance and Schneider, 1970); Pine Cone (Second) [see Alexander, 1970]
Style: Realistic, often with Mid-Century Modern shapes
Standard Color(s): Blue, brown, or green
Typical Marks: Molded (raised-relief) marks, including "Roseville" (script), shape number, and size. Some pieces are die-impressed "PINE CONE," shape number, and size.

Pine Cone Modern is mentioned in the minutes of an April 4, 1952, meeting of Roseville's board of directors. At the time, the factory planned to introduce this "adaptation of the old 'Pine Cone' line" in July 1952. Instead, a series of complicated financial misfortunes delayed the new line for more than a year.

When the new 38-piece line was ready, Roseville advertised, "At last! You've waited for it … Now see it at leading gift shows!" (*Gift and Art Buyer*, August 1953: 27). Four examples of Pine Cone Modern were illustrated: a 472-6" fan vase, a 479-7" bud vase, a 426-6" bowl, and a 485-10" pitcher. The company boasted: "The majestic splendor of evergreen forests is brought to colorful beauty in this newest of Roseville creations, Pine Cone."

By the time factory brochures were prepared, Pine Cone Modern had proven its salability enough to see the addition of at least 13 new designs. All were numbered in the 400s, even those shapes that were reissued (or adapted) from the 1935 Pine Cone line. Pine Cone Modern appears to have sold very well until the factory was sold in the summer of 1954. Most "Pine Cone collectors" seek Pine Cone Modern as avidly as the original Pine Cone designs.

There are no known factory stock pages for Pine Cone Modern. The factory brochure shows 51 shapes:

PINE CONE MODERN

Shape No.	Description	Reference/Notes
400	-4" jardiniere	Bomm 258 (row 8, item 2)
401	-6" jardiniere	Bomm 258 (row 8, item 4)
402	-8" jardiniere	Bomm 259
403	-10" jardiniere	Bomm 259
405	-8" jardiniere & pedestal	Bomm 254 (row 4, item 6)
406	-10" jardiniere & pedestal	Bomm 254 (row 4, item 7)

Shape No.	Description	Reference/Notes
408	-6" basket	Bomm 258 (row 4, item 4)
409	-8" basket	Bomm 258 (row 4, item 3)
410	-10" basket	Bomm 258 (row 4, item 2)
411	-10" basket	Bomm 258 (row 4, item 1)
414	-5" tumbler	Bomm 254 (row 4, item 1)
415	-2 qt. pitcher	Bomm 254 (row 1, item 1)
416	-18" ewer	Bomm 254 (row 4, item 4)
421	-6" cornucopia	Bomm 254 (row 3, item 3)
422	-8" cornucopia	Bomm 254 (row 2, item 1)
425	-6" bowl	Bomm 258 (row 2, item 1)
426	-6" bowl	Bomm 258 (row 1, item 2)
427	-8" bowl	Bomm 258 (row 1, item 3)
428	-8" bowl	Bomm 258 (row 1, item 1)
429	-10" bowl	Bomm 258 (row 3, item 3)
430	-12" bowl	Bomm 258 (row 2, item 2)
431	-15" bowl, canoe shape	Bomm 258 (row 3, item 2)
432	-12" bowl	Bomm 258 (row 2, item 3)
433	-12" bowl	Bomm 258 (row 3, item 1)
439	-8" bookend	Bomm 254 (row 4, item 3) Shape number nearly illegible; may not be accurate
441	-4" rose bowl	Bomm 258 (row 6, item 3)
451	-4" candlestick	Bomm 258 (row 1, item 4)
454	-7" planter, bathtub shape	Bomm 258 (row 6, item 2)
455	-6" planter	Bomm 258 (row 5, item 1)
456	-6" planter	Bomm 258 (row 6, item 4)
457	-7" planter	Bomm 258 (row 7, item 2)
458F	-5" planter	Bomm 258 (row 6, item 1)
459	bookend planter	Bomm 259
461	hanging basket	Bomm 258 (row 8, item 1)
462	double serving tray	Bomm 258 (row 5, item 2)
466	triple wall bucket	Bomm 254 (row 4, item 2)
468	-8" window box	Bomm 258 (row 5, item 3)
469	-12" window box	Bomm 258 (row 8, item 3)
472	-6" fan vase	Bomm 254 (row 3, item 2)
473	-8" double vase	Bomm 254 (row 2, item 3)
479	-7" bud vase	Bomm 254 (row 3, item 1)
480	-7" vase	Bomm 254 (row 2, item 4)
485	-10" ewer	Bomm 254 (row 1, item 3)
490	-8" vase	Bomm 254 (row 2, item 1)
491	-10" vase	Bomm 254 (row 1, item 2)
492	-12" gladiola vase	Bomm 254 (row 1, item 4)
493	-12" vase	Bomm 254 (row 1, item 5)
497	candy dish	Bomm 258 (row 7, item 1)
498	cigarette holder	Bomm 258 (row 7, item 5)
499	ashtray	Bomm 258 (row 7, items 3, 4)
1499	hostess set (one 497 candy dish, one 498 cigarette holder, two 499 ashtrays, available as boxed set)	Bomm 259

Pine Cone Modern. 473-8" double vase, green; 490-8" vase, green. *Courtesy of John Ross Dougar.* **$250–300, $325–375.** Roseville called shape 473 a "novelty flower holder."

Pine Cone Modern. Pair, 451-4" candlesticks, blue; 431-15" bowl, canoe shape, blue. *Auclair collection.* **$350–400 (pair), $500–600**

Pine Cone Modern. 458-5" planter, brown, molded (raised-relief) marks; 458F-5" planter, brown, die-impressed only PINE CONE and 458F-5". *Schultz collection.* **$275–325, $300–350.** Except for their different feet, these two shapes are essentially the same. In one factory stock page, the 458F-5" planter is numbered 458-5" (so may be found marked both ways).

Pine Cone Modern. 415-9" pitcher, brown; 462 double serving tray (6" x 13.25"), blue; 441-4" rose bowl, green. *Courtesy of Treadway Gallery.* **$550–650, $350–400, $125–150**

Pine Cone Modern. 432-12" bowl, brown, die-impressed only 432-12". *Auclair collection.* **$325–375**

Pine Cone Modern. Three examples of the 485-10" pitcher, in brown; green; blue. *Auclair collection.* **$400–500, $400–500, $500–600.** In a factory brochure, this shape is called a vase.

POPPY

A Middle Period Line, introduced in 1938

Factory Name(s): Poppy

Style: Realistic

Standard Color(s): Coral ("pink"), green, or gray

Typical Marks: Die-impressed marks, including "Roseville" (script), shape number, and size

In 1938, Roseville buyers were pleased to note that Poppy was "embellished with graceful, flowing poppy decorations" (trade notice, *Gift and Art Buyer*, January 1938: 21). Full blossoms and poppy pods are modeled in medium relief against a smooth background. Round, scroll-like handles adorn many shapes. Stems curve slightly, in a nod to the Art Nouveau period of an earlier generation, when poppies adorned many decorative objects.

Today Poppy is moderately priced, and is a good value for the Middle-Period collector. Since the line is relatively restrained—somewhere between Classical, Art Nouveau, and Art Deco in style—Poppy pieces are versatile enough for many decors.

Although 40 shapes are mentioned in factory advertising, only 37 examples appear in the Poppy stock pages:

POPPY

Shape No.	Description	Shape No.	Description
35	flower frog	866	-6" vase
334	-4" planter	867	-6" vase
335	-6" rose bowl	868	-7" vase
336	-5" bowl	869	-7" vase
337	-8" bowl	870	-8" pillow vase
338	-10" bowl	871	-8" vase
339	-12" bowl	872	-9" vase
340	-14" bowl	873	-9" vase
341	-7" centerpiece	874	-10" vase
347	-10" basket	875	-10" vase
348	-12" basket	876	-10" ewer
358	-5" hanging basket	877	-12" vase
642	-4" jardiniere	878	-15" vase
642	-5" jardiniere	879	-18" floor vase
642	-6" jardiniere	880	-18" ewer
642	-7" jardiniere	1129	candlestick
642	-8" jardiniere & pedestal	1130	-5" candlestick
642	-10" jardiniere & pedestal	1281	-8" wall pocket
643	-5" vase, flower pot shape		

Poppy. 341-7" centerpiece, vase with attached base and candlesticks, green. *Hoppe photograph.* **$250–300**

Poppy. 879-18" floor vase, brown; 873-9" vase, brown. *Auclair collection.* **$950–1200, $250–300.** Perhaps this unusual brown coloring was a short-lived and early glaze treatment for Poppy.

Poppy. 334-4" rose bowl, gray; 348-12" basket, pink; 1130-5" candlestick, pink; 347-10" basket, gray. *Shannon collection.* **$95–125, $375–450, $95–125, $325–375**

Poppy. Pair, 1129 candlesticks, green; 867-6" vase, green. *Hoppe collection.* **$200–250 (pair), $150–200**

PRIMROSE

A Middle Period Line, introduced in 1936

Factory Name(s): Primrose
Style: Realistic
Standard Color(s): Blue, pink, or tan
Typical Marks: Die-impressed marks, including "Roseville" (script), shape number, and size

The curvaceous stems of Primrose are reminiscent of the 1890s, when the Art Nouveau style was in its prime. Shapes are usually symmetrical, and of a generally classical shape. A few designs are angular or stylized enough to merit the term Art Deco. Reviewers of Primrose admired its "pleasing dainty florals done in white against splendid colored backgrounds" (trade notice, *Crockery and Glass Journal,* January 1936: 65).

Like Poppy, Primrose is typically a moderately price Middle-Period line. As is often true nowadays, the pink and blue pieces usually outsell the tan.

In the factory stock pages, 37 examples of Primrose are shown:

Primrose. 771-12" vase, blue. *Shannon collection.* **$375–450**

PRIMROSE

Shape No.	Description	Shape No.	Description
22	-4" flower frog	760	-6" vase
125	-6" cornucopia	761	-6" vase
260	-5" ferner	762	-7" vase
284	-4" planter	763	-7" vase
285	-6" rose bowl	764	-7" vase
286	-9" bowl	765	-8" pillow vase
287	-12" x 7" bowl	766	-8" vase
341	-10" basket	767	-8" vase
354	-5" hanging basket	768	-8" vase
381	-10" window box	769	-9" vase
634	-4" jardiniere	770	-10" vase
634	-5" jardiniere	771	-12" vase
634	-6" jardiniere	772	-14" vase
634	-7" jardiniere	772	-14" x 10" sand jar
634	-8" jardiniere	773	-21" x 10" umbrella stand
634	-8" jardiniere & pedestal	1105	-4.5" candlestick
634	-9" jardiniere	1113	-5.5" triple candelabra
634	-10" jardiniere & pedestal	1277	-8" wall pocket
636	-5" flower pot and saucer		

Primrose. 770-10" vase, tan. *Hoppe collection.* **$250–300**

Primrose. 125-6" cornucopia, tan; 354-5" hanging basket, tan. *Hoppe photograph.* **$95–125, $250–325**

Primrose. 764-7" vase, blue; 1105-4.5" candlestick, pink; 765-8" pillow vase, pink. *Shannon collection.* **$175–225, $95–125, $225–275**

RAYMOR MODERN ARTWARE
A Late Line, introduced in 1953

Designer: Ben Seibel
Factory Name(s): Modern Artware
Collector Nickname(s): Raymor dinnerware (see Purviance and Schneider, 1970); Raymor artware (see Monsen, 1995)
Style: Mid-Century Modern
Standard Color(s): Contemporary White ("white"), gold, or Manhattan Slate ("black")

Typical Marks: Molded (raised-relief) marks, including "raymor modern artware by Roseville" (script), shape number, and size

After the success of Raymor Modern Stoneware, Ben Seibel was asked to design a line of artware to be manufactured by Roseville and distributed by Richards-Morgenthau as part of the latter's "raymor" line. This little-known Mid-Century Modern line was called Raymor Modern Artware. Shapes include vases, bowls, desk accessories, and other decorative pieces.

Today's Roseville collectors are often unfamiliar with this line. Only a few examples have appeared in previous Roseville books—usually misidentified (and undervalued). The black and white colors are valued more highly than the gold.

Caution: Do not confuse Raymor Modern Artware with the dinnerware line Raymor Modern Stoneware.

No factory stock pages are known for Raymor Modern Artware.

Raymor Modern Artware. 29-11" bowl, clam shape, white. *Courtesy of Mark Bassett Antiques.* **$750–950**

Raymor Modern Artware. pair, 5" candlesticks, black, unmarked; 26-16" bowl, black. *Fairfield collection.* **$300–400 (pair), $400–500**

Raymor Modern Artware. Pair, 96 rectangular boxes, black, original metal covers; 9.25" x 4.25" triangular divided tray, black, original metal stand and cover. *Courtesy of Mark Bassett Antiques.* **$200–250 (each), $250–300**

Raymor Modern Artware. 28-8" bowl, gold. *Fairfield collection.* **$150–200**

RAYMOR MODERN STONEWARE
A Late Line, introduced in 1952

Designer: Ben Seibel
Factory Name(s): Modern Stoneware
Collector Nickname(s): Raymor dinnerware (see Purviance and Schneider, 1970); Raymor (see Alexander, 1970)
Style: Mid-Century Modern
Standard Color(s): Autumn Brown ("dark brown"), Avocado Green ("avocado," or "frog skin"), Contemporary White ("white"), Spring Grey ("gray," also called Beach Gray), Terra Cotta ("pumpkin")
Typical Marks: Molded (raised-relief) marks, including "raymor by Roseville" (script), shape number, and size

Freelance designer Ben Seibel had produced lamps and woodenware for the New York City-based "raymor" group before he turned his hand to ceramics. In 1951, through an arrangement with Irving S. Richards (principal owner of Richards-Morgenthau and the "raymor" trademark), Roseville agreed to produce a dinnerware line in the Mid-Century Modern style.

According to a contemporary reviewer, "Modern Stoneware in the Raymor line was designed by Ben Seibel for informal contemporary serving. The six [*sic*] textural glaze colors are terra-cotta, avocado green, Manhattan slate, spring grey, and contemporary white. Plates and soup bowls have tabs for easier handling. The coffee cup has a flat thumb grip. The individual corn server and the celery and olive dish can be used for seafood and sauce or a vegetable and melted butter. Made by the Roseville Pottery Co., Zanesville, Ohio, and distributed by Richards-Morgenthau Co., 225 Fifth Ave., New York" (trade notice, *Gift and Art Buyer*, January 1952: 109).

Raymor dinnerware began to take off, with the unusual serving pieces getting the bulk of the orders. The success took Roseville executives by surprise. In Zanesville, the company's financial resources were being taxed by several unrelated issues, including labor union negotiations. Expecting buyers to place large orders for the flatware (basic place settings of plates, bowls, cups, and saucers), the factory had produced a large quantity of these shapes. To expedite the orders for more unusual shapes would require purchasing specialized equipment—another forbidding investment of dwindling funds.

Despite previous summaries in earlier Roseville books, Raymor Modern Stoneware was very well received by the leading buyers. Through an unfortunate coincidence of timing, factory executives felt unable to solve the various financial difficulties, and by mid-1954 decided to sell the factory.

Today Roseville's Raymor is one of the most desirable of Mid-Century Modern dinnerware lines. In aesthetics, it compares well with Russel Wright's *American Modern*, and is also much more durable. The highest values still go to odd-shaped serving pieces.

There are no known factory stock pages. A factory brochure—reprinted in Huxford (1980), page 152—shows 55 items in the Raymor Modern Stoneware line:

Shape No.	Description	Shape No.	Description
			187 4-qt. bean pot
150	cup	188	bean pot trivet
151	saucer	189	water pitcher
152	dinner plate	190	gravy boat
153	salad plate	191	pickle dish
154	bread and butter plate	192	lug fruit
155	lug soup	193	3-qt. bean pot
156	individual covered ramekin	194	2-qt. bean pot
157	covered sugar	195	individual bean pot
158	covered cream pitcher	196	4-qt. handled casserole
159	stand for sugar and creamer	197	2.5-qt. handled casserole
160	vegetable bowl	198	1.5-qt. handled casserole
161	salad bowl	199	individual casserole
162	individual corn server	200	shirred egg
163	platter	201	double stacked warmer
164	chop platter	202	bun warmer
165	divided vegetable bowl	203	ash tray
166	handled fruit bowl	300	16-pc. set, complete (4 each: items 150, 151, 152, and 154)
167	6-pc. condiment set (items 168–173)		
168	salt shaker		
169	pepper shaker		
170	vinegar cruet		
171	oil cruet		
172	covered jam or relish, with spoon		
173	condiment stand only		
174	tea pot		
175	tea pot trivet		
176	large coffee pot and stand		
177	celery and olive dish		
178	steak platter with well		
179	handled coffee tumbler		
180	3-pc. cheese and relish set		
181	covered butter dish		
182	relish and sandwich tray		
183	medium casserole		
184	medium casserole trivet		
185	large casserole		
186	large casserole trivet		

Raymor Modern Stoneware. Assortment of dinnerware pieces in the Raymor Modern Stoneware line. *Fairfield photograph.*

Raymor Modern Stoneware. 156 individual covered ramekin, green; 158-4.25" creamer, missing its lid, rust. *Shannon collection.* **$40–50, $30–35 (or $50–60 with lid)**

Raymor Modern Stoneware. Set of four 156 covered ramekins, in white, dark brown, pumpkin, and green, in original wire and raffia stand. *Fairfield collection.* **$75–350 (set, including stand)**

Raymor Modern Stoneware. 156-6.5" individual covered ramekin, dark brown; 189-10" water pitcher, dark brown. *Hoppe photograph.* **$30–40, $125–175**

RAYMOR TWO-TONE CASUAL
A Late Line, introduced in 1953

Factory Name(s): Raymor Two-Tone Casual
Collector Nickname(s): Gourmet bowls (see Purvance and
  Schneider, 1970); Glossy Utility Line (see Huxford, 1980);
  Raymor Gourmet (see Bomm, 1998)
Style: Early American
Standard Color(s): Unknown
Typical Marks: Molded (raised-relief) marks, including "raymor,
  Gourmet Service for the Gourmet by Roseville" (or simpler
  marks, on smaller examples), shape number, and size. Some
  pieces—revived from the Glossy Utility Line—are marked
  with an "R," "U.S.A." and the shape number (and sometimes
  size).

This group of Early American-styled products was a late "oven
to table" line—based in part on another late Roseville product,
Glossy Utility Ware. Raymor Two-Tone Casual used conservative
shapes to allow its use either with the Raymor Modern
Stoneware line or with a homemaker's other china and
stemware. Unlike the Glossy ware, Two-Tone Casual uses
semigloss or matte glazes. Lids and linings are usually white, and
the colored pieces typically have white spatter along the outer
rim.

Introduced late in Roseville's history, Raymor Two-Tone Casual
is a little known and scarce line today. Most Raymor collectors would
like one or more examples for their collections, but Ben Seibel's
designs are typically considered more interesting (and therefore
more valuable).

Caution: Do not confuse Raymor Two-Tone Casual with Glossy
Utility Ware.

The only known factory stock page (reprinted in Bomm, page
268) shows 13 shapes in the Raymor Two-Tone Casual line:

RAYMOR TWO-TONE CASUAL

Shape No.	Description
9	1-qt. mixing bowl
10	1.5-qt. mixing bowl (Glossy Utility Ware shape 10)
11	3-qt. mixing bowl (Glossy Utility Ware shape 11)
12	5-qt. mixing bowl (Glossy Utility Ware shape 12)
14	1-pt. pitcher
15	1-qt. pitcher (Glossy Utility Ware shape 15)
16	2-qt. pitcher (Glossy Utility Ware shape 16)
17	2.5-qt. pitcher (Glossy Utility Ware shape 17)
18	2.5-qt. covered baking dish
19	5-qt. covered baking dish
20	2-qt. covered casserole
21	5-qt. covered casserole
	2-pt. covered casserole

Raymor Two-Tone Casual. 20
covered casserole, white and gray,
spatter in white; Raymor Modern
Stoneware 156 ramekin (lid missing),
mottled slate blue; 18 bean pot, white
and pumpkin, spatter in white.
Fairfield collection. **$175–225, $40–
50 (or $60–70 with lid), $150–200.**
The blue color is unusual for Raymor.

ROSECRAFT
An Early Line, introduced by 1921

Factory Name(s): Azurine, Orchid and Turquoise; Rosecraft
Collector Nickname(s): Azurine Orchid Turquoise (see Clifford,
  1968); Rosecraft Black, Rosecraft Colors, and Azurine-Orchid-
  Turquoise (see Alexander, 1970); Florane (see Huxford, 1976);
  Rosecraft (see Buxton, 1977); Rosecraft–Color (see Bomm,
  1998)
Style: Classical
Standard Color(s): Azurine ("dark blue"), Black, Burnt Orange, Old
  Rose, Orchid ("lavender"), Turquoise ("aqua," also called Jade),
  or Yellow
Typical Marks: Early examples of Rosecraft were unmarked. Starting
  about 1923, they were marked with the blue inkstamp Rv logo
  (including most Burnt Orange examples). Many Black examples
  have a paper or foil label, indicating that they date to about
  1927 or later.

Rosecraft went through several transformations during the
1920s. Little wonder that Roseville collectors have been confused
about this line's identity for decades. It is helpful to view Rosecraft
as an extensive revision of an older idea—using different shapes
and colors—Solid Colors.

By 1921, Roseville introduced the new Rosecraft shapes in a
choice of three glossy glazes: Azurine (dark blue), Orchid, and
Turquoise (also called "jade"). In mid-1922, when Roseville
introduced a mirror Black, the line was renamed "Rosecraft" (trade
notice, *Pottery, Glass and Brass Salesman,* July 13, 1922: 15). The
reviewer thought Rosecraft's Black to be "an excellent example of
this color in popular-priced pottery."

In 1923 a semigloss old rose was added, and in 1925, a glossy
yellow. Also in 1925 a matte glaze was introduced that blended
from orange to olive green or brown. Judging from surviving
examples, Burnt Orange appears to have been extremely popular.
(Earlier writers have confused the burnt orange coloring of
Rosecraft with the late line Florane.)

In the mid-1920s Roseville also began producing Lustre glazes. (Azurine has a lustrous quality.) Lustre and Rosecraft, in fact, share many shapes. Perhaps at some point the company viewed Lustre glazes as additional choices within the Rosecraft line. Here, in keeping with tradition, Lustre and Rosecraft shapes are listed separately.

In the factory stock pages, the term Rosecraft itself does not appear, but 102 shapes are shown in one of the Rosecraft glazes:

ROSECRAFT

Shape No.	Description	Reference/Notes
3	-8" comport	Bomm 273
4	-10" comport	Bomm 273
4	-11" covered vase	Bomm 274
10	-5" bowl	Bomm 274
11	-8" comport	Bomm 274
15	-2.5" flower block	Bomm 274
15	-3.5" flower block	Bomm 275
32	-8" bud vase	Bomm 273
33	-10" bud vase	Bomm 273
44	-8" bud vase	Bomm 275
45	-8" vase	Bomm 274
46	-5" double bud vase, gate shape	Bomm 275
66	-7" bowl	Bomm 55
74	-5" bowl	Bomm 271 (from factory drawing)
74	-6" bowl	Bomm 274
74	-8" bowl	Bomm 271 (from factory drawing)
75	-8" bowl	Bomm 273
75	-10" bowl	Bomm 273
83	-5" urn (also a Lustre shape)	Bomm 275
87	-6" vase	Bomm 275
93	-8" bowl	Bomm 55
93	-10" bowl	Bomm 55
93	-12" bowl	Bomm 55
94	-5" rose bowl	Bomm 55
95	-7" bowl	Bomm 55
96	-6" bowl	Bomm 55
108	-5" bowl	Bomm 274
109	-6" vase	Bomm 274
110	-6" bowl	Bomm 274
124	-5" bowl	Bomm 271 (from factory drawing)
124	-6" bowl	Bomm 275
124	-7" bowl	Bomm 271 (from factory drawing)
124	-8" bowl	Bomm 271 (from factory drawing)
129	-5" vase	Bomm 274
158	-5" vase	Bomm 271 (from factory drawing)
165	-6" vase	Bomm 273
166	-8" vase	Bomm 273
167	-10" vase	Bomm 273
168	-12" vase	Bomm 273
175	-5" vase	Bomm 275
175	-8" vase (also a Lustre shape)	Bomm 275
180	-10" vase	Bomm 55
181	-12" vase	Bomm 55
182	-12" vase	Bomm 55
183	-14" vase	Bomm 55
185	-8" vase	Bomm 274
186	-10" vase	Bomm 274
187	-12" vase	Bomm 274
210	-12" vase	Bomm 274
211	-12" vase	Bomm 274
223	-5.5" vase	Bomm 274
225	-12" vase	Bomm 274
227	-13" vase	Bomm 275
243	-8" vase	Bomm 275
244	-6" vase	Bomm 274
245	-6" vase	Bomm 275

Shape No.	Description	Reference/Notes
246	-6" vase	Bomm 274
247	-6" vase	Bomm 275
249	-8" vase	Bomm 275
250	-10" vase	Bomm 275
308	-7" vase	Bomm 271 (from factory drawing)
309	-8" vase	Bomm 271 (from factory drawing)
310	-9" basket (also a Lustre shape)	Bomm 275
311	-7" vase	Bomm 271 (from factory drawing)
313	-11" basket	Bomm 55
314	-9" vase	Bomm 271 (from factory drawing)
314	-11.5" basket	Bomm 55
315	-10" vase	Bomm 271 (from factory drawing)
315	-11" basket	Bomm 55
316	-9.5" basket	Bomm 55
316	-10" vase	Bomm 271 (from factory drawing)
317	-10" vase	Bomm 271 (from factory drawing)
317	-13.5" basket	Bomm 55
318	-8" vase	Bomm 271 (from factory drawing)
318	-13" basket	Bomm 55
319	-8" basket	Bomm 274
319	-12" vase	Bomm 271 (from factory drawing)
335	-8" vase	Bomm 271 (from factory drawing)
336	-9" vase	Bomm 271 (from factory drawing)
337	-10" vase	Bomm 271 (from factory drawing)
338	-12" vase	Bomm 271 (from factory drawing)
339	-15" vase	Bomm 271 (from factory drawing)
351	-12" vase	Bomm 275
598	-4" flower pot and separate saucer	Bomm 271 (from factory drawing)
598	-5" flower pot and separate saucer	Bomm 55
598	-6" flower pot and separate saucer	Bomm 55
598	-7" flower pot and separate saucer	Bomm 271 (from factory drawing)
1017	-8" candlestick	Bomm 273
1018	-10" candlestick	Bomm 273
1029	-3.75" candlestick	Bomm 55
1030	-4" candlestick	Bomm 55
1031	-6" candlestick	Bomm 55
1032	-8" candlestick	Bomm 55
1033	-12" candlestick	Bomm 55
1034	-15" candlestick	Bomm 55
1035	-8" candlestick	Bomm 274
1036	-8" candlestick	Bomm 274
1038	-10" candlestick	Bomm 274
1039	-10" candlestick	Bomm 274
1225	-10" wall pocket	Bomm 274
1236	-9" wall pocket	Bomm 275
1237	-10" wall pocket	Bomm 275

Rosecraft. Pair, 1038-8" candlesticks, turquoise; 1033-12" candlestick, turquoise; 1031-6" candlestick, turquoise. *Hoppe photograph.* **$150–200 (pair), $75–95, $50–60**

Rosecraft. 175-6" vase; 223-5.5" vase; 248-8" vase; 244-6" vase; 319-8" basket. *Courtesy of Cincinnati Art Galleries.* **$125–175, $125–175, $150–200, $125–175, $175–225.** All five of these examples of burnt orange have the blue Rv inkstamp.

Rosecraft. 585-4" urn, black; 319-10" vase, black; 311-7" vase, black. *Hoppe photograph.* **$95–125, $250–300, $150–200**

Rosecraft. 129-5" urn, yellow; 44-8" bud vase, yellow. *Fairfield collection.* **$125–150 (each)**

Rosecraft. 225-12" vase, azurine; 182-12" vase, azurine. *Hoppe photograph.* **$200–250, $275–325**

Rosecraft. 15-3.5" flower block, orchid; 74-8" bowl, orchid. *Hoppe photograph.* **$20–25, $95–125**

Rosecraft. 316-9.5" basket, turquoise, *Nickel and Horvath collection;* 319-8" basket, azurine, *courtesy of McAllister Auctions.* **$200–250, $175–225**

ROYAL CAPRI

A Late Line, introduced ca. 1954

Factory Name(s): Unknown (see below)

Style: Decorative, often with Mid-Century Modern shapes

Standard Color(s): Gilt, with either a mirror or molten ("weeping") texture

Typical Marks: Molded (raised-relief) marks, including "Roseville" (script), shape number, and size. These molded shape numbers are those of the corresponding Late Capri items, not the numbers appearing in the Royal Capri brochure.

According to the Krause family, the glaze used in Royal Capri was developed by George Krause, who was enamored of gilded porcelain and liked the look of this glaze on Roseville shapes. It is unclear whether any Royal Capri was manufactured by Roseville Pottery, since the only published reference is a brochure printed by "P. & E. Decorators, Roseville, Ohio" (reprinted in Bomm 279).

Another plausible explanation of these wares is that Roseville conducted bisque firings, and that the pieces were gilt and marketed in nearby Roseville, by the P. & E. decorating firm. This alternative would make Royal Capri essentially a commercial job—like Hyde Park. If the line was indeed gilt and marketed by Roseville, this invention undoubtedly dates to the final months of operation, during 1954.

In any case, most Roseville collectors are happy to locate an example of this rare line. A total of 21 shapes appear in the Royal Capri brochure (originally in the Krause Family collection). Except for the 3-piece smoking set (shapes GR-1797, GR-1798, and GR-1799), Royal Capri shapes were borrowed from Late Capri. The abbreviation "GR-" was then added to the old shape number to indicate Royal Capri:

ROYAL CAPRI

Shape No.	Description	Shape No.	Description
GR-508	-7" basket	GR-555	-7" planter
GR-525	-5" bowl	GR-556	-6" cornucopia
GR-526	-7" bowl	GR-563	-10" conch shell
GR-527	-7" bowl	GR-578	-7" bud vase
GR-528	-9" bowl	GR-579	-8" bud vase
GR-529	-9" bowl	GR-583	-9" vase
GR-530	-12" bowl	GR-1797	-5" bowl
GR-533	-10" bowl	GR-1798	-3" cigarette holder, kettle shape
GR-534	-16" bowl		
GR-552	-4" rectangular bowl	GR-1799	-5" ashtray, skillet shape
GR-554	-6" planter	GR-C1010	-10" planter

Royal Capri. 556-6" cornucopia; 851-6" bud vase, a glaze trial for Royal Capri line; 598-9" ashtray, shell shape; 554-6" planter; 4" ashtray, unmarked; 508-7" basket; 555-7" planter. *Krause Family collection.* **$200–250, $275–350, $175–225, $150–200, $95–125, $325–375, $200–250**

Royal Capri (glaze trial). 924-4.5" vase, molded (raised) 4. *Nickel and Horvath collection.* **$275–350**

Royal Capri. 526-7" planter; 578-7" bud vase. *Hoppe photograph.* **$200–250 (each)**

ROZANE LINE
A Middle Period Line, introduced by 1920

Factory Name(s): Rozane

Collector Nickname(s): Rozane, or Rozane Line (see Alexander, 1970); Rozane 1917 (see Huxford, 1980)

Style: Edwardian, or Italianate

Standard Color(s): Blue, green, pink, white, or yellow

Typical Marks: Most examples have a distinctive black inkstamp mark, with the words "ROSEVILLE POTTERY" arranged in a semicircle around the line name "ROZANE." Some examples are unmarked.

Rozane Line features a realistically colored floral bouquet, modeled in relief against a "dimpled" or "hammered" background. In *Roseville Pottery: For Love or Money* (1977), Virginia Hillway Buxton attributes some of Rozane Line's "fresh spring-like attitude" to "ice cream colored backgrounds—vanilla white, strawberry pink, mint green, and a soft light blueberry blue" (146). Also known is a pale lemon yellow.

Today, the pattern finds only moderate interest among Roseville collectors, although it was offered for several years, at least through 1921 (advertisement, *Crockery and Glass Journal,* December 16, 1920: 164).

In the factory stock pages, 16 examples are shown:

ROZANE LINE

Shape No.	Description	Shape No.	Description
1	vase	367	-10" window box
1	-6" ferner	588	-5" jardiniere
2	-8" comport	588	-6" jardiniere
102	-12" vase	588	-8" jardiniere
250	-6.25" vase	588	-10" jardiniere & pedestal
251	-5.5" basket	756	-19" x 9" umbrella stand
252	-8" basket	R108	-5.25" vase
330	-6" hanging basket	R110	-6" vase

Rozane Line. 6.5" urn, loop handles, blue, ROZANE inkstamp; 1016-6" candlestick, green, blue inkstamp "1016-6" (no other mark); 588-6" jardiniere, yellow. *Fairfield collection.* **$150–200, $75–95, $175–225.** The inkstamp on the candlestick is comparable to one found on many examples of Vista and some examples of Dogwood (Smooth).

Rozane Line. 6.5" urn, scroll handles, pink; 2-8" comport (6" tall), pink; R110-6" vase, blue. *Shannon collection.* **$125–150 (each)**

Rozane Line. 6.5" pitcher, white; 10" vase, trophy shape, white; 8.5" basket, white. *Shannon collection.* **$175–225, $175–225, $200–250**

Rozane Line. 8" vase, green; 252-8" basket, yellow. *Shannon collection.* **$150–200, $225–275**

ROZANE PATTERN

A Late Line, introduced in 1941

Factory Name(s): Rozane; Rozane Pattern

Collector Nickname(s): Rozane Line (see Purviance and Schneider, 1970); Rozane Pattern (see Alexander, 1970); Rozane Patterns (see Mollring, 1995)

Style: Streamlined Modern, or Classical

Standard Color(s): Burnt Orange ("brown"), Calla Ivory ("green"), or Mountain Blue ("blue")

Typical Marks: Molded (raised-relief) marks, including "Roseville" (script), shape number, and size

A 1941 factory advertisement described Rozane Pattern as "the first decorated line of pottery made by ROSEVILLE in many, many years. Ineptly styled in the American manner, ROZANE is an all purpose line suitable for the decoration of any home" (*Gift and Art Buyer,* January 1941: 2). The line is sometimes based on classical Chinese shapes, and sometimes geometrical—in the spirit of the 1939 World Fair's trylon and perisphere.

The matte mottled glazes blend from a dark base up the body to nearly ivory at the rim. Despite today's interest in the Art Deco style, prices remain moderate to affordable for most shapes.

It appears that around 1953 or 1954, the factory reintroduced this line, using new glossy glazes—rust, periwinkle blue, violet, and off-white. These glazes appear in the only known factory stock page—which may have been left uncolored until Rozane Pattern was revived. (The Roseville factory stock pages are black and white photographs, which were individually hand-tinted in watercolor.)

The Rozane Pattern stock page shows 26 shapes:

ROZANE PATTERN

Shape No.	Description	Shape No.	Description
I	fish ornament	I I	-15" vase
I	-6" vase	44	flower frog
2	cornucopia	395	-9" vase
2	flame ornament	396	-10" bowl
2	-6" vase	397	-14" bowl
3	-8" vase	398	-4" vase
4	-8" vase	398	-6" vase
5	-8" vase	398	-8" vase
6	-9" vase	407	-6" bowl
7	-9" vase	408	-8" bowl
8	-10" vase	409	-12" bowl
9	-10" vase	410	conch shell
10	-12" vase	1144	-3" candlestick

Rozane Pattern. 8-10" vase, blue; 410 conch, blue. *Hoppe photograph.* **$150–200, $125–175**

Rozane Pattern. 2 cornucopia, green; 1-6" vase, brown. *Courtesy of McAllister Auctions.* **$125–150, $75–95**

Rozane Pattern. 2-6" vase, green; 7-9" vase, brown; 6-9" vase, green; 398-6" vase, brown. *Shannon collection.* **$95–125, $125–175, $125–150, $125–150**

Rozane Pattern. 1 ornament, fish and wave, green; 2 ornament, flame, blue. *Bassett collection.* **$125–150 (each)**

Rozane Pattern (Late). Pair, #1 fish ornaments; three 1144-3" candlesticks; 44 flower frog—all in a glossy violet. *Krause Family collection.* **$125–150 (each), $60–75 (each), $95–125**

Rozane Pattern (Late). 1-6" vase; 5-8" vase; 398-4" vase; 396-10" bowl; pair, 1144-3" candlesticks—all in a glossy periwinkle. *Krause Family collection.* **$95–125, $125–150, $125–150, $125–150, $150–175 (pair)**

Rozane Pattern (Late). 3-8" vase, glossy white. *Fairfield collection.* **$125–150.** This glaze resembles one of the experiments that George Krause conducted with glossy white glaze formulas in the 1950s—for patterns like Burmese and Ming Tree.

Rozane Pattern (Late). 9-10" vase; 10-12" vase; 1-6" vase—all in a glossy rust. *Auclair collection.* **$175–225, $200–250, $95–125**

ROZANE ROYAL
An Early Line, introduced by 1901

Factory Name(s): Rozane, Rozane Royal, and perhaps others (such as Hollywood Ware, Home Art, Light Art, etc.)

Collector Nickname(s): Untrimmed Rozane, and Light Art (see Buxton, 1977); Light Rozane (see Huxford, 1980); Rozane Lights (see Mollring, 1995); Rozane–Hollywood Ware (see Bomm, 1998)

Style: Late Victorian

Standard Color(s): Brown, or gray

Typical Marks: Early pieces have the die-impressed line name "ROZANE," the shape number, "R.P. Co." and perhaps other numerals (whose meaning is not known). Some are unmarked. Starting about 1904, the Rozane Ware wafer was used on Rozane Royal and other early artware lines. In about 1905, a more specific Rozane Royal wafer was used. (All of these marks are found on both the Dark and Light versions.)

Like Weller, Owens, and Cambridge, the Roseville Pottery Company introduced Rozane Royal to offer buyers a less expensive alternative to Rookwood's Standard Glaze (and to corner part of their market). The line appears to have been introduced by 1901 under the sometimes generic term "Rozane." In *Introducing Roseville Pottery,* the term "Rozane Royal" has been used consistently, to help readers avoid confusion with Rozane Line, and Rozane Pattern—two completely unrelated Roseville product lines.

Rozane Royal pieces were first airbrushed with background of blended colors. In the case of Rozane Royal (Dark), these colors range from yellow to dark green to brown. Undecorated examples of Rozane Royal (Dark) are known—and may have preceded the decorated pieces. If decorated, hand-painted designs were next applied in slip (an especially prepared clay slurry, mixed with pigment). A transparent honey-colored glaze was then used to coat the entire piece.

By 1905, Rozane Royal (Light) pieces were also offered, with backgrounds shading from white to gray—and sometimes to black. A blue version of Rozane Royal was introduced under the name "Azurean." (For details, see Azurean.) Occasionally a green example of Rozane Royal is reported.

Contrary to expectation, Rozane Royal remained in the factory line well into the teens. An example dated 1917 has been examined by the author. Such a long-lived product line was clearly a major success in its day, and Roseville advertisements shortly after 1900 often have a tone of bragadoccio about them.

Factory records include several stock pages illustrating lines that appear to be identical to Rozane Royal, but that are given unexpected headings, like "Home Art" and "Hollywood Ware." No Roseville pieces have surfaced with either mark. In *Introducing Roseville Pottery,* these products are all treated as one line.

Some writers have speculated that "Home Art" pieces used decal decoration, instead of hand-painting. (This author has never seen such an example.) Another likely explanation of the term is that Roseville wanted to suggest an affordable art line as being appropriate to grace even a middle-class home.

In the case of "Hollywood Ware"—whatever that term meant to Roseville—it does not seem plausible to suggest a connection to

Rozane Royal (Dark). 864-8.25" lemonade pitcher, corn, artist initials "L.M." (Lillie Mitchell), die-impressed ROZANE marks. *Scheytt collection.* **$950–1200**

Rozane Royal (Dark). 968-10.75" vase, wild roses, artist signature "Myers," die-impressed 7. *Fairfield collection.* **$400–500**

e silent-movie scene in California (see Bomm). Instead, it may be
at "Hollywood"—like Bushberry—is a Roseville coinage intended
suggest mahogany or another dark "woody" color. The holly, of
urse, was an appropriate image to conjure for a line that may
ve been introduced at one of the annual glass and china shows in
tsburgh. (They were held in January.)

Today, these Late Victorian products are relatively undervalued.
ollectors prefer pieces with finely painted decoration, preferably
ned by an artist. Landscapes and portraits (either human or
imal) add another zero to the asking price!

The following Rozane Royal inventory indicates which shapes
peared in the 1904, 1905, and 1906 factory catalogs. Other shapes
pear only in the factory stock pages. Only Rozane Royal (Dark)
amples appear in the 1904 and 1905 catalogs. According to the
06 catalog, those shapes marked (L) were also available in Rozane
yal (Light). Altogether, these factory records illustrate a total of 246
ferent shapes decorated as Rozane Royal:

**Rozane Royal
(Dark).** 424-11"
x 31.5" jardiniere
and pedestal,
chrysanthemums,
artist initials WH,
no factory mark.
Stofft collection.
$2200–2500

ROZANE ROYAL

Shape No.	Description	Reference/Notes
424	-12" x 32" jardiniere & pedestal	Bomm 176
438	-8" jardiniere	Bomm 176
457	-4" jardiniere (L only)	Bomm 208
457	-5" jardiniere (L only)	Bomm 208
457	-6" jardiniere (L only)	Bomm 208
457	-7" jardiniere (L only)	Bomm 208
457	-8" jardiniere (L)	Bomm 176
457	-9" jardiniere (L only)	Bomm 208
457	-10" jardiniere (L only)	Bomm 208
457	-12" jardiniere (L only)	Bomm 208
462	-7" jardiniere	Bomm 176
476	-3" jardiniere	Bomm 176
476	-6" x 18.5" jardiniere & pedestal	Bomm 175
476	-7" x 20.5" jardiniere & pedestal	Bomm 175
476	-8" x 23.5" jardiniere & pedestal	Bomm 175
476	-9" x 26.75" or 27" jardiniere & pedestal	Bomm 176
476	-10" x 29.5" jardiniere & pedestal	Bomm 175
476	-12" x 37" jardiniere & pedestal	Bomm 175
626	cuspidor	Bomm 111; see also July 1916 price list (as "Art–Decorated")
715	-23" x 9" umbrella stand	Bomm 176
723	-20" x 8" (or -21" x 9") umbrella stand	Bomm 176; see also July 1916 price list (as "Art")
724	-20" x 9" umbrella stand	Bomm 175; see also July 1916 price list (as "Art")
725	-23" x 10" umbrella stand	See July 1916 price list (as "Art")
804	-2.75" bud vase	Bomm 282 (row 1, item 5)—1905 (as R804), 1906 catalogs
806	-8" vase	Bomm 285 (row 2, item 2)
807	-12.75" or -13" vase	Bomm 284 (row 2, item 3)—1905 (as R807), 1906 catalogs
809	-5.25" bud vase	Bomm 282 (row 1, item 3)
810	-8.75" bud vase	Bomm 285 (row 4, item 6)
811	-8.25" vase	Bomm 285 (row 2, item 3)—1904 catalog
812	-13.5" vase (L)	Bomm 313 (row 5, item 7)—1904, 1906 catalogs
813	-9.75" or -10" vase	Bomm 280 (row 1, item 1)—1904, 1906 catalogs
814	-9.25" or -10" vase (L)	Bomm 280 (row 1, item 4)—1905 (as R814), 1906 catalogs
815	-20" vase (L)	Bomm 285 (row 1, item 1)—1904, 1906 catalogs
816	-15" vase (L)	Bomm 281 (row 4, item 1)—1904, 1905 (as R816), 1906 catalogs
817	-4" bud vase	Bomm 283 (row 2, item 2)
818	-12" vase (L)	Bomm 284 (row 2, item 2)—1906 catalog
821	-8.5" or -9" vase	Bomm 280 (row 1, item 3)—1904, 1906 catalogs
822	-15.75" or -16" vase (L)	Bomm 285 (row 1, item 3)—1906 catalog
823	-6.5" vase (L)	Bomm 282 (row 3, item 2)—1905 (as R823), 1906 catalogs
824	-11.25" vase	Bomm 280 (row 2, item 3)—1905 catalog (as R824)
826	-21" floor vase	Bomm 281 (row 1, item 2)—1906 catalog
827	-9" vase	Bomm 280 (row 1, item 2)—1906 catalog
828	-8.25" ewer	Bomm 285 (row 3, item 6)—1904 catalog
829	-9" ewer	Bomm 285 (row 3, item 5)—1904 catalog
831	-9.75" or -10" vase (L)	Bomm 280 (row 2, item 2)—1904, 1906 catalogs
832	-20" floor vase	Bomm 281 (row 1, item 1)—1904, 1906 catalogs
833	-11" vase	Bomm 285 (row 4, item 3)
834	-6" or -6.5" vase	Bomm 285 (row 2, item 1)—1904 catalog
835	-10.75" bud vase	Bomm 285 (row 4, item 4)
836	-7.5" vase	Bomm 284 (row 5, item 3)
837	-12.25" or -12.75" vase	Bomm 282 (row 2, item 5)—1905 (as R837), 1906 catalogs
838	-7.75" bud vase	Bomm 284 (row 4, item 4)
839	-6.5" bud vase	Bomm 284 (row 4, item 2)
840	-7" bud vase	Bomm 284 (row 4, item 1)
841	-7.5" bud vase	Bomm 282 (row 2, item 2)
842	-8" bud vase	Bomm 284 (row 4, item 4)—1904 catalog

Shape No.	Description	Reference/Notes
843	-7" vase	Bomm 282 (row 3, item 4)—1904, 1905 (as R843), 1906 catalogs
844	-4.5" vase	Bomm 284 (row 3, item 8)
845	-11.5" vase (L)	Bomm 280 (row 2, item 1)—1906 catalog
846	-4" vase	Bomm 283 (row 2, item 4)—1904 catalog
848	-6.75" vase	Bomm 282 (row 1, item 1)
849	-8" bud vase	Bomm 284 (row 4, item 7)
850	-24" floor vase	Bomm 317 (row 2, item 1)—1904, 1906 catalogs
851	-6" bud vase	Bomm 284 (row 3, item 4)
852	-4.5" ewer	Bomm 284 (row 3, item 7)—1904 catalog
853	-5.5" vase	Bomm 282 (row 3, item 3)
854	-16" ewer	Bomm 284 (row 1, item 3)—1904, 1906 catalogs
855	-14" or -14.5" tankard (L)	Bomm 284 (row 1, item 1)—1904, 1905 (as R855), 1906 catalogs
856	-4.5" stein	Bomm 283 (row 3, item 3)
857	-7.5" ewer	Bomm 284 (row 4, item 6)
858	-15" or -16" ewer	Bomm 284 (row 2, item 5)—1905 (as R858), 1906 catalogs
859	-11.5" bud vase	Bomm 285 (row 4, item 5)
860	-4.75" vase	Bomm 283 (row 2, item 3)
861	-16" vase	Bomm 312 (row 1, item 5)—1904, 1906 catalogs
862	-4.5" bud vase	Bomm 284 (row 5, item 6)
863	-21" floor vase	Bomm 281 (row 1, item 3)—1906 catalog
864	-8.5" pitcher	Bomm 283 (row 3, item 1)—1906 catalog
865	-19" floor vase (L)	Bomm 285 (row 1, item 2)—1904, 1905 (as R865), 1906 catalogs
866	-9.5" ewer	Bomm 285 (row 3, item 4)
867	-10.5" vase (L)	Bomm 323 (row 2, item 3)—1904, 1905 (as R867), 1906 catalogs
868	-9" bud vase	Bomm 284 (row 5, item 6)—1906 catalog
869	-10" vase	Bomm 285 (row 3, item 3)
870	-11" ewer	Bomm 282 (row 2, item 4)—1906 catalog
871	-8" vase	Bomm 283 (row 1, item 2)
872	-5.5" vase	Bomm 282 (row 1, item 2)
873	-5" bud vase	Bomm 284 (row 3, item 2)
874	-5.25" vase	Bomm 284 (row 3, item 3)
875	-6" bud vase	Bomm 284 (row 4, item 3)
876	-8.5" vase	Bomm 283 (row 1, item 4)
877	-7.75" vase	Bomm 285 (row 2, item 6)

Shape No.	Description	Reference/Notes
878	-7.5" bud vase	Bomm 303 (row 2, item 5)
879	-10.5" or -11" vase (L)	Bomm 285 (row 3, item 1)—1906 catalog
880	-5" vase	Bomm 284 (row 3, item 1)
881	-6" ewer (L)	Bomm 284 (row 5, item 2)—1906 catalog
882	-9" pillow vase	Bomm 282 (row 3, item 1)—1904, 1906 catalogs
883	-6" or -6.5" ewer	Bomm 284 (row 5, item 1)—1906 catalog
884	-16" or -16.5" tankard (L)	Bomm 284 (row 1, item 5)—1906 catalog
885	-5" candlestick	Bomm 284 (row 3, item 5)
886	-5" stein (L)	Bomm 283 (row 3, item 2)—1906 catalog
887	-16" or -16.5" vase (L)	Bomm 284 (row 1, item 4)—1904, 1906 catalogs
888	-4" jug	Bomm 283 (row 2, item 1)
889	-7" whiskey jug	Bomm 284 (row 5, item 5)—1906 catalog
890	-12.5" tankard (L)	Bomm 284 (row 1, item 2)—1906 catalog
891	-14" vase (L)	Bomm 284 (row 2, item 1)—1904, 1906 catalogs
892	-8.25" vase (L)	Bomm 285 (row 2, item 4)—1906 catalog
893	-12.5" or -13" vase (L)	Bomm 285 (row 4, item 2)—1904, 1906 catalogs
895	-8" ewer	Bomm 282 (row 2, item 3)—1904, 1905 (as R895), 1906 catalogs
896	-8.25" bud vase (L)	Bomm 283 (row 1, item 5)—1905 (as R896), 1906 catalogs
897	-5.5" humidor	Bomm 283 (row 3, item 4)—1906 catalog
898	-13" or -13.5" vase (L)	Bomm 284 (row 2, item 4)—1904, 1905 (as R898), 1906 catalogs
900	-6" tyge (three-handled drinking cup)	Bomm 283 (row 3, item 5)—1906 catalog
901	-9" covered vase	Bomm 283 (row 1, item 3)
902	-11" vase	Bomm 285 (row 4, item 1)
903	-9.25" candlestick (L)	Bomm 283 (row 1, item 1)—1905 (as R903), 1906 catalogs
904	-5" vase	Bomm 282 (row 1, item 4)—1904, 1905 (as R904), 1906 catalogs
905	-10" or -11" ewer	Bomm 285 (row 3, item 2)—1905 (as R905), 1906 catalogs
906	-8" ewer	Bomm 284 (row 5, item 4)—1906 catalog
907	-8.25" vase	Bomm 285 (row 2, item 5)
908	-5.5" vase	Bomm 282 (row 2, item 1)—1906 catalog
909	cuspidor	Bomm 111; see also July 1916 price list (as "Art–Decorated")
910	-22" x 10" umbrella stand	Bomm 176
911	-6.5" vase	Bomm 281 (row 3, item 3)—1906 catalog
912	-6.5" bud vase	Bomm 281 (row 3, item 8)
913	-6" bud vase	Bomm 281 (row 3, item 4)
914	-6" bud vase (same as Majolica shape 205)	Bomm 281 (row 3, item 6)
915	-7" bud vase (same as Majolica shape 206)	Bomm 281 (row 3, item 5)
916	-11" bud vase (same as Majolica shape 200)	Bomm 281 (row 4, item 4)
917	-12.5" bud vase (same as Majolica shape 201)	Bomm 281 (row 4, item 3)
918	-7" bud vase (same as Majolica shape 204)	Bomm 281 (row 3, item 7)
919	-8" bud vase (same as Majolica shape 203)	Bomm 281 (row 4, item 6)
921	-11" tankard (L)	Bomm 281 (row 4, item 1)—1906 catalog
922	-4.5" bud vase	Bomm 281 (row 2, item 3)
923A	-5 vase	Bomm 281 (row 2, item 8)
923B	-5 vase	Bomm 281 (row 2, item 1)
924	-4.5" bud vase	Bomm 281 (row 2, item 2)
925A	-3.5" bud vase	Bomm 281 (row 2, item 5)
925B	-3.5" bud vase	Bomm 281 (row 2, item 6)
926	-3" vase	Bomm 281 (row 3, item 2)
927	-2.5" vase	Bomm 281 (row 3, item 1)
928	-9.5" or -10" vase	Bomm 281 (row 4, item 6)—1906 catalog
929	-4.5" jug	Bomm 281 (row 2, item 4)
930	-5" ewer	Bomm 281 (row 2, item 7)
931	-14.75" vase (L)	Bomm 312 (row 1, item 1)—1904, 1905 (as R931), 1906 catalogs
932	-17" vase (L)	Bomm 311 (row 1, item 3)—1904, 1905 (as R932), 1906 catalogs
933	-13.5" vase (L)	Bomm 311 (row 2, item 2)—1906 catalog
940	-9.5" pitcher	Bomm 303 (row 3, item 2)

Rozane Royal (Dark). "Married" jardiniere and pedestal, 28" overall height. Jardiniere is decorated with nasturtiums, die-impressed "ROZANE" marks, including shape 819; pedestal is decorated with wild roses, artist signed Myers, die-impressed "ROZANE" marks, including shape 516. *Fairfield collection.* **$950–1200 (as shown).** A circa 1903 factory publication shows this shape—in Decorated Artware (Special)—as 416-28". Because the jardiniere is decorated with a different motif from the pedestal, collectors consider this set to be "married."

zane Royal (Dark). 882-9" pillow vase, spaniel with pheasant, artist ned M Timberlake, unmarked. *Krause Family collection.* **$1800–2200**

ape .	Description	Reference/Notes
9	-18" vase	Bomm 314 (row 5, item 3)—1906 catalog
0	-7.5" ewer	Bomm 315 (row 2, item 2)—1906 catalog
4	-21" vase (L)	Bomm 311 (row 1, item 1)—1904, 1906 catalogs
5	-18" vase (L)	Bomm 313 (row 3, item 4)—1905 (as R955), 1906 catalogs
6	-8.5" vase	Bomm 323 (row 2, item 5)—1904, 1906 catalogs
7	-15" vase (L)	Bomm 313 (row 3, item 5)—1906 catalog
8	-11.25" vase	Bomm 282 (row 4, item 6)—1905 (as R958), 1906 catalogs
9	-7" vase (L)	Bomm 313 (row 3, item 7)—1906 catalog
1	-10.5" vase (L)	Bomm 282 (row 4, item 5)—1904, 1906 catalogs
2A	-13.5" vase	Same as Mongol shape M962—1904 catalog
2B	-14" vase	Bomm 314 (row 5, item 1)—1906 catalog
3	-30" floor vase	Bomm 317 (row 2, item 2)—1906 catalog
4	-16.5" tankard (L)	Bomm 316 (row 4, item 6)—1906 catalog
5	-6.5" stein (L)	Bomm 316 (row 3, item 7)—1904, 1906 catalogs
6	-14" tankard (L)	Bomm 316 (row 4, item 5)—1906 catalog
7	-10.75" vase	Bomm 315 (row 5, item 1)—1905 (as R967), 1906 catalogs
3	-10.75" vase	Bomm 315 (row 5, item 5)—1906 catalog
9	-12" bud vase	Bomm 282 (row 4, item 8)—1906 catalog
0	-10" bud vase (L)	Bomm 282 (row 4, item 2)—1905 (as R970), 1906 catalogs
1	-9" vase (L)	Bomm 282 (row 4, item 1)—1906 catalog
2	-8" vase (L)	Bomm 313 (row 4, item 6)—1906 catalog
3	-11.5" vase (L)	Bomm 282 (row 4, item 7)—1906 catalog
4	-11.5" vase (L)	Bomm 282 (row 4, item 9)—1905 (as R974), 1906 catalogs
5	-6.5" bud vase (L)	Bomm 316 (row 3, item 5)—1906 catalog
6	-7" vase	Bomm 303 (row 2, item 2)—1905 (as R976), 1906 catalogs
7	-6.5" bud vase (L)	Bomm 303 (row 2, item 9)—1906 catalog
8	-8.5" vase (L)	Bomm 313 (row 4, item 7)—1906 catalog
9	-7.25" bud vase (L)	Bomm 303 (row 2, item 4)—1906 catalog
0	-5.75" bud vase (L)	Bomm 303 (row 2, item 8)—1905 (as R980), 1906 catalogs
1	-5.25" bud vase (L)	Bomm 303 (row 1, item 3)—1906 catalog (as R981)
2	-8.75" bud vase (L)	Bomm 313 (row 4, item 1)—1905 (as R982), 1906 catalogs
3	-8" bud vase (L)	Bomm 313 (row 4, item 4)—1906 catalog
4	-5.375" or -5.5" bud vase (L)	Bomm 303 (row 1, item 2)—1906 catalog
5	-10" pillow vase (L)	Bomm 282 (row 5, item 1)—1905 (as R985), 1906 catalogs

Shape No.	Description	Reference/Notes
986	-9" pillow vase (L)	Bomm 282 (row 5, item 2)—1906 catalog
987	-8" pillow vase (L)	Bomm 282 (row 5, item 3)—1906 catalog
988	-6.5" pillow vase (L)	Bomm 282 (row 5, item 4)—1906 catalog
989	-5.5" pillow vase (L)	Bomm 282 (row 5, item 5)—1906 catalog
990	-4.75" pillow vase(L)	Bomm 282 (row 5, item 6)—1905 (as R990), 1906 catalogs
991	-3.25" pillow vase	Bomm 315 (row 1, item 1)—1906 catalog
992	-5" pillow vase	Bomm 315 (row 3, item 6)—1906 catalog
993	-8" basket	Bomm 314 (row 3, item 2)—1906 catalog
994	-4" ewer	Bomm 303 (row 1, item 5)—1905 (as R994), 1906 catalogs
995	-4" vase (L)	Bomm 303 (row 1, item 6)—1905 (as R995), 1906 catalogs
996	-8.5" vase	Bomm 314 (row 4, item 4)—1906 catalog
997	-7.25" vase	Bomm 314 (row 4, item 3)—1906 catalog
998	-6.25" vase (L)	Bomm 316 (row 3, item 3)—1905 (as R998), 1906 catalogs
999	-7" bud vase	Bomm 303 (row 2, item 7)—1906 catalog
R1	-7.25" vase (L)	Bomm 303 (row 2, item 3)—1905, 1906 catalogs
R2	-6.5" vase (L)	Bomm 303 (row 2, item 6)—1906 catalog
R3	-10.5" or -11" vase (L)	Bomm 282 (row 4, item 4)—1906 catalog
R4	-9.25" or -9.75" vase	Bomm 303 (row 3, item 3)—1906 catalog
R5	-10.25" or -10.75" vase (L)	Bomm 282 (row 4, item 3)—1906 catalog
R6	-8.25" vase (L)	Bomm 313 (row 4, item 3)—1906 catalog
R7	-12" vase	Bomm 282 (row 4, item 10)—1906 catalog
R8	-12" vase (L)	Bomm 282 (row 4, item 11)—1906 catalog
R9	-16.5" vase (L)	Bomm 311 (row 2, item 4)—1906 catalog
R10	-20" vase (L)	Bomm 312 (row 1, item 3)—1906 catalog
R11	-19" vase (L)	Bomm 311 (row 2, item 3)—1905, 1906 catalogs
R12	-8" vase (L)	Bomm 313 (row 4, item 2)—1906 catalog
R13	-6.5" vase	Bomm 315 (row 1, item 4)—1905, 1906 catalogs
R14	-8.25" vase (L)	Bomm 314 (row 4, item 5)—1905, 1906 catalogs
R15	-11.5" vase (L)	Bomm 323 (row 2, item 8)—1906 catalog
R16	-7.5" ewer (L)	Bomm 313 (row 1, item 7)—1906 catalog
R17	-8.25" or -8.75" vase	Bomm 323 (row 1, item 4)—1906 catalog
R18	-3.5" vase	Bomm 314 (row 1, item 5)—1906 catalog
R19	-5.25" vase	Bomm 323 (row 1, item 3)—1906 catalog
R20	-6.25" vase	Bomm 315 (row 3, item 7)—1906 catalog
R21	-3.25" vase	Bomm 314 (row 1, item 4)—1906 catalog
R22	-3.5" pillow vase (L)	Bomm 303 (row 1, item 7)—1906 catalog
R23	-5.25" bud vase (L)	Bomm 313 (row 1, item 10)—1906 catalog
R25	-12.25" vase (L)	Bomm 313 (row 5, item 3)—1906 catalog
R26	-9.25" vase (L)	Bomm 314 (row 4, item 1)—1906 catalog
R27	-19.5" vase (L)	Bomm 311 (row 1, item 2)—1906 catalog
R28	-10" vase (L)	Bomm 323 (row 2, item 2)—1906 catalog
R29	-14" vase (L)	Bomm 313 (row 3, item 3)—1906 catalog
R30	-11.25" vase	Bomm 316 (row 2, item 5)—1906 catalog
R31	-6" vase (L)	Bomm 315 (row 3, item 2)—1906 catalog
R32	-15.75" vase	Bomm 312 (row 1, item 4)—1906 catalog
R33	-11.5" vase (L)	Bomm 323 (row 3, item 7)—1906 catalog
R34	-11.5" vase (L)	Bomm 323 (row 3, item 8)—1906 catalog
R35	-8.25" vase (L)	Bomm 313 (row 3, item 1)—1906 catalog
R36	-5" bud vase (L)	Bomm 314 (row 2, item 3)—1906 catalog
R37	-9.5" vase	Bomm 314 (row 4, item 2)—1906 catalog
R38	-3" vase (L)	Bomm 314 (row 1, item 3)—1906 catalog
R39	-6.5" vase (L)	Bomm 316 (row 3, item 4)—1906 catalog
R40	-6.5" vase (L)	Bomm 316 (row 3, item 1)—1906 catalog
R41	-5" vase (L)	Bomm 314 (row 2, item 1)—1906 catalog
R42	-17" vase (L)	Bomm 312 (row 1, item 2)—1906 catalog
R43	-7.5" bud vase (L)	Bomm 313 (row 1, item 6)—1906 catalog
R44	-9.5" vase (L)	Bomm 323 (row 2, item 1)—1906 catalog
R45	-11.5" vase (L)	Bomm 323 (row 3, item 6)—1906 catalog
R46	-10.5" vase (L)	Bomm 312 (row 3, item 3)—1906 catalog
R47	-9.5" vase (L)	Bomm 314 (row 4, item 9)—1906 catalog
R48	-9.5" vase (L)	Bomm 312 (row 2, item 6)—1906 catalog
R49	-5" vase (L)	Bomm 314 (row 2, item 5)—1906 catalog
R50	-4" bud vase (L)	Bomm 313 (row 1, item 1)—1906 catalog
R51	-8.25" vase (L)	Bomm 313 (row 4, item 9)—1906 catalog (misprinted as shape 51)
R52	-11.5" vase (L)	Bomm 316 (row 2, item 1)—1906 catalog

Rozane Royal (Dark). *Row 1*: 848-6.75" vase, poppies, artist signed "W. MYS" (Walter Myers), unmarked; 908-5.5" vase, daffodil, artist signature illegible, partial Rozane Ware wafer; 843-7" vase, pansies, artist signed "G. [Gussie] Gerwick," Rozane Royal wafer. **$225–275, $175–225, $300–400.** *Row 2*: 817-4" vase, berries, artist initials "A.G.," die-impressed ROZANE marks; 927-2.5" rose bowl, decorated with matches, suggesting its intended use as a match holder, die-impressed ROZANE marks; 809-5.25" bud vase, daisies, unusually yellow background, die-impressed ROZANE marks. *Scheytt collection.* **$175–225, $125–150, $200–250**

Rozane Royal (Dark) Portraits. 931-14.75" vase, copy of *Mona Lisa*, artist initials "AD" (Anthony Dunlavy), die-impressed ROZANE marks; 931-14.75" lamp, American Indian chief, artist signature "DUNLAVY"; 891-14" vase, poet John Greenleaf Whittier, artist signature "Dunlavy," Rozane Ware wafer. *Mesre and Downey collections.* **$3500–4000, $4000–4500, $3500–4000**

Rozane Royal (Dark, Undecorated). Four examples, each with die-impressed factory marks: 856-4.5" stein; 829-9" ewer; 862-4.5" vase; 838-7.75" bud vase. *Private collection.* **$125–175, $275–350, $125–175, $175–225**

Rozane Royal (Light). 457-5" jardiniere, geranium; 892-8.25" vase, narcissus. *Hoppe collection.* **$225–275, $275–325.** Note the range of background colors possible for Rozane Royal (Light) pieces. Some are known to shade from pink to black or gray.

Rozane Royal (Light). 991-3.25" pillow vase, dark gray to white background, playing cards decoration (a diamond flush), die-impressed 7. *Courtesy of Treadway Gallery.* **$750–950.** The playing cards indicate that the shape might be suitable for holding one or two decks of cards.

Rozane Royal (Light). 9.75" pitcher, grapes, sprigged-on decoration on lip and upper portion of handle, artist initials "HL" (Harry Larzalere), die-impressed 7. *Wagner collection.* **$2000–2500**

Rozane Royal (Light). 983-8" bud vase, rosebuds, artist signature "W. Myers," Rozane Royal wafer. *Private collection.* **$500–600**

Detail of Rozane Royal (Light) pitcher.

RUSSCO
A Middle Period Line, introduced in 1934

Factory Name(s): Russco
Style: Art Deco
Standard Color(s): Blue, Gold, Luster Green ("green"), or Rusk ("salmon")
Typical Marks: Foil labels. (These could be lost, leaving the piece unmarked.) Some have hand-written (crayon) shape numbers.

Like Pauleo (and later, Clemana), Russco was probably named for a member of George F. Young's immediate family—namely, his son Russell. Russell T. Young had served as Roseville president after his father's death in 1920. According to R.T. Young's obituary, the son's presidency ended around 1930 "when he withdrew by reason of differences of opinion with his mother over the matter of policy" (trade notice, *Pottery, Glass and Brass Salesman,* December 20, 1934: 73). His mother, Anna M. Young, was still acting president in 1934, when Russell's health took a turn for the worse. Russco was announced in the fall, and Russell died in December.

Crockery and Glass Journal called Russco a "smooth surface, solid colored line, simply modeled with an appeal in its sheer simplicity," and recommended the "grand art pottery line" for its "splendid colors, interesting shapes and popular prices" (trade notice, September 1934: 23). According to the *Pottery, Glass and Brass Salesman,* "The special feature of the Russco line is a relief treatment of a semi-modern order, and yet which shows a distinct Egyptian influence. This relief extends all the way down the side of every piece in the line. The shapes also carry out this same thought, being angular rather than melting into curves. Yet so well is this worked up that they are thoroughly artistic and pleasing to the eye" (trade notice, September 6, 1934: 8).

The blue and salmon colors are matte glazes. Both the green and yellow glazes gain a crystalline quality from the chemical rutile, which also causes some olive green, or brown mottling. Green examples are often splashed with crystals large enough to resemble snowflakes. About a year later, the Russco line was offered in Ivory—and this could be lined in glossy yellow or blue, color combinations

that have sometimes been mistakenly interpreted as Trial Glazes (trade notice, *CGJ,* September 1935: 27).

Despite a revived interest in the Art Deco style, prices for Russco remain moderate. Highly crystalline examples bring more than the matte glazed examples. In the factory stock pages, 24 different Russco shapes are shown:

RUSSCO

Shape No.	Description	Reference/Notes
15	-2.5" flower block	
15	-3.5" flower block	
107	-8" double vase	
108	-6" vase	
109	-8" vase	
110	-7" cornucopia	Shown only in Ivory stock pages
111	triple cornucopia	Shown only in Ivory stock pages
259	-6" vase	
260	-6" vase	
260	-8" vase	Shown only in Ivory stock pages
260	-12" vase	
337	-10" basket	
694	-7" vase	
695	-8" vase	
696	-8" vase	
697	-8" vase	
698	-9" vase	
699	-9" vase	
700	-10" vase	
701	-10" vase	
702	-12" vase	
703	-15" vase	
1098	-4.5" candlestick	
1101	-4.5" candlestick	Shown only in Ivory stock pages

Russco. 702-12" vase, green. *Bassett collection.* **$300–350**

Russco. 107-8" double bud vase, salmon; 337-10" basket, blue; 695-8" vase, salmon. *Shannon collection.* **$125–150, $200–250, $125–150**

AVONA

A Middle Period Line, introduced in 1929

actory Name(s): Savona

yle: Italianate

andard Color(s): Blue, Green, Salmon, or Yellow

pical Marks: Paper labels. (These could be lost, leaving the piece unmarked.)

In a factory advertisement for Savona, Roseville remarked that eir new product lines allowed homemakers to choose between signs "in the modernistic or in the more conservative patterning" *House and Garden,* April 1929: 152). Of an arrangement using the ore traditional, Italianate pattern Savona, the company boasted, Truly, you will find fascination in the deft artistry of Roseville aftsmen. How effective are these Roseville pieces! How corative! … They are meant for gay flowers and gleaming candles They are meant to be possessed and cherished."

Savona's glazes involve cheerful glossy colors. A few shapes were prrowed from the earlier Volpato line. Many new shapes were so designed in a similar style, involving a carefully detailed ckground. Judging by one of the Experimental Pieces shown in hapter 3, Savona may originally have been conceived as a matte-azed line.

Today the line is fairly difficult to locate, and values are moderate and rising.

In the factory stock pages, 25 examples of Savona are shown:

SAVONA

Shape No.	Description	Shape No.	Description
13	-4" covered bowl	371	-6" vase
14	-4" comport	372	-6" vase
15	-2.5" flower block	373	-8" vase
15	-3.5" flower block	374	-8" vase
102	-6" bowl (Volpato shape)	375	-10" vase
119	-6" comport (Volpato shape)	376	-10" vase
183	-10" bowl	377	-11" vase
184	-12" bowl	378	-8" vase
185	-6" bowl	379	-12" vase
186	-8" bowl	1070	-3.5" candlestick
207	-6" vase (Volpato shape)	1071	-4" candlestick
209	-10" vase (Volpato shape)	1260	-8" wall pocket
222	-12" vase		

Savona. 374-8" vase, green, *courtesy of Robert Bettinger;* 185-6" bowl, blue, *courtesy of Treadway Gallery.* **$250–300, $150–200**

Savona. 379-12" vase, salmon; 13-4" covered vase (8" across handles), yellow; 222-12" vase, green. *Auclair collection.* **$375–425, $275–325, $375–425**

Savona. 377-11" vase, salmon. *Courtesy of McAllister Auctions.* **$325–375**

Savona. 372-6" vase, yellow; 209-10" bud vase, blue; 378-8" vase, salmon. *Fairfield collection.* **$200–250, $275–325, $400–500**

ILHOUETTE

A Late Line, introduced in 1950

ictory Name(s): Silhouette
yle: Mid-Century Modern
andard Color(s): Cameo Green ("turquoise"), Hollyhock Red ("red"), Olive Brown ("tan"), or Snowdrift White ("white")
pical Marks: Molded (raised-relief) marks, including "Roseville" (script), shape number, and size

Roseville's first advertisement for Silhouette was emblazoned ith this heading: "New, Ultra-Modern Shapes Combined with citing, Bold Colors" (*Gift and Art Buyer,* June 1950: 2). Like Panel— ine three decades older—Silhouette pieces have low-relief florals, aves, or female nudes. The name is derived from the fact that the arker backgrounds within each vignette focus our attention on he decorations.

Roseville boasted, "Everything about this fascinating art pottery is trancingly different—the 36 unusual shapes, the sculpture-like ecorative motifs, the satiny smooth finish—yes, and the four new old colors that are a year ahead of anything you'll see." Silhouette's early geometrical "windows" are slightly curved variations on "L" apes, triangles, or trapezoids. Most motifs stray beyond their window d are carved partly into the vessel's otherwise smooth surface.

Today, Silhouette has a new following, and values are on the rise, although the leaf motifs can still be moderately priced.

No factory stock pages are known for Silhouette. The 36 Silhouette shapes all appear in the factory brochure:

SILHOUETTE

Shape No.	Description	Shape No.	Description
708	-6" basket	757	double planter
709	-8" basket	761	-4" hanging basket
710	-10" basket	763	-8" vase
716	-6" ewer	766	-8" wall pocket
717	-10" ewer	768	-8" window box
721	-8" cornucopia	769	-9" window box
722	cornucopia	779	-5" vase
726	-6" planter	780	-6" vase
727	-8" bowl	781	-6" vase
728	-10" bowl	782	-7" vase
729	-12" bowl	783	-7" fan vase
730	-10" window box	784	-8" vase
731	-14" window box	785	-9" vase
740	cigarette box (covered)	786	-9" vase
741	-4" vase	787	-10" vase
742	-6" urn	788	-12" vase
751	-3" candlestick	789	-14" vase
756	planter	799	ashtray

Silhouette. 708-6" basket, aqua; 709-8" basket, burgundy; 722-8" cornucopia, burgundy; 785-9" vase, aqua. *Shannon collection.* **$150–200, $225–275, $125–175, $150–200**

Silhouette. 787-10" vase, rust; 783-7" fan vase, aqua. *Shannon collection.* **$600–700, $500–600**

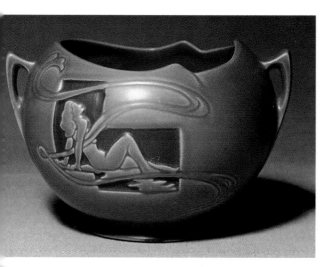

Silhouette. 742-6" urn, nude, rust. *Hoppe photograph.* **$475–550**

Silhouette. 729-12" planter, white; 766-8" wall pocket, white; 717-10" ewer, white; 799 ashtray, white. *Courtesy of McAllister Auctions.* **$150–175, $250–300, $175–225, $75–95**

SNOWBERRY

A Late Line, introduced in 1947

Factory Name(s): Snowberry
Style: Decorative, with some Mid-Century Modern shapes
Standard Color(s): Dusty Rose ("pink"), Fern Green ("green"), or Persian Blue ("blue")
Typical Marks: Molded (raised-relief) marks, including "Roseville" (script), shape number, and size

Like Clematis (1944), Freesia (1945), and Zephyr Lily (1946), Snowberry features low-relief modeled decorations against a partly textured background. Because of World War II, for the fourth year in a row Roseville was not able to produce more than one new product line for 1947.

Unlike those three earlier patterns, Snowberry's "delightful motif of loose, leafy berry clusters" does not seem to have been taken from nature (factory advertisement, *Gift and Art Buyer,* January 1947: 2). Along with the occasional introduction of Mid-Century Modern shapes, Snowberry's fanciful subject matter marks the beginning of the postwar boom and a renewed confidence in the American economy. Still, many shapes are symmetrical. In a new publication titled "How to Decorate with Art Pottery," Roseville featured Snowberry pieces in a variety of room settings, many of which emphasized traditional Early American furniture.

Today, Snowberry has a definite following among collectors, although prices are usually moderate to affordable. Pink and blue are (as usual) the preferred colors.

The Snowberry factory brochure mentions 52 shapes (as the company had advertised in 1946), but only 42 are shown. Comparisons show that this brochure was made by reprinting two of the three known factory stock pages. These pages themselves illustrate only 51 shapes:

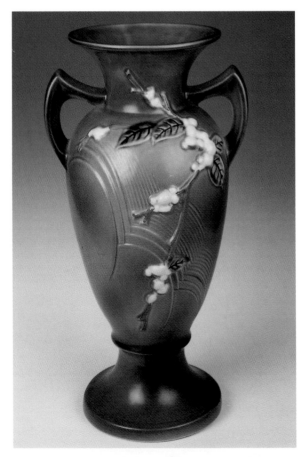

Snowberry. 1V-15" vase, green. *Hoppe collection.* **$500–600**

Shape No.	Description		Shape No.	Description
AT	ashtray		1JP	-8" jardiniere & pedestal
BE	bookend		1PS	-5" flower pot and saucer
BK	-7" basket		1RB	-5" rose bowl
BK	-8" basket		1RB	-6" rose bowl
BK	-10" basket		1S	sugar bowl
BK	-12" basket		1TK	-6" ewer
BL	-8" bowl		1TK	-10" ewer
BL	-14" bowl		1TK	-15" ewer
BL1	-6" bowl		1TP	teapot
BL1	-10" bowl		1UR	-8" vase
BL1	-12" bowl		1V	-6" vase
BL2	-6" bowl		1V	-15" vase
BL2	-10" bowl		1V	-18" vase
BL2	-12" bowl		1V1	-7" bud vase
BV	-7" bud vase		1V1	-8" vase
C	creamer		1V1	-9" vase
CC	-6" cornucopia		1V1	-10" vase
CC	-8" cornucopia		1V1	-12" vase
CS1	-2" candlestick		1V2	-7" vase
CS2	-4.5" candlestick		1V2	-8" vase
FB	-10" bowl		1V2	-9" vase
FH	-6" pillow vase		1V2	-10" vase
FH	-7" fan vase		1V2	-12" vase
HB	-5" hanging basket		1WP	-8" wall pocket
	-4" jardiniere		1WX	-8" x 2.5" window box
	-6" jardiniere			

Snowberry. Pair, 1CS1-2" candlesticks, blue; 1V2-10" vase, blue; 1WX-8" x 2.5" window box, blue; 1FH-7" fan vase, blue. *Courtesy of McAllister Auctions.* **$95–125 (pair), $200–250, $125–175, $150–200.** The abbreviation "FH" stands for "flower holder."

Snowberry. 1J-4" jardiniere, pink; 1V1-8" vase, pink; 1TK-6" ewer, pink. *Courtesy of McAllister Auctions.* **$125–150, $150–200, $125–175.** The abbreviation "TK" stands for "tankard."

Snowberry. 1BK-10" basket, blue; 1BK-7" basket, pink. *Shannon collection.* **$250–300, $175–225**

229

SOLID COLORS
An Early Line, introduced by 1917

Factory Name(s): Unknown (believed to be Solid Colors)
Collector Nickname(s): Matt Color (see Huxford, 1976); Matt Colors (see Buxton, 1977)
Style: Arts and Crafts
Standard Color(s): Matte, semigloss, or glossy colors
Typical Marks: Unmarked. Some have a foil label. (These could be lost, leaving the piece unmarked.)

By 1917, a line called Solid Colors was mentioned in Roseville advertisements. This name must have referred to a group of small vases and planters with impressed linear decorations, shown in one of the untitled factory stock pages. Previous Roseville authors have dubbed these products "Matt Colors," although glossy and semigloss glazes are known too.

Among the colors known are aqua, grayish blue, rose, and tan. One golden tan glaze in this line has mottling similar to that found on the Sandalwood Yellow variety of Capri. This coloring may have a slightly higher value to collectors. Because Solid Colors is affordable today, these pieces can easily be purchased for use in the home.

The only known factory stock page for Solid Colors shows 12 shapes:

SOLID COLORS

Shape No.	Description	Shape No.	Description
22	ashtray	550	-4" jardiniere
236	-3" vase	607	-4" vase
236	-4" vase	608	-6" vase
364	-5" hanging basket	609	-6" vase
548	-4" vase	624	-4" vase
549	-4" vase	625	-5" vase

Solid Colors. 548-4" vase, semimatte turquoise; 625-5" vase, semimatte turquoise; 236-3" vase, semimatte turquoise. *Hoppe photograph.* **$50–60, $60–75, $50–60**

Solid Colors. 607-4" vase, semigloss medium blue; 550-4" vase, glossy grayish blue; 236-3" vase, glossy mauve. *Hoppe photograph.* **$60–75 (each)**

Solid Colors. 607-4" vase, matte mottled tan; 608-6" vase, glossy mauve. *Shannon collection.* **$75–95 (each)**

SUNFLOWER
A Middle Period Line, introduced ca. 1930

Factory Name(s): Sunflower
Style: Arts and Crafts
Standard Color(s): One standard coloring, as described below
Typical Marks: Paper labels. (These could be lost, leaving the piece unmarked.) Some examples have a hand-written (crayon) shape number.

Sunflower seems to date from about 1930. No factory advertisements or trade notices have yet been located. In the mid-1990s a major decorating magazine featured a tastefully decorated

home in which Sunflower was shown in various room settings. Suddenly, values achieved by this already popular Roseville pattern began to soar. The dust is only now beginning to settle.

Sunflower features a repeating motif of a mature sunflower blossom on a curving stem, depicted in low relief against a textured background that blends from brown to green to blue. On a well-molded example, each tiny flower petal is individually defined. Collectors especially love those pieces with a strong blue background area.

As a subject, the sunflower was also popular during the so-called Aesthetic Period, a Japanesque sub-genre of the Art Nouveau. Roseville's Sunflower refers to this period by means of the curvaceous stems. Seen from a distance, the stylized round blooms create a pleasant geometrical pattern, in the spirit of Art Deco. Many collectors consider Sunflower to be Arts and Crafts in style, although clearly the pattern can be useful in other decorating schemes too.

In the factory stock pages, 15 examples of Sunflower are shown:

SUNFLOWER

Shape No.	Description		Shape No.	Description
208	-5" bowl		492	-10" vase
485	-6" vase		493	-9" vase
486	-5" vase		494	-10" vase
487	-7" vase		619	-10" jardiniere & pedestal
488	-6" vase		619	-12" jardiniere
489	-7" vase		770	-20" umbrella stand
490	-8" vase		1265	-7" wall pocket
491	-8" vase			

Sunflower. 5" hanging basket. *Hoppe photograph.* **$1200–1500**

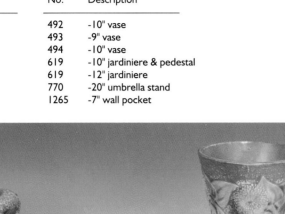

Sunflower. 486-5" vase; 11" window box; 487-7" vase. *Courtesy of McAllister Auctions.* **$600–750, $950–1200, $600–750**

Sunflower. 490-8" vase; 488-6" urn. *annon collection.* **$1200–1500, 750–950**

Sunflower. 485-6" vase; 494-10" vase; 5" vase. *Hoppe photograph.* **$575–650, $1200–1500, $450–550**

SYLVAN

A Middle Period Line, introduced by 1920

Factory Name(s): Unknown (probably Sylvan)
Style: Rustic
Standard Color(s): Bisque colored in shades of tan and green, lined in glossy green
Typical Marks: Unmarked

Contemporary with Dogwood (Smooth), Rozane Line, and Vista, Sylvan is among the first product lines by Frank L.D. Ferrell, who became Roseville's art director in 1918, succeeding Harry Rhead. Sylvan's scarcity today indicates that it may have been the least successful of the four lines. Reminiscent of Ferrell's design for a Peters and Reed line called Moss Aztec, Sylvan may have seemed old-fashioned to 1920 buyers.

The rustic pattern's low-relief carvings depict owls, leaves, hunting dogs, squirrels, foxes, chickens, and cats against a textured background. The exterior surface was airbrushed in green or tan, and then quickly cleaned with a cloth or sponge. This process left some coloring in the crevices, to define the various motifs. Interiors were given a glossy Majolica green glaze to prevent leakage.

Today, collectors avidly hunt examples of this line. Asking prices have a wider range than usual, because fewer market values are available for study.

Roseville advertisements mention a line named Sylvan, although the factory stock pages identified as Sylvan by collectors are not titled. In these factory stock pages, 25 shapes are shown:

SYLVAN

Shape No.	Description	Reference/Notes
225	-4" bowl	
225	-5" bowl	
225	-6" bowl	
325	-4" hanging basket	
325	-5" hanging basket	
325	-6" hanging basket	
325	-7" hanging basket	
325	-8" hanging basket	
325	-10" hanging basket	
362	-11.5" x 6.5" window box	
362	-14" x 8" window box	
362	-16.5" x 8.5" window box	
568	-12" x 33" jardiniere & pedestal	
750	-21" umbrella stand	Bomm 382
S33	-7" x 6" planter	
S34	-5.75" x 5" planter	
S35	-4.5" x 4" planter	
S36	-5.5" x 2.25" bowl	
S37	-4.5" x 1.75" bowl	
S38	-8" x 2.75" x 2.5" window box	
S39	-7" x 5.5" x 2.5" pillow vase	
S40	-6" x 3" x 1.75" bowl	
S41	-7.5" x 3.25" x 2.25" bowl	
S42	-12" x 6.5" x 3" bowl	
	-9.5" vase	

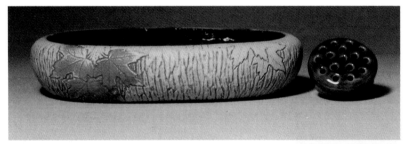

Sylvan. 542-12" bowl, leaves; 15-3.5" flower frog. *Hoppe photograph.* **$350–450, $20–25**

Sylvan. 9.5" vase, shaped like jardiniere and pedestal, fox and chicks. *Hoppe photograph.* **$600–700**

Sylvan. 750-21" umbrella stand, maple leaves. *Hoppe collection.* **$1200–1500**

232

Sylvan. 568-10" jardiniere, hunting dogs. *Hoppe photograph.* **$700–800**

TEASEL

A Middle Period Line, introduced in 1938

Factory Name(s): Teasel

Style: Art Deco

Standard Color(s): Palace Green ("green"), Sunset ("peach"), or Venice Blue ("blue")

Typical Marks: Die-impressed marks, including "Roseville" (script), shape number, and size

In 1938, Roseville announced that Teasel, "our new spring creation," would come in "18 startling shapes" (*Gift and Art Buyer,* April 1938: 2). Each example has a few teasel stems, with the thistle-like flower surrounded by a newly opened leafy bract. Of the genus *Dipsacus,* some varieties of this prickly Old World plant were used to produce a napped texture on fabrics.

Like Pine Cone, Teasel's background surface is left smooth, giving the pattern a Japanese flavor. As an ornament, the simple linear shape of the teasel plants is a provocative and surprising choice for its time. Handles usually involve an oval disk-like protrusion. Rims can be round, or can have stepped details.

Today, Teasel is a moderately priced Middle-Period line, a good choice for the beginning collector. Values are likely to increase in time.

The only known Teasel factory stock page shows all 18 designs:

TEASEL

Shape No.	Description	Shape No.	Description
36	flower frog	884	-8" vase
342	-4" urn	885	-8" pillow vase
343	-6" rose bowl	886	-9" fan vase
344	-8" bowl	887	-10" vase
345	-12" bowl	888	-12" vase
349	-10" basket	889	-15" vase
644	-4" jardiniere	890	-18" ewer
882	-6" vase	1131	candlestick
883	-7" vase		

Teasel. 882-6" vase, peach; 883-7" vase, dark blue; 886-9" fan vase, light crystalline blue (resembling the green Velmoss glaze); 881-6" vase, rust. *Shannon collection.* **$125–150, $175–225, $200–250, $150–175**

Teasel. Pair, 884-8" vases, one peach and the other dark blue. *Krause Family collection.* **$175–225 (each)**

Teasel. 36 flower frog; 644-4" vase, both dark blue. *Hoppe photograph.* **$95–125, $125–150**

Teasel. Pair, 889-15" vases, green. *Ruhoff collection.* **$600–700 (each)**

THORN APPLE
A Middle Period Line, introduced in 1937

Factory Name(s): Thorn Apple
Alternate Spelling(s): Thornapple (see Clifford, 1968)
Style: Realistic, often with classical shapes having Art Deco touches
Standard Color(s): Blue, brown, or pink
Typical Marks: Die-impressed marks, including "Roseville" (script), shape number, and size

Roseville's Thorn Apple was named after the plant it depicts (*Datura stramonium*), a potentially toxic narcotic with funnel-shaped white flowers and prickly seed pods. The plant is modeled in relief against a smooth background. Shapes are typically classical, although some examples have smart Art Deco styling.

Also called "jimsonweed," the thorn apple made an unusual choice as a motif for interior decoration. Like that of several other mid-1930s patterns—notably Poppy and Moss—the subject of Thorn Apple revives an Art Nouveau conceit, symbolizing dreams, hallucinations, ecstasy, and death.

Thorn Apple. 306-5" bowl, blue; 823-12" vase, blue; 812-6" pillow vase, blue. *Hoppe photograph.* **$125–150, $325–375, $150–200**

Modern collectors love Thorn Apple without a thought to such abstract interpretations. The brown coloring may be the most popular, but the others are equally lovely. Values are usually moderate, except for those pieces with extravagant protrusions or delicate handles.

In the factory stock pages, 54 examples of Thorn Apple are shown:

THORN APPLE

Shape No.	Description	Shape No.	Description
3	-5.5" bookend	638	-12" jardiniere & pedestal
29	flower frog	639	-5" flower pot and saucer
30	flower frog	774	-12" x 8" vase
127	-6" cornucopia	775	-14" x 10" vase
252	-5" planter	808	-4" vase
304	-4" vase	809	-5" vase
305	-6" vase	810	-6" vase
306	-5" planter	811	-6" vase
307	-6" bowl	812	-6" pillow vase
308	-7" bowl	813	-7" bud vase
309	-8" bowl	814	-7" vase
310	-10" bowl	815	-7" vase
311	-12" bowl	816	-8" vase
312	centerpiece	817	-8" vase
313	centerpiece	818	-8" vase
342	-10" basket	819	-9" vase
343	-12" basket	820	-9" vase
355	-5" hanging basket	821	-10" vase
356	-4" wall bucket	822	-10" vase
382	-14" window box	823	-12" vase
638	-4" jardiniere	824	-15" vase
638	-5" jardiniere	825	-15" ewer
638	-6" jardiniere	1117	candlestick
638	-7" jardiniere	1118	-4.5" candlestick
638	-8" jardiniere & pedestal	1119	-5" double candelabra
638	-9" jardiniere	1120	-5.5" triple candelabra
638	-10" jardiniere & pedestal	1280	-8" wall pocket

Thorn Apple. 824-15" floor vase, pink. *Fairfield collection.* **$750–950**

Thorn Apple. 816-8" vase, pink; 810-6" vase, blue; 813-7" bud vase, pink. *Shannon collection.* **$200–250, $150–200, $175–225.** The dried seed pod is from a jimsonweed (or "thorn apple").

Thorn Apple. 825-15" ewer, brown; 342-10" basket, brown. *Shannon collection.* **$750–950, $275–350**

TOPEO

A Middle Period Line, introduced in 1934

Factory Name(s): Topeo
Collector Nickname(s): Mowa (see Purviance and Schneider, 1970)
Style: Art Deco (red), or Arts and Crafts (blue)
Standard Color(s): Blue, or Cherry Red ("red")
Typical Marks: Foil labels. (These could be lost, leaving the piece unmarked.) Some have hand-written (crayon) shape numbers.

In 1934, one reviewer called Topeo a "grandly modern" line distinguished by its "handles, built-up and braid-like" (trade notice, *Crockery and Glass Journal,* February 1934: 29). Another writer admired Topeo as a "high-class offering" whose raised decoration "is unique, but has its suggestion in nature" (trade notice, *Pottery, Glass and Brass Salesman,* February 22, 1934: 26).

In its matte-glazed variation, Topeo's beaded, claw-like trim is hand-colored—some portions being pink, to contrast with the blended green and blue background. These matte glazes have a texture resembling that of green Baneda, although in different colors, and appeal to the same group of Arts and Crafts lovers. The deep glossy red Topeo pieces seem more Modernistic, and appeal to those Art Deco aficionados who prefer pink Baneda. As the *PGBS* reviewer observed, "Both are rich, and it is merely a case of which one is preferred."

Prices are usually moderate, although likely to rise. Those interested in collecting a few examples should begin early. The only known Topeo stock page shows 15 examples:

Topeo. 664-12.25" vase, red, silver foil label. *Scheytt collection.* **$500–600**

TOPEO

Shape No.	Description	Shape No.	Description
245	-6" rose bowl	661	-9.25" vase
246	-2.75" bowl	662	-9" vase
246	-3" bowl	663	-10" vase
656	-6" vase	664	-12.25" vase
657	-6.75" vase	665	-14.25" vase
658	-7.25" vase	666	-15" vase
659	-8' vase	1093	4" candlestick
660	-8.25" vase		

Topeo. Pair, 1093-4" candlesticks, blue; 9" bowl, red. *Hoppe collection.* **$175–225 (pair), $225–275**

Topeo. 246-3" bowl, red; 659-8" vase, red. *Hoppe photograph.* **$125–175, $325–375.** The factory notation for this 6" bowl does not follow the typical practice of measuring a bowl's or jardiniere's interior—instead of its height.

Topeo. 660-8.25" vase, blue; 245-6" urn, blue. *Hoppe photograph.* **$325–375, $250–300.** Note the different coloring schemes on the bead-like handles.

TOURMALINE

A Middle Period Line, introduced in 1933

Factory Name(s): Tourmaline
Style: Arts and Crafts, or Art Deco
Standard Color(s): Blue, green, pink and aqua, or yellow
Typical Marks: Foil labels. (These could be lost, leaving the piece unmarked.) Some have hand-written (crayon) shape numbers.

In 1933, a reviewer wrote, "The treat in the Tourmaline line is in the charm of its glaze … and its many and varied treatments" (trade notice, *Crockery and Glass Journal*, March 1933: 25–26). Each shape was available in one of four standard colorings. The line's matte green glaze has a blue-green hue; it is "a combination of light and dark green in a mottle effect." Another matte glaze in Tourmaline is a pink or "rose [that] makes use of nile green at the top and for the lining." Tourmaline's semigloss yellow is a blend of mustard yellow and rust tones. The blue semigloss glaze has subtle crystalline effects and blends several shades of blue with cream and yellow.

Like Ivory, Tourmaline revived a few older designs and also introduced new modernistic shapes. The oval Tourmaline 241-12" bowl was said to be "particularly nice" because it was "deep enough to take care of flowers as well as fruit." The new 614-8" vase was admired for its "graduated stepped-down" design. Derived from a Futura shape, the Tourmaline A429-9" vase had "an interesting base of built-out simulated supports." (Tourmaline's numbering system inserts the letter "A" before those shape numbers borrowed from earlier lines.)

Today, Tourmaline is a moderately affordable choice for the Middle Period collector. Particularly attractive glazes and/or modernistic shapes can command a somewhat higher asking price.

Only one Tourmaline factory stock page is known, and it shows 20 different shapes:

TOURMALINE

Shape No.	Description
152	-6" bowl (Carnelian shape)
238	-5" vase
241	-12" bowl
611	-6" vase
612	-7" vase
613	-8" vase
614	-8" vase
615	-9" vase
616	-10" vase
1089	-4.5" candlestick
A65	-6" pillow vase (Carnelian shape)
A152	-7" bowl (Carnelian shape)
A200	-4" vase (Imperial Glazes shape)
A308	-7" vase (Carnelian shape)
A332	-8" vase (Carnelian shape)
A425	-8" vase (derived from Futura shape)
A429	-9" vase (derived from Futura shape)
A435	-10" vase (Futura shape)
A444	-12" vase (Carnelian shape)
A517	-6" (Earlam shape)

Tourmaline. A308-7" vase, Rosecraft shape, aqua on mottled pink; A65-6" pillow vase, Carnelian shape, aqua on mottled pink. *Shannon collection.* **$150–200 (each)**

Tourmaline. A200-4" urn, Imperial (Glazes) shape, two-tone blue and yellow; A308-7" vase, Rosecraft shape, two-tone blue and yellow. *Hoppe photograph.* **$150–175, $125–150**

Tourmaline. 679-6" vase, also an Ivory shape, mottled green; A444-12" vase, Carnelian shape, mottled green. *Shannon collection.* **$125–150, $325–375**

Tourmaline. Pair, 106-7" cornucopias, also an Ivory shape, rust and gold. *Courtesy of White Pillars Antique Mall.* **$125–175 (each)**

TUSCANY

A Middle Period Line, introduced in 1928

Factory Name(s): Unknown (believed to be Tuscany)
Style: Italianate
Standard Color(s): Gray, green, or pink
Typical Marks: Paper labels. (These could be lost, leaving the piece unmarked.)

Like Baneda, Futura, and Imperial (Glazes), Tuscany can appeal primarily to Arts and Crafts or to Art Deco collectors, depending on the glaze. The first group is typically drawn to Tuscany's feathery matte gray glaze—or to the scarce matte mottled green, which may have been an early glaze, produced for a relatively short period. Art Deco lovers prefer the brightness of Tuscany's semigloss mottled pink.

Each handle in the Tuscany line depicts a large leaf and a cluster of grapes (or berries), hand-colored in pale green and purple. The shapes are often classical and symmetrical, although a few have a geometrical body.

Tuscany is an affordable Middle Period line, and examples are still widely available. The time to buy is now!

In the factory stock pages, 25 examples of Tuscany are shown:

TUSCANY

Shape No.	Description	Shape No.	Description
[15]	[-2.5"] flower block	342	-6" vase
[15]	[-3.5"] flower block	343	-7" vase
66	-5" flower holder	344	-8" vase
67	-4" vase	345	-8" vase
68	-4" vase	346	-9" vase
69	-5" flower holder	347	-10" vase
70	-5" pillow vase	348	-10" vase
71	-6" vase	349	-12" vase
171	-6" comport	1066	-3.5" candlestick
172	-9" bowl	1067	-4" candlestick
173	-10" bowl	1254	-7" wall pocket
174	-12" bowl	1255	-8" wall pocket
341	-5" vase		

Tuscany. 344-8" vase, pink; 342-6" vase, pink. *Shannon collection.* **$250–300, $175–225**

scany. 66-5" combination vase and flower arranger, gray; 349-12" vase, gray; 2-9" bowl, gray. *Fairfield collection.* **$95–125, $375–425, $150–200**

Tuscany. 346-9" vase, green. *Courtesy of Clarabelle Antiques.* **$325–375**

Tuscany. 70-5" pillow vase, hexagonal, pink; 15-3.5" flower block, pink; 341-5" vase, pink; 15-2.5" flower block, pink. *Hoppe collection.* **$150–200, $25–30, $175–225, $20–25**

TILITY WARE
Generic Term for Several Product Lines, from Various Periods

ctory Name(s): Various, including German Cooking Ware, Romafin, Utility Ware, and Venitian. The factory name for some products is unknown, despite occasional descriptive terms (such as "Decorated" or "Decorated Utility Ware") on some factory stock pages.

llector Nickname(s): Various nicknames have been introduced to describe the many Utility Ware products. Sometimes the distinction between Decorated Artware and Utility Ware is difficult to determine. One example is the group of Majolica- or Cornelian-glazed pitchers with low-relief (usually hand decorated) floral or scenic motifs. These have been variously labeled Pitchers (see Alexander, 1970); Early Pitchers (see Huxford, 1976); or Embossed Pitchers (see Buxton, 1977). The 1990s revised edition of Buxton (1977) refers to something called "Brown and White," which may be intended to encompass both German Cooking Ware and its later variation, Romafin. In Bomm (1998), a post-WWII line of Glossy Utility Ware was confused with Raymor Two-Tone Casual.

Alternate Spelling(s): Venetian (see Huxford, 1976)
Style: Folk Art
Standard Color(s): Various, including hand decoration
Typical Marks: Unmarked. Starting in about 1923, a black inkstamp Rv logo appears on banded Creamware items, and on the stylized Lily of the Valley wares. Glossy utility ware pieces have molded (raised relief) marks.

The generic term "Utility Ware" is useful for describing a variety of Roseville products that were intended to be primarily utilitarian, not decorative. This definition should not be applied strictly, because Roseville continually sought new ways to blur the distinction. The factory's products sold consistently well precisely because they served a useful purpose and also had a pleasing appearance.

The product lines of the original factory in Roseville, Ohio, have not been fully identified. But archaeologist and researcher James Murphy (of Columbus, Ohio) has recently discovered shards of Venitian ware at the original plant site. The shards indicates that Venitian was introduced by 1898, when the company bought its first property in Zanesville.

239

In Zanesville, by 1902, the company was producing Utility Ware in a spongeware glaze under the name Cornelian. Several pitchers had repeating leaf designs that some earlier Roseville authors have dubbed "Osiris." (At the factory, these pitchers were numbered B1, B2, and B3.) In a variation of this design, the rows of leaves follow a slight S shape. When glazed as Cornelian, this design was sometimes called "Cornelian Twist." With a hand decorated Majolica glaze, these pitchers may have been nicknamed "Tourist" by Roseville executives (see Bomm, page 131, row 2, item 2).

For a more complete discussion of this category of wares, see "Cornelian." Additional product categories—also discussed separately—that include items of Utility Ware in their lines are Autumn, Creamware, Decorated Artware, and Majolica.

In 1904, Roseville introduced a toilet ware pattern called "Our Ideal." Examples have not been identified. It seems plausible to suspect that the so-called "Ideal" pitchers originated about the same time. These pitchers are colored partly in Creamware and partly in an opaque enamel color, with some minor gilt trim.

In 1906 a new Roseville line of decorative pitchers impressed one reviewer attending the Pittsburgh glass and china show: "Suffice it to say, that some of the dispensers of liquid refreshments would withdraw their offers to fill any jug in town for ten cents if more people chose to send some of the Rozane art pitchers in which to bring the liquids back. They have an underglaze enamel effect on some of those pitchers that is extremely pretty" (China, Glass and Lamps, January 13, 1906: 17). At least some of these new shapes were those pitchers with low-relief designs, such as Wild Rose and Landscape. In 1907 the line was expanded: "The jugs which created such a furor last year are still there, but there are six new ones, the old windmill jug being 'the candy one'" (trade notice, CGL, January 12, 1907: 8). Besides the "underglaze enamel effect" (that is, hand decorated Majolica), these pitchers were also available in Cornelian glazes, with or without hand decoration. Pitcher designs introduced in 1908 seem to include The Boy, Holland, The Owl, and "Teddy Bear, with colors quite in keeping with the design" (trade notice, CGL, January 11, 1908: 11).

The year 1908 also saw a new line of cooking ware by Roseville (trade notice, CGL, January 25, 1908). These baking and serving dishes were usually called "German Cooking Ware" because they imitated a popular import from a region bordering both Germany and France. The "fireproof brown and white lined cooking ware" is mentioned in several Roseville directory listings of the time (see Crockery and Glass Journal, December 22, 1910: 213).

By 1914 another brown and white cookware was introduced under the name Romafin (directory listing, CGJ, July 1, 1914: 28). The text of an undated Roseville pamphlet Romafin: Cooking, Baking and Serving Utensils … (in the Mesre collection) begins, "The Romafin ware is the ware of quality. It is designed with special view to withstanding the hard usage of hotels, cafes and the home.… The small details of shape, design and finish, which add so largely to the beauty and durability of the ware, have all been carefully embodied in our products.… In appearance it is a most pleasing shade of mahogany red, contrasting with a pure white lining, making a fitting ornament and a highly appropriate article for well-appointed table service."

A group of teapots, cast in red clay and glazed in a glossy mirror black, were introduced in 1920 (source: factory advertisement, CGJ, December 16, 1920). The black tea pots continued to be listed among factory products in Roseville's directory listings for 1922–1925. Around 1926, when Carnelian shapes were introduced (and the teapots may have been dropped), the mirror black glaze was added to the Rosecraft line.

During the 1930s, the Volpato glaze was used for a line of Utility Ware pieces having banded decoration in the manner of Creamware. The old Tulip and Landscape pitchers were reissued. An attractive new product line was incised with stylized lilies of the valley, hand decorated in gray and mauve. Shapes included mixing bowls, salad bowls, and pitchers.

Believed to date to the post-WWII era, Roseville's glossy utility line came in blended shades of blue, green, and orange. Some of the "Glossy Utility Ware" shapes were revived in 1953, for use as part of the Raymor Two-Tone Casual line.

Caution: Do not confuse the Holland pieces, which have molded (raised-relief) figures and Majolica glazes, with Creamware. A series of decal decorations, used on Creamware pieces, is known as "Dutch."

In the factory stock pages, at least 87 items are shown that fit into the broad category of Utility Ware. An additional 150 shapes appear in the Romafin catalog:

UTILITY WARE

Creamware (Banded)

Shape No.	Description	Reference/Notes
1	-4" baking dish	Bomm 119
1	-6" baking dish	Bomm 119
1	-8" baking dish	Bomm 119
1	-6" mixing bowl	Bomm 119
1	-8" mixing bowl	Bomm 119
1	-10" mixing bowl	Bomm 119
2	-6" bowl	Bomm 119
2	-8" bowl	Bomm 119
2	-10" bowl	Bomm 119
1309	-3 pt. pitcher	Bomm 119

German Cooking Ware

Shape No.	Description	Reference/Notes
12	-3.5" pudding dish	Also in ca. 1903 "Cornelian Ware" catalog
12	-4.5" pudding dish	Also in ca. 1903 "Cornelian Ware" catalog
12	-5.5" pudding dish	Also in ca. 1903 "Cornelian Ware" catalog
12	-6.5" pudding dish	Also in ca. 1903 "Cornelian Ware" catalog
12	pudding dish	See ca. 1903 "Cornelian Ware" catalog
12	pudding dish	See ca. 1903 "Cornelian Ware" catalog
12	pudding dish	See ca. 1903 "Cornelian Ware" catalog
12	pudding dish	See ca. 1903 "Cornelian Ware" catalog

Glossy Utility Ware

Shape No.	Description	Reference/Notes
10	-6" mixing bowl	Bomm 267
11	-8" mixing bowl	Bomm 267
12	-10" mixing bowl	Bomm 267
13	-11" fruit bowl	Bomm 267
14C	creamer	Bomm 267
14S	sugar bowl	Bomm 267
14T	teapot	Bomm 267
15	-5.5" pitcher	Bomm 267
16	-6.5" pitcher	Bomm 267
17	-7.5" pitcher	Bomm 267

Ideal Pitchers

Shape No.	Description	Shape No.	Description
1	-5 oz. pitcher	5	-5 pt. pitcher
2	-0.75 pt. pitcher	6	-7.25 pt. pitcher
3	-1.75 pt. pitcher	7	-15 pt. pitcher
4	-3.25 pt. pitcher		

Lilies of the Valley

Shape No.	Description	Reference/Notes
3	-6" mixing bowl	Bomm 119
3	-8" mixing bowl	Bomm 119
3	-10" mixing bowl	Bomm 119
4	-9" salad bowl (with 12" underplate)	Bomm 119
1318	-0.5 pt pitcher	Bomm 119
1319	-1.5 pt pitcher	Bomm 119
1320	-4 pt pitcher	Bomm 119

Mounted Casseroles

Shape No.	Description	Reference/Notes
42	-3.25" mounted ramekin	See July 1916 price list
52	-3.5" mounted custard	See July 1916 price list
173	-7" round casserole, shallow	See July 1916 price list
174	-7" or -8" round casserole, shallow	Bomm 164; also in July 1916 price list
174.5	-8" round casserole, shallow	See July 1916 price list
175	-8" round casserole, shallow	See July 1916 price list
183	-7" round casserole, deep	See July 1916 price list
192	-7" oval casserole	See July 1916 price list
193	-8" oval casserole	See July 1916 price list
193.5	-8" oval casserole	Bomm 164
194	-9" oval casserole	See July 1916 price list
194.5	-9" oval casserole	Bomm 164
204	3-pt. casserole	Bomm 164
	7" special casserole	Bomm 164

Miscellaneous Pitchers

Shape No.	Description	Reference/Notes
1	Holland	Bomm 132
2	Holland	Bomm 132; also in July 1916 price list
B1	-1 pt pitcher	Bomm 131
B2	-2 pt pitcher	Bomm 131
B3	-4 pt pitcher	Bomm 131
C3	pitcher	Bomm 132
C4	pitcher	Bomm 132
C7	-2 qt pitcher	Bomm 131
C8	-2 qt pitcher	Bomm 131
D2	-2 qt pitcher	Bomm 131
D3	-3 qt pitcher	Bomm 131
G2	-2 qt pitcher ("The Cow")	Bomm 131
G3	-3 qt pitcher ("The Cow")	Bomm 131
	The Boy	Bomm 131
	The Bridge	Bomm 131
	The Golden Rod	Bomm 131
	The Grape	Bomm 131; also in July 1916 price list
	Iris	Bomm 132; also in July 1916 price list
	Landscape	Bomm 132; also in July 1916 price list
	Owl	Bomm 132
	The Mill	Bomm 131
	Teddy Bear	Bomm 132
	Tulip	Bomm 119 and 131; also in July 1916 price list

Shape No.	Description	Reference/Notes
	The Wild Rose	Bomm 131
	1 pt pitcher (Old Tourist)	Bomm 131
	2 pt pitcher (Old Tourist)	Bomm 131
	3 pt pitcher (Old Tourist)	Bomm 131
	4 pt pitcher (Old Tourist)	Bomm 131
	10-pc. toilet set	See July 1916 price list
	12-pc. toilet set	See July 1916 price list

Romafin

Shape No.	Description
41	1.5 oz. ramekin (2.5" x 1.25")
42	3 oz. ramekin (3.25" x 1.375")
43	5 oz. ramekin (3.5" diameter)
50	3 oz. custard, or individual bean pot (2.5" x 2")
51	5 oz. custard, or individual bean pot (3" x 2.25")
52	6.5 oz. custard, or individual bean pot (3.25" x 2.5")
53	9 oz. custard, or individual bean pot (3.5" x 2.75")
61	2 oz. cocotte (2.875" x 1.25"). Also spelled "cocorte" in factory stock pages (derivation unknown). Bomm 164 .
62	3 oz. cocotte (3.25" x 1.25")
63	4 oz. cocotte (3.75" x 1.25")
64	6 oz. cocotte (4" diameter)
65	8 oz. cocotte (4.5" diameter)
66	10 oz. cocotte (4.75" diameter)
67	12 oz. cocotte (5.25" diameter)
71	2 oz. cocotte with handle (2.375" x 1.25")
72	3 oz. cocotte with handle (3.25" x 1.25")
73	4 oz. cocotte with handle (3.75" x 1.25")
81	4.5" x .75" shirred egg (round)
82	5.5" x 1" shirred egg (round)
83	6.5" x 1.125" shirred egg (round)
84	7.5" shirred egg (round)
85	8.5" shirred egg (round)
91	5" x .875" shirred egg (hotel and dining car special—made to stack)
92	6" x 1" shirred egg (hotel and dining car special—made to stack)
100	.67 pt. mixing bowl (5" diameter)
101	1.5 pt. mixing bowl (6" x 2.75")
102	1 qt. mixing bowl (7" x 3")
103	1.67 qt. mixing bowl (8" x 3.25")
104	2 qt. mixing bowl (9" x 4")
105	3.25 qt. mixing bowl (10" x 4.25")
106	6 qt. mixing bowl (12" x 5")
111	5 oz. pudding dish (4.25" x 1.25")
112	10 oz. pudding dish (5.25" x 1.625")
113	1.5 pt. pudding dish (6.25" x 2")
114	2 pt. pudding dish (7" x 2.25")
115	3 pt. pudding dish (8" x 2.5")
116	4.5 pt. pudding dish (9.25" x 3")
117	8 pt. pudding dish (10.75" x 3.75")
118	10 pt. pudding dish (11.75" x 3.5")
121	8 oz. pudding dish with flange (5.25" x 1.5")
122	1 pt. pudding dish with flange (6.25" x 1.625")
123	1.25 pt. pudding dish with flange (7.25" x 1.75")
124	2 pt. pudding dish with flange (8.25" x 2.5")
125	3.5 pt. pudding dish with flange (9.25" x 2.875")
126	5.5 pt. pudding dish with flange (10.25" x 3.5")
131	8.25" x 1" pie plate
132	9.25" x 1.125" pie plate
133	10.25" x 1.25" pie plate
140	5.5" x 4.25" oval baker, or au gratin dish
141	6" x 4" x 1.25" oval baker, or au gratin dish
142	7" x 5" x 1.25" oval baker, or au gratin dish
143	8" x 5.5" x 1.375" oval baker, or au gratin dish
144	9" x 6.25" x 1.5" oval baker, or au gratin dish
145	10" x 7" x 1.5" oval baker, or au gratin dish
146	11" x 8" x 2" oval baker, or au gratin dish
152	9" x 5.5" x 1" oval shirred egg, or Welsh rarebit dish
153	11" x 6" x 1.25" oval shirred egg, or Welsh rarebit dish
154	12" x 6.5" x 1.5" oval shirred egg, or Welsh rarebit dish

Shape No.	Description
155	13" x 7" x 1.75" oval shirred egg, or Welsh rarebit dish
156	15" x 8" x 2" oval shirred egg, or Welsh rarebit dish
161	12 oz. hotel casserole, round (4.5" x 2.75")
162	1.5 pt. hotel casserole, round (5" x 2.75")
163	3 pt. hotel casserole, round (6.25" x 2.75")
171	12 oz. round casserole, no handles (4.5" x 1.625")
172	1.5 pt. round casserole, no handles (5.5" x 2")
173	2.5 pt. round casserole, no handles (6.25" x 2.5")
174	3.5 pt. round casserole, no handles (7" x 3")
175	5.5 pt. round casserole, no handles (8" x 3.25")
176	8 pt. round casserole, no handles (9" x 4")
181	12 oz. round casserole, tapered bottom (4" x 2")
182	1.5 pt. round casserole, tapered bottom (5" x 2.75")
183	3 pt. round casserole, tapered bottom (6" x 3.5")
184	5.5 pt. round casserole, tapered bottom (7.5" x 4")
185	6 pt. round casserole, tapered bottom (8" x 4.25")
186	8 pt. round casserole, tapered bottom (9.5" x 5")
187	12 pt. round casserole, tapered bottom (10.5" x 5.5")
191	1 pt. deep oval casserole (6" x 4.375" x 2.75")
191.5	1 pt. deep oval casserole, no handle (6" x 4.375" x 2.75")
192	1.5 pt. deep oval casserole (7" x 5" x 3")
192.5	1.5 pt. deep oval casserole, no handle (7" x 5" x 3")
193	2.25 pt. deep oval casserole (8" x 5.75" x 3.625")
193.5	2.25 pt. deep oval casserole, no handle (8" x 5.75" x 3.625")
194	4 pt. deep oval casserole (9" x 6.5" x 4.5")
194.5	4 pt. deep oval casserole, no handle (9" x 6.5" x 4.5")
195	3.5 qt. deep oval casserole (10" x 7.25" x 5.25")
195.5	3.5 qt. deep oval casserole, no handle (10" x 7.25" x 5.25")
196	4.25 qt. deep oval casserole (11" x 8" x 5.75")
196.5	4.25 qt. deep oval casserole, no handle (11" x 8" x 5.75")
197	5 qt. deep oval casserole (12" x 8.75" x 6")
197.5	5 qt. deep oval casserole, no handle (12" x 8.75" x 6")
201	14 oz. bean pot (4" x 3.5")
202	1.25 pt. bean pot (4.25" x 3.5")
203	2 pt. bean pot (4.75" x 4.25")
204	3 pt. bean pot (6" x 5")
205	4 pt. bean pot (7" x 6")
206	bean pot (6.75" diameter)
207	bean pot (7.5" diameter)
211	8 oz. coffee server (4.25" x 2.75")
212	14 oz. coffee server (5.25" x 3.25")
221	3 oz. pitcher (2.625" x 2")
222	4.5 oz. pitcher (3" x 2.25")
223	6 oz. pitcher (3.375" x 2.5")
224	13 oz. pitcher (4" x 2.75")
225	1.25 pt. pitcher (5" x 3.25")
226	2.75 pt. pitcher (6" x 4.25")
226.5	4.5 pt. pitcher
227	6 pt. pitcher (7.25" x 5.5")
231	6 oz. chocolate pot (3.25" x 2.25")
232	10 oz. chocolate pot (4" x 2.5")
233	14 oz. chocolate pot (4.5" x 2.75")

Shape No.	Description
234	1.125 pt. chocolate pot (4.75 x 3.25")
235	1.5 pt. chocolate pot (5.25" x 3.5")
236	2 pt. chocolate pot (5.75" x 4")
241	8 oz. Astor tea pot, black (2.75" x 3.5")
241.5	8 oz. Astor tea pot, black and gold (2.75" x 3.5")
242	10 oz. stein (4" x 2.75")
242.5	16 oz. Astor tea pot, black and gold (3.625" x 4.5")
243	32 oz. Astor tea pot, black (4" x 5.625")
243.5	32 oz. Astor tea pot, black and gold (4" x 5.625")
244	48 oz. Astor tea pot, black (4.75" x 6.25")
244.5	48 oz. Astor tea pot, black and gold (4.75" x 6.25")
245	9 oz. stein (4.25" x 3.5")
251	10 oz. Globe tea pot (3.5" x 2.5")
254	2 pt. Globe tea pot (4.5" x 3.25")
265	2.5 pt. Flat Globe tea pot (4.25" x 4")
275	2.125 pt. Betty tea pot (5" x 3.5")
284	1.75 pt. English tea pot (4.75" x 3")
292	8 oz. Astor tea pot, brown and white (2.75" x 3.5")
293	16 oz. Astor tea pot, brown and white (3.625" x 4.5")
294	32 oz. Astor tea pot, brown and white (4" x 5.625")
295	48 oz. Astor tea pot, brown and white (4.75" x 6.25")
301	10 oz. red clay casserole (4.25" x 1.75")
302	1.75 pt. red clay casserole (6.5" x 2.25")
303	2.75 pt. red clay casserole (7.5" x 2.5")
304	4 pt. red clay casserole (8.5" x 2.75")
311	10 oz. red clay casserole, no cover (4.25" x 1.75")
312	1.75 pt. red clay casserole, no cover (6.5" x 2.25")
313	2.75 pt. red clay casserole, no cover (7.5" x 2.5")
314	4 pt. red clay casserole, no cover (8.5" x 2.75")
321	10 oz. French casserole (4.25" x 1.75")
322	1.75 pt. French casserole (6.5" x 2.25")
323	2.75 pt. French casserole (7.5" x 2.5")
324	4 pt. French casserole (8.5" x 2.75")
331	14 oz. red clay bean pot (4" x 3.5")
332	1.25 pt. red clay bean pot (4.25" x 3.5")
333	2 pt. red clay bean pot (4.75" x 4.25")
334	3 pt. red clay bean pot (6" x 5")
335	4 pt. red clay bean pot (7" x 6")
350	combination tea set
360	combination tea set See July 1916 price list

Toilet Sets

Shape No.	Description	Reference/Notes
	10-pc. Holland toilet set	See July 1916 price list
	12-pc. Holland toilet set	See July 1916 price list

Utility Ware. 13-7" pitcher (7.75" tall), wide blue band, black Rv inkstamp and 13-7; 5-6.75" "ideal" pitcher, opaque glossy blue (an "opac enamel" glaze) and glossy creamware, gilt lines, unmarked. *Fairfield collection.* **$125–150 (each)**

Utility Ware (Banded). 5" baking
pan, narrow gray band; 8" baking pan,
narrow gray band; 10" baking pan,
narrow gray band. *Hoppe photograph.*
$50–75, $75–95, $95–125

Utility Ware (Black Teapots). 244-
3.5" teapot. *Auclair collection.* **$125–
150.** Roseville's black teapots have a
red clay body.

Utility Ware (Black Teapots). 241-3"
teapot; 242-3.25" teapot; 243-3.25"
teapot; 244-3.5" teapot. *Auclair
collection.* **$95–150 (each)**

Utility Ware (German Cooking Ware). 7" teapot; 3" cream pitcher; 8.5" coffee pot.
Hoppe collection. **$75–95, $20–25, $75–95**

Utility Ware (Glossy Colors). Pair, 20-10" cookie jars, golden tan; blue. *Fairfield collection.* **$125–175 (each).** Also known in green.

Utility Ware (Glossy Colors). 14C creamer, orange; 14P teapot, orange; 14S sugar bowl, orange. *Courtesy of Bobby and Joan Joray.* **$40–50, $125–175, $40–50**

Utility Ware (Holland). 4" mug, boy with toy sailboat (obverse shows girl with flowers), hand decorated; 4" mug, standing girl (obverse shows standing boy), blended colors; 4.25" mug, standing boy (obverse shows girl with doll), hand decorated. *Shannon collection.* **$75–95 (each)**

Utility Ware (Holland). 6" pitcher, daughter and mother carrying water, hand decorated; 5" mug, running boy, hand decorated. *Hoppe photograph.* **$125–150, $75–95**

Utility Ware (Lilies of the Valley).
1318-0.5pt. pitcher, 4" tall; 1319-1.5
pt. pitcher, 5.5" tall; 1320-4 pt.
pitcher, 7.25" tall. *Shannon collection.*
$75–95, $95–125, $125–150

Utility Ware (Teddy Bears). 7.5" pitcher, Majolica (Hand Decorated). *Scheytt collection.* **NPD**

Another view of Teddy Bears pitcher.

Utility Ware (Tulip Pitchers). 7.5" pitcher, Volpato glaze;
.5" pitcher, Majolica (Hand Decorated); 7.5" pitcher,
Majolica (Blended Colors). *Shannon collection.* **$225–275
each)**

Utility Ware (Venitian). 9.75" crock, with bail handle, blue.
Shannon collection. **$75–95**

Utility Ware (Venitian). 11" baking dish, brown; 3.5" pudding dish, brown; 9" baking dish, brown. *Hoppe photograph.* **$30–40, $60–75, $25–30**

Utility Ware (Wild Rose Tankards). Left to right: Majolica (Hand Decorated); gold Cornelian; combination of Majolica (Hand Decorated) and blue Cornelian glazes; blue Cornelian; Majolica (Hand Decorated) and gilt. *Shannon collection.* **$200–250 (each).** Although these five tankards use the same mold, they vary slightly in height (from 9" to 9.5"). Such variations are typical for Roseville products.

VASE ASSORTMENT
An Early Product Line, introduced ca. 1903

Factory Name(s): Vase Assortment #60
Style: Late Victorian
Standard Color(s): Unknown
Typical Marks: Unknown. Some examples have a molded (raised-relief) shape number (only).

An early factory stock page illustrates two dissimilar product lines that Roseville sold to wholesalers in pre-packaged groupings, or "assortments." The term "Vase Assortment No. 24" referred to a group of blended-colors Majolica bud vases (shown in *Introducing Roseville Pottery* under "Majolica"). The phrase "Vase Assortment No. 60" identified an entirely different product, which appears to be a sub-category of Decorated Artware.

These vases are typically glossy tan or green, with cream-colored or hand-decorated low-relief floral motifs. The handles and rims have a little gilt tracing. Interiors are glazed in glossy white.

Because Vase Assortment items are seldom found, and never clearly marked Roseville, these pieces can be the "lucky find" of an astute collector shopping the thrift stores and flea markets. Most people who collect early Roseville would like to own at least one example.

The "Vase Assortment" factory stock page shows 12 shapes in this line:

VASE ASSORTMENT

Vase Assortment. 109-7.25" ewer, tan, gilt. *Shannon collection.* **$250–300**

Shape No.	Description	Shape No.	Description
101	vase	108	vase
102	vase	109	ewer
103	vase	110	vase
104	vase	111	ewer
105	vase	112	vase
106	vase		

Left:
Vase Assortment. 106-7.75" vase, green, gilt. *Courtesy of White Pillars Antique Mall.* **$300–350**

Right:
Vase Assortment. 107-8" vase, tan, hand decorated and gilt. *Hoppe collection.* **$350–400**

VELMOSS

A Middle Period Line, introduced in 1935

Factory Name(s): Velmoss
Collector Nickname(s): Velmoss II (see Purviance and Schneider, 1970); Velmoss, Second (see Alexander, 1970); Unidentified (see Huxford, 1976); Velmoss 2 (see Bomm, 1998)
Style: Arts and Crafts (blue, green, and tan), or Art Deco (rose)
Standard Color(s): Blue, green, rose, and tan
Typical Marks: Early examples had foil labels. (These could be lost, leaving the piece unmarked.) Some have hand-written (crayon) shape numbers. Pieces made in 1936 or later have die-impressed marks, including "Roseville" (script), shape number, and size.

Vase Assortment. Two examples of 105-8.5" vase, green, one with hand decorated poppies, both with molded (raised-relief) shape number 105. *Scheytt collection.* **$300–350, $250–300**

Velmoss. 116-8" double bud vase, blue; 115-7" bud vase, cornucopia shape, green; 715-7" vase, blue. *Shannon collection.* **$250–300, $175–225, $225–275**

Like Early Velmoss, the low-relief design used in Velmoss depicts a cluster of leaves and berries. As a reviewer commented in 1935, "the embossment here is somewhat after the nature of a palm leaf, though not an exact copy thereof" (trade notice, *Pottery, Glass and Brass Salesman,* January 10, 1935: 8). The term "velmoss" does not appear in the *Oxford English Dictionary*. Apparently, like the 1937 lines Dawn and Ixia, Velmoss was intended to be decorative, but not to portray an actual plant.

The rose Velmoss pieces have a smooth and fairly uniform matte coloring, which contrasts well with the hand-decorated foliage. The other standard colorings tend to have mottled crystalline effects, and thus appeal to Arts and Crafts collectors. Yet Velmoss remains moderately priced among the Middle Period lines.

The only known factory stock page for Velmoss shows 19 examples:

VELMOSS

Shape No.	Description	Shape No.	Description
115	-7" bud vase	716	-7" vase
116	-8" double bud vase	717	-8" vase
117	-8" double cornucopia	718	-8" vase
119	-10" vase	719	-9" vase
264	-5" vase	720	-10" vase
265	-6" rose bowl	721	-12" vase
266	-8" x 5" bowl	722	-14" vase
266	-12" x 6" bowl	1100	-4.5" candlestick
714	-6" vase	1274	-8" wall pocket
715	-7" vase		

Velmoss. 264-5" vase, tan, gold foil label. *Latta collection.* **$275–325**

Velmoss. 721-12" vase, pink; 714-6" vase, pink. *Hoppe photograph.* **$400–500, $225–275**

Velmoss. 722-14" vase, red crayon shape number 722; 116-8" double bud vase. *Auclair collection.* **$700–800, $325–375.** Neither piece has die-impressed marks, nor are there any trial glaze notations. Perhaps this unusual tan coloring was a short-lived and early glaze treatment for Velmoss.

Velmoss. 264-5" vase, green. *Courtesy of Mark Bassett Antiques.* **$200–250**

VICTORIAN ART POTTERY
A Middle Period Line, introduced ca. 1925

Factory Name(s): Victorian Art Pottery

Collector Nickname(s): Victorian (see Clifford, 1968); Aztec Art, Egyptian, New Hampshire Vintage, or Love Apple (see Buxton, 1977)

Style: Italianate, or Egyptian Revival

Standard Color(s): Brown, chartreuse, or gray

Typical Marks: Most examples have a blue inkstamp Rv logo, although some are unmarked. (In other cases, the inkstamp mark may be obscured by a thick glaze.)

Victorian Art Pottery shapes are classical and symmetrical. Each example has a low-relief carved band near the shoulder. Otherwise, the surfaces are adorned with a smooth monochromatic glaze— usually matte brown or gray. These details give the line an extremely traditional look, even those examples with Egyptian scarab motifs.

Middle Period collectors are not always as taken with Victorian Art Pottery as are collectors of early Roseville. Perhaps the line's name is indeed appropriate. Values are usually a bit higher than those earned by other 1920s Italianate lines.

The only known factory stock page for Victorian Art Pottery shows 12 shapes, in profile only. In this case, the glossy black and white photograph was not hand-painted to illustrate the standard colors and decorations:

VICTORIAN ART POTTERY

Shape No.	Description	Shape No.	Description
132	-4" vase	260	-8" vase
133	-6" rose bowl	261	-8" covered vase
256	-6" vase	262	-10" vase
257	-7" vase	263	-10" vase
258	-7" vase	264	-9.5" vase
259	-7" vase	265	-12" vase

Victorian Art Pottery. 132-4" rose bowl, brown; 258-7" vase, brown. *Hoppe collection.* **$250–300, $450–550**

Victorian Art Pottery. 263-10" vase, gray, blue Rv inkstamp. *Courtesy of Riverfront Antique Mall.* **$700–800**

Victorian Art Pottery. 264-9.5" vase, blue. *Shannon collection.* **$700–800**

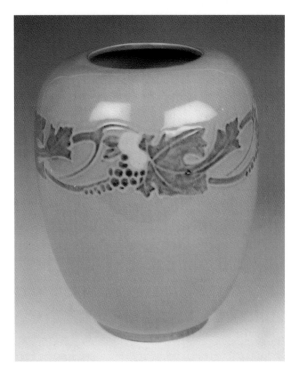

Victorian Art Pottery. 261-8" ginger jar (missing its cover), chartreuse. *Fairfield collection.* **$450–550 (or $550–650 with cover)**

VINTAGE
A Middle Period Line, introduced in 1925

Factory Name(s): Rosecraft Vintage
Style: Italianate, with Art Nouveau stylistic touches
Standard Color(s): Brown, or green
Typical Marks: Most examples have a blue inkstamp Rv logo, although some are unmarked. (In other cases, the inkstamp mark may be obscured by a thick glaze.)

In 1925 Vintage was said to be "adorned with a conventional grape pattern in the darker shades of purple, etc." (trade notice, *Pottery, Glass and Brass Salesman,* August 20, 1925: 17). Actually, the background color is usually a very dark brown, with a ruddy cast. Occasionally, one encounters an example in dark green. Each shape has a low-relief design whose details are hand-painted in pale shades of green and purple. These motifs often follow a "whiplash curve" in the Art Nouveau style.

Vintage pieces are usually classical in shape, and symmetrical. In spirit, they are related to both Victorian Art Pottery and Panel. Collectors of one line are often drawn to the others. Prices are fairly moderate.

In the factory stock pages, 24 examples of Vintage are shown. In Bomm, Vintage shapes are located under "Rosecraft–Vintage":

VINTAGE

Shape No.	Description	Shape No.	Description
9	-3" vase	277	-8" vase
48	-4.5" double bud vase, gate shape	278	-8" vase
		279	-10" vase
139	-3" bowl	280	-12" vase
140	-4" bowl	372	-10" window box
141	-5" bowl	607	-5" jardiniere
142	-6" bowl	607	-6" jardiniere
143	-3" rose bowl	607	-7" jardiniere
144	-6" urn	607	-8" jardiniere
273	-4" vase	607	-9" jardiniere
274	-5" vase	607	-10" jardiniere & pedestal
275	-6" vase	1241	-8" wall pocket
276	-6" vase		

Vintage. 9-3" vase, brown; 144-6" urn, brown; 139-3" bowl, brown; 141-5" x 2" comport, brown. *Hoppe collection.* **$150–175, $175–225, $95–125, $125–150**

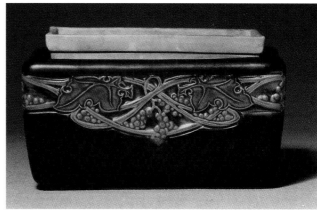

Vintage. 372-10" window box, with liner (raised), brown. *Hoppe photograph.* **$325–375**

Vintage. 607-5.5" jardiniere, green. *Shannon collection.* **$325–375**

Vintage. 8" candlestick, brown; 607-5.5" jardiniere, brown. *Hoppe photograph.* **$150–200, $200–250**

VISTA

A Middle Period Line, introduced ca. 1920

Factory Name(s): Unknown
Collector Nickname(s): Unidentified (see Huxford, 1976); Vista (see Buxton, 1977); Forest (see Huxford, 1980; rev. ed. 1997)
Style: Arts and Crafts
Standard Color(s): One standard coloring, as described below
Typical Marks: Unmarked. Some examples have a blue inkstamp mark giving the shape number and size (only).

Vista is a much beloved line, coveted by both Arts and Crafts lovers and Middle Period collectors. It depicts a scene of palm trees near a body of water, decorated in semigloss pastels—lavender, gray, green, and purple. Vista is attributed to Roseville because it sometimes bears a blue inkstamp shape number that is identical (in typeface) to one occasionally found on Rozane Line and Dogwood (Smooth) pieces. No published references to the line have been located.

In weight, Vista resembles Donatello, Early Carnelian, Early Velmoss, Imperial (Textured), and Mostique. As shown in Chapter 4, the Vista jardiniere appears to have been derived from an Early Carnelian shape. The Vista line probably dates to around 1920—that is, after Rozane Line and Dogwood (Smooth), but before Rosecraft.

Vista. 224-18" floor vase. *Hoppe collection.* **$1500–1800.** Like many Vista pieces, this example has a blue inkstamp mark that provides the shape number and size.

Vista. 15" vase; 132-18" floor vase; 10" vase. *Hoppe photograph.* **$1200–1500, $1800–2200, $650–750**

Vista. 20" umbrella stand. *Hoppe photograph.* **$1800–2200**

Vista. 6.5" basket; 9.5" basket. *Shannon collection.* **$600–700, $750–950**

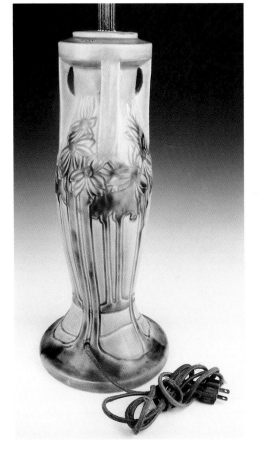

Vista. 8" vase; 130-18" floor vase; 121-15" vase. *Hoppe photograph.* **$500–600, $1500–1800, $1200–1500**

Vista. 134-18" floor vase, drilled for use as lamp, blue inkstamp shape number 134-18". *Merritt collection.* **$750–950 (or $1500–1800 as vase)**

Vista. 12" vase; 8" basket. *Hoppe photograph.* **$950–1200, $750–950**

Vista. 6.5" basket; 126-10" vase. *Hoppe photograph.* **$600–00, $950–1200**

Vista. 4" x 7" fern dish; 6" jardiniere. *Hoppe photograph.* **$275–350, $400–500**

Vista. 12" vase; 8" basket. *Hoppe photograph.* **950–1200, $750–950**

Vista. 531-7" hanging basket; 531-6" hanging basket. *Hoppe photograph.* **$600–700, $450–550**

VOLPATO

A Middle Period Line, introduced in 1922

Factory Name(s): Volpato Ware; Volpato
Style: Italianate
Standard Color(s): Glossy buff
Typical Marks: Early examples were unmarked. About 1922, some were marked with a die-impressed Rv logo. Starting about 1923, paper labels were used. (These could be lost, leaving the pieces unmarked.)

Roseville's Volpato line was so named to honor a Venetian potter who worked in the late 18th century. According to a 1922 trade notice, Giovanni Volpato made "a beautiful line of faience noteworthy for the classic lines of its shapes, the artistry of its sculptural embossments, as well as for the excellence of its potting. This ware turned out by Volpato was in a rich cream tone" (trade notice, *Pottery, Glass and Brass Salesman,* July 13, 1922: 15). As today's collectors can easily recognize, these features characterize the Roseville line too.

Roseville's Volpato line was said to be "classic in form and decoration, featuring particularly the art of Greece at the time of Pericles" (trade notice, *PGBS,* March 29, 1923: 17). Volpato has both smooth and fluted sections, and is usually accented with rose garlands. The translucent glossy glaze allows the buff-colored Zanesville clay to show through. As noted elsewhere, the Volpato glaze was also used on selected 1930s Creamware and Utility Ware items.

In the factory stock pages, 33 examples of Volpato are shown:

VOLPATO

Shape No.	Description	Shape No.	Description
2	-5.5" vase	189	-7" vase
3	-8" covered vase	190	-9" vase
5	-10" covered vase	191	-10" vase
12	-8" bowl	192	-12" vase
13	-10" bowl	206	-6" vase
97	-4" vase	207	-6" vase
98	-5" bowl	208	-8" vase
99	-5" bowl	209	-10" vase
100	-6" bowl	599	-6" flower pot and saucer
101	-6" bowl	1039	-8" candlestick
102	-6" bowl	1040	-8" candlestick
103	-8" bowl	1041	-10" candlestick
104	-10" bowl	1042	-10" candlestick
105	-14" bowl	1043	-12" candlestick
119	-6" comport	1046	-10" candlestick
120	-8" bowl	1047	-12" candlestick
188	-5" vase		

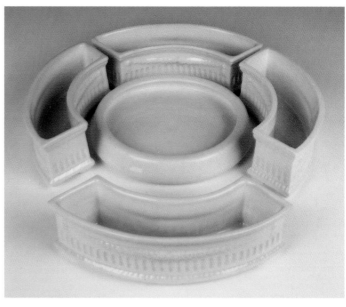

Volpato. Set, consisting of 7.5" centerpiece base and four curved 2.5" x 8" planters. *Fairfield collection.* **$400–500 (set)**

Volpato. 189-7" vase, die-impressed Rv logo. *Merritt collection.* **$200–250**

Volpato. Pair, 1041-10" candlesticks, black paper labels; 12-8" comport. *Fairfield collection.* **$400–500 (pair), $225–275**

Volpato. 105-14" x 9" bowl. *Courtesy of McAllister Auctions.* **$225–275**

WATER LILY

A Late Line, introduced in 1943

Factory Name(s): Water Lily
Style: Realistic, often with angular handles
Standard Color(s): Ciel Blue ("blue"), Rose ("pink"), or Walnut Brown ("brown")
Typical Marks: Molded (raised-relief) marks, including "Roseville" (script), shape number, and size

In 1943 Roseville announced "one of the most beautiful of all decorative art pottery patterns, Water Lily ... a gorgeous new floral motif by the makers of America's fastest-selling decorative art pottery" (advertisement, *Gift and Art Buyer,* January 1943: 2). Having met with market forecasters during 1942, the factory noted that Water Lily was available in "the year's most in-favor decorator colors."

Except for the extravagant handles, Water Lily designs are relatively conservative. Backgrounds are textured, and each water lily is portrayed against a mass of leaves and closed blooms. Bowl rims are often irregular, following the silhouette of the topmost petals. Water Lily basket designs evoke the Mid-Century Modern style.

Today, collectors tend to prefer the pink coloration, although blue and brown Water Lily examples also have a following. Values are moderate to affordable.

Although factory advertising mentions 50 shapes, only 48 Water Lily designs are shown in the factory stock pages:

Water Lily. 82-14" vase, blue; 84-16" vase, blue. *Hoppe collection.* **$350–400, $450–550**

WATER LILY

Shape No.	Description	Shape No.	Description	Shape No.	Description
	-8" cookie jar	82	-14" vase	441	-10" bowl
10	-6" ewer	83	-15" vase	442	-10" bowl
11	-10" ewer	84	-16" vase	443	-12" bowl
12	bookend	85	-18" floor vase	444	-14" bowl
12	-15" ewer	174	-6" vase	445	-6" conch shell
48	flower holder	175	-8" vase	468	-5" hanging basket
71	-4" vase	176	-6" planter	663	-3" jardiniere
72	-6" vase	177	-6" cornucopia	663	-4" jardiniere
73	-6" vase	178	-8" cornucopia	663	-5" jardiniere
74	-7" vase	380	-8" basket	663	-8" jardiniere & pedestal
75	-7" vase	381	-10" basket	663	-10" jardiniere & pedestal
76	-8" vase	382	-12" basket	664	-5" flower pot and saucer
77	-8" vase	437	-4" rose bowl		
78	-9" vase	437	-6" rose bowl	1154	-2" candlestick
79	-9" vase	438	-8" conch shell	1155	-4.5" candlestick
80	-10" vase	439	-6" bowl		
81	-12" vase	440	-8" bowl		

Water Lily. 78-9" vase, brown. *Courtesy of McAllister Auctions.* **$200–250**

Water Lily. 381-10" basket, pink; 174-6" vase, brown; 71-4" vase, brown. *Shannon collection.* **$250–300, $150–200, $95–125**

Water Lily. 663-5" jardiniere, blue; 439-6" bowl, blue; 77-8" vase, blue; 437-6" rose bowl, blue. *Hoppe collection.* **$125–150, $95–125, $175–225, $125–150**

WHITE ROSE
A Late Line, introduced in 1940

Factory Name(s): White Rose
Style: Realistic, often with Art Deco stylistic touches
Standard Color(s): Ciel Blue ("blue"), Coral ("pink"), or Verdi Brown ("brown")
Typical Marks: Molded (raised-relief) marks, including "Roseville" (script), shape number, and size

Roseville advertisements reveal the factory's pride in their 1940 line White Rose: "Universally the most esteemed flower, the Rose inspires the new motif for this elegant pattern" (advertisement, *Gift and Art Buyer,* June 1940: 2). Most shapes depict two overlapping roses on one side, and a single rose on the obverse. Backgrounds are partly textured, and many pieces have an Art Deco feel.

Along with the more extravagant pattern Bleeding Heart, White Rose was one of the first lines designed and produced during Roseville's so-called "late period." The late period of Roseville had begun in 1938 with the death of Anna Young, and the subsequent presidency of her son-in-law Fenwick S. Clement. Clement served in this office until his retirement in 1945. During his difficult wartime presidency, the factory was able to produce little more than a dozen new lines.

Predictably, today's collector chooses the pastel pink and white colorings over the brown. Values are generally moderate, making White Rose a good choice for someone just starting a Roseville collection.

Factory advertising mentioned that White Rose consisted of 58 shapes, but only 56 appear in the factory stock pages:

WHITE ROSE

Shape No.	Description	Shape No.	Description
1	cornucopia	392	-10" bowl
1	-C cream	393	-12" bowl
1	-S sugar	394	-14" bowl
1	-T teapot	463	-5" hanging basket
7	bookend	653	-3" jardiniere
41	flower frog	653	-4" jardiniere
143	-6" cornucopia	653	-5" jardiniere
144	-8" cornucopia	653	-6" jardiniere
145	-8" double cornucopia	653	-7" jardiniere
146	-6" vase	653	-8" jardiniere & pedestal
147	-8" vase	653	-10" jardiniere & pedestal
148	double bud vase, gate shape	654	-5" flower pot and saucer
362	-8" basket	978	-4" vase
363	-10" basket	979	-6" vase
364	-12" basket	980	-6" vase
382	-9" window box	981	-6" ewer
387	-4" rose bowl	982	-7" vase
388	-7" urn	983	-7" vase
389	-6" bowl	984	-8" pillow vase
390	-8" bowl	985	-8" vase
391	-10" bowl	986	-9" vase
		987	-9" fan vase
		988	-10" vase
		990	-10" ewer
		991	-12" vase
		992	-15" vase
		993	-15" ewer
		994	-18" floor vase
		995	-7" bud vase
		1141	candlestick
		1142	4.5" candlestick
		1143	double candelabra
		1288	-6" wall pocket
		1289	-8" wall pocket
		1324	pitcher

White Rose. 148-4.5" double bud vase, gate shape, blue; 995-9" bud vase, blue; 978-4" vase, blue. *Hoppe photograph.* **$125–150, $95–125, $75–95**

White Rose. 983-7" vase, brown; 990-10" ewer, pink; 982-7" vase, brown. *Shannon collection.* **$150–200, $275–325, $150–200**

White Rose. 382-9" window box, blue; pair, 7 bookends, blue; 387-4" rose bowl, blue. *Hoppe collection.* **$125–175, $225–275 (pair), $95–125**

White Rose. 1C creamer, pink; 1T teapot, pink; 1S sugar bowl, pink. *Auclair collection.* **$75–95, $325–375, $75–95**

WINCRAFT
A Late Line, introduced in 1948

Factory Name(s): Wincraft
Collector Nickname(s): Glossy White Rose, Bushberry, or Glossy line (see Purviance and Schneider, 1970); Pine Cone II (see Buxton, 1977)
Style: Mid-Century Modern
Standard Color(s): Apricot ("tan"), Azure Blue ("blue"), or Chartreuse ("green")
Typical Marks: Molded (raised-relief) marks, including "Roseville" (script), shape number, and size

With Wincraft, Roseville's final president—Robert Windisch, son-in-law to F.S. Clement—made his presence unmistakably known. Finally, the privations of World War II were being succeeded by a postwar economic "boom" and a general feeling of increasing prosperity. With the success of Roseville's 1948 Wincraft line, the factory would no longer be restricted to producing only one new line a year, as it had been since 1944.

The earliest known Wincraft advertisement reads, "Once in a blue moon is born an art pottery creation with the completely arresting appeal of WINCRAFT. For here is new, unusual ceramic beauty graciously expressed in twenty-six distinctive art pieces, each a separate and fascinating style" (*Gift and Art Buyer,* December 1947: 2). Six months later, Roseville boasted that "WINCRAFT is wholly new … **original**. It combines graceful contours in the modern manner with blended color tones of surpassing beauty. Each piece is a separate style with varying floral motif, glorified by a unique high-luster mottled glaze" (advertisement, *The Gift and Art Buyer,* May 1948: 2).

By July, Roseville could call Wincraft "America's fastest-selling decorative art pottery line! The overwhelming acceptance of Wincraft has inspired the addition of new and more beautiful items to the line, which is now comprised of forty-seven pieces in three color choices" (advertisement, *House and Garden,* July 1948: 120).

The Wincraft glazes also reflected Windisch's approach. Instead of using matte glazes (as longtime art director Frank Ferrell preferred), he chose to produce the line in glossy mottled colors. Nearly every year after that, Windisch would oversee the production of both a new matte and a new glossy line. In 1948, showing considerable foresight, factory executives decided to name the line Wincraft after their current president, Robert Windisch.

During the 1970s, Roseville researchers often had difficulty identifying the line. Even today, beginners can become confused by the variety of floral motifs used in Wincraft. (Some of the more difficult distinctions are illustrated in Chapter 4.)

Nowadays Wincraft has begun to find an appreciative audience, both among Roseville collectors and for those who decorate in the Mid-Century Modern style. The tan and blue colorings usually sell higher than the green, and prices are beginning to rise. Everyone naturally wants an example of the panther vase (shape 290).

No factory stock pages are known for Wincraft. In the two factory brochures, 51 examples of Wincraft are shown:

WINCRAFT

Shape No.	Description	Reference/Notes
208	-8" basket	
209	-12" basket	
210	-12" basket	
216	-8" ewer	Originally 2TK-8"
217	-6" ewer	
218	-18" ewer	
221	-8" cornucopia	
222	-8" cornucopia	
226	-8" bowl	
227	-10" bowl	
228	-12" bowl	
229	-14" bowl	
230	-7" tray	
231	-10" bowl	
232	-12" bowl	
233	-14" bowl	
240	-B cigarette box	
240	-T ashtray	
241	-6" vase	
242	-8" vase	
250	-C cream	
250	-P chocolate pot	
250	-S sugar	
251	-3" candlestick	Originally 2CS1
252	-4" candlestick	
253	triple candelabra	
256	-5" vase, flower pot shape	Originally 2PT
257	-6" planter	
259	-6" bookend	
261	-6" hanging basket	
263	-14" vase	
266	-5" wall bucket	
267	-5" wall pocket	
268	-12" window box	
271	-C cream	
271	-P teapot	
271	-S sugar	
272	-6" fan vase	
273	-8" fan vase	Originally 2FH-8"
274	-7" vase	
275	-12" pillow vase	
281	-6" bud vase	
282	-8" vase	
283	-8" vase	Originally 2V2-8"
284	-10" vase	Originally 2V1-10"
285	-10" vase	Originally 2V2-10"
286	-12" vase	
287	-12" vase	
288	-15" vase	
289	-18" floor vase	
290	-11" vase	

Wincraft. Pair, 222-8" cornucopias, one green and one apricot. *Krause Family collection.* **$125–150 (each)**

Wincraft. Pair, 221-8" cornucopias, blue; pair, 252 candlesticks, blue; pair, 259 bookends, blue. *Courtesy of McAllister Auctions.* **$95–125 (each), $75–95 (pair), $175–225 (pair)**

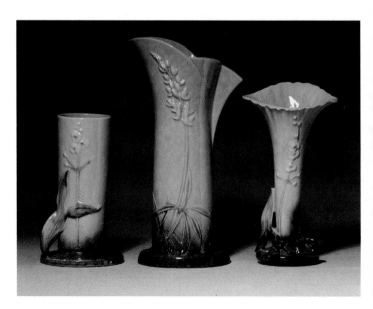

Wincraft. 285-10" vase, chartreuse; 288-15" vase, chartreuse; 286-12" vase, chartreuse. *Hoppe photograph.* **$150–200, $375–450, $175–225**

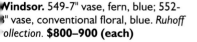

Vincraft. 242-8" vase, chartreuse; 289-18" floor vase, tan. *Shannon collection.* **$125–175, $450–550**

WINDSOR

A Middle Period Line, introduced in 1931

Factory Name(s): Windsor Ware
Style: Art Deco
Standard Color(s): Blue, or rust ("brown")
Typical Marks: Paper labels. (These could be lost, leaving the piece unmarked.)
   Some examples have a hand-written (crayon) shape number.

Windsor is an elegant line with the simplicity of classic French Art Deco. Introduced in 1931, the pattern is sometimes viewed as having two personalities. Some examples feature detailed designs portraying fern leaves. Most Windsor shapes, however, present highly conventionalized motifs with the appearance of having been incised into the moist clay.

The two most readily available colorings involve matte mottled glazes that seem related to the Ferella and Falline glazes. Sometimes Windsor is found in a glossy blue instead, a glaze that may have been produced for only a short time. The fern leaves are hand decorated in green. Other motifs can be green or yellow (or both). As one reviewer noted, Windsor is "a decorative line showing an attractive but not too obtrusive semi-conventionalized motif on the side" (trade notice, *Pottery, Glass and Brass Salesman,* August 13, 1931: 13).

Although the prices for Ferella and Falline tend to be higher than those achieved by Windsor, this line appeals to essentially the same group of collectors. Expect to pay a little extra for an example with crisply outlined decorations.

The only known factory stock page shows 15 shapes in the Windsor line:

Windsor. 549-7" vase, fern, blue; 552-8" vase, conventional floral, blue. *Ruhoff collection.* **$800–900 (each)**

WINDSOR

Shape No.	Description	Shape No.	Description
224	-10" bowl	548	-7" vase
329	-4" basket	549	-7' vase
330	-5" basket	550	-7" vase
331	-8" basket	551	-7" vase
545	-5" vase	552	-8" vase
546	-6" vase	553	-9" vase
547	-6" vase	554	-10" vase
		1084	-4" candlestick

Windsor. 7" bowl, conventional berries and leaves, brown. *Courtesy of Mark Bassett Antiques.* **$250–300**

Windsor. 224-10" bowl, glossy blue. *Courtesy of Jack Brooks.* **$400–500.** The opening of this bowl measures 10" x 6.75", but the outer dimensions are 16" x 10.25". Remember to measure Roseville bowls and jardinieres across the opening.

Windsor. 549-7" vase, fern, brown; 547-6" vase, geometrical motifs, brown; 550-7.25" vase, conventional branch, brown. *Shannon collection.* **$800–900, $400–500, $800–900**

Windsor. 331-8" basket, blue; 545-5" vase, blue; 548-7" vase, blue. *Shannon collection.* **$800–900, $550–650, $600–700**

WISTERIA
A Middle Period Line, introduced in 1933

Factory Name(s): Unknown (probably Wistaria)
Style: Realistic
Standard Color(s): Blue, or brown
Typical Marks: Foil labels. (These could be lost, leaving the piece unmarked.) Some have hand-written (crayon) shape numbers.

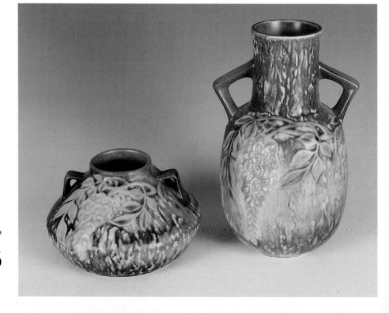

Wisteria. 629-4" vase, blue; 638-9" vase, brown. *Shannon collection.* **$400–500, $700–800**

During the early 20th century, "Wistaria" appears to have been the preferred spelling for this fragrant southern flower. When Wisteria was advertised in 1933, one reviewer called it "a new fancy line… set off with relief motifs" (trade notice, *Pottery, Glass and Brass Salesman*, August 17, 1933: 9). Another reviewer commented that 'the wistaria runs down the side with its orchidy color blending in with the dripped-color, ranging from your darker shades on top downward to your lighter shades at the base" (trade notice, *Crockery and Glass Journal*, September 1933: 21).

Backgrounds are textured, and background colors blend from green to either blue or brown. Modern collectors predictably prefer the blue, when given an alternative. Prices are on the rise, and crisp examples can be relatively expensive.

The only known Wisteria factory stock page shows 16 examples:

Wisteria. 8" vase, brown; 635-8" vase, blue. *Shannon collection.* **$800–900, $700–800**

WISTERIA

Shape No.	Description
242	-4" vase
243	-9" x 5" bowl
629	-4" vase
630	-6" vase
631	-6" vase
632	-5" vase
633	-8" vase
634	-7" vase
635	-8" vase
636	-8" vase
637	-6.5" vase
638	-9" vase
639	-10" vase
640	-12" vase
641	-15" vase
1091	-4" candlestick

Wisteria. 10" vase, blue; 636-8" vase, blue; 640-12" vase, blue. *Schultz collection.* **$950–1200, $800–900, $1500–1800**

Wisteria. 633-8" vase, blue; 632-5" vase, blue. *Ross collection.* **$800–900, $500–600**

WOODLAND
An Early Line, introduced in 1905

Factory Name(s): Rozane Woodland
Style: Japonisme
Standard Color(s): Various enamel colors, against a bisque background
Typical Marks: Most examples have a Woodland wafer. Some are unmarked.

According to the 1905 catalog, Woodland was inspired by "Old Celadon" ware from China, which

> like Woodland, was decorated by incising either floral or conventional designs in the moist clay, or 'biscuit,' after moulding, and was further ornamented with studs or dots.... and scattered with little laminae of mica, or sometimes picked with tiny points, almost imperceptible.

> ... Woodland has not the mica. The laminae mentioned, however, are daintily picked into the surface of the softly shaded mat background, lending just an agreeable relief from its plainness ... while the enameled designs stand out in pleasant contrast ... usually in foliage hues ...

Although no published references document Gazo Foudji's contribution to Woodland, he was surely the line's designer, as he had been for the related Fudji and Fujiyama wares.

Woodland motifs include chrysanthemums, clover, daisies, dandelions, lilies of the valley, foliage, mistletoe, poppies, and thistles. The 1905 catalog illustrates a few of the conventional decorations available on Woodland. These are extremely rare today, and would be easy to mistake for Fudji.

In general, Woodland motifs are less detailed than Fudji designs. Even more characteristic of Woodland are the pin-pricked backgrounds, which often blend from gray to tan or buff. Values are high, and many collectors are eager to acquire an example for their collection.

No factory stock pages are known for Woodland. In the 1905 catalog, 16 different examples are illustrated. In Bomm, Woodland is located under "Rozane–Woodland."

WOODLAND

Shape No.	Description
W2	-6.5" vase (Rozane Royal shape R2)
W3	-10.5" vase (Rozane Royal shape R3)
W6	-8.25" vase (Rozane Royal shape R6)
W15	-10.25" vase (Rozane Royal shape R5)
W893	-12.5" vase (Rozane Royal shape 893)
W955	-15" vase (Rozane Royal shape 955)
W961	-10.5" vase (Rozane Royal shape 961)
W969	-12" bud vase (Rozane Royal shape 969)
W971	-9" vase (Rozane Royal shape 971)
W973	-11.5" vase (Rozane Royal shape 973)
W974	-11.5" vase (Rozane Royal shape 974)
W976	-6.5" vase (Rozane Royal shape 975)
W978	-8.5" vase (Rozane Royal shape 978)
W933	-16.5" vase (Rozane Royal shape R9)
W997	-7.25" vase (Rozane Royal shape 997)
W999	-7" vase (Rozane Royal shape 999)

Woodland. 4" x 5.25" letter holder, Rozane Ware wafer; 8.25" vase, Woodland wafer. *Nickel and Horvath collection.* **$650–750, $950–1200**

Woodland. R5-10" vase, daisies, Woodland wafer; 975-6.5" vase, Woodland wafer. *Shannon collection.* **$950–1200, $700–800**

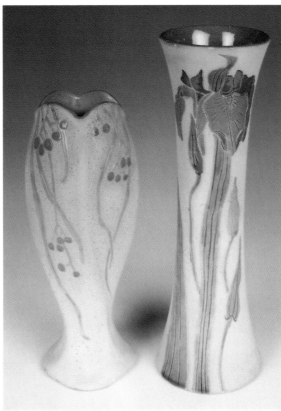

Far left:
Woodland. 7" vase, poppies, partial Rozane Ware wafer. *Courtesy of McAllister Auctions.* **$750–950**

Left:
Woodland. 8.75" vase, Woodland wafer; 10.25" vase, Rozane Ware wafer. *Fairfield collection.* **$750–950, $950–1200**

ZEPHYR LILY

A Late Line, introduced in 1946

Factory Name(s): Zephyr Lily Pattern (or Zephyr Lily)
Style: Realistic
Standard Color(s): Bermuda Blue ("blue"), Evergreen ("green"), or Sienna ("brown")
Typical Marks: Molded (raised-relief) marks, including "Roseville" (script), shape number, and size

Roseville called Zephyr Lily "a lovely floral design of unusual grace, beauty and refinement" (advertisement, *Gift and Art Buyer,* January 1946: 2). The motif depicts a flower of the genus *Zephyranthes,* which is native to the tropical regions of the Americas. This line marked the second year in a row during which Roseville could offer only one new line—probably due to wartime conditions. The new line was advertised in each issue of *Gift and Art Buyer,* from January through November, although delivery was not available until late June.

Today, Zephyr Lily remains moderate to affordable. Shapes are based on classical designs, with the addition of curved handles with knob-like termination at the vessel. A few shapes hint at the Mid-Century Modern style, but many seem conservative to advanced collectors.

In the factory stock pages, 51 examples of Zephyr Lily are shown:

Zephyr Lily. 141-15" vase, blue. *Hoppe collection.* **$700–800**

ZEPHYR LILY

Shape No.	Description		Shape No.	Description
5	-8" cookie jar		204	-8" cornucopia
7	-C creamer		205	-6" fan vase
7	-S sugar		206	-7" fan vase
7	-T teapot		393	-7" basket
8	-10" comport		394	-8" basket
16	bookend		395	-10" basket
22	-6" ewer		470	-5" planter
23	-10" ewer		471	-6" vase
24	-15" ewer		472	-5" hanging basket
29	ashtray		472	-6" bowl
130	-6" vase		473	-6" bowl
131	-7" vase		474	-8" bowl
132	-7" vase		475	-10" bowl
133	-8" vase		476	-10" bowl
134	-8" vase		477	-12" tray
135	-9" vase		478	-12" bowl
136	-9" vase		479	-14" bowl
137	-10" vase		671	-4" jardiniere
138	-10" vase		671	-6" jardiniere
139	-12" vase		671	-8" jardiniere & pedestal
140	-12" vase		672	-5" flower pot and saucer
141	-15" vase		1162	-2" candlestick
142	-18" floor vase		1163	-4.5" candlestick
201	-7" bud vase		1237	-8" wall pocket
202	-8" vase		1393	-8" window box
203	-6" cornucopia			

Zephyr Lily. 132-7" vase, green; 22-6" ewer, brown. *Shannon collection.* **$150–200, $125–175**

Zephyr Lily. 206-7" fan vase, green; pair, 16 bookends, green; 395-10" basket, green; 671-4" jardiniere, green. *Courtesy of McAllister Auctions.* **$150–200, $225–275 (pair), $275–325, $125–150**

Zephyr Lily. 137-10" vase, brown; 202-8" vase, blue; 24-15" ewer, brown. *Courtesy of McAllister Auctions.* **$175–225, $175–225, $600–700**

Chapter 7
FACTORY MARKS
AND ARTIST SIGNATURES

Even though a more accurate chronology of the Roseville lines beginning to be worked out (see Chapter 5), researchers must sometimes make educated guesses about the chronology of factory marks and products. Many think that the various Rozane Ware wafers date to about 1905, when five of these product lines were shown in a small factory catalog. If so, would unmarked examples of Egypto, Mara, Mongol, and Woodland be older than 1905? We can only speculate.

At various times, the factory adopted fairly standard trademarks. Apart from the die-impressed Rozane marks and the subsequent wafer marks, the earliest such trademark to see consistent use was a blue inkstamped "Rv" monogram. This mark, introduced by 1923, is in the form of a capital letter "R" within which is embedded a lower-case "v." It characterizes many of the Italianate lines—whether with cream-colored or dark brown matte glazes.

Around 1927, a new trademark came into play in the form of a paper label. The shield-shaped dark gray and black label bears the legend ROSEVILLE POTTERY. Most of these labels have a somewhat triangular shape, with truncated corners. A rounded urn-shaped paper label is shown in a ca. 1927 Roseville booklet, but is seldom seen. Along with an occasional crayon shape number, these paper labels (when present) are the only factory mark known to occur on Futura, Tuscany, Earlam, and other lines.

Even after 1933, when silver and gold foil labels were introduced, the paper labels may occasionally have been used. Foil labels (found in two sizes) are characteristic of such lines as Cherry Blossom, Tourmaline, Laurel, Russco, and Morning Glory.

The year 1936 saw the introduction of a die-impressed trademark with the word "Roseville" in script, along with the shape number and size. Variations on these standard marks were used for the rest of the factory's history. Starting in 1940, the marks were incorporated into the designs in raised-relief lettering.

The more popular Roseville lines could stay in production long enough to outlive a trademark. For example, both Ivory and Pine Cone were introduced during a time when the factory used only labels. Pieces made between 1936 and 1939 have impressed marks. Any example with a raised-relief mark was made in 1940 or later.

Artist signatures are said to add value to early Roseville examples. If the artist is well-known and well-regarded, this is more likely to be true. Quality of artwork, however, is the main criterion. The photographs will help beginners locate artist signatures and initials, which can crop up unexpectedly in unobtrusive places. Consider them a plus if the artwork (or shape) is particularly pleasing. Artist marks and biographies are particularly difficult to research. Despite our admiration for their work, many of these artisans in their day were viewed merely as "decorators" (and were paid accordingly).

Venitian Mark. This molded (raised-relief) mark was found on an example of Utility Ware (Venitian). It reads "Venitian, Fire Proof."

Molded (Raised-Relief) Shape Number. This mark was found on an example of Vase Assortment.

Die-Impressed "ROZANE." Another example of this mark, arranged in a semicircle.

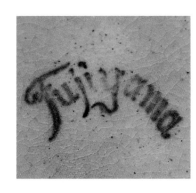

"Fujiyama" Inkstamp, 1905. This inkstamp with artistic lettering was the only mark on an example of Fujiyama.

Die-Impressed "ROZANE." The earliest examples of Rozane Royal (Dark) are typically marked in this manner. Beneath the word "ROZANE" is the shape number (862), followed by the abbreviation "R P Co" (for Roseville Pottery Company). The meaning of the other marks is unknown—perhaps referring to kilns, choice of background colors, or firing schedules. The age of this mark is unknown, although we can find the term "ROZANE ART" in the letterhead of Roseville letters dated 1898, in the minutes of the Board of Directors.

Inkstamp TRPCo Monogram. These marks were found on an example of Modern Art. The "T" in this monogram represents the word "The." A shape number (444) is also present, both as a blue inkstamp and as a die-impressed mark.

Rozane Ware Wafer. This wafer was found on an example of Rozane Royal (Dark). It is believed to have been introduced before 1904.

Die-Impressed "ROZANE." Another example of this mark, using a different typeface. Here, the "o" in the abbreviation "R P Co" is illegible because of the glaze.

"Chloron" Inkstamp, 1905. This inkstamp with artistic lettering was found on an example of Chloron. The mark can be die-impressed instead of inkstamp.

Rozane Ware Paper Label. This scarce paper label was found on an example of Della Robbia.

ozane Ware Wafer. This wafer was found n an example of Della Robbia, along with the and-incised artist initials EB.

Egypto Wafer. This wafer was found on an Egypto version of the E60 "Goethe" candlestick, along with a paper price tag (blank) and raised marks reading "The Roseville Pottery Co., Zanesville, O."

ozane Royal Wafer. This wafer was found n an example of Rozane Royal (Dark).

Mara Wafer. This wafer was found on an example of Mara.

Early Price Tag. This paper label was found on an example of Crystalis. The "#9" may be the factory shape number. The retail price appears to be $5.00. The meaning of the other marks is not known.

Mongol Wafer. This wafer was found on a tall and delicate vase, a shape that is not shown in the factory records.

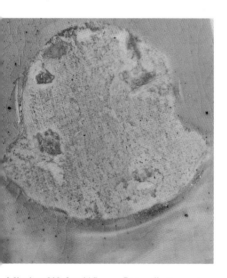

Missing Wafer. When a Roseville inspector ecided this piece was a factory second, he roke off the Rozane Royal wafer, leaving an nglazed section there. Sometimes a partial afer is found—also denoting a factory econd.

Woodland Wafer. This wafer was found on an example of Woodland.

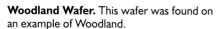

Hand-Painted Black Ink "ROZANE POTTERY." This mark was found on an example of Olympic.

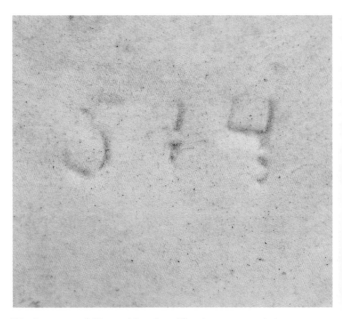

Olympic Marks. These marks were found on an example of Olympic. The title of the scene is shown, along with the name of the line and the phrase "Rozane Pottery," all hand-lettered in black ink. The die-impressed numeral 56 is probably a shape number.

Die-Impressed Shape Number. This die-impressed shape number was found on an example of Old Ivory (Tinted).

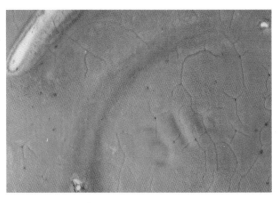

Die-Impressed Shape Number. This die-impressed shape number (316) was found on an early example of Matt Green.

Hand-Lettered Black Ink "ROSEVILLE." These marks were found on an example of Creamware (Persian). The shape number (557) was also die-impressed.

Olympic Marks. These marks were found on an example of Olympic. The line name and title are hand-lettered in black ink. The larger notations were added later, presumably by a collector.

Raised Factory Name. These raised marks were found on a Creamware version of the E60 "Goethe" candlestick.

Hand-Lettered "Mercian" Marks. These black ink marks were found on an example of Creamware, whose decoration has been nicknamed "Mercian" (meaning unknown). The shape number (545) is die-impressed above the ink markings.

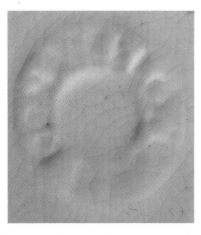

Donatello Mark. This distinctive molded (raised-relief) mark is found on a few Donatello shapes.

Three-Line Inkstamp Mark (Version 1). This mark reads "Roseville Pottery Co., Zanesville, O." and was found on an example of Creamware (Advertising).

Hand-Incised Shape Number. This hand-incised shape number (16) was found on an example of Early Carnelian.

Pauleo Marks. Today, many examples of Pauleo bear neither the molded (raised-relief) Pauleo wafer, nor the Pauleo paper label. This example is distinctive in having both marks. A hand-incised shape number is also present, although partly obscured by the (partial) label.

Three-Line Inkstamp Mark (Version 2). This mark reads "Roseville Pottery, Zanesville, O." and was found on an example of Creamware (Advertising).

Paper Label. This rectangular paper label was found on an example of Antique Matt Green.

Inkstamp Mark from the Rozane Line. Many pieces of Rozane Line bear this black inkstamp mark, reading "Roseville Pottery" and "Rozane."

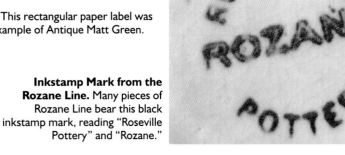

Blue Inkstamp Shape Number and Size. These marks were found on an example of Vista. Similar marks are occasionally found on Dogwood (Smooth).

Die-Impressed Rv Logo. This die-impressed Rv logo was found on an example of Lustre and has also been observed on Volpato. It is believed to date to about 1922.

Black Paper Label. This label was found on an example of Carnelian (Glazes). The shape number (310) is hand-lettered in orange crayon. Above it is a very faint blue inkstamp Rv logo, applied earlier—when the piece was ready to be fired as Carnelian (Drip).

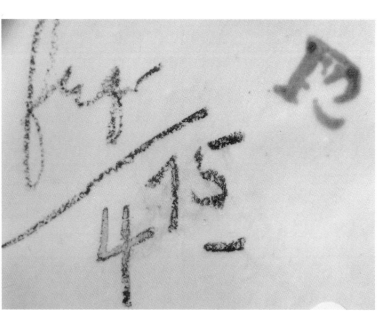

Blue Inkstamp Rv Logo. This blue inkstamp Rv logo was found on an example of Panel and is the trademark that was introduced in about 1923. Also present is the original retail price ($4.75), hand-lettered in black crayon. The meaning of the other mark is not known.

Foil Label. This label was found on an example of Baneda. The meaning of the other mark (a faint hand-written blue numeral 9) is not known.

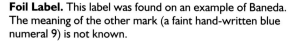

Black Inkstamp of Rv Logo. This black inkstamp Rv logo was found on a glossy example of Creamware (Juvenile) and dates to the mid 1920s. The other mark may be a shape number.

...e-Impressed "Roseville" (script), Shape Number, and Size. These marks were **...**und on an example of Ixia and illustrate the trademark introduced in 1936. Note that a **...**otograph of die-impressed Roseville marks can produce the optical illusion of being **...**lded (raised) marks. In reality, they are embedded slightly into the surface of the clay **...**fore bisque firing.

Molded (Raised-Relief) "R," "U.S.A.," and Shape Number. Molded (raised-relief) marks like these appear on only three examples of glossy Creamware (Juvenile). They are believed to date to the mid 1930s.

Molded (Raised-Relief) "R" (script), "U.S.A.," and Shape Number. These molded (raised-relief) mark like these were found on a Florane sand jar. (The white spots are hard-water deposits.)

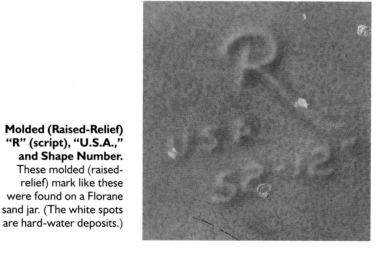

...lded (Raised-Relief) "Roseville" (script), "U.S.A.," Shape ...mber, and Size. These marks were found on a Trial Glaze **...**ample of Clematis and illustrate the trademark introduced in **...**40. The trial glaze notations are hand-written in black crayon. The **...**ters "wht" may be an abbreviation for "white"; the other marks **...**obably refer to glaze formulas.

Molded (Raised-Relief) "U.S.A." These were the only marks found on a White Rose hanging basket.

Molded (Raised-Relief) Marks on Mock Orange. These molded (raised-relief) marks appear on most examples of Mock Orange. Pieces with a small base may omit the term "Mock Orange" or may be unmarked.

Below:
Molded (Raised-Relief) Marks on Raymor Modern Artware. These molded (raised-relief) marks appear on most examples of Raymor Modern Artware. Examples of Raymor Modern Stoneware are usually marked "raymor by Roseville." Pieces with a small base are sometimes marked "R R," followed by the shape number and size.

Molded (Raised-Relief) Marks on Lotus. These molded (raised-relief) marks appear on most examples of Lotus. Pieces with a small base may be marked with only a script "L" and the shape number and size.

Die-Impressed Marks on Pine Cone Modern. As shown here, some examples of Pine Cone Modern are die-impressed "PINE CONE," followed by the shape number and size. Most examples have only the molded (raised) marks typical of post-1940 Roseville: the words "Roseville" (script) and "U.S.A." (block letters), and the shape number.

Molded (Raised-Relief) Roseville (script) and "U.S.A." These molded (raised-relief) marks were found on an example of Late Capri.

Molded (Raised-Relief) Marks on Raymor Two-Tone Casual. Similar molded (raised) markings appear on serving pieces in the Raymor Two-Tone Casual line.

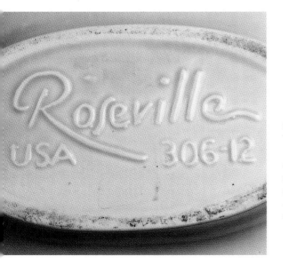

Molded (Raised-Relief) Marks on Keynote. These molded (raised-relief) marks are found on Keynote. Note the slightly different typeface, the missing periods in "USA," and the missing symbol for inches after the "12"— changes made after the sale of the Roseville trademarks in 1954.

and-Painted Artist Signature. This unusually clear hand-painted artist nature (L. Mitchell) was found on an example of Rozane Royal (Dark), near the ot.

Molded (Raised-Relief) Marks on Pasadena Planters. These molded (raised-relief) marks are found on most Pasadena Planters. Pieces with a small base may omit the term "PASADENA PLANTERS."

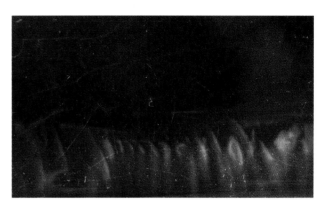

Hand-Painted Artist Signature. This blurry hand-painted signature (M. Timberlake) was found on an example of Rozane Royal (Dark), near the foot. The yellow slip used for the signature melted a bit during the final firing. Some signatures are completely illegible.

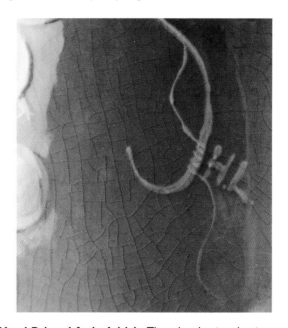

Hand-Painted Artist Initials. These hand-painted artist initials (HL) were found on an example of Rozane Royal (Light), near the decoration under the handle. This mark may be the signature of Harry Larzalere.

Hand-Painted Artist Initials. These hand-painted artist initials (G.H.) were found on an example of Rozane Royal (Dark), near the decoration. As is often the case with artist-signed Roseville, the artist's identity is unknown.

Hand-Incised Artist Signature. This rare artist signature (Gazo Foudji) was found on an unusual early piece, with an aventurine glaze. Although most artist signatures in Roseville occur on the decorated surface, here the signature is on the base, just below the Rozane Ware wafer.

Squeezebag Artist Initial. This squeezebag artist initial (R) was found on an example of Aztec, near the foot. The owner would like to think it to be the work of Harry (or better yet, Frederick Hurten) Rhead.

Hand-Incised Artist Signature. This hand-incised artist signature (E. Dutro) was found on an example of Della Robbia, near a handle.

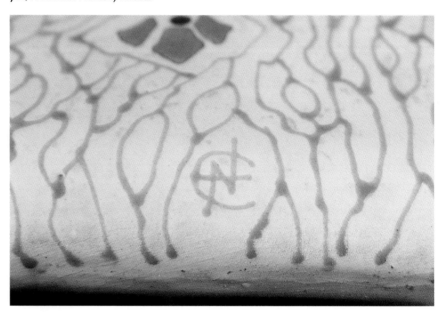

Squeezebag Artist Monogram. This squeezebag artist monogram (either NE, or EN) was found on an example of Fudji, near the foot. An artist mark is easy to overlook on an example of Fudji!

Hand-Incised Artist Initials. These hand-incised artist initials (F.H.B.) were found on a bisque-fired experimental piece. Like many Roseville experimentals, this piece is the work of modeler Frank H. Barks.

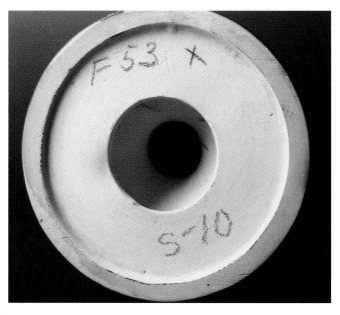

Crayon Notations on a Lamp. These hand-written crayon glaze notations were the only marks on a Roseville lamp. Because many Roseville lamps do not correspond to any standard line, these marks do not mean that a trial glaze was used—and they were not experimental pieces either. Expect the unexpected! (Incidentally, at Roseville Pottery, the letter "X" was **not** used to mark factory seconds. Usually found under the glaze, the letter "X" at Roseville appears to indicate a specific firing schedule.)

Vintage Store Label. During the 1940s, Hatcher's was a retail department store that sold Roseville Pottery. Some collectors think these vintage store labels add value to a piece—particularly if the particular label has sentimental value for the collector.

Crayon Notations on a Wincraft Piece. The hand-written crayon notation "SPEC" (an abbreviation for "special"?) was found on the base of a Wincraft basket. The piece appears to have a standard coloring. Perhaps this notation was used to mark the final "proof" piece after a series of glaze trials.

Collector's Label. Some collectors (and dealers) mark their inventory with special labels or other marks. The "White Pillars Museum" label is widely known, and many older collectors think it adds value to a piece. During the 1960s and 1970s, Zanesville pottery collector–researchers Evan and Louise Purviance welcomed visitors to view their collection in a "museum" setting. Their museum "gift shop" doubled as a retail outlet for selling American art pottery. When the couple eventually sold their collection, most pieces were marked with this label. (An unknown quantity of additional, previously unused "White Pillars Museum" labels is believed to have been sold with the collection.)

Appendix 1
Similar Products
by Roseville's Competitors

During the first quarter of the 20th century, the pottery trade in America was a booming business. Companies were interested in products that sold. When one firm came up with a new idea that caught on, other potteries were quick to produce a similar line. Inspired by the success of Rookwood's hand-decorated Standard Glaze pieces, several other Ohio potteries—including Roseville—developed a less expensive but similar line. A few years later, when Matt Green was in vogue, everyone wanted to sell a matte green pottery—from Rookwood to Hampshire, and from Roseville to Teco. Decorated creamware had a vogue during the Edwardian Age. The so-called "German" cooking wares were made by various firms, particularly after World War I restricted imports from abroad.

Two Ohio potteries whose decorative artware lines were introduced during the 1930s should **not** be confused with the Roseville Pottery Company (of Zanesville, Ohio)—namely, the Robinson Ransbottom Pottery Company ("R.R.P. Co.") and the Ungemach Pottery Company ("U.P. Co."). Even though Roseville Pottery's products look nothing like the wares of either R.R.P. Co. or U.P. Co., beginners continue to misidentify these pieces as "ROSEVILLE" on the Internet and in the shops. The confusion derives in part from the factory marks: certain products of both companies have die-impressed marks that include the abbreviated factory name and the factory location, worded as ROSEVILLE, O., simply ROSEVILLE, or in some cases ROSEVILLE, OHIO. (For line drawings of typical RRPCo and UPCo marks, see Lois Lehner's useful reference book, *Lehner's Encyclopedia of U.S. Marks on Pottery, Porcelain and Clay.*)

This chapter illustrates some of those products—many without a factory mark—that might resemble Roseville to a beginner, but that were instead made by one of Roseville's competitors. To learn more about these other American firms, look for the newly revised edition of Ralph and Terry Kovel's *Kovels' American Art Pottery* (New York: Crown, 1993). Of the available introductory works on American art pottery, the Kovels' book is still the most comprehensive, giving balanced coverage to factories, university ceramic programs, studio potters, and tile makers.

Arc-en-Ceil Pottery. 6.75" vase, gilt, die-impressed shape number 501. *Merritt collection.* **$250–300.** This Zanesville pottery operated from about 1903 to 1905. Marked examples are also known. Except for the size, the shape is identical to Roseville's Chloron C23-8" vase. Perhaps Arc-en-Ceil used a finished Roseville vase as their starting point, making a mold from it, recasting, decorating, and firing. Such a process generally causes the later "copy" to be about 10% shorter than its original.

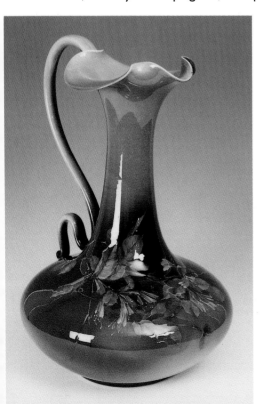

Left:
Rookwood Pottery's Standard Glaze. 12.75" Rookwood ewer 469A, dated 1889, honeysuckle vine on a light colored background, white clay body, artist signed ARV (Albert R. Valentien). *Private collection.* **$950–1200.** This piece was accompanied by a faded pencil note claiming that the ewer was a "World's Fair Prize piece" and previously owned by "the President of W.F." (Such stories are difficult to prove; even well-established provenance seldom affects the value of a piece of pottery.)

Right:
Weller Pottery, Jap Birdimal Line. Weller 4" Jap Birdimal vase, slip-decorated geese in flight. *Courtesy of Jane Langol Antiques.* **$300–400.** This line was designed by Frederick Hurten Rhead before he came to work at Roseville. Some examples are unmarked.

Weller Pottery, Dickensware Lines. Weller 9.75" Dickensware I (glossy) vase, hand-carved scene of partly clothed female in garden; Weller 9.75" Dickensware II (matte) vase, hand-carved figures in classical draperies, walking through wooded meadow. *Courtesy of Cincinnati Art Galleries.* **$1200–1500, $1500–2000.**

Left:
Weller Pottery, Fudzi Line. 11.75" vase, poppies, unmarked. *Courtesy of Mike Nickel and Cindy Horvath.* **$1200–1500.** This Weller line was designed by Gazo Foudji and closely resembles Foudji's lines for Roseville—Woodland and Fudji. All are highly sought by collectors.

Right:
Matte Green Pottery by Weller and Owens. Weller 10.5" vase, in the form of a tiger lily; Owens 8.75" vase, four buttress-like feet. *Wagner collection.* **$950–1200, $750–950**

Matte Green Pottery by Brush. 10.5" jardiniere, rich matte green, Egyptian scene of pyramids and Sphinx, oxen, family traveling on bull, unmarked. *Private collection.* **$500–600**

Child's Creamware Plate by Booths, Ltd. (England). 7.5" rolled-edge plate, circus animals (elephant, monkey, trained dog), unmarked. *Scheytt collection.* **$125–150.** This plate was once thought to be an unusual example of Roseville Creamware (Juvenile), which might have increased its value tenfold. For an almost identical example, see Booths advertisement, *Pottery, Glass and Brass Salesman,* December 19, 1929: 176.

Brush Pottery, "Venetian" Line. 7" jardiniere, no mark. *Zanesville Art Center* A5817. **NPD.** This decorated creamware line by Brush should not be confused with Roseville Creamware (Persian).

Some Weller Pottery Lines. Fairfield bowl (*not* Roseville Donatello); Weller creamware (*not* Roseville creamware); Lustre candlesticks (*not* Roseville Lustre). *Fairfield collection.* **$125–150, $40–50, $75–95 (pair).** It is easy to mistake the products of one Zanesville company for those of a competitor. When there is *any* doubt, use the term "attribution" in written descriptions. Or mark such an item "Roseville?" in your inventory.

"German" Cooking Ware. 5.5" pitcher, unmarked, maker unknown. *Fairfield collection.* **$50–60.** This utilitarian ware was produced by a number of American companies, all of which copied a popular German (and French) crockery of the time. Because the shape does not appear in Roseville factory records, it may be the work of another American pottery—such as Weller or Cambridge. Collectors have great difficulty identifying the various makers, and values are quite low.

Weller Pottery, Bronze Ware and Cloudburst Lustre Lines. Weller 11" Bronze Ware vase, unmarked; Weller 7.5" Cloudburst Lustre vase, unmarked. *Courtesy of Treadway Gallery.* **$500–600, $300–400.** Do not mistake these Weller products for Roseville Pauleo.

Left:
Peters and Reed Pottery (Zanesville, OH). 10.25" vase, glossy blue with sponge-applied black decorations, brick red clay, unmarked. *Courtesy of Vera Kaufman.* **$150–200.** Do not mistake this Peters and Reed line for Roseville Pauleo.

Burley-Winter Pottery (Zanesville, OH). 6.25" vase 54, matte mottled rust and green; 7.5" vase 45, matte mottled ivory and mint green. *Courtesy of Medina Antique Mall.* **$50–60, $75–95.** This Burley-Winter line is sometimes mistaken for Roseville's Carnelian (Glazes).

Right:
Royal Haeger Ashtray for Hyde Park. Ashtray, biomorphic shape, glossy mottled blue, white clay. *Hoppe photograph.* **$10–15.** Roseville items for Hyde Park have a buff clay body, with glazes resembling those of Artwood.

Appendix 2
Reproductions, Fakes, and Fantasy Pieces

This appendix illustrates some of the "copycats" that beginners might mistake for Roseville pieces. During the middle to late 1930s, George Rumrill hired Red Wing Pottery of Red Wing, Minnesota, to produce pottery for him to market under the brand name "RumRill Pottery." Several RumRill catalogs are reprinted in Ray Reiss's *Red Wing Art Pottery: Including Pottery Made for RumRill* (Chicago: Ray Reiss, 1996). Studying them shows that RumRill Pottery borrowed designs from various sources—including Roseville—altering some shapes slightly and reissuing others. Fortunately, RumRill's glazes are distinctive and unlike those used by Roseville.

Although not illustrated in *Introducing Roseville Pottery*, several other potteries also issued Roseville-like pieces during the 1930s, including Shawnee, whose wares are often marked simply "U.S.A." Occasionally one finds a pot that was made by another 1930s American pottery, but that is being offered for sale with a Roseville label (and a Roseville price tag).

At some time, one or more Japanese firms began making reproductions and imitations of Roseville shapes in a brittle white clay body. Modeling and glazing were done quickly and without the finesse that is associated with Roseville Pottery. These pieces were originally inkstamped "MADE IN JAPAN," although the mark has sometimes been removed through repeated washing or the use of a strong cleaning solution.

The recent Chinese reproductions, imitations, and fantasy pieces—meant to look like Roseville—are marked with molded (raised-relief) characters, even when the original Roseville line was not marked in that manner. The clay body tends to have a gray coloring, and is lighter in weight than that used by Roseville. The first Chinese copies had inferior glazes that do not resemble Roseville glazes in the least. As the Chinese copyists gain experience, and with instructions from their American "bosses," their glazes and marks are getting close enough to Roseville's that some pieces might actually fool a beginner.

Fortunately, up-to-date information about these troublesome Chinese copycats can be viewed at the Internet website: <www.inch.com/~kteneyck/roseville.html>. (Thanks a million, Karen!) **Neither the Chinese nor the Japanese pieces have any value to most Roseville collectors.** The figures cited are approximately equal to the retail value suggested by the American importers of these products.

In recent years, one or more unscrupulous potters have been making nearly identical copies of old Ohio art pottery pieces. Among the items believed to have been forged are some Hull Bowknot and Red Riding Hood items, the Watt Policeman cookie jar, the Roseville Panel nude wall pocket (sometimes glazed in white and aqua), a 6" Roseville La Rose vase, and several Weller Pop-eyed Dogs. These pieces often employ a buff-colored clay, but their weight is not quite the same as that of the original piece. (None of these examples is illustrated in *Introducing Roseville Pottery*.)

New attempts to deceive and exploit beginners are likely to be discovered from time to time. As you can see from the values in this book, they do not seriously affect the prices, nor the collecting market. The best defense is to make friends with people who love pottery as much as you do. Information about copycats circulates quickly.

Readers interested in learning about a wide variety of reproductions may want to subscribe to *Antique & Collectors Reproduction News*, the source that "broke the story" of the Chinese copycats of Roseville in 1997. This important monthly newsletter is also available in annual book versions (for 1995 through 1998). Ceramic subjects in the 1998 volume include Roseville Pottery, Van Briggle Pottery, Red Riding Hood, Royal Dux, Nippon porcelain, historical creamware, cookie jars, and RS Prussia–Suhl–Germany. Other 1998 subjects range from beaded purses and Keen Kutter tools to Titanic artifacts. For a one-year subscription, send $32 to ACRN, P.O. Box 12130-MB, Des Moines, IA 50312; or call 1-800-227-5531 (9 am – 5 pm Central, Mondays–Fridays).

RumRill Pottery by Red Wing, 1938. 8.75" RumRill Pottery vase 375 (*not* a Roseville Tuscany 345-8" vase), die-impressed 375; 5.5" RumRill Pottery vase 360 (*not* a Roseville Sunflower 6" vase), die-impressed 360. *Jacklitch collection.* **$100–125 (RumRill), $60–75 (RumRill).** In the 1938 RumRill catalog, vase 375 is shown with the "Grecian Group" and vase 360 with the "Florentine Group." As you can see, RumRill Pottery (mostly made by Red Wing Pottery, of Red Wing, Minnesota) sometimes reintroduced copies (or near copies) of older designs by other companies. **Do not mistake these pots for Trial Glaze pieces by Roseville!**

RumRill Pottery versus Roseville. Roseville Lombardy 350-6" vase, unmarked; 6.5" RumRill Pottery vase 390, unmarked. *Auclair collection.* **$125–150 (Roseville), $40–50 (RumRill).** In the 1938 RumRill catalog, vase 390 is shown with the "Fluted Group." RumRill pieces were marked with either RumRill or Red Wing paper labels (which could be lost, leaving the piece without a factory mark). Most examples have a die-impressed shape number.

Monmouth Pottery Vase, 1930s. Monmouth Pottery 8" vase, matte mottled reddish brown. *Auclair collection.* **$40–50 (Monmouth).** In making this vase, Monmouth Pottery (Monmouth, Illinois) did not intend to imitate Roseville products. Like Roseville, the Monmouth company marked its wares with paper labels. Sometime later, an unscrupulous seller affixed a *Roseville* label to the piece, clearly with the intention to deceive.

The Bottom of the Monmouth Vase.

Coors Pottery. Coors Pottery 12" vase, matte white with glossy blue lining, inkstamp mark. *Courtesy of Len Boucher.* **$150–200.** Always glazed in solid colors, this early 1930s Colorado piece was derived from the Roseville Futura 410-12" vase.

Japanese Reproductions. 4.25" vase, inkstamp "MADE IN JAPAN"; Roseville Montacello 555-4" vase, aqua; Roseville Montacello 579-4.75" vase, brown; 4.75" vase, inkstamp "MADE IN JAPAN." *Shannon collection.* **$20–25 (copy), $275–350 (Roseville), $275–350 (Roseville), $15–20 (copy).**

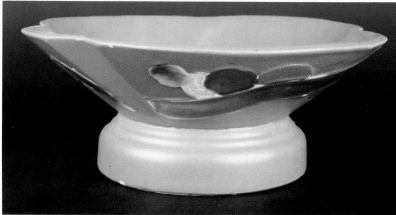

Japanese Reproduction. 9" x 3.5" bowl (*not* a Roseville Futura 187-7" bowl), inkstamp "MADE IN JAPAN," several small chips. *Latta collection.* **$5–10**

Roseville Futura. Roseville Futura 197-6" bowl, unmarked. *Courtesy of Treadway Gallery.* **$500–600 (Roseville).** This piece measures 5.5" tall. Do not rely merely on size to distinguish the original from the copy!

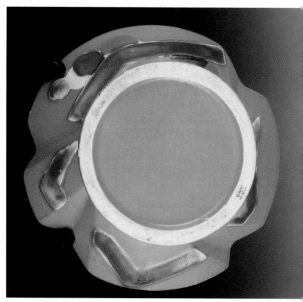

Marks and Bottom of a Japanese Reproduction.

Japanese Fantasy Piece and Reproduction. 7.75" bowl, brown and green, inkstamp "MADE IN JAPAN"; 5.25" vase, brown and green, unmarked. *Private collection.* **$25–30 (copy), $30–40 (copy).** The bowl shown here is a fantasy piece, since Roseville never made this shape—which is clearly intended to resemble Futura. Compare the "value" of the Japanese vase to the value of the actual Roseville Futura piece.

Japanese Imitation. 7" vase, brown and black on white, inkstamp "MADE IN JAPAN"; Roseville Laurel 673-8" vase, green. *Hoppe photograph.* **$30–40 (copy), $400–500 (Roseville).** Because of its non-standard size and glazes, this example is unlikely to cause much confusion.

Japanese Imitation. 7" bowl (*not* a Roseville Velmoss 266-5" x 8" bowl), glossy blue and green, inkstamp "MADE IN JAPAN." *Hoppe photograph.* **$20–25 (copy).** Because of its non-standard size and glazes, this example is unlikely to cause much confusion.

Chinese Reproductions. 4.25" fan vase (*not* a Roseville Jonquil 93-4.5" fan vase), marked "Roseville" (script); 5.75" vase (*not* a Roseville Fuchsia 892-6" vase), marked "Roseville" (script) and C–892-6". *Courtesy of an antiques and collectibles mega-mall.* **$25–30 (each).** Roseville's Jonquil line was made during a period when the factory used paper labels. At Roseville, molded (raised-relief) marks were not introduced until 1940.

Marks from the Chinese Fuchsia-Type Vase. Note the reversed "9" in the shape number. Roseville Fuchsia shape numbers do not begin with the letter "C."

Chinese Imitation. 8.5" wall pocket (*not* a Roseville Luffa 1272-8" wall pocket), marked "Roseville" (script) and -8-1/2". *Hoppe collection.* **$25–30**

Chinese Imitations. Three 8.5" vases (*not* Roseville Experimental pieces), each marked "Roseville" (script). *Courtesy of an antiques and collectibles mega-mall.* **$25–30 (each).** These vases are poorly made— clearly molded and not hand-carved like an actual Roseville Experimental. Sometimes they are found with a dark blue glaze, instead of the pumpkin color shown.

Marks from the Chinese Luffa-Type Wall Pocket. Roseville's Luffa pattern was introduced in 1934, when the factory marked their products with foil labels (which could be lost, leaving the piece unmarked). Luffa was never marked with the word "Roseville." In 1940 and later, when molded (raised-relief) marks *were* used at Roseville, the marks *never* quoted a size without providing a shape number.

Chinese Imitations. 13" vase (*not* a Roseville Luffa 691-12" vase), marked "Roseville" (script) and -13" (only); 16" ewer (*not* a Roseville Zephyr Lily 24-15" ewer), marked "Roseville" (script), "U.S.A." (partly removed), and 24-15". *Courtesy of an antiques and collectibles mega-mall.* **$25–30 (each)**

Marks from the Chinese Luffa-Type Vase. See the comments on the marks from a Chinese wall pocket.

Marks from the Chinese Zephyr Lily-Type Ewer. The "U.S.A." mark was probably defaced when the Chinese copycat realized that this mark might complicate their legal relationship with U.S. customs.

Chinese Imitations. 10.5" basket (*not* a Roseville Foxglove 375-12" basket), marked "Roseville" (script) and 375-12"; 6.25" bowl (*not* a Roseville Peony 428-6" bowl), marked "Roseville" (script) and 428-6"; 7.5" vase (*not* a Roseville Snowberry 1V2-7" vase), marked "Roseville" (script). *Courtesy of an antiques and collectibles mega-mall.* **$25–30 (each).** The price tag on the vase shown here was marked "Roseville" and "Bittersweet" (instead of "Snowberry").

Chinese Imitation and Fantasy Pieces. 7.5" vase (*not* Roseville Magnolia), marked "Roseville" (script) and 90-7"; 5.75" watering can (*not* Roseville Magnolia), marked "Roseville" and 180-5". *Courtesy of an antiques and collectibles mega-mall.* **$25–30 (each).** The watering can is a fantasy piece, since Roseville never made water cans (in any line!). **Note:** The seller's price tags say "Roseville" too, but the prices themselves are both less than $25. **When you think a price is too good to be true, maybe you should think again.**

Marks from the Chinese Foxglove-Type Basket. Note the impressed circle on this base, over which the copycat has placed a "Roseville" mark. This bottom is completely unlike any made at the Roseville Pottery.

Fantasy Piece. 14" vase (*not* Roseville Woodland), glossy white, decorated with red tulip, gilt rim, and stippled background, hand-written black ink marks "ROSEVILLE POTTERY" and "ROZANE WARE," maker unknown. *Courtesy of Norm Haas.* **$30-35**

Imitation of Roseville Blackberry. 7.5" vase (*not* a Roseville Blackberry 575-8" vase), tan and green drip on matte white, unmarked. *Harris collection.* **$10–15.** The maker of this imitation piece is not known.

Marks from the Woodland-Type Fantasy Piece. It must have taken considerable time and effort to hand-letter these marks.

Selected Bibliography

Alexander, Donald E. *Roseville Pottery for Collectors*. Richmond, IN: Donald E. Alexander, 1970. 68-page paperback.

Bomm, Jack and Nancy. *Roseville Pottery in All Its Splendor*. Gas City, IN: L-W Book Sales, 1998. [Essential reference guide.]

Buxton, Virginia Hillway. *Roseville Pottery: For Love ... or Money*. Nashville: Tymbre Hill, 1977. In ca. 1996, Buxton reprinted this book in a limited edition, and included a new chapter at the end.

Clifford, Richard A. *Roseville Art Pottery*. Winfield, KS: Andenken Publishing Co., 1968. 44-page paperback.

Dale, Sharon. *Frederick Hurten Rhead: An English Potter in America*. Erie, PA: Erie Art Museum, 1986. [Recommended.]

Evans, Paul. *Art Pottery of the United States ... 1974; 2nd rev. ed.* New York: Lewis and Feingold, 1987. [Highly recommended.]

Humphries, John W. *A Price Guide to Roseville Pottery by the Numbers*. No city indicated, CA: John W. Humphries, 1999. 34-page booklet.

Huxford, Sharon and Bob. *The Collectors Encyclopedia of Roseville Pottery*. First series. 1976; rptd. Paducah, KY: Collector Books, 1998.

Huxford, Sharon and Bob. *The Collectors Encyclopedia of Roseville Pottery*. Second series. 1980; rptd. Paducah, KY: Collector Books, 1998.

Kovel, Ralph and Terry. *Kovels' American Art Pottery: The Collector's Guide to Makers, Marks, and Factory Histories*. 1974; rev. New York: Crown, 1993. [Highly recommended.]

Lehner, Lois. *Lehner's Encyclopedia of U.S. Marks on Pottery, Porcelain and Clay*. Paducah, KY: Collector Books, 1988. [Essential reference guide.]

Mollring, Gloria and James Mollring. *Roseville Pottery: Collector's Price Guide*. 5th edition. Lockford, CA: Gloria Mollring, 1999. 263-page spiral-bound paperback.

Monsen, Randall B. *Collectors' Compendium of Roseville Pottery*. Volume I. Vienna, VA: Monsen and Baer, 1995. [Recommended.]

Monsen, Randall B. *Collectors' Compendium of Roseville Pottery*. Volume II. Vienna, VA: Monsen and Baer, 1997.

Perry, Barbara A. *American Art Pottery: From the Collection of Everson Museum of Art*. New York: Abrams, 1997. [Recommended.]

Purviance, Louise and Evan, and Norris F. Schneider. *Roseville Art Pottery in Color*. Des Moines: Wallace-Homestead, 1970. 52-page spiral-bound booklet (counting cover).

Roseville Pottery Company. Various factory documents, in the collections of the Ohio Historical Society; Moses Mesre; Frank Shannon; and Ed and June Wagner.

Sigafoose, Dick. *American Art Pottery: Identification and Values ...* Paducah, KY: Collector Books, 1998.

Snook, Josh and Anna. *Roseville Donatello Pottery*. Lebanon, PA: Josh Snook, 1975.

Index to Roseville Products